the BELIEVER'S HANDBOOK

the BELIEVER'S HANDBOOK

Lester Sumrall

WHITAKER HOUSE

Editor's note: This book has been edited for the modern reader. Words, expressions, and sentence structure have been updated for clarity and readability.

THE BELIEVER'S HANDBOOK
Titles included in this anthology:

The Names of God	ISBN: 0-88368-224-9	© 1993 by Lester Sumrall
The Gifts and Ministries		
of the Holy Spirit	ISBN: 0-88368-236-2	© 1993 by Lester Sumrall
Angels to Help You	ISBN: 0-88368-564-7	© 1993 by Lester Sumrall
Demons: The Answer Book	ISBN: 0-88368-329-6	© 1993 by Lester Sumrall
60 Things God Said about Sex	ISBN: 0-88386-770-4	© 1993 by Lester Sumrall

ISBN: 0-88368-852-2
Printed in the United States of America
© 2002 by Whitaker House

Whitaker House
30 Hunt Valley Circle
New Kensington, PA 15068
visit our website at: www.whitakerhouse.com

Library of Congress Cataloging-in-Publication Data
Sumrall, Lester Frank, 1913–1996
   The believer's handbook / Lester Sumrall.
      p. cm.
   ISBN 0-88368-852-2 (pbk. : alk. paper)
   1. Theology, Doctrinal—Popular works. I. Title.
   BT77 .S783 2003
   230—dc21   2002154129

1 2 3 4 5 6 7 8 9 10 11 12 / 10 09 08 07 06 05 04 03 02

Contents

The Names of God

Contents

1
What's in a Name?

The great poet William Shakespeare once posed this question:

> What's in a name? That which we call a rose
> By any other name would smell as sweet.

And most people today would agree. Our modern society places little significance on the meaning of a name. Parents usually name their children after beloved relatives or well-known persons. Sometimes they pick a child's name merely because it "sounds good." But seldom would they give any thought to the meaning of a name.

Yet names do mean something. Ideally, they correspond directly to the one designated by the name. For example, did you know that the name *Kenneth* comes from the Greek word meaning "to know"? So a person named Kenneth is supposed to be knowledgeable. Since the name *Diana* comes from the Greek word meaning "of a god," a girl with that name is supposed to be "simply divine" in her beauty or other qualities. Other people's names are derived from words of the ancient Greek, Latin, Norse, or other languages. And most of those names have some special meaning.

The same is true of place names. You probably know, for example, that the name *Philadelphia* means "city of brotherly love." It comes from the Greek words *phileo* ("to love") and *delphos* ("city"). The name Jerusalem means "city of peace," being derived from the Hebrew word *shalom* ("peace"). There is probably some significance behind the name of your town or city.

My point is simply this: While it may have been all right for Shakespeare to shrug off the importance of a name, we should not take names so lightly. Often a name provides an important clue to the nature of a person or place.

This is certainly true of God. The Bible refers to God by many different names, and each one reveals some aspect of God's character or His relationship with us. The translators who gave us the King James Version and other English versions of the Bible simply translate His name as "God" or "LORD"; but significantly, several Greek or Hebrew names are used in the original manuscripts. If you want to become a serious student of the Word of God, you should be familiar with those Greek and Hebrew names because they contain a wealth of truth about the wonderful God we serve.

God's Credentials

For centuries, people did not know the name of God. That may come as a surprise to you, but it's true. When God walked with Adam and Eve in the Garden of Eden, it wasn't necessary for them to know His name because they knew Him intimately. They did not need to call upon Him or invoke Him in prayer for He was their daily companion. Then they disobeyed Him and were driven out of the garden, forced to make a living by the sweat of their brow and the labor of their hands. They and their descendants began offering sacrifices to Him and calling upon Him in prayer.[1] In fact, Genesis 4:26 says it was not until the birth of Adam's grandson Enos that men began *"to call upon the name of the LORD."* The Bible says Adam was one hundred and thirty years old when Seth was born (see Genesis 5:3), and Seth was one hundred and five years old when his son Enos was born (see Genesis 5:6). So for over two hundred years, despite the Fall, men and women did not find it necessary to call on God by name. They were still that aware of His presence.

I often wish that we could regain that intimate state of communion with the Lord! In my own prayer life, I have felt very near to Him at times—so near that it was not necessary to offer Him any formal prayer. It was enough just to be in His presence. The Bible says, *"Draw nigh to God, and he will draw nigh to you"* (James 4:8), and that's the kind of experience He has given me in prayer. Yet none of us has regained the depth of intimacy with the Lord that would let us worship Him heart-to-heart, as Adam's family did.

Paul knew that one day he would meet God. He affirmed, *"Then shall I know even as also I am known"* (1 Cor. 13:12). All of us look forward to such a day. But for now we are limited by our human imperfections and the distractions of this carnal world. We must shut the door of our prayer closets and focus our thoughts on God if we are to have any fellowship with Him. The human race has needed to pray this way ever since the days of Enos.

Humankind fell into deep corruption in the centuries that followed Adam. Finally, God had to destroy most of the human race with a worldwide flood, saving only a godly man named Noah and his family in one last effort to salvage humanity. The Bible says that when the flood waters receded and Noah's great wooden ark came to rest on Mount Ararat, he left the ark to build an altar and offer sacrifices to God. (See Genesis 8:18–21.) He wanted to make a fresh beginning for the human race, and he started by worshipping God.

Centuries later, God spoke to a godly man named Abram and invited him to leave his native homeland (in what is now Iran) and travel to Canaan. As soon as Abram arrived in that land, he also built an altar and offered sacrifices to God. (See Genesis 12:7.)

Notice how important the worship of God was to these men. Each of them celebrated the landmark events of his life by building an altar, burning a sacrifice on it, and uttering praise to God. Worship was a way of life for them. Yet God had to remind them who He was again and again.

He put a rainbow in the sky to remind Noah that He was a benevolent God and would never again destroy the earth with

11

water. (See Genesis 9:14–17.) When Abram worshipped Him, He said, *"Fear not, Abram: I am thy shield, and thy exceeding great reward"* (Gen. 15:1). He also said, *"I am the* LORD *that brought thee out of Ur of the Chaldees, to give thee this land to inherit it"* (Gen. 15:7). Finally He said, *"I am the Almighty God; walk before me, and be thou perfect"* (Gen. 17:1). It was as if God had to present His credentials every time He talked with them because they kept forgetting who He was.

"The God My Folks Worshipped"

When Abraham's grandson Jacob dreamed of a ladder reaching to the throne of heaven, God said to him, *"I am the* LORD *God of Abraham thy father, and the God of Isaac* [Jacob's immediate father]: *the land whereon thou liest, to thee will I give it, and to thy seed"* (Gen. 28:13).[2] God had already promised the land to Abraham and his descendants; now He would fulfill that promise to Jacob and his immediate family.

But God had to keep reminding Jacob of who He was. When Jacob went to work for his Uncle Laban in the land of Haran, God spoke to him in another dream and said, *"I am the God of Bethel, where thou anointedst the pillar, and where thou vowedst a vow unto me: now arise, get thee out from this land, and return unto the land of thy kindred"* (Gen. 31:13).[3] Yet when Jacob talked about God, notice how he referred to Him: *"the God of my father, the God of Abraham, and the fear of Isaac"* (Gen. 31:42) and *"the God of Abraham, and the God of Nahor, the God of their father"* (Gen. 31:53).

If Jacob ever knew God's name, he seems to have forgotten it! He referred to Him only as "the God my folks always worshipped."

I'm afraid this is the only way many people identify God today. "Sure, I know God," they say. "My folks have worshipped Him for years. He and I are not personal friends, but He's a good friend of my parents." Yet there is a world of difference between knowing God and knowing *about* God. Someone who knows Him only as "the God my folks worshipped" simply knows *about* Him. We need to become so intimately acquainted with God that we fall on our knees and say with Thomas, *"My Lord and my God"* (John 20:28).

Of course, Jacob may have referred to God as "the God of Abraham and Isaac" as a gesture of respect. He may have been underscoring the fact that God had been faithful to his forefathers and was also faithful to him. Some Bible commentators interpret Jacob's words this way.

But I think Jacob's spiritual "track record" says otherwise. He was a cunning, deceitful man who tricked his older brother out of his birthright and made off with part of his uncle's flocks. Only in times of crisis did Jacob turn to God. Jacob's brother Esau learned he was coming home and went out to meet him. Jacob was desperate. He wailed to the *"God of my father Abraham, and God of my father Isaac, the* LORD *which saidst unto me, Return unto thy country"* (Gen. 32:9). Jacob still was on very formal terms with God, not friendly terms.

Only after Jacob's faith had been tested a great deal more, did God appear to him again and say, *"Thy name shall not be called any more Jacob, but Israel shall be thy name"* (Gen. 35:10). The Hebrew name *Israel* literally means "ruling with God."

> *And God said unto him, I am God Almighty: be fruitful and multiply; a nation and a company of nations shall be of thee, and kings shall come out of thy loins.* (Gen. 35:11)[4]

Not only did God give Jacob a new name, but He revealed more of His own divine nature to him. He revealed that He was all-powerful and able to do anything He promised to do. So His vow to bring *"a nation and a company of nations"* out of this man was no casual promise.

It carried the authority of an omnipotent God, a God whom Jacob had come to trust.

"Tell Them 'I Am That I Am' Sent You"

I am giving you a quick review of God's early relationship with humanity so that you can see how individuals tried to perceive God. Sometimes people had a special name for God (as we'll see in the following chapters); sometimes they could only refer to God in terms of something He had done for them. Through it all, humankind was reaching out to God, trying to understand who He was and that He should be worshipped. We see this occurring most vividly about four hundred years after the death of Jacob (or Israel), when God called a man named Moses to lead Jacob's descendants out of Egypt.

Moses himself was an Israelite who fled from Egypt after he murdered a government official. He was tending the flocks of his father-in-law in the craggy wastelands of the Sinai Peninsula when God appeared to him. To make sure that Moses recognized Him for who He was, God appeared in a bush that burned without being consumed. That sight was bound to attract a shepherd's attention! So Moses said, *"I will now turn aside, and see this great sight, why the bush is not burnt"* (Exod. 3:3). And as he came near to the bush, he heard God in the midst of it, saying, *"put off thy shoes from off thy feet, for the place whereon thou standest is holy ground"* (v. 5).

God explained to Moses that He had appeared previously to Abraham, Isaac, and Jacob (v. 6). Then He gave Moses the task of returning to Egypt and confronting the Pharaoh himself to demand the release of the Israelite slaves.

Moses was scared. He tried to make excuses to God. He said, *"Behold, when I come unto the children of Israel, and shall say unto them, The God of your fathers hath sent me unto you; and they shall say to me, What is his name? what shall I say unto them?"* (v. 13). Here was the supreme test of God's intentions. If God really meant business with Moses, He would reveal His name. Otherwise, Moses would know the relationship with God was only casual. He would only be able to know God "at a distance," and perhaps God would leave him when the going got tough.

But God gave Moses a name for Himself. He said, *"Thus shalt thou say unto the children of Israel, I AM hath sent me unto you"* (v. 14). The Hebrew word *(yhwh)* that God gave him is a puzzle, even to Bible scholars today. It has no clear-cut, simple translation. The closest it has been translated is "I am who I am." In the next chapter, we'll explore what these words conveyed to the Israelites when Moses carried the message to them. But notice how eager Moses was to identify God. He wanted to know God's name because the name would tell him something about the very nature of God.

A Name, Not a "Handle"

Several major highways converge in South Bend. We get a large amount of heavy truck traffic through our city, some going right past the Christian Center where I am pastor. The truckers have developed their own special jargon for us on the citizens' band radio, and I overhear them using some of that CB lingo at local restaurants.

A very common CB term is "handle." Truckers use that word when they want to get the name another trucker goes by. They say, "What's your handle?"

I suppose they use "handle" because that's what a name does for them; it lets them get hold of someone they know. To use that old cliché, a name lets them "get a handle" on their friends.

If you ever visit the Philippines and hear the jungle tribesmen call upon their gods for help, you'll discover that the names of the gods are supposed to have magic power. These people believe that when they invoke the name of a certain god, he must come and do their bidding—whether or not he wants to! Like many pagans, they believe a god is a kind of supernatural serving boy who will jump to help them the moment they snap their fingers.

But the true God is not like that. He is the sovereign Ruler of the universe, who expects us to serve Him—not the other way around! So when we call upon the name of God, we are using a "handle" to bring Him to us. He will help us only if we have followed His commandments; He will put His promises into effect only if we have met the conditions of those promises.

On the Day of Pentecost, Peter said, *"Whosoever shall call on the name of the Lord shall be saved"* (Acts 2:21). Three thousand people did. When the apostles Peter and John met a lame man at the gate of the temple, Peter said, *"In the name of Jesus Christ of Nazareth rise up and walk"* (Acts 3:6), and the man did. Peter's testimony was that *"through faith in his name [Jesus] hath made this man strong"* (Acts 3:16). Later the apostles asked God *"that signs and wonders may be done by the name of thy holy child Jesus"* (Acts 4:30), and an earthquake shook the place where they were assembled (v. 31).

This was no magic. These men were not ordering God around by using His "handle." Not by any means! They received God's blessing only because they were obedient to God in every way, including the manner in which they prayed. God instructed them to pray in His name; that's what we are expected to do as followers of Jesus Christ. But that in itself would not force God to do something against His will, nor would it force Him to bless someone unworthy of a blessing.

When the Israelites fled to the shore of the Red Sea, Moses commanded them to stand still and called upon the Lord to fight back the pursuing Egyptian army. God did not do what Moses asked, however, because He had a better plan in mind. *"And the LORD said unto Moses, Wherefore criest thou unto me? speak unto the children of Israel, that they go forward"* (Exod. 14:15). So Moses urged his people to run toward the sea itself, and God divided the waters so they could pass through on dry ground.

When the pagan armies of Ai defeated the Israelites, Joshua threw himself on the ground and said,

> *Alas, O Lord GOD, wherefore hast thou at all brought this people over Jordan, to deliver us into the hand of the Amorites, to destroy us? would to God we had been content, and dwelt on the other side Jordan! O Lord, what shall I say, when Israel turneth their backs before their enemies!* (Josh. 7:7–8)

But God saw the situation differently.

> *And the LORD said unto Joshua, Get thee up; wherefore liest thou thus upon thy face? Israel hath sinned, and they have also transgressed my covenant which I commanded them: for they have even taken of the accursed thing, and have also stolen, and dissembled also, and*

they have put it even among their own stuff. Therefore the children of Israel could not stand before their enemies, but turned their backs before their enemies, because they were accursed: neither will I be with you any more, except ye destroy the accursed from among you.
(Josh. 7:10–12)

God refuses to bless people who are clinging to their sins. As a pastor, I talk with many people who expect God to treat them kindly, even though they often disobey Him. They seem to think that God is a kind of "Daddy Warbucks" who will give them everything they desire, no matter what they do. But they are wrong. God is not a "soft touch." He is not deceived by the glib tongues of people who promise Him the moon but fail to deliver. He is not a foolish God.

He blesses people if they meet His conditions, not just because they call upon Him. As Billy Graham says:

> There is one thing God's love cannot do. It cannot forgive the unrepentant sinner....God will not force Himself on any man against his will. A person can hear a message about the love of God and say, "No, I won't have it," and God will let him go on in his sin to slavery and judgment.[5]

So it is with the prayer of a disobedient person. That person may plead with God and try to claim the promises of God. As long as he or she disobeys God, however, that individual can expect no help, God will not be ordered around by the whims of man. He will not put aside His own will to do our will.

A Blessing, Not a Curse

While some people use God's name in prayer, others use His name in cursing. They seem to think that God's name adds weight to their temper tantrums. It doesn't; in fact, it shows how little they know of God.

If those who curse in God's name really knew Him, they would know that He said, *"Thou shalt not take the name of the LORD thy God in vain; for the LORD will not hold him guiltless that taketh his name in vain"* (Exod. 20:7). This is one of the most commonly violated of the Ten Commandments because people do not know what it means.

The word *vain* normally means "selfish pride" or "conceit." When we say that a person is vain, we mean this person is puffed up with pride. This is an arrogant kind of attitude that says, "I'm better than everyone else."

To "take the Lord's name in vain," means to use His name for your own selfish purposes. Some people swear oaths casually in God's name, as if God lent His authority to their word. They say, "God knows that I've done thus-and-so." What vanity! Others exclaim, "Oh God!" at the slightest provocation, as if they were on chummy terms with Him. What conceit! Still others angrily tell God to damn someone or something that irritates them at the moment, as if God were taking orders from them. What blasphemous pride!

But there is another, more subtle kind of "taking God's name in vain"—a kind many Christians practice. That is the vain habit of pronouncing God's condemnation against something that God does not condemn. Some Christians—including some preachers—denounce in God's name things they don't happen to like.

For example, I remember a time when many preachers denounced the cutting of a woman's hair; they said it was a worldly, sinful practice. Some preachers harangued their people about the "sin" of drinking coffee or tea. Others railed about women who wore lipstick; they said it was a *"superfluity of naughtiness"* (James 1:21).

Now there's nothing wrong with denouncing sin, so long as God's Word really says it is sin. But when you try to distort God's Word to make *everything that you don't like* a sin, you are using God's name in vain, just as much as the infidel who swears the most vile oaths in God's name. The Bible commentator Bo Reicke summed it up well:

> Unhappily the tongue of many pretended Christians (James 3:91) has assumed a double function. With the same

tongue believers bless God and curse men, who are created in the image of God....In their eagerness to appear as prophets of doom they believe that it is part of the Christian message to pronounce curses upon degraded mankind....There is an absolute difference in kind between the true Christian message and the expression of the poisonous tongue. Bitter dissatisfaction has nothing to do with the gospel, and it is impossible to oscillate between the one and the other.[6]

God's name is a word of blessing not a curse. We should never invoke God's name to accomplish our own selfish ends, even if we can think of some "good" reason to justify it. God's name is holy. It should be spoken reverently. It should be invoked only for the most godly purposes. God's name should not be a part of someone's "gutter talk." It also should not be the high-caliber "shell" that explodes in some preacher's barrage against his personal peeves. God's name is meant to bring hope, healing, and happiness to all people. Let's be sure we use His name to that end.

"Tell Me That Name Again"

This book discusses some of the Hebrew names for God, names used in the Old Testament. But we should also take a brief look at the names of God's Son, Jesus Christ, who is God incarnate, God in the flesh. The names of Jesus tell us a great deal about His character as He ministered on this earth. We can draw a great deal of comfort from meditating upon the names of Jesus because they remind us again of His deep love for us. Bill and Gloria Gaither penned these beautiful lines:

> Jesus, Jesus, Jesus!
> There's just something about that name!
> Master, Savior, Jesus!
> Like the fragrance after the rain.*

*From "There's Something about that Name" by William J. & Gloria Gaither. © 1970 by William J. Gaither. International copyright secured. All rights reserved. Used by permission of The Benson Company, Inc., Nashville.

And that should be the testimony of every Christian, should it not? There's no earthly name to compare with the name of our precious Jesus, who died to save us from our sins. What then are some of the names that the New Testament uses to refer to Him?

Jesus. The Greek name *Jesus* comes from the Hebrew name *Yeshua,* which means "God the Savior" or "God is salvation." In our English Old Testament, it is the name *Joshua.* This is the name most commonly used in the New Testament to refer to Him. It's the name His mother Mary gave to Him because the angel of God revealed to her that He would *"save his people from their sins"* (Matt. 1:21).

Christ. This Greek name means "the anointed One," and that is also what the Hebrew name *Messiah* means. So when the Bible speaks of "Jesus Christ," it literally means "Jesus the Messiah" or "Our Savior, the Anointed One." In Old Testament times, new kings and prophets were anointed with holy oil to show that God had chosen them for a special purpose. Although Jesus was not (as far as we know) anointed with oil at the beginning of His ministry, He was anointed with God's Holy Spirit. (See Luke 3:21–22.)

Immanuel. In Hebrew, this name means "God (is) with us." The prophet Isaiah announced that the promised Messiah of God would be called by this name (see Isaiah 7:14), indicating that He would be God in the flesh. Matthew says that Jesus fulfilled this prophecy (see Matthew 1:23), although He was not commonly called by this name. Perhaps this was because the average Jew of Jesus' day was not able to grasp the miracle of the Incarnation.

Master. The New Testament records that Jesus' disciples called Him by several Greek names that the King James Version translates as "Master." The most common of these was *didaskalos,* meaning "Teacher." Another was *kurios,* meaning "lord" or "overseer." The gospel of Matthew tells us that a certain scribe once came to Jesus and said, *"Master [didaskalos], I will follow thee whithersoever thou goest"* (Matt. 8:19). Jesus replied, *"The foxes have holes, and the birds of the air have nests; but the Son of man hath not where to lay his head"* (v. 20). Jesus knew that if this man thought He was merely a great teacher about to form a prestigious corps of Jewish scholars, the man would be greatly disappointed. Jesus and His followers were destined to suffer and even die for the truth He came to proclaim.

Paul, in his letter to the Colossians, said, *"Masters, give unto your servants that which is just and equal; knowing that ye also have a Master [kurios] in heaven"* (Col. 4: 1). He portrays Jesus as a just and compassionate Master who provides the most basic needs of His servants.

Son of God. When the angel appeared to Mary and predicted Jesus' birth, he said, *"That Holy One who is to be born will be called the Son of God"* (Luke 1:35 NKJV). Jesus' followers often addressed Him as "the Son of God" (compare Matthew 16:16; John 11:27). So did unbelievers (see Mark 14:61), and even demons. (See Luke 4:41.)

Son of Man. Jesus most often used this name to refer to Himself. He was keenly aware of being both God and man, and perhaps wanted to stress the reality of His incarnation to all who heard Him. Even though He called Himself the "Son of man," Jesus did not hide the fact of His divine nature and power. For example, as Jesus foretold the end times, He said, *"Then shall all the tribes of the earth mourn, and they shall see the Son of man coming in the clouds of heaven with power and great glory"* (Matt. 24:30). Surely He was no ordinary man! He was and is, at once, both God and Man.

Redeemer. We often use this name to refer to Jesus, but did you know it is not used in the New Testament? It is only found in the Old. The Hebrew word *gaal* ("redeemer") literally means "one who redeems someone from jail." Job looked forward to the day when his Messiah would purchase his soul's release from death. He said, *"For I know that my redeemer liveth, and that he shall stand at the latter day upon the earth"* (Job 19:25). He was referring, of course, to Jesus Christ.

The Bible has many other names for Jesus, each one revealing a bit more of His unique character and ministry. We don't have space to examine all of them, but I thought you might like this brief background on some of the more familiar names for Jesus. He is, after all, the eternal Son of God of human flesh. So the names of Jesus are names of the Son of God. They tell us something about the One who came to reveal God the Father.

Unlocking the Treasure

Bible students have long been fascinated by the unique role of names in the Scriptures. Perhaps names have little importance to today's man on the street, but they had great importance to the people living at the time the Bible was written. In the introduction to Robert Young's well-known *Analytical Concordance to the Bible,* we find this interesting comment:

> In Scripture, a name is much more than an identifying tag. It denotes the essence and character of a person or thing. Jesus told His disciples, "And he shall be hated of all men for my Name's sake...." Surely Christians were persecuted for more than the literal name of Jesus. Similarly, the Psalmist often refers to those who love "the name of the Lord" (e.g., Ps. 5:11), but it would be ridiculous to think that someone could love the name of the Lord without loving the Lord Himself.[7]

In over sixty years of evangelistic work, I have done considerable Bible study. Again and again, I am surprised to find new insights as I examine the names of God. Each name is like a golden key, ready to unlock a treasure of truth to the inquiring mind.

Thus, in the following pages I want to share some of the discoveries I have made in my studies. My goal is not to make you a biblical "egghead," spouting off Hebrew phrases to impress your friends. Vanity is not my purpose, and it should not be yours. But I trust you will draw closer to the Lord Himself as you learn more about Him through this study. And if you have not yet become a newborn child of God through the saving blood of His Son, Jesus Christ, I pray this volume will inspire you to take that step.

Notes

1. The Bible does not specifically say that Adam and Eve offered sacrifices to God. The Bible first records sacrifices made by their sons, Cain and Abel. (See Genesis 4.) But we must assume that the parents taught their sons about God and showed them how to worship Him.

2. God gave Abram a new name, Abraham, literally meaning "father of a multitude" (Gen. 17:5). Obviously, God saw great significance in a name!

3. When Jacob woke up from his dream of the ladder, he set up a stone pillar and worshipped the Lord there, calling it *Beth-el* (literally, "house of God").

4. In chapter 5, we will see that this phrase "God Almighty" actually became a Hebrew name for God.

5. Billy Graham, *Till Armageddon: A Perspective on Suffering* (Waco, Tex.: Word Books, 1981), pp. 46–47.

6. Bo Reicke, "The Epistles of James, Peter, and Jude," *The Anchor Bible*, Vol. 37 (Garden City, N.Y.: Doubleday and Company, 1964), pp. 39–40.

7. Robert Young, *Young's Analytical Concordance to the Bible*, rev. by William B. Stevenson and David Wimbish (Nashville: Thomas Nelson Publishers, 1980), p. vii.

2

The LORD
(Yahweh/Jehovah)

I n the first chapter, we saw that God told Moses, *"Thus shalt thou say unto the children of Israel, I AM hath sent me unto you"* (Exod. 3:14). The Hebrew name that God used to identify Himself here, as we have mentioned, is a puzzle and a mystery to Bible scholars even today. There is no other name like it in all of the ancient Hebrew literature. And the Jewish scribes who copied the manuscripts of the Bible felt the name was so holy that they did not even pronounce it. They wrote it without the vowels, because it was never to be spoken aloud.

Whenever you find the name LORD written in small capitals like this in the King James Version of the Bible, it represents this name that God revealed to Moses. The Bible first records this name in Genesis 2:4. Moses wrote the first five books of the Bible (sometimes called the Pentateuch), probably during the forty years that the Israelites wandered in the wilderness. By that time, he knew this intriguing name of God, so he used it to record the very earliest history of the human race in Genesis.

What clues do we have to the meaning of this mysterious name? First, the Hebrew manuscripts tell us that the consonants of the name were YHWH. That's all. We don't know for sure what vowels were supposed to be inserted in that word; it could have been pronounced "Yowoh" or "Yehwah" or several other ways. Bishop Clement of Alexandria, writing in the third century A.D., noted that the name was pronounced

"Yaoweh." Theodoret of Cyprus, a century later, said that the Samaritans pronounced it "Yabeh." Third-century manuscripts found in Egypt confirm this latter pronunciation.[1] Based on such information, scholars have come to assume that the name of God was pronounced "Yahweh."

But if the Jews thought this name was too holy to pronounce, what did they do when they read the Scriptures aloud? Did they just skip the name of God?

No, they took the vowels from the Hebrew name Adonai ("Lord") and inserted them in the name YHWH to make *YaHoWaH*. (We pronounce it "Jehovah.") Since this word is really a combination of the Hebrew names for "God" and "Lord," we might say that it means "Lord God."

So much for this little excursion into the mechanics of Hebrew. We still have a tough question to answer: What does the name mean?

The word *Yahweh* came from a Hebrew verb that means "to be." The name appears to have meant "I AM." That seems very simple. But think about the deep implications of that simple name.

The God Who Always Is

The Bible tells how Abraham made a covenant with Abimelech, a ruler of the Canaanites, because Abimelech saw that God blessed everything Abraham did. (See Genesis 21:22.) As a part of their treaty, Abimelech agreed to return to Abraham what he had stolen from him. So they called the place *Beersheba*, meaning "well of the oath." The Bible says that Abraham planted a grove of trees at that place as a memorial to their treaty, *"and called there on the name of the* LORD, *the everlasting God"* (Gen. 21:33).

God told Moses that He was the God who always had been, and who always would be. He was the eternal God. No matter what might happen in the world, and even in the entire universe, God would continue to live and reign as God. In his notes to *The Criswell Study Bible*, Dr. W. A. Criswell comments:

> God exists in a way that no one or anything else does.
> His [supreme] nature is implied by His ever-present existence
> without beginning or ending. He is the only God who exists,
> and all other existence is dependent upon His uncaused exis-
> tence.[2]

The other nations of Moses' day worshipped perishable gods.
Egypt, the most powerful nation in that part of the world, worshipped animals such as monkeys, alligators, cats—even beetles!
The Egyptians thought these animals and insects represented
the gods of the universe. For instance, the falcon represented Re,
the sun god. When one of these animals died, it was given a
very stately burial. Archaeologists have found thousands of cat
mummies, bird mummies, and mummies of other animals considered sacred. The Egyptians *worshipped* these things. Yet their
gods perished.

Imagine how radical Moses' message to his people must have
been! He returned to Egypt from the sun-parched wilderness of
the Sinai to tell the Israelites, "I AM has sent me." The God who
had always lived and always would live—who had always been
God and always would be God—had sent Moses.

The message was startling then, and it's just as startling
today.

America worships the present day. Television commercials
try to convince us that any new product must be better than
all of the competition. Political leaders scour the country for
new faces every election year, hoping to attract voters with their
"new-and-improved" candidates. Families plan their budgets
one week at a time (if they plan at all), because they think the
present is all that matters. That's the mindset of modern America: Live today to the fullest, for there may be no tomorrow.

Therefore, modern Americans are reluctant to follow an eternal God. They feel uncomfortable with the idea that God stakes
His claim on all of our future plans, as well as today's. They don't
like a long-term commitment to anyone; they certainly don't
want to worship anyone. These people want a disposable way of
life, one they can rearrange or discard at their slightest whim.
So they sneer at the Bible-preaching ministers of *Yahweh,* just as

the Israelite slaves must have sneered at Moses when he came to promise their deliverance. An unchanging God? An everlasting covenant with God? A lifelong commitment to God? Why, that sounds like a foreign language! Yet that is the claim placed upon our lives by the great "I AM."

The Self-Sufficient God

God was never created by some greater power. He was never conjured up by some human mind. He depends upon no one and nothing to continue living; He will live forever. One Bible commentator explains it this way:

> "I AM THAT I AM" signifies that He is self-existent, the only real being and the source of all reality; that He is self sufficient.[3]

We human beings may talk of being self-sufficient, but we don't know what that really means. During the early years of this nation, settlers pushed into the forests of Appalachia to build crude log cabins and to carve little farms out of the wilderness. They felt self-sufficient. But the family members still depended on one another to make clothes, cut firewood, draw water, harvest crops, and do all the things necessary to sustain life. The pioneers were not really self-sufficient.

Today we read of young families who have abandoned urban life to go "back to nature." They have bought little tracts of land in the forest, just as their ancestors did. Now they are building solar-heated log cabins and they are raising hybrid vegetables. But still they are not self-sufficient. They depend upon one another—and upon those of us who have remained in the cities—to provide these supplies they need to build their homes.

Individuals depend upon other individuals, families upon other families, and nations upon other nations. But God depends upon no one. He never gets hungry or shivers in the cold. He will never die of old age or suffer for lack of medical help. He is God!

The Real God

Religious hucksters have invaded human society. Fakes, quacks, and charlatans set up false gods, or make false claims about the true God, to make a reputation for themselves and reap a handsome profit. Self-professed healers often demand that people pay them large sums of money before they pray for their victims' healing. Money-grabbing "gurus" use every sort of gimmick imaginable to reap profits from their ministry. They succeed because man is so desperate to find the one true God, and to follow Him.

The God who spoke to Moses out of the burning bush was real. He said His name is "I AM," not "I am supposed to be" or "Some people think I am." God needs no one to make extravagant claims for Him. He doesn't need to be sold, glamorized, or promoted by anyone. He will be worshipped for what He is, not for the image that someone may fabricate of Him.

When the Russian cosmonaut Yuri Gagarin peered out through the window of his space capsule into the depths of space, he said he did not see God. He felt his failure to see God was a vindication of his atheistic belief that God is a figment of the capitalist imagination, a fable used to pacify the working class. The communist leaders of Russia ridiculed our faith because they thought it was just make-believe. They said, "If there really were a God, we could see and touch Him. But we can't. So He must not be real."

The minds of such people are so clouded by unbelief that they cannot search for God with any objectivity. But if they could put aside their prejudices, they would notice that many things in our world cannot be seen, touched, or measured with instruments. Yet we know these things exist.

Take the force of gravity, for instance. No one would say that gravity is just a fairy tale, but who can *see* gravity? Sure, we see the *effects* of gravity every day. If you trip over a rock, you fall on your face. If you let go of a bag of groceries, it falls to the ground. If you nudge your telephone off the edge of your desk, it falls. In space travel, the effect of gravity—acceleration—is measured in "g's." When we see these things, we know that the force of gravity is at work. But we cannot see gravity itself. We can't touch it. We can't detect it even on the most sophisticated sensing devices. We can only watch its effects.

Likewise, we cannot see, touch, or measure God—but we can see the effects of His activity in our world. We can see people's lives transformed when they surrender themselves to Him. We can see miracles of healing. We can watch the marvelous cycles of the natural world, which keeps renewing itself and preserving itself year after year as if guided by some unseen Person. Yes, we see the effects of God's actions. We know by His revealed Word that they are the results of His activity. So we know that He is real.

Moses had no doubt about that. Moses had never read one word of Holy Scripture (because none had yet been written), but he could see the flames engulfing that bush. He had never heard a sermon, yet he could hear the voice of God. He could hardly remember the testimony of his ancestors who had seen God at work, yet he saw God perform mighty miracles before his own eyes. This was enough to convince Moses that God was no figment of his imagination. As God said, "I AM."

The Unchangeable God

In my boyhood home of Louisiana, we referred to a very old person by saying, "He's as old as the hills." That was just a figure of speech, of course; no human being is as old as the mountains.

But God is. In fact, He is much older than the mountains because He "Is" from everlasting to everlasting. He made the hills!

People change with age. Their hair turns gray and falls out; their skin wrinkles and toughens; their bones become brittle. And every person will eventually die.

We may not realize it, but the "hills" are always changing, too. Geologists say that the mountains are shifting and buckling under the pressure of great forces within the earth. Wind, rain, and ice wear the mountains away. Man's earthmoving machines whittle away the mountain's profile to make a highway or a shopping center. Every hill changes with age.

But God is older than any human being. He is older than any of the hills. In fact, God is *"from everlasting to everlasting"* (Ps. 90:2). There was never a time when God the Father, Son, and Holy Spirit was not. And God never changes. He just "IS."

This is hard enough to comprehend concerning the Father. But consider for a moment how this applies to Jesus, and the truth of God's name *Yahweh* becomes even more awesome. Jesus is the second person of the triune, or threefold God. So when the Bible says God is *"from everlasting to everlasting,"* it also means that Jesus Christ exists *"from everlasting to everlasting."* The eternal Son of the Father has lived since the very beginning and will live forever. The Bible says of Him:

> *In the beginning was the Word, and the Word was with God, and the Word was God. The same was in the beginning with God....He was in the world, and the world was made by him, and the world knew him not. He came unto his own, and his own received him not.*
> (John 1:1–2, 10–11)

We can hardly imagine how anyone could reject God in human flesh. Jesus was a common man, a neighbor; but He was also the everlasting God. Yet many of Jesus' kinsmen did exactly that. They rejected Him. They spat upon Him. They demanded that He be crucified.

> *But as many as received him, to them gave he power to become the sons of God, even to them that believe on his name: which were born, not of blood, nor of the will of the flesh, nor of the will of man, but of God. And the Word was made flesh, and dwelt among us, (and we beheld his glory).*
> (John 1:12–14)

Jesus Christ is *Yahweh,* the God who "IS" from endless time before and beyond all time to come. He is our Master and Savior forever.

And the Holy Spirit exists from eternity to eternity. There never was and there never will be a time when He does not proceed eternally from the Father. In fact, Jesus offers Himself to the Father through the "eternal Spirit":

> *How much more shall the blood of Christ, who through the eternal Spirit offered himself without spot to God, purge your conscience from dead works to serve the living God?* (Heb. 9:14)

The Self-Fulfilled God

Talk with a college student about career plans, and you'll get some interesting answers. "I'm going to be a physician," says one; "I'm going to be a civil engineer," says another; "I'm going to sell widgets," says a third, and so on. But come back to those same people ten years after they graduate from school, and ask what they have become. The answers will probably be quite different. The "physician" may have become a veterinarian; the "civil engineer" may have become a politician; the "widget salesman" may have become an advertising executive. None of us knows what the future holds for us; that's one of the most exciting and exasperating things about being human.

But there has never been any question about what God the Father, Son, and Holy Spirit would be. God is only what He wills to be—God!

God wills to be righteous, and He is. He wills to be merciful, and He is. He wills to be all-powerful, and He is. Nothing can hinder God from becoming what He wills. He "IS" God, the perfect fulfillment of all that He wills to be.

In the late 1960s and early 1970s, some prominent theologians advocated a new teaching that they called "process theology." The leading thinker of this new movement was the philosopher Alfred North Whitehead. One review of Whitehead's work said:

> His God is not like the God of traditional [Christian belief], a static or perfect Being but is process. He is becoming so that

he has something in common with the living God of biblical faith. But critics...doubt that Whitehead's God can be identified with the God of Christian faith.[4]

I myself certainly doubt Whitehead's ideas. If God were always changing, evolving into some better sort of God, how could we ever be sure of our relationship with Him? Why, we would live in a nightmare world where we could not trust any of His natural laws. If God intended such anarchy, however, we must discard the Holy Bible. God's Word says concerning the Son that He is *"the same yesterday, and to day, and for ever"* (Heb. 13:8). God's Word is sure. The testimony of God's very name reminds us that He "IS" all that we could ever hope He would be, and all He might ever will to be. He "IS" the fulfillment of His own perfect will. He is not a God "in process," but a perfect, unchanging God.

Much Revealed—Much Hidden

Despite all of the insights that we can discern through examining God's name *Yahweh,* we must admit that we still do not understand everything about God's character. God's nature is far more mysterious than our minds can completely comprehend. Referring to the title *Yahweh,* one commentator says:

> The name preserves much of His nature hidden from curious and presumptuous enquiry. We cannot by searching find Him out (cf. Prov. 30:4).[5]

And so it must always be with God. The more of Himself that He reveals to us, the more remains hidden from our view. I'm sure that when Moses withdrew from that burning bush, slipped back into his sandals, and returned to Jethro's flocks, he still had many unanswered questions about God. God promised to go with Moses and his brother, who would act as his translator, when they went back to Egypt. However, there was very little more Moses knew about this One who spoke amidst the flame. But Moses acted on what he did know and obeyed God.

God may be trying to change something in your life. He may be telling you to leave your present job and undertake a new venture that would glorify Him. He may want you to heal a broken relationship in your family. He may call you to surrender an incurable illness to Him so that He can heal you. Whatever He is saying, you may hesitate to obey Him because you want to know more. But you shouldn't hesitate. If God expected us to wait until we understood *everything* about Him, no one would ever serve Him! The human mind has never fully understood God.

The apostle Paul said, *"And without controversy great is the mystery of godliness"* (1 Tim. 3:16). Even when he tried to explain the *"deep things of God"* (1 Cor. 2:10 NKJV), he confessed, *"No one knows the things of God except the Spirit of God"* (v. 11 NKJV). At the end of the familiar "Love Chapter," Paul stated, *"For now we see [God] in a mirror, dimly, but then face to face. Now I know in part, but then I shall know just as I also am known"* (1 Cor. 13:12 NKJV). Yet Paul's lack of complete understanding did not prevent him from doing great things for God. He was ready to obey the heavenly Father despite his incomplete knowledge of Him.

When I give an altar call at the end of a worship service at the Christian Center, people may walk down the aisles to commit their lives to Jesus Christ. Yet if I asked those people to explain the Trinity, the Incarnation, or some other deep truth of God, they probably couldn't do so! That's all right. The church has always called these things "mysteries." Thank God. *"By grace you have been saved through faith"* (Eph. 2:8), and not through knowledge or understanding.

The name *Yahweh* tells us much about God. It leaves much more shrouded in mystery. But like Moses, we don't need to let the mystery keep us from serving God as we ought.

Notes

1. B. W Anderson, "God, Names of," *The Interpreter's Dictionary of the Bible,* Vol. 2 (Nashville: Abingdon Press, 1962), p. 409.

2. W. A. Criswell, ed., *The Criswell Study Bible* (Nashville: Thomas Nelson Publishers, 1979), p. 75.

3. Francis Davidson, ed., *The New Bible Commentary* (Grand Rapids, Mich.: William B. Eerdmans Publishing Company, 1954), p. 109.

4. William E. Hordern, *A Layman's Guide to Protestant Theology* (New York: The Macmillan Company, 1968), p. 248.

5. Davidson, p. 15.

3
The LORD Is God
(Jehovah-Elohim)

One verse of the Creation account has puzzled and intrigued many Bible readers, because it shows that God is more than one person. That verse is Genesis 1:26:

*And God said, Let **us** make man in **our** image, after **our** likeness: and let them have dominion over the fish of the sea, and over the fowl of the air.* (emphasis added)

We Christians understand that "us" and "our" refer to the Trinity. The verse reveals that God is three persons in one nature—Father, Son, and Holy Spirit. In Old Testament times, before the birth of Jesus Christ, people did not understand in the way we do today that God is one nature in three persons. But they did know that God was more than one person.

The name He used to identify Himself was *Elohim* (pronounced "el-o-HEEM"). This is a name "reflecting divine majesty and power."[1] In fact, Bible scholars often call it the "plural of majesty." [2] The Bible sometimes uses the word *elohim* to refer to any number of "gods," such as the pagan gods of the Canaanites. (See Exodus 20:3.) But most often *Elohim* is a proper name for the one true God, suggesting His unique nature as the three-in-one God. Yet the name means more than this.

Mercy versus Justice!

The Jewish scholar Samuel Sandmel says, "The ancient Rabbis...had asserted that Elohim emphasized God's mercy, while Yahve [Yahweh] emphasized His strict justice."[3] The ancient rabbis came to this conclusion after comparing passages in the Bible that use the name *Yahweh* with other passages that use the name *Elohim*. Here are some comparisons:

Yahweh

Gen. 6:3 *"And the* LORD *[Yahweh] said, My spirit shall not always strive with man, for that he also is flesh: yet his days shall be an hundred and twenty years."*

Gen. 15:4 *"And, behold, the word of the* LORD *[Yahweh] came unto him, saying, This* [Ishmael] *shall not be thine heir; but he that shall come forth out of thine own bowels shall be thine heir."*

Gen. 30:27 *"And Laban said unto him, I pray thee, if I have found favour in thine eyes, tarry: for I have learned by experience that the* LORD *[Yahweh] hath blessed me for thy sake."*

Elohim

Gen. 1:28 *"And God [Elohim] blessed them, and God said unto them, Be fruitful, and multiply, and replenish the earth, and subdue it."*

Gen. 17:3, 6 *"And Abram fell on his face: and God [Elohim] talked with him, saying....And I will make thee exceeding fruitful, and I will make nations of thee, and kings shall come out of thee."*

Gen. 30:17 *"And God hearkened unto Leah, and she conceived."*

There does seem to be a contrast between those passages that use *Yahweh* and those that use *Elohim*. But we could quote many other verses that stress God's mercy and call Him *Yahweh*, alongside with other verses that stress His justice and call Him *Elohim*. So the rabbis' theory about these names, although there is some truth to it, does not seem completely accurate.

Then what does the name *Elohim* mean, as far as God is concerned? Why call Him *Elohim* when so many other names might be used?

A God Worthy of Worship

I gave you a clue to the answer at the very beginning of this chapter when I mentioned that the name *elohim* referred to the pagan gods of Old Testament times. *Elohim* basically means "something (or someone) that is worshipped." The *elohim* were the things most revered and honored by ancient man.

Most ancient peoples worshipped false gods. For example, the Canaanites worshipped bulls and lambs because they thought these animals were fertility gods. The Canaanites wanted plentiful crops and they hoped to bear many children. So they bowed down before symbols of fertility in hopes of becoming fertile. The bulls and lambs they worshipped were their *elohim*.

In a previous chapter, I mentioned how the Egyptians worshipped all sorts of animals and insects. These things were far inferior to God, but they served as the Egyptians' false gods. They were the Egyptians' objects of worship, their *elohim*. When Moses' father-in-law, Jethro, saw God deliver the Israelites from Egypt, he confessed, *"Now I know that the LORD [Yahweh] is greater than all gods [elohim]: for in the thing wherein they dealt proudly he was above them"* (Exod. 18:11). King David said to God, *"And what one nation in the earth is like thy people…which thou redeemedst to thee from Egypt, from the nations and their gods [elohim]?"* (2 Sam. 7:23).

God proved that these pagan idols were false by showing His people that He alone had power. Yet pagan people continued to serve their *elohim*: They continued to worship God's creatures in place of the Creator Himself. And God punished them for their idolatry.

For since the creation of the world His invisible attributes are clearly seen, being understood by the things that are made…so that they are without excuse, because, although they knew God, they did not glorify Him as God, nor were thankful, but became futile in their thoughts, and their foolish hearts were darkened. Professing to be wise, they became fools, and changed the glory of the incorruptible God into an image made like corruptible man; and birds and four-footed animals and creeping things. Therefore God also gave them up to uncleanness,...who exchanged the truth of God for the lie, and worshiped and served the creature rather than the Creator, who is blessed forever. Amen. (Rom. 1:20–25 NKJV)[4]

Our modern word *worship* comes from the Old English word, *weorthscipe,* meaning "to attribute worth" to something. That's what the pagan peoples did to their *elohim;* they believed their idols had great power to influence their everyday lives. They boasted about what their idols did for them. They believed their idols could cure diseases, provide food, deliver them from military foes, and do any number of other things. So they bowed the knee to their *elohim,* their "worthy things," and praised all that these idols were supposed to do.

But the Israelites knew that only Yahweh is worthy of praise. Only the one true God could do the things these pagans claimed their idols would do. God told the Israelites that He was the true *Elohim,* the only One to be worshipped. In fact, He often referred to Himself as *Jehovah-Elohim,* a name that literally meant "the LORD IS God" Our Bible translators usually render it as simply, "the LORD God" Here are some examples from the Old Testament:

This is the account of the heavens and the earth when they were created, in the day that the LORD God [Jehovah-Elohim] made earth and heaven. (Gen. 2:4 NASB)

The LORD God [Jehovah-Elohim] made tunics of skins for Adam and his wife and clothed them. (Gen. 3:21 NEB)

[Moses said,] *But as for you and your servants, I know that you do not yet fear the LORD God [Jehovah-Elohim].*
(Exod. 9:30 RSV)

Notice that the title *Elohim* ("God," or "One to Be Worshipped") is attached to God's proper name *Jehovah* as if it were a surname. In the English language, many surnames like "Smith," "Cooper," or "Taylor" originated this way. If a man was a black-smith, his customers began calling him "John the Smith" or "John Smith." If a woman was a barrel-maker (or cooper), they might call her "Jane the Cooper" or "Jane Cooper." So the people of Israel began calling Yahweh "LORD the God," or simply "LORD God." The meaning of that name became crystal-clear on Mount Sinai when God gave Moses the first of the Ten Command-ments:

> *Thou shalt not make unto thee any graven image, or any likeness of any thing that is in heaven above, or that is in the earth beneath, or that is in the water under the earth: Thou shalt not bow down thyself to them, nor serve them: for I* **the** LORD **thy God** *am a jealous God, visiting the iniquity of the fathers upon the children…and showing mercy unto thousands of them that love me, and keep my command-ments.* (Exod. 20:4–6, emphasis added)

God expects to be worshipped. He is pleased when we wor-ship Him as He ought to be worshipped. But He grows angry with anyone who neglects worshipping Him properly.

A Lost Discipline

We modern Americans have sadly neglected the worship of God. I think it is time for us to confess that worship is a lost dis-cipline here.

The public's casual attitude toward church attendance indi-cates this neglect. On a typical Sunday morning, you can drive through a suburban community and see most homeowners mowing the lawn, washing the car, playing touch football— doing all sorts of things *except* going to church! Yet if you took the time to question those same people about their spiritual lives, many of them would say they are "church members." Some would even say they are Christians. Yet their Sunday activities prove that they worship other things besides the one true God they profess to worship. They worship the gods of personal plea-sure, recreation, and money.

Another indicator of the sad state of our worship habits is the attitudes of people who *do* attend church. Most churchgoers love to hear a professional musician or a well-known author give a testimony. When the sermon begins, however, they lounge back in their seats and doze off to sleep. These desultory church folk like sanctuary "entertainment," but they don't care to have their souls fed.

One reason for this is the sad state of preaching in America. Most pastors are not really proclaiming the Word; they're dishing up predigested pabulum from current devotional magazines, or they are expounding their favorite psychological theories. But *"the word of God is quick, and powerful, and sharper than any twoedged sword, piercing even to the dividing asunder of soul and spirit,...and is a discerner of the thoughts and intents of the heart"* (Heb. 4:12). When Jesus Christ is preached with the power of the Holy Spirit, people can't help but stay awake! They become aware of what the Bible has to say to them. Why, they might even have to leave the room because they can't stand the conviction they feel! The fact that this seldom happens in our churches is a bitter commentary on the shoddiness of American preaching as well as on the indifference of the American churchgoer.

Once, a shipbuilder attended a preaching service of that fiery eighteenth-century evangelist George Whitefield. "I can usually construct a whole ship during a sermon," he said, "but with Whitefield I couldn't even lay the keel." May God give us more preachers who will preach the Word with such force and fervor that they hold the attention of their congregations like that!

Another indicator of the sad state of American worship is the ineffectuality of most prayers. Why aren't more prayers answered? Has God stopped working in the lives of His people? Aren't Christians praying steadfastly enough? Aren't they praying aright? I suspect the problem isn't with God, but with us.

So little time is given to focused, fervent prayer in the typical American worship service! At best, you might hear a five-minute litany of prayer by the pastor, as he runs down the list of sick and needy people in the church. They become no more than "shopping list" prayers. The Bible says that after Jesus ascended into heaven, His disciples returned to Jerusalem and *"continued with one accord in prayer and supplication"* until the Day of Pentecost (Acts 1:14). They prayed constantly until they got what they were waiting for—the power of the Holy Spirit. Their entire worship service was devoted to prayer. Every aspect of their life for those ten days involved prayer. And God answered their prayer.

I believe that revival will come to churches in America only if Christians devote themselves to prayer. Flashy visitation programs won't bring revival, and neither will slick Madison Avenue advertising gimmicks. The only thing that will open the church to a fresh infilling of the Holy Spirit's power is constant, faithful prayer. Yet such prayer is conspicuously absent from most of our worship services.

Dick Eastman of the World Literature Crusade used to hold seminars on prayer. He called prayer time "The Hour That Changes the World." Matthew 26:40 speaks of Jesus' return from His prayer vigil in Gethsemane. When He found Peter sleeping, Jesus said, *"What, could ye not watch with me one hour?"* After Dick read this verse, he wondered what would happen if he dedicated one hour each day to prayer—nothing but prayer. He tried it and began to see remarkable things happen in his ministry. He recommended such prayer to his friends and colleagues, and they too were blessed. Now he travels about the country, holding seminars on prayer. His program is based on the idea that Christ deserves at least one undisturbed hour of our day in prayer.

Think what might happen if Christians spent even half an hour in prayer every Sunday when they came together for worship. Why, we might witness another Day of Pentecost—another mighty outpouring of God's Spirit!

I said earlier that I believed worship is a lost discipline for most American Christians. Worship is a discipline, you know. It does not come naturally for carnal human beings. In most church services we are much too concerned about comfortable seating, or the golf game we want to play, or the pot roast that's in the oven to truly focus our thoughts on God. But *worship must be concentrated.* It must be focused. If we intend to "attribute worth" to God, we must put everything else out of our minds and hearts. Archbishop Fenelon, writing in the seventeenth century, grasped this idea when he wrote,

> The love of God...desires that self should be forgotten, that it should be counted as nothing, that God might be all in all. God knows that it is best for us when self is trampled under foot and broken as an idol, in order that He might live within us, and make us after His will....So let that vain, complaining babbler—self-love—be silenced, that in the stillness of the soul we may listen to God.[5]

How to Worship as We Ought

If we truly believe that God is *Jehovah-Elohim,* we should start worshipping Him *"in spirit and in truth"* (John 4:23). We should worship Him wholeheartedly Let me suggest some ways that you can improve your worship to God.

1. *Study the Word of God.* Notice I said, "study," not just "read" the Bible. There's a world of difference between the two. A Bible student comes to the Word of God with a real hunger to learn more of God's will for his life. He reads the Bible prayerfully, thoughtfully, and meditatively He takes time to absorb what Scripture says and to apply the Word to current problems in his life. Job said, *"I have esteemed the words of his mouth more than my necessary food"* (Job 23:12). The apostle Peter said, *"As newborn babes, desire the sincere milk of the word, that ye may grow thereby"* (1 Pet. 2:2). And the Bible gives ample proof that God can use His written Word to bring revival among His people if they will but study it.

2. *Obey what you read in the Word of God.* This seems so simple that it almost goes without saying. But the great majority of Christians ignore this simple rule. They read the Bible, then slap the Book closed and walk away.

> *But be ye doers of the word, and not hearers only, deceiving your own selves. For if any be a hearer of the word, and not a doer, he is like unto a man beholding his natural face in a glass: for he beholdeth himself, and goeth his way, and straightway forgetteth what manner of man he was.* (James 1:22–24)

If your spiritual life is weak, it may be because you've disregarded what God's Word admonishes you to do. Begin obeying Scripture, and you'll be able to worship more freely. You'll be better able to enjoy His presence.

3. *Confess that He is God and you are His servant.* Again, this seems so simple, but many Christians keep trying to make themselves God, and to make God their servant. A. W. Tozer touched on this problem when he wrote:

> Before the Spirit of God can work creatively in our hearts, He must condemn and slay the "flesh" within us; that is, He must have our full consent to displace our natural self with the Person of Christ....Nothing that comes from God will minister to my pride of self-congratulation. If I am tempted to be complacent and to feel superior because I have had a remarkable vision or an advanced spiritual experience, I should go at once to my knees and repent of the whole thing. I have fallen a victim to the enemy.[6]

When self keeps God off the throne of your life, you are bound to have a discouraging worship experience because you are really worshipping yourself instead of God. You must be able to say with Paul, *"I die daily"* (1 Cor. 15:31), and *"I am crucified with Christ: nevertheless I live; yet not I, but Christ liveth in me: and the life which I now live in the flesh I live by the faith of the Son of God, who loved me, and gave himself for me"* (Gal. 2:20). We must truly let Christ, not ourselves, reign in our hearts if we want to have a meaningful life of worship.

4. *Make peace with any Christian who is at odds with you.* Jesus said, *"Therefore if thou bring thy gift to the altar, and there rememberest that thy brother hath ought against thee; leave there thy gift before the altar, and go thy way; first be reconciled to thy brother, and then come and offer thy gift"* (Matt. 5:23–24). Did you ever feel that your prayers were getting no higher than the ceiling? Maybe that was because you had a conflict with some other Christian. Jesus says you need to settle your problems with other Christians before you pray at the altar of God—even if you're not the one who's upset. Notice that he said, *"If thy brother hath aught against thee."*

I wonder what would happen in our Sunday morning worship services if pastors began the prayer time by saying, "We're going to pause for a minute to let you iron out any problems you have with your brothers and sisters here. Then we'll pray." In the worship services of the early church, the kiss of peace always preceded Communion, to give the people the opportunity to make certain they were reconciled to one another. I think we would be pleasantly surprised at what God could do were His people to establish such peace with each other.

5. *Begin your prayer with praise.* So many Christians give the Lord a perfunctory "thank you" at the start of prayer, just as a prelude to the "real" business of *asking* God for things. They remind me of someone who curtly doffs his hat to a stranger and then asks for a handout. God doesn't appreciate that sort of "courtesy"!

Make sure you start your prayer with genuine praise of God. Praise Him for being who He is. Praise Him for what He has done in your life. Praise Him for what He has promised to do in the future. Put your petitions out of your mind for the time being; just focus your thoughts on God and let your praises flow. The psalmist said, *"Enter into his gates with thanksgiving, and into his courts with praise: be thankful unto him, and bless his name"* (Ps. 100:4). That's still good advice.

6. *Make specific prayer requests.* There is a proper time in each prayer for bringing your requests to God—after you have truly praised Him and meditated on who He is. When the time for petitions is come, make sure you are specific. Don't say, "Lord, bless my children." Let Him know *in what way* you believe they need to be blessed. Tell Him if they need to be saved, healed, aided with their finances, or anything else. Don't say, "Lord, work out this problem that I have." Let Him know *in what way* you need His help in resolving it. Indicate that you've wrestled with this problem and tried to discern His will in the matter before you approached Him with your requests. The Bible says, *"The effectual fervent prayer of a righteous man availeth much"* (James 5:16). That word *effectual* means that you should pray for specific "effects," specific results that you feel are in keeping with

the will of God. A vague, general prayer probably indicates that you're really not too concerned about the outcome of your request.

7. *Make "quiet space" for God.* Modern lifestyles leave little room for quiet meditation, and most of us have forgotten what an hour of silence feels like. A friend of mine once spent a day at a Catholic retreat center to meditate and pray. The first few hours were very uncomfortable, he said. Know why? Because he could hear no radio, television, or telephone! It was called a discipline of silence. "I felt like I was on another planet," he remembered.

The saints of past centuries knew the value of having quiet tunes with the Lord. They retired to their prayer closets or to a secluded hillside every day just to talk with Him. God told the people of Israel, *"In returning and rest shall ye be saved; in quietness and in confidence shall be your strength: and ye would not"* (Isa. 30:15). If you will take time to make some "quiet spaces" for meditating, praying, and worshipping God, you will find far more strength in your spirit than you have now.

Call Others to Worship

Followers of the ancient Persian cult of Ahura-Mazda believed they should keep their pagan "truth" to themselves, so they did not invite outsiders to their worship services. The same was true of those infamous heretics of the early church, the Gnostics. Other offbeat groups throughout the intervening centuries have tried to keep mystic secrets of their religion to themselves.

But the followers of *Jehovah-Elohim* do just the opposite. They invite their unbelieving friends to join them in worshipping God. In fact, they believe that evangelism—calling others to God—is a key part of their own worship. If He is truly *Elohim,* the One worthy of worship, then all people ought to worship Him.

Thus saith God the LORD, he that created the heavens, and stretched them out; he that spread forth the earth, and that which cometh out of it; he that giveth breath unto the people upon it, and spirit to them that walk therein: I the LORD have called thee in righteousness, and

45

> *will hold thine hand, and will keep thee, and give thee for a covenant*
> *of the people, for a light of the Gentiles; to open the blind eyes, to bring*
> *out the prisoners from the prison....I am the* LORD: *that is my name:*
> *and my glory will I not give to another, neither my praise to graven*
> *images.* (Isa. 42:5–8)

We twentieth-century Christians are tempted to think that we don't need to tell others about God. Tenderhearted intellectuals say that everyone is entitled to his own belief; therefore, there's no need for evangelism. So there has been a sharp decline in missionary work. Major denominations are shutting down mission schools and hospitals; they're now sending money to aid the "economic development" of foreign nations.

In fact, the only Christian groups that have increased their force of missionaries to the field these days are the independent, evangelical churches, according to a recent article in *Christianity Today*. We still believe God is supposed to be worshipped by the entire world, not just white Anglo-Saxon Protestants who make more than $20,000 a year. In that article Harold Lindsell commented:

> Many factors have contributed to the serious loss of missionaries among the traditional ecumenical denominations. However...these figures are a rough index of the depth of confliction about basic Christian doctrine—the nature of the gospel, the lostness of mankind apart from Christ, and the necessity of obeying biblical mandates. [7]

We do have a mandate from God, a mandate to call the entire world to Him. Christ said, *"Go ye therefore, and teach all nations, baptizing them in the name of the Father, and of the Son, and of the Holy Ghost"* (Matt. 28:19). So our worship will never be complete until we tell others that the Lord is the one true God indeed, God in three persons, God of all the world, and worthy of our deepest devotion.

Notes

1. Francis Brown, S. R. Driver, and Charles A. Briggs, eds., *A Hebrew and English Lexicon of the Old Testament* (Oxford: Oxford University Press, 1972), p. 43.

2. B. W Anderson, "God, Names of," *The Interpreter's Dictionary of the Bible,* Vol. 2 (Nashville: Abingdon Press, 1962), p. 413.

3. Samuel Sandmel, *The Hebrew Scriptures* (New York: Alfred A. Knopf, 1963), p. 329.

4. For more insight into how these nations ignored God, see my book, *Where Was God When Pagan Religions Began?* (Nashville: Thomas Nelson Publishers, 1980).

5. Fenelon, *Let Go* (New Kensington, Pa.: Whitaker House, 1973), p. 52.

6. A. W. Tozer, *The Best of A. W. Tozer,* ed. by Warren W. Wiersbe (Grand Rapids, Mich.: Baker Book House, 1978), pp. 189–190.

7. Harold Lindsell, "The Major Denominations Are Jumping Ship." *Christianity Today,* (September 18, 1981), p. 16.

4

The LORD God Most High
(Jehovah-Elyon)

Jehovah-Elyon should elicit praise upon praise from the fervent believer. This name for God is used about forty times in the Old Testament. It first appears in Genesis 14, in which King Melchizedek of Salem praises Abram's valiant rescue of his nephew Lot. Melchizedek said,

> *Blessed be Abram of the most high God, possessor of heaven and earth: and blessed be the most high God, which hath delivered thine enemies into thy hand.* (Gen. 14:19–20)

This name *Elyon* literally means "supreme God" or "most loved God." Notice why Melchizedek believes God is the "most high." and the "possessor of heaven and earth." He points out to Abram in verse 20 that God *"hath delivered thine enemies into thy hand."* And when you consider the frightful odds that Abram was up against—three hundred and eighteen household servants to fight the armies of the mightiest nations of that day (vv. 1, 14)—you realize how great Abram's God had to be!

Pagan kings believed their gods helped them in battle. If they were defeated, they believed it was because their enemy's god was stronger than their own. So Melchizedek knew he spoke on good authority when he said Abram served "the most high God," *Elyon.*

An Unlikely Victor

To get a better idea of the magnitude of Abram's victory, notice that he had to pursue his enemies from the vicinity of Beersheba (in southern Canaan) to Dan, then divide his meager force of three hundred and eighteen men to keep on chasing the enemy by night to Damascus. (See Genesis 14:13–15.) Even today, if a tourist party in Beersheba wakes early in the morning and boards a bus or van for Damascus, it will be nightfall by the time they arrive. This was a long and perilous journey over rough terrain. Yet Abram made the trip. He pitted his tiny band of soldiers against larger armies. And he won! Surely he was serving "the most high God."

Since Abram had also captured the war booty that his enemies had taken from Sodom and Gomorrah, the king of Sodom went out to meet Abram as he returned from battle. The king of Sodom offered Abram a deal. He said, *"Give me the persons* [i.e., the slaves], *and take the goods to thyself"* (v. 21). But Abram refused. He said,

> I have lift up mine hand unto the LORD, the most high God [*Jehovah-Elyon*], *the possessor of heaven and earth, That I will not take from a thread even to a shoelatchet, and that I will not take any thing that is thine, lest thou shouldest say, I have made Abram rich.* (vv. 22–23)

Abram gave God all the credit for the victory he had won, and he would give God all the credit for the material blessings he would receive. When the day came that God would bless him with herds, land, and other kinds of wealth, Abram wanted no one to say, "I made Abram what he is today." So he gave the war booty back to the king of Sodom.

How about you? Is your life a "rags to riches" story? If it is, to whom do you give the credit—to God or man? I have led some very wealthy businessmen to the Lord Jesus Christ; every one of them then started giving God the credit for their wealth. Before Jesus took over their lives, they boasted of their keen business sense and "lucky breaks"; but after Jesus took over, they gave God all the credit for their prosperity. That's the way it should be.

Abram gave God all the credit for his success. He wanted his ungodly neighbors to see how God blessed him; he wanted them to realize that he served "the Lord the most high God."

A Self-Made Man?

The attitude of Lot, Abram's nephew, was just the opposite of his uncle's. Lot kept trying to prove that he could make a successful life for himself, with no help from anyone else. He wanted to prove he could be a "self-made man."

When Uncle Abram let him choose his own portion of the land, Lot chose the best portion in hopes of making a great name for himself. The Bible says, *"Lot…pitched his tent toward Sodom. But the men of Sodom were wicked and sinners before the LORD exceedingly"* (Gen. 13:12–13). Lot chose to live in an area good for trading, despite the moral corruption that the "cities of the plain" might bring to his family.

Then Sodom and Gomorrah fell to their enemies, and Lot was carried off by the pagan armies of the East. Abram rescued him but turned over all the flocks and other possessions to the king of Sodom. So Lot lost everything he owned. At that point, the wisest thing Lot could have done would have been to say, "I see, Uncle Abram, that when I'm with you, I'm on the winning side. When I'm with you, God blesses me. And when I try to make it on my own, I'm a slave."

But he didn't. He went right back to the city of Sodom, got a house for his family, and tried to eke out a living in that hellhole of corruption.

Soon God decided to destroy Sodom and Gomorrah, and He warned Lot to get out before it was too late. (See Genesis 19.) Lot took his family to the city of Zoar as God rained fiery brimstone upon Sodom and Gomorrah, scorching them from the face of the earth forever. You'll remember that Lot lost his wife in the process. When she disobeyed God and looked back at her hometown, God turned her into a pillar of salt.

You would think that by now Lot would have learned his lesson. After these cliff-hanger escapes, he should have known that he ought to trust *Jehovah-Elyon* to bless his life, instead of trying to bless himself.

But no, Lot soon decided to take his two daughters and retreat to a nearby mountain cave. Apparently, he intended to spend the rest of his life there as a hermit. What a classic portrait of human despair! When a man fails to succeed at his own plans for self-conceited success, all he wants is a lonely place to sulk. If he can't have the congratulations of others, he certainly doesn't want their pity. He would rather be forgotten. That's what Lot wanted to do: hide and be forgotten.

Do you see the contrast between Lot and his Uncle Abram? One man tried to make something of himself, the other let the most high God make something of him. And which one succeeded?

Let's return to that conversation between Abram and Melchizedek, because it reveals two important facts about the most high God. Look again at what Melchizedek says in Genesis 14:19: *"Blessed be Abram of the most high God, possessor of heaven and earth."* Because God is the Most High, He owns everything in creation. In fact, He created it to begin with! So it's easy to see how God can control every situation of our lives. He owns the universe. He's in charge of everything in it.

We once needed to build an important building for our ministry, and the state government required us to have two driveway exits. So the contractor approached the man who owned the adjacent property and asked to buy more of the property so we could meet the building code. The owner, however, did not want to sell.

Now this fellow was an elderly farmer. The ground we wanted to buy from him was open farmland. He would soon be dead, and the property would be of no use to him. But he would not sell. "They'll never get even a little bit of this land from me!" he said.

His attitude didn't bother me personally. I always say, "The Lord's will be done." We just didn't erect the building. But can you imagine the tragedy of thinking like that man! Why, none of us really own anything. When I die, my body will be put in a casket and buried six feet under; that's all the earthly "possession" that will be left to Lester Sumrall. I don't really own anything in this world. I'm just allowed to use some things for a little while, to bring glory to the Lord. He's the One who really owns it all.

The Bible says that Abram *"gave him tithes of all"* (Gen. 14:20) because He realized God owned it all. He gave a tenth of the war spoils to this king-priest, as an offering to God, because he knew God really owned everything he had. This is the Bible's first reference to tithing and it comes at a most appropriate place in Scripture. We begin to tithe our money and other material goods to the Lord's work when we realize that the most high God owns it all.

The Deliverer

Notice the second thing Melchizedek said about the most high God: *"And blessed be the most high God, which hath delivered thine enemies into thy hand"* (v. 20). Not only does God own all things and all people, but he delivers them into the hands of His people.

Think about that for a moment: Did you realize that God will deliver your enemies into your hands?

I think this is the thing most people don't understand about the ministry of deliverance. They know how much they would like to be delivered from sin, from illness, from demon possession, and so on. They want to escape from these things, and God offers them a way of escape. But there's another kind of deliverance that He promises, too. He promises to subdue certain problems His people experience.

God may not remove that malignant cancer from your body, but He will deliver the fear of cancer into your hands. He will give victory over the fear. God may not remove the hateful temper of your husband or wife, but He will deliver that temper into your hands. He will give you victory over it.

Hundreds of people have asked me to pray that God would deliver them from smoking, drinking, taking drugs, and any number of other things. Yet they're surprised at how God delivers them. The cigarettes, booze, and drugs are still there; the temptation still faces them. But God gives them victory over the temptation. He delivers the enemies into their hands. Hallelujah!

Many people already have deliverance from their problems, but they don't claim it. Now what do I mean by that? I mean it's not enough to dream about deliverance from your problem. It's not enough to read your Bible and say, "My, look how God used to deliver people from this." You must claim God's promise to be *Jehovah-Elyon* in your life, and say, "I am delivered!" And you must keep on reminding yourself that God *has* delivered the enemy into your hand.

God Is Greater

We may be so impressed by human achievements that we overlook the greatness of God Himself. You think I'm exaggerating, but it's true.

Many people have made a religion of modern technology; they think that scientists' ingenious minds can solve any problem that confronts them. They think they have no need for God; that, in fact, God only exists in the imagination of gullible people.

I'll agree that the human mind has achieved some marvelous things in recent years. Today I can leave New York or Washington on a magnificent supersonic plane and arrive in London less than three hours later. (The trip used to take nearly a month by boat.) I can sit down at a desktop computer, punch a few buttons, and call up thousands of facts about the stock market or medical science or any other area of interest to me. Those facts are stored on a plastic disc no bigger than a dinner plate. I can stand before a TV camera and preach a sermon, while my picture and the sound of my voice are instantaneously transmitted to millions of homes through a satellite hovering far above the earth. What a marvelous age in which to live!

But all of these marvels are just a taste of the infinite marvels God will reveal to us in eternity. God's mind is far greater than those He created. The Bible says, *"Eye hath not seen, nor ear heard, neither have entered into the heart of man, the things which God hath prepared for them that love him"* (1 Cor. 2:9).

We Christians are going to live with God forever, in continuous awe of His majesty and glory. We will serve the most high God throughout eternity. I'm so glad that the most high God, *Jehovah-Elyon,* was not only Abram's God: He's the God of every born-again believer today.

God revealed Himself to Abram as *Jehovah-Elyon* in a moment of victory. At the moment of final victory, when Christ conquers Satan once and for all, the saints of God will certainly look heavenward and exclaim that He is greater than anyone else or any other power. He is truly the most high God, *Jehovah-Elyon.*

5
The Almighty God
(El-Shaddai)

Genesis 17 tells how God appeared to Abram just after the birth of Ishmael, reminding him that they still had a covenant together. Abram was ninety-nine years old when this conversation began (v. 1), but he had turned one hundred by the time it ended (v. 17). So it must have been quite a prayer meeting! Notice what happened:

> *And when Abram was ninety years old and nine, the LORD appeared to Abram, and said unto him, I am the Almighty God [El-Shaddai]; walk before me, and be thou perfect. And I will make my covenant between me and thee, and will multiply thee exceedingly. And Abram fell on his face: and God talked with him.* (Gen. 17:1–3)

Here God reveals another of His names to the man that He promised would be the father of mighty nations. God was teaching Abram more and more about Himself by giving him these different names for God. Each name had its own particular meaning, and revealed more of God's nature. The name "God Almighty," or *El-Shaddai* in the Hebrew, emphasizes God's ability to handle any situation that confronts His people. Dr. W. A. Criswell notes that *El-Shaddai*

> ...is a further enrichment of the supreme name YAHWEH. "El" is the singular form of *Elohim,* and "Shaddai" is literally "sufficient" or "self-sufficient"; therefore, it is rendered "almighty." The "almightiness" and "self-sufficiency" of YAHWEH are

adequate for Him to deal victoriously and even destructively with His enemies.[1]

God wanted Abram to know He was in control of every situation. Abram might feel discouraged about trekking across the Near East to find the Promised Land; he might feel defeated by the prospect of fighting the strong warriors of Canaan to get the inheritance God had offered him. But God said there was no reason to feel discouraged and defeated. Abram just needed to remember that *El-Shaddai* would take care of him. The almighty God would not let his mission fail.

Satan wanted to destroy the nation of Israel even before it got started, so he threw all of his powers against Abram. The name Satan means "the Accuser," and Satan did his best to accuse Abram of failing. I can imagine Satan whispering into Abram's ear, "How can God make you a great nation? You have no children of your own, except for this boy you conceived in an illicit affair with your servant girl. You think God will use him to make a 'holy nation'? That's a laugh!"

Satan tries to destroy us from within, you see. He can give us physical trouble, and he can give us much opposition in the work we try to do for the Lord. But the frontline for the battleground, as far as Satan is concerned, is your mind. He knows that if he can defeat your thoughts, he'll defeat your faith. He wants to make you skeptical of God's promises. So he seizes on every setback and problem as an accusation to bring to your mind; he begins whispering doubt in your ear. That's what he tried to do with Abram.

But God told Abram, *"I am the Almighty God."* In other words, he said, "Abram, you see a lot of obstacles ahead. You see only the problems. But I'm bigger than any of your problems, and I'll fulfill my promises to you despite all the problems, if you'll turn them over to Me."

How many times God has had to remind me of that! I've been a minister of the gospel all my adult life, first as a foreign missionary and now as a pastor. Believe me, Satan works on nobody more than he works on a pastor or a missionary! He knows that if he can defeat God's leaders, he can defeat all of God's people.

So he works overtime at feeding doubts into my mind, and I've come close to being discouraged many times. But, praise God, the Almighty reminds me that He's able to take care of whatever trouble I'm facing! He may not show me *how* He's going to do it; He doesn't have to show me. He only reminds me that He is the almighty God, more powerful than any problem in my life. That's enough to lift the mist of defeat.

Confessing God's Power

So-called Christian psychologists often tell people to confess their weaknesses. Doing so allows you to be more human, they say. If you confess your weakness, you won't feel defeated so often because you'll know you're entitled to a few slip-ups.

The Bible does say that we are weak, humanly speaking. Paul admitted that Christians have the treasure of God's righteousness in *"earthen vessels"* (2 Cor. 4:7)—clay pots that are liable to crack and break altogether. That's why we must rely on the Holy Spirit to give us God's own power every day. But if we concentrate on our weaknesses, rather than on the might of God, we set a limit on what God can do through us. Satan tried to make Abram believe he could never carry out God's plan because he was too old, too weak, and too travel-weary. But Abram stood his ground. He believed God. He may have looked weak, but his faith wasn't weak at all, and his God certainly wasn't weak. He was on God's side, and nobody is weak on God's side.

I'm not talking here about confessing sins. Certainly when we transgress God's law, we should confess and ask His forgiveness. (See 1 John 1:8–9.) I'm speaking here of lack of *faith*.

Here's something Satan hopes you never find out: *You're only as weak as you confess to be.* If you spend all your time talking about how weak you are, you set a puny human limit for the power of God. You've programmed yourself for failure. But the more you confess God's power, the more He can do for you.

Al Oerter was a track-and-field athlete who won the gold medal for discus throwing in the 1956 Olympics in Melbourne and the 1960 Olympics in Rome. He decided to try again at the 1964 Tokyo Olympics. His top competitor in Tokyo was a powerful Czech who had beat Al's old record just with his practice throws.

A week before the Olympics, Al tore the cartilage off the right side of his rib cage in a field practice accident. He had trouble with a cervical disc and had to wear a neck collar to keep it from hurting. Somehow he managed to qualify for the finals, but he had so much pain that his doctor advised him to drop out.

Don't make a fool of yourself, an inner voice whispered. *You've got an excuse. Withdraw!*

But Al Oerter suited up for the competition. He felt he had to try, in spite of the pain. When it came time for Al to throw the discus, he stepped into the ring and prayed, "God, give me strength."

His first toss was not particularly good, but it was good enough to get him into the last string of finalists. He had three more chances. His next throw was a failure, and the pain in his side and neck got worse.

But Al trusted the Lord to provide the strength he didn't have. He stepped back into the ring and threw the discus one more time. It sailed over 200 feet down the field for a new world record—and Al's third gold medal. Looking back on that day, Al said, "The important thing for all of us to remember is that wherever we want to go in life, we won't get there unless we bend all our efforts—mental, physical, and spiritual—toward that end."[2]

What do you do when you face a problem that's bigger than you can handle? Do you confess your weakness? Or do you confess God's power? You ought to do both. You ought to let God be "God Almighty" in your life.

Honoring an Almighty God

If God is all-powerful and all-sufficient, and we are just *"earthen vessels,"* that raises another dilemma: How can we possibly have fellowship with Him? How can God tolerate us? God answered those questions for Abram when He said, *"Walk before me, and be thou perfect"* (Gen. 17:1).

God Almighty expects His people to live differently than everyone else. Many people today who think they know God go on living like the rest of the world. Women who claim to be God-fearing Christians still dress like Jezebel, prancing their endowments seductively before the eyes of men. But God wants us to know that we walk before Him. Our actions and thoughts are under the scrutiny of God Almighty, so they should not be like the actions and thoughts of carnal, unregenerate sinners. God's people can't live like Sodomites without being destroyed along with Sodom. (See Matthew 11:20–24.)

When God says, *"Be thou perfect,"* He is referring to moral perfection. He means we should live clean and godly lives before Him. Christian, don't sin against God and try to excuse yourself by saying, "Oh well, I'm only human." You're redeemed! You're a child of God! You are in union with Jesus Christ. Look like it, walk like it, talk like it, and live like it. That's the only way you can honor the almighty God you serve, and it's the only way He will continue to have fellowship with you.

Christian businessman J. Daniel Hess writes:

> God is the Creator, the Definer of the good, the Maker of reality, the Head of the divine kingdom. All of our work and each of our obligations are subjected to the claims of God's creation and God's kingdom. To fulfill those obligations, we become servants of Christ.[3]

In other words, the only way we can fulfill God's design for our lives is to obey Him. That's true on the job, at home, in the school board meeting, riding a plane—wherever you are. God expects you to "walk before Him, and be perfect."

God blesses people who "walk before Him" in moral purity. The second time Jacob and his sons needed grain from Egypt, Jacob sent them there with twice as much money as they had been charged before, plus the money they had found in their bags, which they thought was *"an oversight"* (Gen. 43:12). And Jacob said, *"God Almighty [El-Shaddai] give you mercy before the man, that he may send away your other brother, and Benjamin"* (Gen. 43:14). He believed that if his sons did what was right, God the Almighty would bless them.

When Jacob called his sons to his deathbed for a final blessing he said to Joseph, *"The archers have sorely grieved him, and shot at him, and hated him: but his bow abode in strength, and the arms of his hands were made strong by the hands of the mighty God of Jacob....Even by the God of thy father, who shall help thee; and by the Almighty [Shaddai], who shall bless thee"* (Gen. 49:23–25). Jacob knew God would bless Joseph because the young man had done what was right, regardless of what his brothers had done to him. God the Almighty honors those who honor Him with a holy life.

Notice that God first told Abram to "be perfect," *then* He will "make a covenant" with us; if we don't, He offers us nothing.

There's no telling what wonderful things God would do in our lives if we started doing all that He tells us to do. The moment we question God, however, we blunt His blessings. When God gives us an order and promises to bless us if we carry out that order, we shouldn't say, "Now wait a minute, Lord. Just how are you going to do this?" The person of faith must walk in simple confidence that the Lord will do what He has said He will do.

One night as I prayed to the Lord, He told me that He wanted me to win a million souls for Him. Imagine that! Why, I would have been thrilled to win even a hundred souls for the Lord—but a million! Yet when God says that He's going to do a certain thing, we'd better believe Him. And I believe He's going to bless my ministry in just that way, if I keep on obeying Him.

God—The Beginning of Greatness

I'm sure that if Abraham told his neighbors what God had promised to do for him, they would have thought he was crazy. A great nation would come of this wizened old tent-dweller? This century-old codger would have more sons by his ninety-year-old wife? I'm sure Abraham's friends would have laughed at the very thought; it would have seemed so preposterous, so impossible.

But God needs men and women who are willing to be considered crazy for His sake. The Lord needs Christians who will stand up with Paul and say, *"We are fools for Christ's sake, but ye are wise in Christ"* (1 Cor. 4: 10). The only way this world will learn the truth of the gospel is if people like you and I will "stick our necks out" to believe what God promises.

That's what Abraham did. (God gave him a new name.) At first he, too, thought God's promise was laughable; but he went right ahead and believed it. Sarah, his wife, said, *"God hath made me to laugh, so that all that hear will laugh with me"* (Gen. 21:6). And she said, *"Who would have said unto Abraham, that Sarah should have given children suck? for I have born him a son in his old age"* (v. 7). Only God could have promised them such a thing. Anyone else would have found it impossible to fulfill such a promise, but *"with God all things are possible"* (Matt. 19:26).

If I had told the people of my congregation twenty years ago what God would do with our radio and TV ministry, they would have burst out laughing. Who could have believed that He would give us the ownership of eight TV stations, plus a radio station? Who would have believed that we would make hundreds of audiocassettes and videocassettes of our worship services each week to send to people around the world? Who would have believed that our basement would be jammed full of printing presses, mailing machines, and complex electronic gear? Who would have believed that we would operate our own Christian college, which sends missionaries around the globe? Nobody would have believed it. But all these things have come to pass by the grace of the Lord. We had better believe Jesus when He says, *"With God all things are possible."*

The prophet Isaiah predicted that God would send His Anointed One to deliver the nation of Israel from all their enemies, especially the spiritual enemy of Satan. But Isaiah also said, *"Who hath believed our report? and to whom is the arm of the LORD revealed?"* (Isa. 53:1). The answer was simple—only the ones who had courage enough to believe that God does what He says He will do. Believers may be accounted fools, as far as the world is concerned, but they are wise in the eyes of the Lord. They are the ones who will see *"the arm of the LORD revealed"* in mighty and wondrous works.

When I was a boy, we had lots of wall mottoes hanging in our home. Each one had a Bible verse or some other statement designed to strengthen our faith. And one of those wall mottoes said, "I am the El-Shaddai." If a visitor didn't know what that meant, my mother could take an hour to tell him. I still remember how excited she would become as she told how great, how wonderful, and how powerful God really is.

My friend, you and I need to rejoice in God's greatness today. We need to remind ourselves that He is indeed El-Shaddai, "God the Almighty," and that He can handle any problem that faces us. It's so easy to have puny faith because we assume God is puny. We secretly think He's not able to make much difference in our lives. But when we realize that He is the almighty God, the all-powerful Ruler of the Universe, we begin to see wonderful things happen in our lives. Our faith becomes great as we realize God is great.

Dr. Robert H. Schuller tells of a tourist who walked down a seaside pier one afternoon and saw a fisherman pull in a big fish, measure it, and throw it back in the ocean. This intrigued the tourist, so he kept watching. Soon the fisherman caught a much smaller fish, measured it, and dropped it in his bucket. He kept doing this for some time—throwing the big fish back, keeping the little fish. So the tourist asked him why he did this.

"Why," the fisherman said, "because my frying pan is only ten inches across!"[4]

Are you doing that with God's promises? Are you "throwing back" the overwhelming miracles that He wants to do in your life, and "keeping" only the small, believable things that He promises? Let God be *El-Shaddai* in your life! Let Him be the almighty God that He can be! Put your trust in His infinite greatness, and He'll make you what He wants you to be!

Pay careful attention to what God promised Abraham in Genesis 17:8:

*And I will give unto thee, and to thy seed after thee, the land wherein thou art a stranger, all the land of Canaan, for **an everlasting possession**; and I will be their God.* (emphasis added)

God granted Abraham the entire land of Canaan as an everlasting possession for him and his family. The Jews have been evicted from that land time and again, but they always come back because it belongs to them. *God honored Abraham's faith by giving him the only permanent real estate grant on the face of the earth.* That's how great God is!

The diplomats of the United Nations have bent all their human wisdom to solving the problem of dividing up the land of Palestine. They're not sure how much land should go to Israel, how much to Jordan, how much to Egypt, and how much to the Palestine Liberation Front. But there's only one problem with all their debating and political maneuvering! God says the land will always belong to Israel. I don't say that because I'm pro-Israel or anti-Palestinian; I say that because the Word of God says it. God is great enough to back up His promise to Abraham, and He will do so long after the United Nations has disbanded. And He will make His promise stick, because He is *El-Shaddai.*

God gave Abraham two sons, Ishmael and Isaac. Ishmael was the ancestor of the Arab people, while Isaac was the ancestor of the Jews. These two groups of people account for much of the material wealth in our world today. I'm not saying this to draw attention to the Jews or Arabs, but to draw attention to the One who made them what they are. God the Almighty has not failed in His promise to the descendants of Ishmael and Isaac, even today. And He's going to keep His promises for all eternity.

God blesses the people who believe He is as great as He really is. God even blesses the children of people who believe.

I know liberal theologians would deny the above statement, nevertheless it's true. It would be interesting to make a study of the top officers of the "Fortune 500" companies, and see how many of them are the sons and daughters of devout, godly parents. I think you'd find a surprisingly large number of them are. (I'm acquainted with some of these people, so I know my statement is not just a "shot in the dark.") Make a survey of the members of Congress, the governors of our states, and the other top political leaders of our nation, and I think you'll find that most of them grew up in God-fearing, God-honoring homes. I have talked with some of the chief political leaders of our land, and most of them say that their parents prayed for them. Their parents said, "Lord, I claim your promises. Bless my children." And the Lord did.

So no matter how simplistic it may sound, I repeat it to you: *God blesses people who believe He is as great as He really is. Furthermore, He blesses their children. "For He remembered His holy promise, And Abraham His servant. He brought out His people with joy, His chosen ones with gladness"* (Ps. 105:42–43 NKJV).

Obey His Word—Claim His Power

Of course, these promises didn't just fall into the lap of Abraham's children. They had to stay true to God's covenant with Abraham before He could bless them as He desired. *"And God said unto Abraham, Thou shalt keep my covenant therefore, thou, and thy seed after thee in their generations. This is my covenant, which ye shall keep, between me and you and thy seed after thee"* (Gen. 17:9–10).

"Brother Sumrall," you say, "do you expect me to believe that all the Jews have obeyed God's covenant?" Of course not. In fact, history proves that most of the Jews rejected God's covenant and denied His own beloved Son who came to die for them. But a few were faithful, and God kept blessing the nation because of them. When God predicted the doom of Israel at the hands of the marauding Assyrians and Babylonians, He said,

> *I will also leave in the midst of thee an afflicted and poor people, and they shall trust in the name of the LORD. The remnant of Israel shall not do iniquity, nor speak lies; neither shall a deceitful tongue be found in their mouth: for they shall feed and lie down, and none shall make them afraid.* (Zeph. 3:12–13)

This faithful remnant of the Jews kept God's covenant alive. They were the reason God continued to bless the Jews, even when the majority of them turned away from Him. Their enemies would triumph over them for a time, but in the end *"the residue of my people shall spoil them, and the remnant of my people shall possess them"* (Zeph. 2:9). Though most Jews disobeyed God and disregarded His covenant, enough were loyal to keep open the channel to His covenant blessings. Today there are thousands of Jewish Christians—Jews who have accepted Jesus as their Messiah—living in the land of Israel. They are living by God's New Covenant, sealed with the blood of Christ. We can expect God to keep on blessing Israel materially because of their faithfulness.

And what about the descendants of Ishmael? How do we account for the tremendous power that the Arabs have today?

Again, we must trace it back to a faithful remnant who have kept Abraham's covenant with God. Granted, they are the "black sheep" of the covenantal family because of Ishmael's illegitimate descent from Abraham. Nevertheless, they belong to that family. Though they are not saved, the fact that God is blessing them indicates that some of them must still be faithful to Him. Bible scholar Dr. William Smith notes:

> The sons of Ishmael peopled the north and west of the Arabian peninsula, and eventually formed the chief element of the Arab nation, the wandering Bedoin tribes. They are now mostly Mohammedans, who look to him [i.e., Mohammed] as their spiritual father, as the Jews look to Abraham.[5]

But remember that Mohammed was not born until the sixth century A.D. What happened to Ishmael's descendants until that time? Many of them became Christians! In fact, Mohammed had to convert several Christian communities in Arabia before he could consolidate his power there.[6] Mohammed had so many Christian friends that his Islamic doctrine was actually "a theology which partook of elements of Judaism, Christianity, and Arabian heathenism."[7] Many of Ishmael's descendants were won to Christ during the six hundred years before Mohammed's fanatical campaign.

Mohammed tried to wipe out Christianity in Arabia, but he failed. There are still a few small, strong, tenacious Christian communities in Egypt, Iran, Saudi Arabia, and the other oil-rich Arab nations of the Middle East. Is it really a coincidence, then, that God has blessed these nations? I think not.

God the Almighty, *El-Shaddai,* is far greater than any political theory or economic system or social utopia. God blesses those who are faithful to Him, even when His blessing contradicts human logic. And in the case of the Jews and Arabs, we see God blessing the descendants of one man who, by all human odds, would have been long forgotten in the dust of history except for one thing, *"Abraham believed God, and it was accounted to him for righteousness"* (James 2:23 NKJV).

Do you believe God is almighty? Do you believe God will give you *"every good and perfect gift"* that you need to serve Him (James 1:17)? Then be ready for God to do some marvelous things in your life and in the lives of your children.

Notes

1. W. A. Criswell, ed., *The Criswell Study Bible* (Nashville: Thomas Nelson Publishers, 1979), p. 27.

2. Al Oerter, "The Challenge," *Guideposts* (April 1980), p. 5.

3. J. Daniel Hess, *Ethics in Business and Labor* (Scottdale, Pa.: Herald Press, 1977), p. 64.

4. Robert H. Schuller, *You Can Become the Person You Want to Be* (Old Tappan, N.J.: Spire Books, 1976), p. 21.

5. William Smith, *A Dictionary of the Bible,* ed. and rev. by E. N. and M. A. Peloubet (Nashville: Thomas Nelson Publishers, 1979), p. 269.

6. William M. Miller, *A Christian's Response to Islam* (Wheaton, Ill.: Tyndale House Publishers, Inc., 1980), p. 35.

7. Howard F. Vos, *Highlights of Church History* (Chicago: Moody Press, 1960), p. 53.

6

The LORD Will Provide

(Jehovah-Jireh)

I n the hour when Abraham's faith was tested more severely, God revealed another of His names. This name encouraged Abraham's faith and should encourage our faith today. The name is *Jehovah-Jireh*, which means "the LORD will provide." Turn to Genesis 21:33 to pick up the story of Abraham.

> *And Abraham planted a grove in Beersheba, and called there on the name of the LORD, the everlasting God. And Abraham sojourned in the Philistines' land many days. And it came to pass after these things, that God did tempt Abraham.* (Gen. 21:33–22:1)

The word *tempt* is not a very good rendering of what the Hebrew manuscript says here. Other versions say that God *"tested"* Abraham (RSV, NASB, TLB). God never tempts a person to sin.

> *And [God] said unto him, Abraham: and he said, Behold, here I am. And he said, Take now thy son, thine only son Isaac, whom thou lovest, and get thee into the land of Moriah; and offer him there for a burnt offering upon one of the mountains which I will tell thee of.* (Gen. 22:1–2)

The region of Moriah is where Jerusalem is now located. At least seven hills, or "mounts," form the citadel of the city.

I well remember visiting Jerusalem with a tour guide some years ago. He said to me, "Isn't it interesting that Abraham found the right hill for his sacrifice? Because if he hadn't, he would have found no ram there" (compare Genesis 22:13). God had one ram prepared for Abraham, and one hill where He wanted Abraham to offer his sacrifice. Abraham didn't know he'd found the right hill until he had gotten there. Aren't you glad that God is wiser than we are?

God provided a specific place for Abraham to worship Him. I believe God still does that for His people. I believe certain people are supposed to be worshipping in the Christian Center, where I am pastor; when they worship elsewhere, they don't get the blessing they would have received at the Center. Likewise I know some people have tried worshipping in my congregation who should have been worshipping elsewhere. Sometimes I've had to tell them so. They didn't realize what a blessing they missed until they worshipped with the people God intended them to worship with, and in the way He intended them to worship. God's plans for us are that specific.

> *And Abraham rose up early in the morning, and saddled his ass, and took two of his young men with him, and Isaac his son, and clave the wood for the burnt offering, and rose up, and went unto the place of which God had told him.* (v. 3)

Abraham was ready to obey the Lord. He didn't say, "Now listen, Lord, it will take me a few days to get things ready." God told him what to do, and the very next morning Abraham set out to do it.

If you study the lives of other spiritual giants, you will find they were like Abraham in this respect. They never hesitated to do what God told them. They never consulted with their friends before deciding whether to obey the Lord. Suppose Abraham had called his oldest servant and said, "Eleazar, you're my chief counselor here. Someday I'm planning to send you to find a wife for my son Isaac. But the Lord says I should take Isaac over into Moriah and burn him on an altar there. What do you think I should do?"

The servant probably would have said, "Well! If you do what you think the Lord's told you to do, we won't have anyone to find a wife for! Have you gone crazy?"

Friend, if you depend only on other people to tell you God's will for your life, you will miss His will every time. As long as you keep tugging at your friend's shirttail saying, "What do you think I should do?" you make it that much harder for God to speak to you. I believe the Holy Spirit guides us both from within and from without, in a marvelous way. He does not have to knock us down with thunderbolts to get God's message across; He just indicates the direction in which we should go, and the open doors we should follow. Then He leaves the rest to us. (That is not to say that we are to neglect the wise counsel of more mature Christians, such as our elders. Hebrews 13:17 says to *"obey them that have the rule over you* [spiritually], *and submit yourselves: for they watch for your souls."*)

I believe that every child of God is living in the will of God, unless he or she has rebelled against it consciously. I don't believe the will of God is some dark, unfathomable secret that requires you to weep and scream in order to find it. As long as you are obeying the inner direction of His Spirit and have the inner peace that He gives to His obedient children, you don't need to consult every Tom, Dick, and Harry before you decide to act.

I have seen this in my own experience as a father. A father can't follow his children everywhere they go; if he tried, he would wear himself out. He must trust them to obey him even when he's out of sight. Only when his children rebel openly against his will or ignore his will does the father need to discipline them.

Always remember that God is your loving Father. He doesn't hound you with His will; He simply reveals His will to you, then trusts you to follow it. And the only time you'll feel His chastening hand of punishment is when you violate or ignore His will.

Notice what Abraham did next:

Then on the third day Abraham lifted up his eyes, and saw the place afar off. And Abraham said unto his young men, Abide ye here with the ass; and I and the lad will go yonder and worship, and come again to you. (Gen. 22:4–5)

The journey from Beersheba to Moriah was long and difficult. No wonder Abraham took two servant boys with him! But when they arrived at the place of worship, he left the servants with his donkey. God had commanded that the sacrifice be offered by him and his son alone. Yet he confidently said that they would *"come again"* to the servants. Now what did he mean by that? He meant that he believed his son would live, no matter what happened on top of that rocky hill. I can imagine him saying, "Lord, even if my son goes up in flames, I'll command those ashes to stand up straight and walk back down the hill with me." That was faith! Abraham knew God had promised him a son—in fact, had promised a long line of descendants to him—so he knew his son would live.

> *And Abraham took the wood of the burnt offering, and laid it upon Isaac his son; and he took the fire in his hand, and a knife; and they went both of them together. And Isaac spake unto Abraham his father, and said, My father: and he said, Here am I, my son. And he said, Behold the fire and the wood: but where is the lamb for a burnt offering? And Abraham said, My son, God will provide [Jehovah-Jireh] himself a lamb for a burnt offering: so they went both of them together.*
> (vv. 6–8)

What an amazing exhibition of faith! With a knife in his hand and the flames billowing from his torch, he told his son, *"God will provide himself a lamb for a burnt offering."*

> *And they came to the place which God had told him of; and Abraham built an altar there, and laid the wood in order, and bound Isaac his son, and laid him on the altar upon the wood.*
> (v. 9)

At this point, Abraham's faith had to become Isaac's faith as well. The old man had promised that God would provide a sacrifice, and now he laid his own son upon the sacrificial trough. I imagine he must have whispered in Isaac's ear, "Don't be afraid, Son. Go with me all the way and don't be afraid. And if you feel a little frightened, just close your eyes and think of Jehovah."

> *And Abraham stretched forth his hand, and took the knife to slay his son. And the angel of the* LORD *called unto him out of heaven, and said, Abraham, Abraham: and he said, Here am I. And he said, Lay not thine hand upon the lad, neither do thou any thing unto him: for now I know that thou fearest God, seeing thou hast not withheld thy son, thine only son from me.* (vv. 10–12)

God's messenger brought a stay of execution at the last possible moment. Abraham's faith was tested to capacity, and proved strong. God regarded that faith by sparing his son Isaac.

> *And Abraham lifted up his eyes, and looked, and behold behind him a ram caught in a thicket by his horns: and Abraham went and took the ram, and offered him up for a burnt offering in the stead of his son. And Abraham called the name of that place Jehovahjireh.* (v. 13–14)

Today the Mosque of Omar stands on the spot where Abraham is said to have made this historic sacrifice. Under the dome of that mosque is a massive stone, the Stone of Abraham, with a large cave at the base of it. Tradition says that King Solomon offered animal sacrifices here, letting the blood flow down into the cave. We do not know whether that is true, but we do know that when Abraham and Isaac stood on that spot, there were no buildings there. Nothing obstructed their view of the seven hills of Moriah. They could see the hill of Golgotha, just a few hundred feet away, where Jesus Christ would offer His life as the final and complete sacrifice for man's sins. Jesus would tell the Jews, *"Your father Abraham rejoiced to see my day: and he saw it, and was glad"* (John 8:56).

Oh, what a day of rejoicing that must have been! How jubilant Abraham and Isaac must have been as they raised their hands heavenward and exclaimed, *"Jehovah-Jireh:* The LORD will provide!"

Not only was Jehovah-Jireh their name for that place; we might say it was their name for God. For at that moment they knew God was the Provider of all they needed. He had provided the Lamb that all mankind would need for sacrifice. *Jehovah-Jireh:* "The LORD will provide!"

His Provision for You

When soldiers march into battle, they carry provisions in their knapsacks—food, water, and vitamins—to give their bodies strength for the conflict.

Whether or not you realize it, God gives you provisions for the spiritual battles you face. When you surrender your life to Christ and let Him take full control, you become a soldier in the Lord's army. As the famed missionary Hudson Taylor once said, "God's work done in God's way cannot fail to have God's provision."

On the very night He was betrayed, Jesus asked His disciples, *"When I sent you without purse, and scrip, and shoes, lacked ye any thing? And they said, Nothing"* (Luke 22:35). God provided the food, clothing, and money that these first evangelists needed when they set out to tell the world about Jesus. The same is true today. God provides what His servants need to serve Him.

I am a living testimony to that fact. Everything that I have today came from the Lord's hand. In fact, I owe my very life to Him, because I have been on the brink of death twice and He has cured me miraculously. In each instance I found that when I committed myself to serve Him with every fiber of my being, He gave me the health and strength to survive.

Today some people drive past our property in South Bend and say, "My, doesn't Brother Sumrall have a beautiful house?" That's true, but it reflects no credit on Lester Sumrall; all the credit goes to the Lord, who provided that house for me. Some people walk through our television studios at South Bend or Indianapolis and exclaim, "Well, Brother Sumrall has certainly spared no expense here!" I agree: it's expensive to do a first-class job of television ministry. Our equipment, however, is no credit to me; it's a credit to the Lord who provided it.

The Lord will provide everything a Christian needs to tell unsaved friends about Jesus. Whether it's something material or spiritual, obvious or hidden—the right book to loan or true insight into what that one needs to hear—regardless of what is needed, the Lord will provide it, as long as you use His provision to service Him.

And God is able to make all grace abound toward you; that ye, always having all sufficiency in all things, may abound to every good work: (As it is written, He hath dispersed abroad; he hath given to the poor: his righteousness remaineth for ever. Now he that ministereth seed to the sower both minister bread for your food, and multiply your seed sown, and increase the fruits of your righteousness).
(2 Cor. 9:8–10)

Notice the promise that God gives us in those three short verses of Scripture:

God will "minister seed to the sower." When you commit yourself to be a witness for the Lord, He will give you a message to share. If you're the wife of an unsaved man, God will show you how to tell your mate about Jesus. If you're a Christian teacher in the public schools, God will show you how to be a shining witness in the classroom. If you're a young preacher in your first pastorate, God will give you those sermon outlines and open the Scriptures to your understanding. No matter where you plan to "sow" the gospel, you can be sure that God will give you the "seed."

God will "minister bread for your food." This is the kind of provision Hudson Taylor was talking about, and the kind I have experienced myself. The psalmist said, *"I have been young, and now am old; yet have I not seen the righteous forsaken, nor his seed begging bread"* (Ps. 37:2 5). That was true long before the days of food stamps and Social Security, it's still true today. God doesn't let His people go hungry. He doesn't let them wear ragged tatters for clothes. He doesn't abandon them to die of exposure in the snow. God provides for the physical needs of His children.[1]

God will "multiply your seed sown." In other words, God will take care of convicting the hearts of unsaved people that hear the gospel from you. Don't feel discouraged if your unsaved friends don't clamor to become Christians. Your job is to tell them about Jesus. Then God's Holy Spirit can begin His convicting work in their lives. (See John 16:8–11.) He will bring fruit from the seed that you sow.

God will "increase the fruits of your righteousness." He promises not only to multiply the fruit of your witnessing, but the fruit of

ᴗy of living. James 3:18 says, *"The fruit of righteousness*
⟋eace of them that make peace." And Galatians 5:22-23, 25
.t the fruit of the Spirit is love, joy, peace, longsuffering, gentle-
⟋oodness, faith, meekness, temperance: against such there is no
..If we live in the Spirit, let us also walk in the Spirit." The fruit of
ᵣnteousness, then, is the outward manifestation of being filled
ᵥith God's Holy Spirit. One who is so filled evidences all of the
godly attitudes described above. God will cause these attitudes
to emerge in your life as you serve Him.

These are God's provisions for you if you are one of His chil-
dren. You can enjoy these provisions only if you are His child.
And how do you become His child? Jesus explained that to the
Jewish leader Nicodemus, saying:

> *Except a man be born of water and of the Spirit, he cannot enter into*
> *the kingdom of God. That which is born of the flesh is flesh; and that*
> *which is born of the Spirit is spirit. Marvel not that I said unto thee,*
> *Ye must be born again.* (John 3:5-7)

That's how you get these previous provisions of God—by
being "born again" through the cleansing water of salvation and
the empowering Spirit of Christ. You must repent of your sins,
claim Jesus as your only Savior, and let Him fill you with His
Holy Spirit. When you join the ranks of the reborn, you inherit
all the precious provisions of God.

God also provides for us in the midst of trouble. Billy Graham
has said:

> I seriously doubt if we will ever understand our trials and
> adversities until we are safety in heaven. Then when we look
> back we are going to be absolutely amazed at how God took
> care of us and blessed us even in the storms of life. We face
> dangers every day of which we are not even aware.[2]

Yes, God will provide the help we need to live our lives for
Him. He will provide the patience to endure hardships for His
sake. And finally, He will provide an eternal home for us around
His heavenly throne. *Jehovah-Jireh:* The LORD will provide!

Notes

1. Someone naturally asks, "What about the Christians in East Africa who are starving to death? Or the Christians in India and the Caribbean who have no homes? Doesn't God provide for them?" I would say, Yes. God does provide for them, but the people who are in a position to deliver the goods in His name do not always follow His instructions. I'm afraid that many of us Americans are sitting on top of God's provision for our Christian brothers and sisters in those other countries and refusing to share that provision as we should. God will hold us responsible.

2. Billy Graham, *Till Armageddon: A Perspective on Suffering* (Waco, Tex.: Word Books, 1981), p. 168.

7

The LORD Is Healer
(Jehovah-Repheka)

G od made our bodies, and God is able to heal them and keep them healthy when we meet His conditions by obeying His instructions. God demonstrated this to the children of Israel as Moses led them out of bondage in Egypt.

Exodus chapter 15 tells how the Israelites rejoiced to see God deliver them from the Egyptians. You'll remember that God parted the Red Sea so they could cross over on dry ground, then He let the waters come flooding in upon the pursuing Egyptian hordes. What a day of victory that was! And the Israelites celebrated with singing and dancing, with Moses' sister Miriam leading the festivities. (See Exodus 15:20–21.) But three days later, when they were unable to find good drinking water, the Israelites started grumbling. (See verses 22–24.)

Isn't that just like fickle human nature? We forget God's goodness so easily. But in this moment of distress, God spoke to His people through Moses and revealed another name for Himself, a name that would encourage them for years to come:

> *There he made for them a statute and an ordinance, and there he proved them, and said, If thou wilt diligently hearken to the voice of the LORD thy God, and wilt do that which is right in his sight, and wilt give ear to his commandments, and keep all his statutes, I will put none of these diseases upon thee, which I have brought upon the Egyptians: for I am the LORD that healeth thee [Jehovah-Repheka].*
> (Exod. 15:25–26)

Notice that God said, "I am the Lord who heals you *if* you'll do what I've told you to do." His promise came with a requirement, a condition that the Israelites had to meet if they wanted Him to heal them.

The "Why?" Question

Many people come to my study and ask such questions as these: "Brother Sumrall, why haven't I been healed?" "Why did my mother die?" "Why was my baby born retarded?"

We all have a lot of "why?" questions. I have plenty of my own. Not all of them will be answered in this life. They will have to wait until we join the Lord in heaven. But Exodus 15:26 gives some insight into many of the questions we have about healing.

So many of our "why" questions would be answered if we only looked at the way we live, and compared it with the standard of living required by the Word of God. Then we would realize that we are not living up to God's conditions.

Most people read the *benefits* promised in God's Word, but they fail to read the *conditions* attached to them. And that's usually the reason they can't figure out why no healing has come.

If an insurance salesman comes to your house and offers you a policy for a million dollars, he won't start his sales pitch by telling you how much you'll have to pay to get such coverage. He'll start by selling you on how much you'll get from it. That's his job. He will say, "If you ever get sick, we'll pay you so much money every day; we'll take care of all your hospital bills; we'll pay the doctor everything you owe. If you get laid off work, we'll pay you so much workman's compensation." And so on and so on. Only when you get excited enough to "sign on the dotted line" will he tell you about the premiums you have to pay. He knows you'd much rather think about the benefits.

That's what the children of Israel were doing. They must have thought, "Isn't it fantastic to have all these benefits that the Lord is going to give us?" But they would rather pay no attention to the requirements He gave them; they would rather not think about doing *"that which is right in his sight,"* or *"giving ear to all his commandments,"* or *"keeping all his statutes."*

We are the same way, of course. We are so eager to get God's benefits that we forget what He requires of us. So we go a couple of steps forward in our Christian life, then slide back a step. We get saved and start testifying like a zealot, then fizzle when the first bit of trouble comes along. If we would just stick to the Word of God and obey what He tells us to do in it, God would bless us.

God intended for all His children to be healthy. Adam and Eve were created perfect, without ailments. Even though we rejected God's goodness and rejected the health He offers (through the Fall), He was merciful and gave us healing instead.

Someone is bound to say, "What about the faithful Christians who keep on suffering? What about people who are serving the Lord with all their hearts, but still don't get healed?"

People like Joni Eareckson-Tada have struggled with this question deeply. Her only answer is that God knows what He is doing. She is being made Christlike, and God is being glorified in her infirmities, more than He would be glorified in her physical healing. The same was true for Paul. (See 2 Corinthians 12:7–9.) We may not fully understand how this is to our benefit or how God can be glorified in this way, but He is. There are special cases in which God demonstrates His love through giving patience and strength instead of healing. God wants His people to be healthy—spiritually and physically. So sometimes He is healing (perfecting) our spiritual lives first. He wants His ailing people to be healed. The overarching will of God is to heal us of all our diseases, that He may be glorified by our healing.

Looking to Christ

Numbers 21 describes a situation in which God proved His healing mercy to the children of Israel. They had been wandering in the wilderness for a long time without getting into the Promised Land, and they started to grumble again. They said to Moses, *"Wherefore have ye brought us up out of Egypt to die in the wilderness? for there is no bread, neither is there any water; and our soul loatheth this light bread"* (Num. 21:5).

God was giving them manna from heaven. In their rebelliousness, however, they said, "We don't care for it." They were saying, "Thanks for the meat, Lord, but we want filet mignon." They forgot that God was supplying their needs; they started complaining and begging for some of their wants.

So the Lord allowed fiery serpents to attack their camp. Many Israelites were bitten and died. Suddenly the survivors realized how well-off they had been before. They came to Moses and said, *"We have sinned, for we have spoken against the* Lord, *and against thee"* (v. 7).

So Moses prayed for the people. The Lord instructed him to make a serpent of brass and set it upon a pole in the midst of their camp, promising that anyone who was bitten by a snake could look upon that snake and live. The Lord would heal the victims of the snakebites.

The notes to the Scofield Bible indicate that the serpents represented sin, while brass represented divine judgment (as in the brazen altar). Therefore, according to Scofield, the brass serpent represented Christ—God who became sin on our behalf. Jesus Himself pointed out this connection when He said to Nicodemus:

And as Moses lifted up the serpent in the wilderness, even so must the Son of man be lifted up: that whosoever believeth in him should not perish, but have eternal life. (John 3:14–15)

The Israelites were to look at the brass serpent and receive healing; we are to look unto Christ and receive healing. All of our healing—physical or spiritual—comes from the Lord.

It's so hard to get people to understand this. They travel all over the country to faith-healing services; they listen to tapes about healing; they buy all the latest books about healing; they take herb cures and every other kind of treatment that promises healing. But there is no healing virtue in these things. There is no healing virtue in an evangelist, in a church, or in a theory of any kind. There is healing virtue only in Christ; only He was made sin for us. Sin is the cause of all our suffering. Sometimes suffering comes to us because of Adam's sin; sometimes it comes because of some more immediate transgression. But sin is always the cause of suffering. And Christ took all of our sins to the cross. He suffered in our place, so that *"with his stripes we are healed"* (Isa. 53:5).

Jesus said, *"And I, if I be lifted up from the earth, will draw all men unto me"* (John 12:32). Maybe church attendance is sluggish because people seldom see Jesus lifted up in our churches. We read in the newspapers that a congregation is about to launch a two-million-dollar building program, or that a certain preacher has just started a new series of prophecy lectures, or that a musical group is about to have a spectacular concert. But we seldom see Jesus lifted up. We seldom hear testimonies of how He has cast demons out of someone. We seldom hear about other ways He has worked in people's lives. Is it any wonder, then, that people are so indifferent to the church?

God's Word is true. God does heal people today. God does save sinful souls today. God does cast out evil spirits today. I know He does because I see Him doing it!

Denying God's Promises

I recall an article in one of our leading evangelical magazines a couple of years ago, debating whether God still grants the gifts of the Spirit today. (The gifts of the Spirit, of course, are listed several times in Paul's letters; they include such things as preaching, teaching, prophecy, and healing. See the list in 1 Corinthians 12:4–11, for example.) On the "pro" side of the debate was an Episcopal priest. He believed that God still gives Holy Spirit gifts to His people today, including the gift of healing. On the "con" side of the argument was a well-known evangelist. He felt that God stopped giving these gifts to His people long ago because we don't need them anymore.

I wonder what a person like this evangelist does when he gets sick? Does he say, "I know this sickness must come from you, Lord, so I'm going to pray for more sickness"? Does he say,

"Please don't make me well, Lord, because that would be a bad testimony"? I doubt it. Even the people who deny God's promise of healing will turn to Him for healing when they get ill.

Others deny that God will heal *certain kinds* of illness. For example, if they have an emotional problem they don't go to the church for prayer; they go to a mental health clinic or a psychiatrist. If a friend or relative goes insane, they would never call a pastor to pray for that person. They seem to think that God can ease pain or heal a broken family, but mental disorders are too big for Him! So they cut themselves off from God's blessings.

Or how about the people who think God can't cure a common cold? They testify about what God can do for serious illnesses, then turn around and say, "Guess I'd better not send my children to school this week. They'll catch the flu from everybody else." Or they may say, "I'll probably come down with a cold, like everybody at work. It's that time of year." They talk like that all through the week, then come to church a couple of hours on Sunday and expect to have their faith lifted!

If we are the children of God, let's start acting like it. Let's not say what the rest of the world is saying; let's not buy the skepticism of everyone else. We don't need to expect a heart attack to strike us down, or a tumor to kill us. We worship *Jehovah-Repheka,* the Lord who heals. So let's start taking Him at His Word.

Is Pain Your God?

Ill people become depressed very easily. They grow weary of the daily suffering. They tend to feel defeated by their illness; they fail to look to the Lord, who can conquer their illness. Visit the cancer ward in your local hospital, talk with some of the patients, and you'll see what I mean. It's not easy to struggle with pain for months, even years, without seeing some improvement. After a while, the sufferer wants to give up.

In a case like that, healing can only begin when the sufferer shakes off the depression and begins expecting to be healed. Norman Cousins, former editor of *Saturday Review,* tells about an experience he had with a serious illness.[1] He was stricken with a rare disease that destroys the muscles and joints. His doctors said they couldn't cure him; only about five percent of the victims ever recovered, and no one knew why they did.

But Mr. Cousins didn't give up. He decided he was going to get better. He decided he was going to be one of the five percent who survived. He read all the medical articles he could find about his illness; in fact, he became an expert on it. He recommended that his doctor give him a treatment that had never been tried before, and it worked. He recovered.

So far as I know, Mr. Cousins doesn't claim to be a Christian. He didn't call on the Lord to be healed, though I'm sure his healing came from the Lord. *"Every good gift and every perfect gift is from...the Father"* (James 1:17). The important thing we can learn from his experience is this: *He did not surrender to his illness.* He decided he was going to get well, and he never let go of that goal.

So often I've heard Christians say from their hospital beds, "I guess it's just the Lord's will for me to die." Yet they are young, gifted, capable people who could give many more years to the Lord's work. They give up so easily. They surrender to the pain. They let their illness become the master of their lives.

Either pain is your god, or God is your God. Either circumstance is your god, or God is your God. Which is it?

God made us free moral agents with the power to choose what we will do with our lives. But I'm amazed at the choices most people make! We can choose to believe in God, but most people choose not to. We can choose to be saved from our sins, but most people choose not to. We can choose to be healed of our illnesses, but most people choose not to. I'm afraid that, for most people, the freedom to choose a miracle is so scary that they choose to suffer and die without it.

When you surrender to your circumstances, or you give in to your disease, it means you're afraid to live on the front lines of the spiritual battlefield. You head for the rear to patch yourself up after you've been beaten. That's where too many Christians spend their time—getting "patched up" from what the devil has done to them all week long. People come to me and say, "Pastor, pray for me. The devil's really been after me this week."

How about it? Is the devil influencing your life, or is God in charge of it? Is the tormentor in control, or is the Healer in control? You must decide. The depression, sorrow, and confusion that Satan gives will come upon you only if you let them come upon you.

Praise God for being *Jehovah-Repheka.* Thank Him for being the One who *"healeth all thy diseases."* Then claim His healing for *your* life today!

Notes

1. Norman Cousins, *Anatomy of an Illness* (New York: W. W. Norton and Company, 1979).

8
The LORD Is Our Righteousness
(Jehovah -Tsidqenu)

I am amazed when I talk with brilliant scientists who work with the mysteries of life in their laboratories and yet curse the coworkers beside them. I am puzzled that genius-level astronomers and physicists can explore the depths of space and yet care nothing about the bums on Skid Row. I am dismayed to see a mechanic adjust the fine workings of his automobile and yet scream all sorts of insults at his wife. The psalmist said, *"The heavens declare the glory of God; and the firmament showeth his handiwork"* (Ps. 19:1). Yet millions of people gaze upon miracles every day and fail to see God. They don't change their lives one whit; they are irascible sinners, day in and day out.

Jesus said that this natural world reveals the heavenly Father who made it, whether sinful humanity realizes that or not. Moreover, the Bible says God will hold us accountable for the corrupt way that we live in the face of this abundant evidence of God's existence. (See Romans 1.) God is a holy, righteous God; and He expects us to be righteous as well.

God's Evidence and Man's Verdict

Josh McDowell has written a tremendous book entitled *Evidence That Demands a Verdict,* in which he lists dozens of proofs that God exists.[1] I hope you read that book someday; it will inspire and challenge you. But even if you never read McDowell's book, you read God's own book of "proofs" every day because you live in the world He created. Jesus said,

Behold the fowls of the air: for they sow not, neither do they reap, nor gather into barns; yet your heavenly Father feedeth them. Are ye not much better than they?...And why take ye thought for raiment? Consider the lilies of the field, how they grow; they toil not, neither do they spin: and yet I say unto you, That even Solomon in all his glory was not arrayed like one of these. Wherefore, if God so clothe the grass of the field, which to day is, and to morrow is cast into the oven, shall he not much more clothe you, O ye of little faith?

(Matt. 6:26, 28–30 NKJV)

The order of the natural world shows that Someone is in charge of things; Someone cares about every detail of the universe, even to the feeding of the sparrows. Logic would say that these birds should have died long ago of hunger and exposure, but they haven't. The theory of evolution would say that plants as tender and delicate as the lilies would have been crowded out by tough, aggressive weeds; but they haven't. Someone cares for the sparrows and lilies. That Someone is God, and He cares for you even more.

Yet many people study the wonders of this intricate world every day and never perceive God. A prize-winning scientist recently boasted:

A Designer is a natural, appealing, and altogether human explanation of the biological world. But, as Darwin and Wallace showed, there is another way, equally appealing, equally human, and far more appealing: natural selection [i.e., evolution], which makes the music of life more beautiful as the aeons pass.[2]

Obviously, this man's careful study of nature did not automatically make him believe in God. This attitude is fairly common among scientists today.

That is why God revealed Himself to His people in dramatic, unmistakable ways—like through the burning bush. That is also why God revealed His written Word to us, to explain what the natural world means in case we fail to perceive who is behind it all!

One thing should be clear: God likes order and harmony. He made such a beautifully well-ordered world because He likes to arrange things that way. The same is true of human society; He wants order and harmony among people because that will protect the creatures He made and allow them to serve Him as they should. God gave His people laws to make sure they live in an orderly way. He punishes their unlawful, immoral conduct because He knows it will destroy all of us if He allows it to go unchecked. Divine law and moral decency are safeguards for the survival of humankind; they help to insure that men and women can live as God intended, without undue harm befalling them.

Man's Mechanism for Self-Destruction

But humankind is not inclined to follow God's law. Isn't that strange? Canadian geese follow their instincts and fly south for the winter, salmon follow their instincts and swim upstream to spawn, but the human race won't follow God's natural order for their life. People disregard God's law. They insist on living their own way, regardless of what God says is best. The result? People tend to destroy themselves, like a missile with a mechanism for self-destruction that blows itself up when it strays off course. The human race is destroying itself by straying from God's revealed law.

One sign of that self-destruction is the rise of militarism in our world. I believe military leaders will be held accountable for the frightful atrocities they are inflicting, either directly or indirectly, upon innocent families. When I think of the billions of dollars spent on weapons each year—dollars that could have been spent on food and clothing for millions of needy people around the world—my heart is dismayed. I'm sure God is angry. The destroyers of earth spend so much to devise new instruments of war, when the real need of individuals is to understand and love other people! What a pathetic sign of human carnality! But Christ will return to this world soon, to destroy the destroyers. Jesus said, *"All who take the sword will perish by the sword"*

(Matt 26:52 NKJV). This is the destiny of everyone who defies God's gospel of peace.

Death is also the destiny of the less aggressive enemies of God. Whom do I mean by that? I mean everyone who disobeys God in less obvious ways, or who simply neglects to obey the mandates of His word; in other words, everyone who sins against God. Scripture says, *"For the wages of sin is death, but the gift of God is eternal life in Christ Jesus our Lord"* (Rom. 6:23 NKJV). Sin is any willful transgression of God's law, so a person may sin by defying what God says or just by ignoring what He says. But God's Word is clear and direct; God's commands are easy to understand. We can be sure that any man or woman who disobeys His Word will reap the consequences.

I have visited city missions in some of the great metropolitan areas of our nation; and in every one of them, I have found pathetic portraits of this human self-destruction through sin. Whether in Chicago, New York, Los Angeles, or right here in South Bend, the story of sin-wrecked lives is repeated again and again.

A boy drops out of school to feed his drug habit. He "graduates" from marijuana to cocaine, and from cocaine to heroin or one of the other hard drugs. He must rob stores and mug innocent pedestrians to get enough money to buy his "fix" every day. His arms and legs are scarred with the tracks of the needle. His eyes are bloodshot with fatigue. His breath is vile. He may be fortunate to find his way into a rescue mission where Christian people can help him get right with the Lord and kick his drug habit. Otherwise he is destined to die in the gutter before he is thirty.

A girl begins running with the crowd that likes to drink. She goes to every party she can find, cracking off-color jokes and wheedling as many beers as she can get. She frequents the neighborhood bars, soliciting drinks from the other customers and even selling sexual favors for a drink. Her habit deepens. Her nerves become raw. Like the drug addict, she is doomed to die unless someone leads her to the Lord and helps her to "dry out."

A man or woman who tries to live without God is committing suicide. It may be a slow and painful death, but the end result is certain: *"The wages of sin is death."* People destroy themselves when they ignore the clear testimony of God seen in the world He has created and in the written Word He has inspired. They are *"without excuse"* for rebelling against Him (Rom. 1:20), and they must pay the penalty.

Corrupt Leadership

Lay people are not the only ones who ignore God's commands. Even spiritual leaders, the so-called "anointed of the Lord," can be guilty of disobeying God's law. And when spiritual leaders fall into sin, they pay the same price—death.

At one of the telethons for our TV station in Miami, a precious Christian couple came to me. "Brother Sumrall, will you pray for us?" they pleaded. "We belong to one of the largest churches in southern Florida, and our pastor has been caught in adultery. Three women in the congregation have given signed statements that the pastor has committed adultery with them. He wants us to have a business meeting with him tonight to discuss these things. But we don't know what to do." Tears were running down their cheeks. I would guess they were in their fifties, handsomely dressed, and they were on their way to this important meeting with their pastor. The situation was grievous.

God expects the leaders of His church to live clean, righteous lives before His people. Christians must have holy leaders. And when we don't have them, the Bible says,

> *Woe be unto the pastors that destroy and scatter the sheep of my pasture! saith the LORD....Ye have scattered my flock, and driven them away, and have not visited them: behold, I will visit upon you the evil of your doings, saith the LORD.*　　　　　　　　　(Jer. 23:1–2)

God will not leave His church in the hands of corrupt leaders. He will not let ungodly men and women pervert the morals of His people. Not by any means! Notice what God says in that same passage:

> *Behold, the days come, saith the* LORD, *that I will raise unto David a righteous Branch, and a King shall reign and prosper, and shall execute judgment and justice in the earth.* (Jer. 23:5)

The "Branch," of course, is Jesus Christ. He has fulfilled this prophecy in one sense by being born from the lineage of David. But the real thrust of this prophecy will be fulfilled when Christ returns to rule the world. He will snatch the church from the hands of every ungodly leader who pretends to be leading her in His name. He will expose these frauds for what they really are, and give them their just reward.

> *In his days Judah shall be saved, and Israel shall dwell safely: and this is his name whereby he shall be called,* THE LORD OUR RIGHTEOUSNESS. (v. 6)

What a majestic thought! "The LORD our righteousness"! All heaven and earth will rejoice in His righteousness. All people will realize that any righteousness Christians have is merely the "imputed" righteousness of Christ. (See Romans 4:13–25.) They will know that He is *Jehovah-Tsidqenu,* "the LORD our righteousness." This is the name God's people will use to hail Christ when He returns.

The rest of Jeremiah 23 presents a sad commentary on human society, for it predicts that both prophet and priest will become morally profane.

> *For both prophet and priest are profane; yea, in my house have I found their wickedness, saith the* LORD. *Wherefore their way shall be unto them as slippery ways in the darkness: they shall be driven on, and fall therein: for I will bring evil upon them.* (vv. 11–12)

I believe there is a tremendous amount of sin in the pulpits of America today.

God, however, wants to become our righteousness; He wants to give us the holiness that we can never achieve on our own. He has already done it. He has already saved our soul from the pit of hell by sending His Son, Jesus, to die in our place. Jesus' death on the cross cleanses us of our moral impurity when we surrender our lives to Him and say, "I confess I can't live as I should. Take over my life, Lord. Make me what You want me to be."

Then when we enter the gates of heaven, we won't say, "We're here because we've been so good." No, we'll walk through those gates singing a new song: "The LORD is our righteousness." He has made everything right with God the Father, with our fellow-man, and even with our innermost selves. He has straightened out our lives.

Don't Wait to Get Right

Now some people may think, "I'll just wait until the Millennium to live a holy life. That's when the Lord will reign, isn't it? So that's when I'll let Him make me perfect."

Well, I have some exciting news for you! You don't have to wait! God is ready to make you perfect, *right now!*

God the Father demands an upright, holy life of all His people. He expects them to be *"a peculiar people, zealous of good works"* (Tit. 2:14).

God the Son died on the cross so we could become those *"peculiar,"* holy people. He purified us by sacrificing His own body and blood on Calvary. (See 1 John 1:7.) We need only confess our sin and accept His sacrifice to receive the righteousness He offers.

God the Spirit keeps guiding us on the path of moral rightness. When Paul rebuked the immorality of the Christians at Corinth, he said, *"Do you not know that you are the temple of God and that the Spirit of God dwells in you?"* (1 Cor. 3:16 NKJV). When the Spirit dwells within, He shows us how to keep our *"temple"* clean.

It's not necessary for you to wait until the Lord Jesus returns before you get your moral life straightened out. In fact, it's downright dangerous to wait. You can live in God's righteousness now, and *"to him who knows to do good and does not do it, to him it is sin"* (James 4:17 NKJV).

Hal Lindsey closes his classic book on prophecy, *The Late Great Planet Earth,* with a reminder that none of us should wait to live as God has told us to:

> We should make it our aim to trust Christ to work in us a life of true righteousness. We all grow in this, so don't get discouraged or forget that God accepts us as we are. He wants our hearts to be constantly set toward pleasing Him and have faith to trust Him to help us.[3]

Granted, none of us will be completely perfect until our raptured bodies go to heaven. But we can have the righteousness of God, through Christ, at this very moment. God expects us to have it because He expects His church—the family of all the saved—to be *"a glorious church, not having spot, or wrinkle, or any such thing; but that it should be holy and without blemish"* (Eph. 5:27).

We can have that kind of life only when we surrender to Jesus Christ, "the LORD our righteousness."

Notes

1. Josh McDowell, *Evidence That Demands a Verdict* (San Bernardino, Calif.: Campus Crusade for Christ, 1971).

2. Carl Sagan, *Cosmos* (New York: Random House, 1980), p. 29.

3. Hal Lindsey and C. C. Carlson, *The Late Great Planet Earth* (Grand Rapids, Mich.: Zondervan Publishing House, 1970), p. 187.

9

The LORD of Hosts
(Jehovah-Tsebaoth)

B efore mankind was on the face of this earth, cosmic battles took place. The beginning of all war was not on this earth, it was in heaven. Michael, God's warring archangel, and the armies of God fought against Lucifer and his angels. Revelation 12 outlines the battle and how Lucifer with one-third of the angels were cast out of heaven to the earth. These fallen angels are the demons that torment humans until this day.

> *And there was war in heaven: Michael and his angels fought against the dragon; and the dragon fought and his angels, and prevailed not; neither was their place found any more in heaven. And the great dragon was cast out, that old serpent, called the Devil, and Satan, which deceiveth the whole world: he was cast out into the earth, and his angels were cast out with him.* (Rev. 12:7–9)

War in Heaven

This was the beginning of all war in heaven when an angel, a created being, decided to be like the Creator.

> *How art thou fallen from heaven, O Lucifer, son of the morning! how art thou cut down to the ground, which didst weaken the nations! For thou hast said in thine heart, I will ascend into heaven, I will exalt my throne above the stars of God: I will sit also upon the mount of the congregation, in the sides of the north: I will ascend above the heights of the clouds; I will be like the most High.* (Isaiah 14:12–14)

Ezekiel gives us a further illumination of Lucifer's fall.

> *Son of man, take up a lamentation upon the king of Tyrus, and say unto him, Thus saith the Lord GOD; Thou sealest up the sum, full of wisdom, and perfect in beauty. Thou hast been in Eden the garden of God; every precious stone was thy covering, the sardius, topaz, and the diamond, the beryl, the onyx, and the jasper, the sapphire, the emerald, and the carbuncle, and gold: the workmanship of thy tabrets and of thy pipes was prepared in thee in the day that thou wast created. Thou art the anointed cherub that covereth; and I have set thee so: thou wast upon the holy mountain of God; thou hast walked up and down in the midst of the stones of fire. Thou wast perfect in thy ways from the day that thou wast created, till iniquity was found in thee.* (Ezek. 28:12–15)

God reminded Lucifer of the position and the blessings he forfeited because he sinned against the Most High. War arose in heaven that had to be fought and terminated.

Let us examine God's function in the area of war.

Archangels of the LORD of Hosts

In the structure of heaven, God created archangels: Gabriel, Michael, and Lucifer.

Gabriel is in charge of heaven's telecommunications. Scripture records three instances where Gabriel appeared to humans. It was Gabriel who brought the word to Mary concerning the birth of Jesus (Luke 1:26). Gabriel appeared to Zachariah in Luke 1:18 regarding John the Baptist's birth and ministry. Gabriel also spoke to Daniel about end-time prophecy in Daniel chapters 8 and 9.

Michael is the warrior angel. When Daniel prayed, he entered into spiritual warfare:

> *But the prince of the kingdom of Persia withstood me one and twenty days: but, lo, Michael, one of the chief princes, came to help me; and I remained there with the kings of Persia.* (Dan. 10:13)

Satan became personified in kingships such as in Babylon, Persia, and Greece; and he designated these kingdoms as his domain (Dan. 10:20).

Lucifer was the archangel in charge of song and praise in heaven; however, he rebelled. The angel who led worship decided he was as great as God and would elevate himself.

O LORD of hosts, God of Israel, that dwellest between the cherubims, thou art the God, even thou alone, of all the kingdoms of the earth: thou hast made heaven and earth. (Isa. 37:16)

The LORD of Hosts Is a Warrior

The term LORD of Hosts is cited 282 times in the Word of God. It is a military term meaning "God of Battles."

As birds flying, so will the LORD of hosts defend Jerusalem; defending also he will deliver it; and passing over he will preserve it. (Isa. 31:5)

Our God is a Warrior. He is a Fighter, and we are in His army. When He comes, riding upon a white horse, His army will be with him to battle the Antichrist (Rev. 19:14). As children of the LORD of Hosts, we are following after the One who wins every battle.

A struggle is not bad if it's for a good thing. God wants warriors who stand up for Him in the face of the enemy so that the lost may be saved.

One reason we see weakness in the body of Christ is because we often fail to acknowledge the LORD of Hosts, the God of Battles. Many Christians think that once they are saved, their battle with sin and Satan is over. But actually, the call to salvation is a call to enlist in God's army and war against the spirits of darkness and their activity in this world.

We must understand His character to appreciate the LORD of Hosts. The LORD of Battles can tell us exactly how to stand against the strategies of the enemy. He can counsel us on how to fight and how to win our victories.

This also cometh forth from the LORD of hosts, which is wonderful in counsel, and excellent in working. (Isa. 28:29)

Lord of Sabaoth, "The LORD of Armies"

The LORD of Hosts is referred to in the New Testament as the LORD of Armies:

> *Behold, the hire of the labourers who have reaped down your fields, which is of you kept back by fraud, crieth: and the cries of them which have reaped are entered into the ears of the Lord of sabaoth.*
>
> (James 5:4)

> *And as Esaias said before, Except the Lord of Sabaoth had left us a seed, we had been as Sodoma, and been made like unto Gomorrha.*
>
> (Rom. 9:29)

If it were not for God's holiness in defeating the devil for us through Jesus Christ at Calvary, we would be eternally lost in sin. He is the LORD of Armies who wins the battles for us.

The LORD of Hosts Keeps His Promises

Every year Elkanah and his barren wife, Hannah, traveled to Shiloh to bring their sacrifice and offerings before the LORD of Hosts. In great need and intense prayer, Hannah made a commitment to the LORD of Hosts:

> *And she vowed a vow, and said, O LORD of hosts, if thou wilt indeed look on the affliction of thine handmaid, and remember me, and not forget thine handmaid, but wilt give unto thine handmaid a man child, then I will give him unto the LORD all the days of his life, and there shall no razor come upon his head.* (1 Sam. 1:11)

The LORD of Hosts heard Hannah's cry, and the great prophet Samuel was conceived. Samuel was pivotal in the plan of God. He consummated a dispensation of 450 years and fifteen judges and ended the era when he anointed David, the warrior, as King of Israel (Acts 13:20).

> *For the LORD of hosts hath purposed, and who shall disannul it? and his hand is stretched out, and who shall turn it back?* (Isa. 14:27)

David Knew the LORD of Hosts

David not only knew Jehovah-Rohi as his Shepherd, he also recognized Jehovah-Tsebaoth—the LORD of Hosts. David trusted in God's ability to fight his enemies and win his battles for him. He became the champion of his nation and a legend in his own time through the LORD of Hosts.

> *Then said David to the Philistine, Thou comest to me with a sword, and with a spear, and with a shield: but I come to thee in the name of the LORD of hosts, the God of the armies of Israel, whom thou hast defied. This day will the LORD deliver thee into mine hand; and I will smite thee, and take thine head from thee; and I will give the carcases of the host of the Philistines this day unto the fowls of the air, and to the wild beasts of the earth; that all the earth may know that there is a God in Israel. And all this assembly shall know that the LORD saveth not with sword and spear: for the battle is the Lord's, and he will give you into our hands.* (1 Sam. 17:45–47)

David's bold response to Goliath was a response of faith in the LORD of Hosts. In the book of Psalms, David referred to the LORD of Hosts fifteen times. He knew the LORD of Hosts could bring him the blessings he needed. *"O LORD of hosts, blessed is the man that trusteth in thee"* (Ps. 84:12).

The LORD of Hosts Judges Nations

> *But, O LORD of hosts, that judgest righteously, that triest the reins and the heart, let me see thy vengeance on them: for unto thee have I revealed my cause.* (Jer. 11:20)

> *For the day of the LORD of hosts shall be upon every one that is proud and lofty, and upon every one that is lifted up; and he shall be brought low.* (Isa. 2:12)

> *And I will come near to you to judgment; and I will be a swift witness against the sorcerers, and against the adulterers, and against false swearers, and against those that oppress the hireling in his wages, the*

widow, and the fatherless, and that turn aside the stranger from his right, and fear not me, saith the LORD *of hosts.* (Mal. 3:5)

God is speaking against transgressors, rebellious people who will not serve Him.

The Soviet Union fought God for over seventy years with their lips and actions. Today it is torn asunder from within, and is reaping what it has sown.

America has experienced God's blessings only because our forefathers loved and served Him. They attended church and hated sin. Because of this, our generation is reaping a harvest that we didn't plant. One day our children will reap the harvest we are now planting; so let's be deliberate in what we plant before the LORD of Hosts.

"Their Redeemer is strong; the LORD *of hosts is his name: he shall thoroughly plead their cause, that he may give rest to the land, and disquiet the inhabitants of Babylon"* (Jer. 50:34).

The LORD's Hosts Have a Captain

Not only does the LORD of Hosts have volunteers in His army. He has a Captain.

And it came to pass, when Joshua was by Jericho, that he lifted up his eyes and looked, and, behold, there stood a man over against him with his sword drawn in his hand: and Joshua went unto him, and said unto him, Art thou for us, or for our adversaries? And he said, Nay; but as captain of the host of the LORD *am I now come. And Joshua fell on his face to the earth, and did worship, and said unto him, What saith my lord unto his servant? And the captain of the* LORD's *host said unto Joshua, Loose thy shoe from off thy foot; for the place whereon thou standest is holy. And Joshua did so.* (Josh. 5:13–15)

We know that this person with a sword in his hand was not an angel because angels refuse worship. Only the Most High is worthy of praise; however, this Mighty One commanded Joshua to worship Him. The Captain of God's hosts is Jesus Christ.

When the children of Israel faced their first battle after coming into the Promised Land, the Lord of Hosts took over the warfare.

Archaeologists have discovered that the walls of Jericho did not fall east or west, they fell straight down. It's no wonder. When Jesus hits any wall, it must come down!

> *Thus saith the Lord the King of Israel, and his redeemer the Lord of hosts; I am the first, and I am the last; and beside me there is no God.*
> (Isaiah 44:6)

Jesus teaches His people how to fight. For the church, this means spiritual warfare.

We Are in Spiritual Warfare

It is very interesting that the first instrument used against man after he sinned in Genesis chapter 3 was an angel with a sword. This indicates that cosmic warfare is ongoing.

> *So he drove out the man; and he placed at the east of the garden of Eden Cherubims, and a flaming sword which turned every way, to keep the way of the tree of life.* (Gen. 3:24)

> *For we wrestle not against flesh and blood, but against principalities, against powers, against the rulers of the darkness of this world, against spiritual wickedness in high places.* (Eph. 6:12)

Our warfare is spiritual. It is not against people, but against the powers of darkness. Some Christians refuse to get into the area of spiritual warfare, and some have been carried away by extremes.

Many have become weary practicing spiritual warfare. They are fighting the devil and trying to win a battle that is already won. What they need to do is to shout and rejoice in God. Jesus triumphed over Satan and destroyed his works at Calvary. Satan's only weapon now against mankind is deception.

"And having spoiled principalities and powers, he made a show of them openly, triumphing over them in it" (Col. 2:15).

When man tries to enter into a personal conflict against Satan using human strength, he can never win. But we must exercise spiritual warfare according to the Word of God. James 4:7 admonishes us, *"Submit yourselves therefore to God. Resist the devil, and he will flee from you."*

You and I have the victory because of Jesus. We function and operate through His successes and through His victories. Our victories are not accomplished through human manipulation, but by the LORD of Hosts. He is the One who has defeated the devil! He is the Almighty God!

Anchor your trust in the LORD of Hosts. Depend upon Him. He is the LORD of Battles. He is the LORD of Victories. Call on Him by His Name, and ask Him to do what He is capable of doing. Say, "Lord, You are the Mighty Deliverer. I've got some enemies. Go get 'em!"

I believe that in these last days, spiritual warfare will be intensified. More and more, wickedness and viciousness will come against us. The body of Christ is going to bless the world. We are going to stand up with Jesus in all of His strength and win every battle!

For thus saith the LORD *of hosts; Yet once, it is a little while, and I will shake the heavens, and the earth, and the sea, and the dry land; and I will shake all nations, and the desire of all nations shall come: and I will fill this house with glory, saith the* LORD *of hosts. The silver is mine, and the gold is mine, saith the* LORD *of hosts. The glory of this latter house shall be greater than of the former, saith the* LORD *of hosts: and in this place will I give peace, saith the* LORD *of hosts.*
(Hag. 2:6–9)

10
The LORD Is Conqueror
(Jehovah-Nissi)

In previous chapters, we have studied the names of God that He revealed to individuals such as Melchizedek, Abraham, and Moses at some crisis in their lives. The following chapters are a bit different because they will discuss place names that Old Testament people gave to certain places to declare what they learned about God there.

Turn in your Bible to Exodus 17. This chapter tells how the children of Israel pitched their tents at Rephidim after years of wandering through the wilderness. If you check a Bible atlas, you will find that Rephidim is a rugged desert Place near Mount Horeb. Water is scarce there, and the Bible says that when the Israelites arrived at Rephidim, *"there was no water for the people to drink"* (Exod. 17:1). The people were weary of wandering, the armies of Amalek were pressing down upon them, and there was not so much as a drop of good drinking water for them. They felt utterly defeated. So they started complaining to Moses once again.

If you are a pastor, you probably know exactly how Moses felt. A congregation goes through its "dry desert places," just as the Israelites did. At times, the people of God run up against one dead end after another and one problem after another. There seems to be no relief in sight. They come to their pastor with a complaining spirit and say, "Do we have to keep on going? Do we have to keep on fighting this battle for the Lord? Looks like the Lord has given up on us, so let's admit we're licked."

Defeatism is a curse. It can overwhelm God's people and make them lay down their weapons, even before the battle has begun. Moses, however, was not about to be defeated. He took the problem straight to the Lord and cried, *"What shall I do unto this people? they be almost ready to stone me"* (Exod. 17:4). He didn't lean on his own human wisdom. He didn't run to some textbook on church administration, or to some leadership expert. He turned to the Lord. In effect, he said, "You brought us out here, Lord. Now you will have to take care of us. So what do you want me to do?"

If more of God's leaders did that today, we would see fewer people leaving the church, disgusted because of the trouble they find there. God himself gives us the best answers when God's people run up against a problem.

God told Moses what to do. He directed Moses to a certain rock and told him to strike the rock with the staff that he had used to part the Red Sea. Moses did as God told him, and water gushed out of the rock to give the Israelites plenty to drink.

This occured not a moment too soon because the Amalekites descended upon them. (See verse 8.) Moses turned to his commander-in-chief, Joshua, and told him to muster an army against these invaders: *"Choose us out men, and go out, fight with Amalek: to morrow I will stand on the top of the hill with the rod of God in mine hand"* (v. 9). The armies of Amalek had come out to destroy the Israelites, but Moses knew God wanted them to enter the Promised Land. So nobody could stop them. Nobody could destroy them. You can be sure that no one can destroy you one moment before God is through using you. If He has called you to evangelize the continent of Africa (as He did with David Livingstone), you can be sure He won't let you die until you've gone to Africa and preached the Word. If God has called you to live in another country (as He did with the Israelites), you can be sure you won't be destroyed before you get a chance to set up housekeeping there.

Moses knew that, so he wasn't afraid. He told Joshua that he would stand atop the mountain and raise the rod of God to remind the Israelites who was fighting for them that day. Aaron and Hur had to help him hold up his hands, but he kept his promise. And God kept His. The Israelites defeated the Amalekites that day. Moses then built an altar to commemorate the great victory they had won. Notice what the Bible says about that monument:

> *And Moses built an altar, and called the name of it Jehovahnissi* ["the LORD my banner"]: *for he said, Because the LORD hath sworn that the LORD will have war with Amalek from generation to generation.*
> (vv. 15–16)

Jehovah-Nissi—what an unusual thing to say about God! This name means "the LORD is my banner," or "the LORD is my sign of conquest." In other words, Moses used this name to declare that God would always conquer the foes of His people. So long as Moses and the Israelites followed the LORD, they would have victory. He would defeat the Amalekites and any other pagan people who tried to thwart His purpose and plan.

What's Your Banner?

People march under different "banners" today. They put their trust in different things; they give credit for their success to different things. What do you credit for making you who you are today?

Perhaps you credit your brains. You think you acquired the wonderful mate you live with, the fancy home you live in, the swanky car you drive, and the well-paying job you have with brains! After every new business deal, you think to yourself, "Am I not clever? Didn't I outfox them again?" You go through life under the banner of "Brains" or "Intellect." You tell other people that you got where you are today by "outsmarting" your competitors.

Or perhaps you credit your success to your physical strength or your great physique. Perhaps your friends have said, "He's as strong as an ox," and you like that reputation. You want to convince your boss and everyone else that you have more endurance than other people, so you like to work overtime. You like to tackle the toughest assignments. You like to show everyone how much physical stamina you have. And then you like to say, in mock modesty, "I can handle it." You're marching under the banner of "Brawn" or "Strength."

Perhaps your banner is money, or arrogance, or "knowing the right people." You credit these things for the successes you have in life. They are the banners you hold up as you march on to your personal victories.

But all these things will fail you someday. Advancing age will weaken your brain and rob your muscles of strength. Inflation will suck your money out of the bank. Fickle human nature will turn your friends against you. Repeated failures will give a hollow ring to your arrogance. March under any of these banners, and you will follow it to defeat.

God's Rightful Place—In Front

Moses learned that when he followed God, he conquered. When he let God blaze the trail before him, he had victory. Moses learned to let God be his leader from bondage to the Promised Land. And so should we.

Christians fail to have victory in life when they won't let God be their banner. Sometimes they want God to follow along behind them, blessing whatever they decide to do. They pray, "Lord, bless what I do today in your name." But that kind of attitude puts God in the wrong place. It puts Him in the chuck-wagon, bringing up the rear of the battle column, when He should be the Captain at the front of the column.

Ken Forsch, a pitcher for the Houston Astros baseball team, had to learn this lesson the hard way. During the 1977 playing season, he injured his right arm. Although the doctors and trainers were able to relieve the pain, he lost most of the strength he needed in that arm. For the rest of the season, he was a lousy pitcher.

He did no better at the start of the 1978 season. Every time he came to the mound, batters usually got an easy hit. Ken put himself through a grueling series of exercises to toughen his muscles, trying to regain the strength of his grip. But he didn't improve. His wife and friends prayed for him because they knew his career might soon be over.

After another dismal failure in a game against Pittsburgh, Ken went back to his hotel room and collapsed in despair. He knew all too well that the problem was too much for him to handle. He just couldn't go on in his own strength.

In quiet acceptance, he bowed his head and turned the problem over to the Lord—to do with as *He* wished. And he slept peacefully.

Soon the Astros met the Montreal Expos in a doubleheader. The first game tied and went into the twelfth inning with bases loaded. Then Ken was called to pitch. He promptly struck out three men and won the game. In the second game, he was called to pitch at the bottom of the eighth inning. He helped the Astros win again. After that, his coach put Ken back in the starting lineup, and he won eight of the next ten games.

On the second day of the 1979 season, Ken pitched his first no-hitter, against Atlanta. Thinking back on that experience, Ken realized what his struggle had been. He had been insistent on doing things his way, deliberately refusing to think about what God might have in mind. But Ken learned well that when he asked God to take charge, He worked his life out even better than he could have imagined.

That's what Moses and the Israelites learned at Rephidim. God the Banner must always be in front of our lives, leading the way, if we are going to have victory.

Four Kinds of Victory

God gives us many kinds of victory. Listing all of them would be impossible in the brief space I have here, so let me point out four kinds of victory that I think every Christian should possess.

1. *God gives us victory over sin.* First John 1:7 says, *"But if we walk in the light, as he is in the light, we have fellowship one with*

another, and the blood of Jesus Christ his Son cleanseth us from all sin."
Notice the Bible says He cleanses us from *"all sin."* He gives us
victory over every sin in our lives. He doesn't give us just a partial cleansing of sin; He washes it all away.

We had a friend on one of our Holy Land tours who stopped
smoking about ten times in eleven days! I'm always puzzled to
see Christians "get the victory" so many times over the same
sin. I believe that when we have victory over sin, it ought to
be permanent. When we knock the devil out of our lives and
he starts to get up again, we should put a foot on him and
say "Listen, you're down! You're out! You're finished in Jesus'
name!" We don't need to repeat our victory over sin again and
again because Jesus is our Banner. He has won the victory for us.
We only need to claim that victory to make it ours all the time.

2. *God gives us victory over habit slavery.* This is related to our
victory over sin. Jesus said, *"If the Son therefore shall make you free,
ye shall be free indeed"* (John 8:36). No longer are we bound to the
habits that hinder us from serving the Lord. Whether it's smoking drinking or even compulsive coffee-sipping—whatever the
habit may be, Christ can set us free. We no longer need to be
enslaved to our habits.

3. *God gives us victory over self.* Galatians 2:20 says, *"I am crucified with Christ: nevertheless I live; yet not I, but Christ liveth in
me."* Here the Bible refers to our victory over the dictates of
self-desire.

Lucifer was an angel of God who rebelled against God
because he couldn't do things his own way. He was cast out of
heaven because God would not let him follow his own willful
impulses (see Isaiah 14:12–20). Ever since that time, he has tried
to deceive man into following the same kind of error. He has
tried to convince us that our own self-conceited wisdom is better
than God's wisdom. Satan's deception is a lie straight from the
pit of hell, but God gives us the victory over it. Jesus said, *"If any
man will come after me, let him deny himself, and take up his cross,
and follow me"* (Matt. 16:24). He gives us the power to conquer
self-desire and self-will and to submit ourselves to the will of
almighty God.

4. *God gives us victory over sorrow.* Job provides the classic example of man's struggle with sorrow. Job had so many problems that he couldn't understand, and these were perplexing because he suffered these problems while being faithful to God.

Every one of us has problems we don't understand. Life is not always easy. But if we put our trust in the Lord God our banner, He will give us victory over the sorrow that would otherwise overwhelm us. He keeps us from groveling in grief over our problems.

I once received a ten-page letter from a friend I had met when I was a young preacher in Oklahoma. The letter described how I had baptized several people in the Arkansas River while holding a series of meetings at a country schoolhouse. My correspondent recounted how her father had made her walk eight miles every night to the schoolhouse to hear my preaching. But she had not accepted the Lord. She later married and moved to California. The night she wrote the letter, she had tried to jump off the Oakland Bridge to commit suicide. But the police had caught her.

"I want to kill myself," she told me, "because my life has been nothing but sorrow."

Here was a woman who literally had been baptized in sorrow. She heard the gospel and had an opportunity to give her heart to the Lord. But she never did so, and she has been defeated by sorrow ever since.

My book on grief tells how I struggled with a heavy grief in my own life—the deaths of five close friends in a plane crash.[2] God gave me victory over that grief. He kept me from drowning in sorrow. And I know from that personal experience that He is *Jehovah-Nissi,* "the LORD my banner," even in the face of sorrow.

Let God give you the victory today. No matter what threatens to defeat you in life, you can know that God is the Conqueror who marches on before you. If you're willing to follow Him and give Him the credit for your victory, He will let you triumph every time.

Notes

1. Ken Forsch, "Have It Your Way, Lord." *Guideposts.* (April 1981), pp. 30–31.

2. Lester Sumrall, *You Can Conquer Grief Before It Conquers You* (Nashville: Thomas Nelson Publishers, 1981).

11

The LORD Is Peace
(Jehovah-Shalom)

During World War II, I spent three months preaching in what was then the eastern regions of Poland. I traveled through Minsk to Vilna, all the way to the Russian border. What a hair-raising experience that was! At times we could hear the hoofs of the cavalry troops nearby, and my interpreter would hush my preaching. The house in which I was preaching would be completely silent. We knew that if the soldiers found that many people assembled in one place, we would all be thrown in jail.

Can you imagine how you would feel to be thrown in jail for praising the Lord?

I have preached to Christians in the jails of China. These people often had nothing but bamboo stakes for walls and a dirt floor to sleep on. They were lucky to get anything to eat. Many of them starved or were tortured to death for their faith.

Can you imagine how you would feel worshipping the Lord under those conditions?

Yet it seems that God revealed precious things about Himself to the Israelites when they worshipped Him in times of trouble. He disclosed a new name for Himself—a name that helped them understand Him better—in a time of national crisis. We find another example of this in Judges 6. This chapter opens by telling how the Midianites were destroying the fields and villages of the Israelites, making life utterly miserable for them. The Midianites wanted to drive them out of Canaan once and for all.

And [the Midianites] *encamped against them, and destroyed the increase of the earth, till thou come unto Gaza, and left no sustenance for Israel, neither sheep, nor ox, nor ass. For they came up with their cattle and their tents, and they came as grasshoppers for multitude; for both they and their camels were without number: and they entered into the land to destroy it.* (vv. 4–5)

So God sent a prophet to the Israelites. The Bible doesn't even record his name (see verse 8), just his message. He said:

Thus saith the Lord *God of Israel, I brought you up from Egypt, and brought you forth out of the house of bondage; and I delivered you out of the hand of the Egyptians, and out of the hand of all that oppressed you, and drave them out from before you, and gave you their land; and I said unto you, I am the* Lord *your God; fear not the gods of the Amorites, in whose land ye dwell: but ye have not obeyed my voice.* (vv. 8–10)

The Israelites were worried about their enemies. But God said, "Wait a minute. Don't you remember how I brought you out of Egypt? Don't you remember the victories I gave you over the Canaanites when you first entered this land? Didn't I tell you not to be afraid of the pagan gods of these people? You're in this mess because you forgot My promises. You're afraid because you've forgotten how powerful I am."

The Power of Praise

God was reminding the Israelites of one of the most neglected spiritual truths: the power of praise. Many times we become so anxious to enlist God's help for a certain problem that we forget to thank Him for what He has already done about it. And when the problem is solved, we tend to say, "Oh well, I would have gotten those blessings anyway."

When I tell people how God healed me of tuberculosis when I was a boy, they often say, "You probably would have been healed anyway." But the doctor didn't think so. When he came to our home and examined me, he wrote out my death certificate and left it on my father's desk. "The boy can't live two more hours," he said. "You had better start digging his grave."

But God performed a miracle for me. God healed me. And I will always give Him the praise for that.

When I face an especially tough problem and begin praying about it, I start by praising God for what He's already done. My friend Merlin Carothers does the same thing. He's written several books on the power of praise.[1] As a chaplain in the Army, he found the best advice he could give men about their prayer life was this: *Start by praising God for what He's already done!* You will be surprised at the tremendous spiritual power unleashed in a thankful heart.

This prophet of God mentioned in Judges recalled the marvelous things God had done for the Israelites. In that time of national crisis, God had him preach a sermon on thankfulness. God would begin to give victory when the hearts of His people were thankful.

"The Lord Is Peace"

Then God sent an angel to draft a farm boy named Gideon into military duty. God called Gideon to be the captain of a new army that would go out to fight the Midianites. Gideon saw himself as a most unlikely candidate for that job, so God had to give him some miraculous signs to prove He was serious about the call. (See Judges 6:15–22.) At last Gideon was convinced. He accepted God's call. And he erected an altar on the spot as a monument to what God had told him:

> *Then Gideon built an altar there unto the* Lord, *and called it Jehovah-shalom* [the Lord *is Peace*]: *unto this day it is yet in Ophrah of the Abiezrites.* (v. 24)

What a striking name for that place! "The Lord is peace." Despite the terrible threat of the Midianite army and the meager strength of the Israelite militia that Gideon could rally against them—despite that dreadful prospect of war, Gideon knew that "the Lord is peace."

If you want to live a double life, looking oh-so-religious in church on Sunday but living like the devil the rest of the week, God will let you do that. However, you will have no peace living that way. And you will face eternal damnation in the end for living that way. But God gives you that choice.

On the other hand, if you want to plunge into the Christian life, and if you want to love the Lord with all your heart, He will be everything to you that He was to Gideon and to the other heroes of the Bible. Scripture tells us that He is *"the same yesterday, and to day, and for ever"* (Heb. 13:8). He will be the same God to you that He was to Gideon if you are willing to serve Him faithfully.

The rest of Judges 6 and 7 tells how God brought military peace to Israel through Gideon. You probably remember the story from your childhood Sunday school lessons. Gideon began by gathering an army of thirty-two thousand men. But God told him to keep weeding out the cowardly and clumsy until he had a force of only three hundred men. With those three hundred, some clay lamps and some trumpets, Gideon routed the Midianites from their camp and sent them scurrying back home without fighting at all! *"Thus was Midian subdued before the children of Israel, so that they lifted up their heads no more. And the country was in quietness forty years in the days of Gideon"* (Judg. 8:28).

God can bring peace to a nation. America needs His peace today, just as much as Israel needed it. Our greatest conflict is not with Iran or Libya or even with the Soviet Union; our greatest conflict is with the greedy hearts of our own people. Americans are at war with themselves. They are trying to get all they can for themselves, even if they have to destroy each other to do it. Because of greed, even when America has a bumper crop of wheat, the price of bread is not reduced by one penny. In the District of Columbia, Los Angeles County, and other parts of the country, the divorce rate is now higher than the marriage rate because of human lust and pride. This nation is in turmoil because our people are ruled by their sinful nature. Only the Lord God can change our nature. Only He can bring peace to our country.

You may say, "I don't believe that. I just don't see any evidence of what you're talking about." That's just because your soul is sick with sin and needs to be healed. You need to let the Holy Spirit of God *"purge your conscience from dead works to serve the living God"* (Heb. 9:14). Greed, lust, and pride are *"dead works."* They will give you constant agony in this life and eternal torment hereafter. You need to let the Lord purge those things out of your life so you can serve Him and have peace forevermore.

Emotional Peace

God can give a nation military peace. He also can give you a spirit of peace that comes when you know you are saved. But there's another kind of peace He can give, and perhaps it is the kind of peace you need. I'm talking about emotional peace.

Many people live controlled by their emotions. They are like waves in the ocean, sloshing up and down all the time. In the morning they may be "up," and in the afternoon they may be "down." A man comes home from work and isn't sure what condition the house will be in because he doesn't know whether his wife's emotions have been "up" or "down" today. That's pathetic. But many people live that way today. If they get up from bed feeling depressed, they wallow in depression all day. If they get charged with excitement by a bonus in their paycheck, they feel happy for awhile. Soon, however, their emotions change; and their outlook on life sloshes back the other way.

God does not intend for us to live defeated emotional lives. Notice what Paul said to his friends in Corinth, people who were apt to let their emotions run their lives:

> But thanks be to God, which giveth us the victory through our Lord Jesus Christ. Therefore, my beloved brethren, be ye stedfast, unmoveable, always abounding in the work of the Lord, forasmuch as ye know that your labour is not in vain in the Lord. (1 Cor. 15:57–58)

We should be *"stedfast"* and *"unmoveable"* in our emotions; we should be *"always abounding in the work of the Lord."* God expects

His people to live victoriously and confidently. We can't live that way on our own, but we can live that way through the grace of God, *"which giveth us the victory through our Lord Jesus Christ."*

"Brother Sumrall," you say, "does that mean we are not going to have any problems?"

No, the Bible doesn't mean that at all. But it does mean that when problems come, God will give us confidence to face those problems. He will be *Jehovah-Shalom* in our lives. He will be our peace.

Notes

1. Merlin R. Carothers, *Prison to Praise: A Radical Prayer Concept for Changing Lives* (Plainfield, N.J.: Logos International, 1970); *Power in Praise* (Plainfield, N.J.: Logos International, 1972).

12

The LORD Is There
(Jehovah-Shamah)

The last verse of Ezekiel's prophecy gives us an intriguing name for God. Notice what the prophet says concerning the nature of the New Jerusalem that God revealed to him in a vision:

> *It was round about eighteen thousand measures: and the name of the city from that day shall be, The LORD is there [Jehovah-Shamah].*
> (Ezek. 48:35)

God revealed that this would be the name of the Holy City when He restores her to her former glory: *Jehovah-Shamah,* "The LORD is there." But this is not only a name for the New Jerusalem; this is a name that reveals much about the nature of God Himself.

The Lord Has Been There

First, the name reveals that God chooses to dwell in the Holy City. The Bible shows how God picked the ancient city of Jerusalem to be the scene of many crucial events. Here Abraham met the priest-king Melchizedek who blessed him and interceded to God for him. (See Genesis 14:18–19.) Here David brought the ark of the covenant when he recaptured the land of Canaan from the Philistines. (See 2 Samuel 6:12–19.) Here David and Solomon placed the seat of their government. (See 2 Samuel 5:5–9.)

Here the returning Jews erected a new temple and reestablished the sacrificial worship of God. (See Ezra 1:1–4.) Here Jesus performed many miracles, taught in the temple and was crucified.

The Bible calls Jerusalem *"the throne of the* L<small>ORD</small>*"* (Jer. 3:17), predicting that God will create a New Jerusalem to be the seat of Christ's power at the end of time. (See Revelation 21.) It is only natural, then, for the New Jerusalem to be called *Jehovah-Shamah.* The Lord has been there, physically and spiritually, and He will reign in the New Jerusalem forever.

If you have ever visited present-day Jerusalem, you know how exciting it is to walk the streets that Jesus and His disciples walked. No wonder this city attracts more pilgrims than any other religious site in the world! The air seems to tingle with the drama of biblical events. Only the most hardened heart can visit that city without sensing the atmosphere of divine purpose.

I have led several tours of the Holy Land, and I must confess that Jerusalem is my favorite stop on that tour. Every time we cross that last hill and the city comes into view, the morning sun glimmering on its bleached stone ramparts, my spine tingles with excitement. I feel like saying, *"Jehovah-Shamah,* the L<small>ORD</small> is there," for He is there in a unique way.

The Lord Will Be There—With Us!

Second, the name *Jehovah-Shamah* reminds us that God chooses to live among men. The New Jerusalem that Ezekiel saw was to be no ghost town; it will be teeming with God's people. The saints of all the ages will live there and worship the Lamb, *"and they shall reign for ever and ever"* (Rev. 22:5).

This is not the place to begin a detailed study of Bible prophecy. But let me at least say this: I believe the Lord Jesus Christ is coming back to this earth. I believe He will conquer Satan and all of his devilish servants once and for all. I believe He will set up His kingdom, and all of the saved peoples of earth will reign with Him. And I believe all suffering, sorrow, and pain will be abolished in that kingdom. People will no longer struggle to make a living, but will live to praise the Son of God.

Do you know why I believe these things? Because the Bible teaches them. Read the books of Ezekiel and Daniel, or the great book of Revelation, and you will see the ultimate plan of God described in vivid detail. The Lord will be there in His Kingdom, and we will be with Him! What a glorious thought!

The Lord Is Here—Now!

Third, and most important for our lives today, the name *Jehovah-Shamah* reminds us that the Lord is already living among His people. He is already reigning in your heart if you are a Christian. He has already set up His throne in your life if you have surrendered your life to Him. Other people wear T-shirts promoting their favorite beer or tennis shoes, but a Christian's life should advertise who lives within. A Christian's life should say just as boldly as a T-shirt does, *"Jehovah-Shamah,* the LORD is there."

The Lord enters your life at the moment you are saved. If you are a Christian, think back to how you felt when you were converted. Didn't you feel marvelous? I was saved on the night God healed me of tuberculosis as a teenager, and I shall never forget the incredible joy that flooded my heart. Christ entered my heart that night.

But later I slipped into a bad attitude that the Lord had to correct. He called me to the ministry, but I started grumbling about "having to preach." At times I even growled at the people who came to hear me, because I would rather have preached to an empty house than to preach to real live people who could hear my mistakes. I was born again, but I had not been filled with God's Holy Spirit. When I finally received His Spirit, He cleansed that foul attitude from my life. He gave me a new love for my people, and a new zeal for the work I had been called to. "The Lord was there" in an even more powerful way when I was baptized with the Holy Spirit.

I see similarities between my experience and the progress of America. Our nation has changed dramatically in the past one hundred fifty years. In the early days of America, its people were lean and strong. Most men could chop down a mighty oak with their bare hands. But today most men are so flabby that they can't even split kindling for the fireplace. We have changed spiritually, too. In the early days, a person who was saved had some dramatic changes occur in his life. He or she shed old, sinful habits and started living like the "new creature" God intended him or her to be (2 Cor. 5:17).

Today, however, most people think that "getting saved" is a nice little ritual that they ought to go through, but they don't think their lives should change much because of it. They cling to the filthy habits they had before. They make excuses for not witnessing, not tithing, and not even attending worship services. When someone got saved in the camp meetings of a hundred fifty years ago, God saved him through and through; today we have thousands of people who are satisfied to be half-saved Christians. They confess Jesus with their lips, but you can't see any change in their lives.

Now I don't depreciate what God is doing in people's lives today. I know His Holy Spirit is still at work. I see Him at work in my own congregation and in many congregations I have visited. But I do think that the vast majority of professing Christians have not surrendered themselves completely to the Lord's control. And I think these halfhearted Christians make a mockery of the truth when they point to their own lives and say, "The Lord is here." Because He's *not* there in any obvious way.

I think of Charles G. Finney, who practiced law in upstate New York over a century ago. Finney had attended some camp meeting services and heard what the Lord could do with a life that was fully surrendered to Him. Finney had professed to be a Christian, and he could see some changes in his life that had occurred since he was converted. But he couldn't really say that the Lord owned him completely. Charles Finney still had control of his own life, and as long as he did, he knew that God would withhold His full blessing.

One day Finney felt so convicted about his spiritual life that he locked the door of his law office, walked down the street, and climbed a wooded hill to be alone. He knelt down with the

Lord and surrendered himself completely to the Holy Spirit of God. That was the beginning of a marvelous ministry for young Finney. He began preaching at great city-wide evangelistic rallies throughout the eastern United States. Finney's name has gone down in history as one of the greatest preachers this nation has ever known, because he was willing to get himself out of the driver's seat and let the Lord take command. The Lord was there.

The Lord can do the same with you. If you're willing to "present your body as a living sacrifice" on the altar of full commitment to the Lord, He will fill your life with Himself. He will let His Spirit shine out through your life. Your friends will no longer see the spirit of John Smith or Mary Doe in all that you do; they'll see the Spirit of Christ. The Lord will be there—in you!

The Lord Is There in Trouble

How wonderful it is to be able to say, "I have a refuge from my problems. I have Someone I can turn to. I have a Friend to comfort me, no matter what happens." That's exactly what the Lord promises to you.

The Bible says,

> *God is our refuge and strength, A very present help in trouble. Therefore we will not fear, Even though the earth be removed, And though the mountains be carried into the midst of the sea; though its waters roar and be troubled, Though the mountains shake with its swelling.*
> (Ps. 46:1–3 NKJV)

Everything in your world may turn upside down, but the Lord will still be there to comfort and help you. That's one of the most precious promises of His word, and many times He has proven that promise to me.

As I mentioned earlier, a few years ago I lost five of my closest friends in a plane wreck.[1] The grief of that day seemed greater than I could bear. But the Lord stood by me, even then. He encouraged me when I thought I could not preach because of my sorrow. He ministered to me through the words of my wife and family and the members of my congregation. There are still times a lump forms in my throat when I think of that tragedy. But the Lord reminds me that He still loves me, and that He has those departed friends in glory with Him now.

But there is a greater friend than even our closest human ones. The Bible says, *"A man who has friends must himself be friendly, But there is a friend who sticks closer than a brother"* (Prov. 18:24 NKJV).

That Friend is Jesus Christ. You may have many friends, and think that they'll come to your aid when you have trouble. But you might discover that most of them are "fair weather friends." They like you and help you so long as you are prospering. But when you fall into trouble, they seem to disappear. Jesus never does. He *"sticks closer than a brother,"* even when the rest of your friends abandon you. The Lord is there in time of trouble.

The Lord Is There in Loneliness

I must confess that I can't remember when I have ever felt lonely. Until I was seventeen years old, I was surrounded by a strong family. Then I accepted Jesus Christ as my Savior, and He's been with me ever since. He has given me friends everywhere I have traveled, because He made me part of the wonderful family of God.

When I'm in China, I think I'm Chinese. When I'm in the Philippines, I think I'm a Filipino. (I almost have to look in a mirror to realize that I'm not!) Seriously, I have found such a natural fellowship with God's people in every country of the world that I can't remember being alone as long as I have ministered in His name.

But I know that loneliness is a painful problem for many people. I have visited widows who sit at their living room windows and stare blankly for hours on end. I have met with cancer patients who seldom see their friends or relatives, and college students whose families seem to have forgotten them. We live in an age of callused hearts, when people seem to have lost the love of family and friends that was so common just one generation ago. Millions of people are lonely because no one takes time to say, "I care about you."

But the Lord cares.

The Bible says, *"For the Lord GOD will help me; therefore shall I not be confounded....He is near that justifieth me; who will contend with me? let us stand together"* (Isa. 50:7–8). Again it says, *"Thou art near, O LORD; and all thy commandments are truth"* (Ps. 119:151). And again, *"Seek ye the LORD while he may be found, call ye upon him while he is near"* (Isa. 55:6). Can there be any doubt that the Lord is with you today, whether you recognize Him or not? He cares for you. He wants to help you. He is closer to you than any human being because He made you and His Spirit is speaking to you. But as long as you reject Him, you will feel lonely. You won't actually *be* alone, but you'll *feel* lonely because you shun the God who is there.

Francis A. Schaeffer has written a book titled *He Is There, and He Is Not Silent.* I think there's a marvelous truth in that title. The God we serve is *Jehovah-Shamah,* the LORD who is there, and He speaks to every one of us in our innermost spirits. Some choose to reject Him. They call themselves atheists, agnostics, or something else. But all of their high-flown intellectual arguments against the existence of God do not change the fact that He is there, within us. He is not silent. The gospel songwriter William J. Kirkpatrick put it beautifully when he penned these lines:

> Jesus, my Savior, is all things to me,
> Oh, what a wonderful Savior is He;
> Guiding protecting, o'er life's rolling sea,
> Mighty Deliverer—Jesus for me.
>
> Jesus in sickness, Jesus in health,
> Jesus in poverty, comfort or wealth,
> Sunshine or tempest, whatever it be,
> He is my safety—Jesus for me.
>
> Jesus in sorrow, in joy, or in pain,
> Jesus my Treasure in loss or in gain,
> Constant Companion, where'er I may be,
> Living or dying—Jesus for me!

Jesus *is Jehovah-Shamah,* the Lord who is there when we need Him most. He is like an invisible Companion who tries to gain your attention and prove that He is "for you." But you must accept Him and acknowledge Him.

The Lord Is There in Persecution

I have often been persecuted because of my ministry. When I was a missionary in Tibet, the Buddhist officials tried to drive me out of the country. When I was a pastor in the Philippines, the witch doctors tried to ban me from their villages. Even as a pastor in South Bend, I am sometimes persecuted. Politicians don't always like the stand I take on contemporary issues, and they try to silence me. Businessmen have tried to take control of the LeSEA ministry. I have been pressured and threatened. But, praise God, I have always known that the Lord would help me through all of those troubles.

Jesus warned His disciples:

> *There is no man that hath left house, or brethren, or sisters, or father, or mother, or wife, or children, or lands, for my sake, and the gospel's, but he shall receive an hundredfold now in this time, houses, and brethren, and sisters, and mothers, and children, and lands, **with persecutions**; and in the world to come eternal life.*
> (Mark 10:29–30, emphasis added)

You see, Jesus wanted them to know what they could expect: a house (He will always provide shelter somewhere); brothers, sisters, mothers, and children (spiritually speaking); lands (when and if they are needed); *"with persecutions."* We Christians will have great privileges, yes; but we will endure persecution along the way. We should expect persecution. And we should know that the Lord is with us, even in the time of persecution.

If you're a Christian, you need to develop such a close relationship with the Lord that you'll be ready for persecution. You need to *digest* the Word of God so that you'll know what to do when you are persecuted. You need to be so fortified with God's

Word and Spirit that you'll be able to thrive when persecution comes. You need to be ready to say, "This will drive me closer to the Lord. This will make me more mature in the Lord. Thank you for this trouble, Lord, because I know you mean it for my good."

As I mentioned in an earlier chapter, when I was a boy, Christian families decorated their homes with Scripture mottoes. You don't see many of them these days. They were often made out of painted cardboard with velvet letters. I remember sitting around our dinner table and seeing Mother point to a motto on the wall that said, "Christ is the Head of this house; the unseen Guest at every meal; the silent Listener to every conversation." That simple motto reminded us that the Lord was there, living with us, no matter how hard the going might get. (And believe me, the going got pretty tough during the Great Depression!)

I have often said on my television program that if you are what God wants you to be, and if you're doing what God wants you to do, when the devil calls on you he'll just get a busy signal! But if you're idle, or if you're doing something that is not ordained of the Lord, the devil gets an "open line" to talk with you.

Friend, let the motto over your home be *Jehovah-Shamah,* "the LORD is there. " Keep well occupied with the work of the Lord by reading His Word and devoting yourself to prayer. If you'll do that, the Lord will make you the person that you should be in His sight.

My Prayer for You

O Lord, we know that everything in our lives will work out for Your glory if You are in them. We're so glad that You are the Lord who is always present in our lives. And we pray that we would acknowledge Your presence more fully by the way we live.

Lord, I thank You for the unsaved person who may be reading these words. I pray that You will convict this person of his or her sins and make him or her realize how desperate is the need to exalt You as the Lord of life. Forgive that sinner and take control of that heart right now.

And Lord, I thank You for the halfhearted Christian who may be reading these lines. May that person yearn to be Yours completely. Let him or her surrender all the things that have been held back from you, and let him or her turn the controls of that life over to You. Fill that one with Your Holy Spirit so that the world can look at that life and say, "Jehovah-Shamah, the Lord is there." And for that we will give You the praise.

Remember, the Lord of Hosts is there to fight your battles for you!

"What Must I Do to Be Saved?"

The apostle Paul and his missionary partner, Silas, were imprisoned at Philippi for preaching about Jesus. While in prison, they prayed and sang praises to God *"and the prisoners heard them"* (Acts 16:25). They were witnesses for the Lord, even in prison. While they were singing and praying, an angel of the Lord shook the prison with a strong earthquake. The keeper of the prison woke up, thinking all the prisoners must have escaped. So he drew his sword to commit suicide. But Paul cried, *"Do thyself no harm: for we are all here"* (Acts 16:28).

The prisonkeeper got a torch and ran into their prison cell, falling at their feet with fear. He cried, *"Sirs, what must I do to be saved?"* (Acts 16:30).

That has been the question of humanity since the very beginning of time: *What must I do to be saved from my sin? What must I do to be delivered from the fear and heartache that I have?* Paul and Silas were ready to answer the prisonkeeper. They said, *"Believe on the Lord Jesus Christ, and thou shalt be saved, and thy house"* (v. 31).

Now if Jesus was just another religious teacher, this advice would have been useless. The world has known plenty of religious teachers, but none of them have been able to save people from sin, fear, heartache, and death. Can you imagine how silly Paul and Silas would have sounded if they had said, "Believe on Socrates, and thou shalt be saved"? What if they had said, "Believe on Buddha, and thou shalt be saved"? Why, that would be ridiculous! No amount of religious teaching can save a person from sin.

But Paul and Silas said, *"Believe on the Lord Jesus Christ, and thou shalt be saved."* The apostle Peter said, *"Neither is there salvation in any other: for there is none other name under heaven given among men, whereby we must be saved"* (Acts 4:12). The apostle John said, *"Your sins are forgiven you for his name's sake"* (1 John 2:12).

The name of Jesus is powerful because Jesus Himself is powerful. Only He can save us from our sins, because He is God in the flesh. All the names of God that we have studied in this book apply to Jesus, because He is God. He is righteous; He is almighty; He is conqueror; He is healer. Every one of those attributes is true of Jesus Christ, because He is God Himself.

Perhaps you are asking the question that the Philippian jailer asked. Perhaps the burdens of your life are more than you can bear. You may be asking, "How can I be saved from the mess I'm in? How can I be delivered from the heartache of living like I do?"

If so, I have good news for you! It's the same good news that Paul and Silas gave the jailer: Believe on the Lord Jesus Christ, and you will be saved. Your whole family can be saved if all of you will turn your lives over to Him.

Steps to Salvation

Here are some simple steps that you can follow to accept the Lord Jesus Christ right where you are:

1. *Repent of your sins.* The word *repent* means "to turn away from." When John the Baptist introduced Jesus to the people of his day, he said, *"Turn away from your sins...because the Kingdom of heaven is near!"* (Matt. 3:2 TEV). Peter said, *"Each of you must turn away from his sins and be baptized in the name of Jesus Christ, so that your sins will be forgiven"* (Acts 2:38 TEV). That's your first step to being saved. Admit that you have been sinning against God, and decide that you want to turn away from that sinful way of life.

2. *Confess that Jesus is your Savior.* In other words, admit that Jesus is the only One who can save you from your sins. He died on the cross of Calvary so you would not have to die in sin. You cannot earn your way into heaven by trying to do good; you can only trust Him to save you with His sacrificial blood. You need to confess that fact to Him, and confess it to your friends. The Bible says, *"That if thou shalt confess with thy mouth the Lord Jesus,*

and shalt believe in thine heart that God hath raised him from the dead, thou shalt be saved" (Rom. 10:9).

3. *Believe that God will give you eternal life because you have placed your trust in Jesus.* This involves more than just accepting with your mind what the Bible says about Jesus. It means accepting God's promise with your whole heart, mind, and strength. Satan will try to make you doubt God's promise, but God never goes back on His Word. *"And this is the promise that he hath promised us, even eternal life"* (1 John 2:25).

You can take these steps right now, wherever you are. Salvation must be settled between you and God, and you can do that without anyone else helping you. But if you have trouble getting started with your prayer to Him, you might try this simple prayer:

Lord, I know that I am a sinner. I'm not living as You want me to live, and I can never live that way in my own strength. But Lord, I want to put sin out of my life once and for all, and begin living for You. So please forgive me for what I've done.

I believe You can save me from my sins, because You died on the cross and rose again. I confess that Your precious blood can cleanse the sin from my life. Only You can make me the person I ought to be. So I surrender my life to You.

Thank you for listening to my prayer, Lord. And thank you so much for the eternal life You have given me through Your death and resurrection from the grave. I give You all the praise for what You are going to do in my new life I believe Your Word when it says I am "a new creature" now. I believe all the old things have passed away, and I am now completely different [2 Cor. 5:17]. Thank you for making me new, Lord. Amen.

I hope that is your prayer today. I am praying that this study will cause you to accept Jesus as your Savior if you haven't already. When you do, you will praise Him along with the hymn writer Edward Perronet who said:

> All hail the power of Jesus' name!
> Let angels prostrate fall;
> Bring forth the royal diadem,
> And crown Him Lord of all!

The Gifts and Ministries
of the Holy Spirit

Contents

Dedication

This study on the gifts and ministries of the Holy Spirit is dedicated to the late Howard Carter of London, England.

While Rev. Carter was serving time in prison as a conscientious objector during World War I, he spent many hours in prayer and study of the Word of God. It was there that these glorious truths regarding the gifts of the Spirit were revealed to him.

I lived with Howard Carter for a number of years and knew personally how he was persecuted by religious leaders because of these truths. Yet today his explanation of the gifts of the Spirit is accepted and enjoyed by millions of people of all denominations throughout the world.

Many times I was highly honored to hear him lecture and answer questions on the gifts of the Spirit. The entire charismatic world today owes the treasure of this teaching to this dedicated man to whom God revealed the identity, definition, and operation of the gifts of the Holy Spirit.

I certainly do thank God for my having known Howard Carter, for the privilege of living with him, and for the truths that I am permitted to share with you because of this friend of years past.

Preface

As we begin this study into the gifts and ministries of the Holy Spirit, I cannot emphasize strongly enough the need for information on this subject. As I so often say when teaching, God cannot bless ignorance; He can only bless intelligence.

Do you wish to have faith? I am quite sure that you do. Then you must realize this fact: You can have faith only in relation to your knowledge of God. The same principle stands true with regard to the gifts and ministries of the Holy Spirit. These gifts and ministries function with greatest accuracy through people who understand them.

The purpose in this study is to define the gifts and ministries of the Holy Spirit and to reveal their operations in the body of Christ today.

If God's Holy Spirit is to function fully in our lives, we must have an open heart and a consuming desire to know all we can about the nature and role of the Holy Spirit—His gifts and His ministries to the body of Christ. It is my earnest prayer that this book will be a helpful tool in fulfilling your need.

Part I
Gifts of the Holy Spirit

Now concerning spiritual gifts, brethren, I would not have you igno-rant. Ye know that ye were Gentiles, carried away unto these dumb idols, even as ye were led. Wherefore I give you to understand, that no man speaking by the Spirit of God calleth Jesus accursed: and that no man can say that Jesus is the Lord, but by the Holy Ghost. Now there are diversities of gifts, but the same Spirit. And there are differ-ences of administrations, but the same Lord. And there are diversities of operations, but it is the same God which worketh all in all. But the manifestation of the Spirit is given to every man to profit withal. For to one is given by the Spirit the word of wisdom; to another the word of knowledge by the same Spirit; to another faith by the same Spirit; to another the gifts of healing by the same Spirit; to another the work-ing of miracles; to another prophecy; to another discerning of spirits; to another divers kinds of tongues; to another the interpretation of tongues: but all these worketh that one and the selfsame Spirit, divid-ing to every man severally as he will. (1 Corinthians 12:1–11)

Introduction

There is no other subject so pertinent to the world scene today as the operation of spiritual gifts in the body of Christ. The gifts of the Spirit—the weapons of our warfare—can destroy any force the devil might use against the body of Christ.

I want you to realize how tremendous the gifts of the Spirit can be as they function in your life. You are a candidate for these gifts—not for one gift only, but for all nine of them.

A number of years ago in a simple wooden building in Tennessee, God showed me a vision. (I have experienced only two in my entire life.) In this vision I saw millions of people marching past me into eternity. At that time God made me to know that I was called to minister to the entire world.

At that same time in London, England, a man I had never heard of—Rev. Howard Carter—also received a special message from God, saying he would travel and minister throughout the world. Howard Carter was then president of Hampstead Bible College in North London. At that time God also told him, "I have a companion for you. He will come from afar. He will be a stranger when he comes, and these are the words he will say." This message from God so impressed Rev. Carter that he recorded word for word what God had said to him.

At the time Howard Carter came to minister in this country, I was preaching an open-air revival for a church in the state of Oklahoma. One morning as I was kneeling in prayer under a tree, the Lord spoke these words to my heart: "Close this meeting today and go to Eureka Springs." Eureka Springs is a town in Arkansas about two hundred miles away.

Immediately, I went to the sponsoring pastor's house and told him my plans. This man, much older than I and very severe, scolded me for wanting to close the meeting and said he would never recommend me to other pastors.

So, leaving the angry pastor behind, I headed for Eureka Springs.

In Eureka Springs, I found the great camp meeting in which an Englishman, who turned out to be Howard Carter, was speaking. The meeting hall was packed with people. When Rev. Carter finished ministering, he walked out to the sidewalk and began greeting the people. When he reached me, words began to flow out of my mouth. They were the same words God had spoken to him in London almost eighteen months before.

"Brother Carter," I said, "I will do what you do and I will go where you go. If you travel by plane, I will do likewise. If you go by train, so will I. If you walk, I will walk." With these words God fulfilled to the letter the message He had given Rev. Carter in London.

Because I didn't realize what was happening, I became upset with myself for saying foolish things to a stranger. But Rev. Carter sensed something very different, so he took hold of my hand. When he did, I said, "When you are old, I will help you. I will strengthen you and bless you."

And this I did, until the time he went to be with God in heaven.

Rev. Carter invited me to his hotel room and read from his book of prophecies. He read the words that God had revealed to him that I would say. Through this amazing experience, I realized that the Word of Wisdom is true, that God can show us the future. There in Eureka Springs we lifted our hearts and thanked God that He would speak to us in these last days. In that moment there began a most remarkable friendship. Howard Carter and I traveled throughout the world ministering together—he as a teacher, I as an evangelist—and blessing multitudes of people.

The Night Vision

Here you can see the functioning of the Word of God's Wisdom. God did not reveal everything to me. All He did at first was show me a dying world. That night I made my commitment and began to get myself ready to minister to the whole world. Then He took me one step at a time.

I was so excited that day that I left without asking Howard Carter where he was going, and I forgot to give him my address. Within one hour, I had lost him! It was through the gifts of the Spirit that I found him again.

My sister was traveling with me in evangelistic work at the time, so I drove her to our parents' home. While there, I intended to sell my car and find Howard Carter—wherever he might be in the world. With the Depression on, selling a car was not an easy task. And getting a passport in those days was quite an experience. The only place I could get one was Washington, D.C., and they issued them just as quickly or slowly as they wanted.

It was three months before I could get everything done, and by that time I had no idea where Mr. Carter was. Some people said he had gone to China, others said Japan, still others said India. Finally, I asked the Lord, "Lord, where is this man?" His answer was interesting. All He said was: "Go to the bottom and work up." (God often leads us like that. If He told us the whole story, we would know too much.)

So I started at "the bottom." I found a British boat headed for Australia and got on board. Twenty-one days later the boat docked in Wellington, New Zealand. When I stepped off the boat, I had no idea where Howard Carter was; but determined to find him for fellowship, I began looking for a Full Gospel church. To my amazement, Howard Carter was in New Zealand!

Mr. Carter was attending a minister's retreat in the mountains where there was no communication of any kind. While Mr. Carter was in prayer, God moved again by the gifts of the Spirit. He later told me the following story:

It seems that a day earlier, Mr. Carter was praying, "Lord, over three months ago you gave me a young man, but I have lost him."

The Lord said, "No, you haven't."

"But, Lord, I haven't heard from him since."

The Lord said, "He is in Wellington harbor right now on a boat. Tomorrow morning he will leave that boat, looking for a church, so send the pastor down with a note to him. Tell him you will meet him in Australia."

Mr. Carter walked out where the pastors were and asked, "Which one of you is from the city of Wellington?"

When a man raised his hand, Mr. Carter said to him, "Tomorrow morning there will be a young man at your house. His name is Lester Sumrall. He will be asking for me. Tell him I'll meet him in Australia. Will you give him my personal card?"

The next morning, I started looking around town. After two or three hours I arrived at a little white chapel on the hill. When the pastor answered the door, I said, "I am Lester Sumrall. I am from America. You don't know me."

He said, "Yes, I do. Howard Carter told me you would be here. Here is a note from him to you."

Together we saw the working of the gifts of the Spirit in a most wonderful way in our lives. Rev. Carter had these gifts functioning almost constantly in his ministry, never foolishly, but for great things. God put us together as a team, and we went around the world as teacher and evangelist, winning many souls to Jesus, setting up Bible schools, doing all the things God wanted us to do.

Through my relationship with Howard Carter I gained a firsthand knowledge of the operation of the Holy Spirit. I heard him teach on this subject, not just once or twice, but many times. In Indonesia, Australia, China, Japan, Poland, England, South America, and the United States, I heard this man share with people about the gifts of the Spirit. I never wearied of it. Each time he would lecture, I was engrossed. Because of that experience, I am able to bring you knowledge that others may not be fortunate enough to have.

The Gifts and Ministries of the Holy Spirit

When Howard Carter laid hands on me, he said, "The spiritual life and the faith that is within my heart, I put into you." I trembled throughout my total being as that man of God, twice my age, laid his hands on me to transmit to me the faith that was in his own heart.

I believe God ordained that segment of my past so I could share with the body of Christ today in a direct line from the one who in these modern times found these gifts by the power of the Holy Spirit. God planted them within him. Before Howard Carter's time, people misunderstood and minimized the gifts of the Spirit. They said the gift of faith meant just to believe for something. If you had the gift of the word of wisdom, they assumed that meant you were just clever or smart. Howard Carter recognized these as *sign gifts* from God, and he defined them. Today multiplied millions of people have accepted the truth as it was revealed to his heart.

I believe God wants to accomplish His work supernaturally on the face of the earth. He wants to take natural people and work supernaturally through them to bring about a mighty surge of His power, just the way He worked through Howard Carter. I challenge you to make yourself ready for Him to use you in this wonderful moment in which we live today.

1
Nature and Role of the Holy Spirit

To accurately study the work of the Holy Spirit, we must begin with the book of Genesis, the first book of the Bible. First Corinthians 12:1–11 includes the first mention in the New Testament of the *works* of the Holy Spirit, which are the *gifts* of the Spirit; but in the book of Genesis we see the Holy Spirit introduced in pristine grandeur—an exciting and thrilling display of the Holy Spirit as He functions best.

In the very first verses of the Bible, we read:

In the beginning God created the heaven and the earth. And the earth was without form, and void; and darkness was upon the face of the deep. And the Spirit of God moved upon the face of the waters. And God said, Let there be light: and there was light. (Gen. 1:1–3)

The functioning of the Holy Spirit as demonstrated in the early Christian church is not new. He had been working with human beings for 4,000 years prior to the Christian era, and He has been working in the church for the 2,000 years since. The Holy Spirit has been very busy functioning in behalf of mankind for 6,000 years. He knows our problems; He knows the answers; and we need these answers from Him.

Omnipotence of the Spirit

When we think of the functioning of the Holy Spirit in the creation of the world, we think of omnipotence. The Holy Spirit was omnipotent, all-powerful. Out of the chaos that existed in the beginning, He brought cosmos. God spoke, and His Word had to be obeyed! The Spirit of God moved upon the desolation, and there came forth that which was beautiful for God and for man.

Omnipresence of the Spirit

In His creative powers the Holy Spirit is omnipotent. In His universality He is omnipresent. Psalm 139:7 says this: *"Whither shall I go from thy spirit? or whither shall I flee from thy presence?"* Here David is saying to God, "Where could I go to escape the presence of Your Spirit?" It is impossible to flee from the presence of the Holy Spirit. Perhaps you found that to be true when you were running away from your convictions. God "dogged" you until He got you—and He can do it again and again!

The Holy Spirit is universal in the fulfilling of His operations. He possesses all power and He is everywhere. There is no place that the gifts of the Spirit will not work. They will function anywhere, whether it is in Asia, South America, Europe, or right where you are now.

In Genesis 6:3, we find how God said in words of convicting strength and power that His Spirit would not always strive with man. The Holy Spirit strives to bring man into a place of reconciliation with God. Imagine that happening from Genesis and continuing through Revelation. The Holy Spirit has a fullness of ministry whose chief exercise is to cause men to come to God. Jesus, in speaking to us of the functionings of the Holy Spirit, told us that the Holy Spirit would be a comfort to us and that He would relate the things He heard in the heavens. He would relate those things you say to God and then tell you what God says in reply.

It is the Holy Spirit who moves back and forth, bringing communication from our hearts to God and from God's heart to us. He is accustomed to striving with men's hearts. When you feel within you a craving and a desire to be more like God and to live a holy life, that is the moving and the functioning of the Holy Spirit in your behalf.

Poured Out upon All Flesh

During this present age, the dispensation of grace, God is pouring out of His Spirit upon all flesh. *"And it shall come to pass in the last days, saith God, I will pour out of my Spirit upon all flesh"* (Acts 2:17). Here is the central theme of this study: The Spirit of God will be poured out upon us. We will experience the infilling of the Spirit of God; and as the infilling of the Spirit of God comes, these gifts will automatically flow.

I will tell you how these gifts came to start functioning in my life. You may be interested to know that they were born, not in a moment of jubilation or victory in my life, but in a moment of great attrition. They were born in a moment when I was downcast and almost broken, which only made me realize the greatness and majesty of God. I came to know the thrill of having God in my own heart and life. I believe it will be exciting to you, too, as the power of the Holy Spirit comes upon you and the gifts of the Spirit begin to function in your life.

If the gifts of the Spirit were not for you, it would be wrong for me to discuss them in this way. If they were only for the hierarchy of the church—for the bishops and the archbishops—then you and I might as well discuss something else. We would need to study a subject that is available to us, something we can use in our everyday lives, something that can help with our everyday burdens and trials and cares. God wants it to work, and it *will* work. It *does* work.

"In the last days…I will pour out of my Spirit upon all flesh." "All flesh" means men, women, young people—all cultures, all languages, all people—whether lowborn or highborn, well-educated or ignorant.

The fact that God is willing at this time to pour out His Spirit upon all flesh makes this study imperative. We are at a moment when, more than ever before in the history of man, the power of the Holy Spirit is being poured out. I don't want to be left in a dry corner; I want to be standing right in the middle of the deluge! I want the blessing of God in its fullest. I want to be in the middle of the spout where the glory comes out!

Speaking of the Holy Spirit, Jesus said, *"Howbeit when he, the Spirit of truth, is come, he will guide you into all truth: for he shall not speak of himself; but whatsoever he shall hear, that shall he speak: and he will show you things to come"* (John 16:13).

One of the functions of the Holy Spirit is to bring to our hearts a revelation of the future. If we need to know things that are to come to pass, and the ways in which they will come to pass, the Holy Spirit is the One to reveal them. We need not go to a fortune-teller or to an astrologer. We can go directly to the Holy Spirit. We have a prophecy from our Lord and Savior that the Holy Spirit will be the One to show us things to come.

The Holy Spirit is our guide into all truth, the revealer of things to come. The Holy Spirit is living in His own dispensation today—separate from the dispensation of innocence, the dispensation of conscience, the dispensation of human government, the dispensation of promise, and the dispensation of the Law. We are now living in the dispensation of the grace of the Holy Spirit; and while living in His own dispensation with Him, we can expect His movements to be greater than ever before.

Able Ministers

In 1 Peter 4:10, we read these beautiful words: *"As every man hath received the gift, even so minister the same one to another."* To me this is one of the most precious verses of Scripture that has been delivered to us from the Word of God. Those who have received the gifts should minister the same.

I believe that anything that has been given to us was given to us from God to share. God does not dig holes and bury things. He is not a cover-up man; that is the devil's business. God is a *revealer*, a revealer of the interior workings of human beings. This great message of the gifts of the Holy Spirit is something that should be shared. That is the purpose of this writing.

I encourage you to become a sharer and to share everything you receive. In fact, the way to get this message to grow in your own spirit is to start talking to others about the things you have learned. As you talk about them, there will almost immediately be an increase of knowledge on your own part. As you give, you receive. The Bible says that those who water are watered. As you give out, you will receive back. That is especially true as we study the Word of God. Those who have received the gift should minister the same. This is the desire of my own heart.

I have shared these preliminary thoughts relating to the Spirit of God for a specific reason: The deeper I can place the foundations of this truth, the stronger your tower of strength will be, and I want it to be very strong!

In 2 Corinthians 3:6, the Word of God says we should be able ministers, giving life. I would say that the deep purpose of these lessons would be for us to become able ministers of truth, giving life—spiritual life, dynamic life—to those with whom we come in contact.

2
Charismatic Renewal

Possibly the most spiritual revolution since the Protestant Reformation is taking place in the world at this moment. This is a tremendous statement, but one that I believe to be true. A new force has appeared within Christian ranks today. Nothing has so stirred and excited the entire Christian world during our generation as the movement referred to as the "charismatic renewal."

Unlimited by authority and unconcerned about the organized church, this ecumenical following, which is composed of many colorful backgrounds, is marching toward an experience that is completely in line and in total harmony with New Testament truth.

The "charismatic renewal" is said to be the fastest growing religious movement since New Testament days, having grown quickly and in many directions. People from every Christian denominational background are coming together, equally eager to receive truth on the charismatic gifts of the Holy Spirit.

During the first half of the twentieth century, the most despised segment of the Christian church was known as "Pentecostalism." Suddenly these Pentecostals have become the most important spiritual factor on the face of the earth.

In the decade of the 1960s multitudes within the so-called traditional churches—Catholics, Episcopalians, Lutherans, Methodists, Baptists, and others—started receiving the infilling of the Holy Spirit, just as was experienced by the early disciples on the day of Pentecost, evidenced by a phenomenon called "speaking in other tongues."

"Tongues" is a spiritual language coming from the spiritual person—not from the "soulical" parts (the mind), but from the spirit. The words spoken cannot be understood by the mind. In this experience God gives the speaker what is termed a "heavenly language," or a "prayer language."

It was a remarkable and amazing event to the protestant world when Catholics began to move in spiritual realities, bypassing the entire fundamental and orthodox denominations, and entering into the ranks of the Pentecostals—those who believed the whole Bible to be the Full Gospel. When the Spirit began to move them into the salvation rank of regeneration, they went on into the fullness of the baptism of the Holy Spirit. To me it is remarkable that they did not stop halfway. They did not stop on second base, but ran on around. If they were going to have anything, they would have it all—and they received, much to the amazement of millions of people!

Multitudes of people in this charismatic renewal meet in colleges, in private homes, in borrowed halls. They meet in the most unlikely and unusual places to worship their God and His beloved Son, the Lord Jesus Christ. The gifts of the Spirit function wherever they meet—whether it is in a church, a home, an office building, an auditorium, or a convention hall.

This clearly demonstrates that God has no holy places. He will meet you anywhere—the home, the factory, the street—wherever you are.

Charisma Today

Many people teach that after the day of Pentecost, the phenomena of "charisma" ceased. For people to say that God cannot do today what He was doing 2,000 years ago shows me they do not know the God I know. My God can do anything today that He did then. We are not eating the leftovers of a feast; we are taking in the whole menu. We are getting in on the best and the biggest that the world has ever known.

The Gifts and Ministries of the Holy Spirit

Proof of this is in Acts, chapter 2. On the day of Pentecost Peter stood and spontaneously began to preach. Under the anointing of the Holy Spirit, he laid open the Word of God and preached with such strength and power that the people trembled at his words. When he had finished speaking, verse 37 says of the people who heard:

> Now when they heard this, they were pricked in their heart, and said unto Peter and to the rest of the apostles, Men and brethren, what shall we do?

Peter's response was simple:

> Then Peter said unto them, Repent, and be baptized every one of you in the name of Jesus Christ for the remission of sins, and ye shall receive the gift of the Holy Ghost. For the promise is unto you, and to your children, and to all that are afar off, even as many as the Lord our God shall call. (Acts 2:38–39)

In this scripture passage we find the New Testament promise of God to all those who will heed His instructions:

1. *Repent*—the witness of the blood.
2. *Be baptized*—water baptism as a sign of cleansing from sin.
3. *Receive the Holy Spirit*—the evidence of the Spirit.

Who is this promise for?

When Peter was speaking to these people, he said, *"For the promise is unto you, and to your children."* The promise had already passed beyond the apostles to those people there before him, then on to their children. But that is not all Peter said. He continued with these important words: *"and to all that are afar off, even as many as the Lord our God shall call."* That's you and me!

On the day of Pentecost we have the direct promise that what God did at that moment He would never cease to do. The promise was for them, for their children, for all those afar off, even as many as God would call.

Since the call of God is the call to repentance, as long as God is saving people, He will also be filling them with His precious Holy Spirit.

Charismatics today provide the footings in the body of Christ for what God began 2,000 years ago. We are living in that glorious moment prophesied by Joel:

> *And it shall come to pass afterward, that I will pour out my spirit upon all flesh; and your sons and your daughters shall prophesy, your old men shall dream dreams, your young men shall see visions: and also upon the servants and upon the handmaids in those days will I pour out my spirit.* (Joel 2:28–29)

In the body of Christ today we have the old, the young, and the middle-aged, which is the way it ought to be.

Fruit of the Charismatic Blessing

The charismatic experience, the charisma, has certain benefits and blessings that accompany it.

Love of God's Word

There comes into your life a love for the Word of God that you have never before experienced. The Bible, which seemed to you like a dead book of religious history, suddenly comes alive and seems more relevant than the morning news.

Stewardship

Another fruit of this charisma is a level of stewardship previously unknown. I have found the charismatics to be a remarkable people of stewardship. Throughout the world it is the same. The more they give, the more God gives.

Facing Up To Sin

A third fruit of the charismatic experience is the ability to face up to sin and to confess it. So many religious people try to hide from their sins by making excuses for their behavior.

The Gifts and Ministries of the Holy Spirit

No people in the world face up to reality like the charismatics. If there is sin in their lives, they just come out with it and say, "I'm sorry." Then they receive their forgiveness and become cleansed.

Evangelistic Compassion

Another fruit of the charismatic way is a tremendous growth in evangelistic compassion for others. You will not find another people who love so deeply and so wonderfully as the charismatics—the people who have become identified with the gifts of the Holy Spirit. These people of evangelistic compassion will go throughout the world, teaching and preaching the Gospel because it is in their hearts to do so.

Reaching Out to Others

Another fruit of the charisma is special ministry and service to people in the field of counseling. Charismatics are free to talk to people and help them, because they have a spirit of counseling. They know what to say and how to help those in need.

Joy and Happiness

Charismatics are a singing people, and singing will do special things for you. The Bible says, *"A merry heart doeth good like a medicine"* (Prov. 17:22). There is a spirit inside charismatics that says, *"Rejoice in the Lord alway: and again I say, Rejoice"* (Phil. 4:4). The move of God is evident today by the joy in our hearts, the melody that is within us.

Physical Healing

If you want to hear many outstanding experiences in healing, spend some time with people who are filled with the Spirit of God. You will hear testimonies of healings like you have never heard before.

3
Sign Gifts of the Holy Spirit

The *charisma* is a spiritual phenomenon, unique to our time, one that has been met with tremendous response by millions of people throughout the world.

The word *charisma* is a Greek word that means "spiritual gift"—not natural or carnal or "soulical," but spiritual—freely given to us by God. In its characteristic usage *charisma* denotes an extraordinary ability that is bestowed upon a human being by the infinite strength and power of the third person of the Trinity, who is called the Holy Spirit. This spiritual gift is bestowed as a special service to the body of Christ.

These gifts from God to the local church are what we call "sign gifts." They are supernatural endowments that God places within our lives. The third person of the Trinity is the Governor who brings them in, situates them, chooses which we will have, and lets them flow out through us into the world.

Regarding the living body of the New Testament church in these last days, Jesus Christ said, *"And the gates of hell shall not prevail against it"* (Matt. 16:18). We have come to the titanic contest between good and evil. For us to be the kind of people God wants in these trying times, we must have the gifts of the Spirit. It is imperative that we be qualified spiritually—that we know about spiritual gifts, understand them, and be able to use them wisely as the Lord wills.

These charisma gifts of the Spirit are the weapons of our warfare. If we have these gifts functioning within us, they become our battle axes, our guns, our swords, our spears—all the artillery we need to destroy the works and the powers of the devil.

The Gifts and Ministries of the Holy Spirit

The gifts of the Spirit are not tender little gifts. They are dynamic, dangerous, warlike. You will understand this more as we get into our study and show, in particular, how the gifts have functioned in the Word of God and how they still function today.

These are the special weapons that you will be able to handle dexterously. Some people will not understand you and may call you a fanatic, but that might not be such a bad word after all. In my hometown of South Bend, Indiana, we have great "fanatics." They are Notre Dame "fanatics," or "fans," which only means they get excited about the football games. You and I are also "fans"—fans of the Lord Jesus Christ. We get excited about Him, and we don't mind saying so!

The gifts of the Spirit are the weapons God gives us to fight and win our battles. We must never underestimate their strength, their power, and their usefulness; but we must study them deeply and continuously until they function through us. First, we learn of their existence and we say, "Lord, thank You for the knowledge we have." Then we learn how to avail ourselves of them. Next, we learn about their proper usage. In some bodies of believers, the gifts of the Spirit are misused; and misuse of the gifts will only cause them to cease functioning.

In this study I want to provide you with a firm foundation on the work of the Holy Spirit. I want you to be able to answer any question about spiritual gifts; but more than just explain them to people, I want you to put them into operation both in your personal life and in the local body where you worship. These spiritual gifts should function through you with great wisdom, so that God is pleased with you.

Spiritual gifts are not the icing on the cake or the meringue on the pie; they are the weapons of our warfare. The gifts of the Spirit are not designed just to make you different from other people. They are given to equip you for God's service.

Many people say they would like to have God's power and God's gifts, so they can sit down in a rocking chair and rock themselves right into eternity. But God will not give you the weapons of His warfare so that you can sit in a rocking chair. As long as you are in a rocking chair, you have no need of the gifts.

Spiritual gifts spring up mightily out in the highways and byways—out where the people are. Look at the life of Jesus. The gifts of the Spirit came into operation when He faced the people, such as the Gadarene demoniac. (See Luke 8:26–36.) That was a very frightening situation. When Jesus met certain situations, He had to know things that normally could not be known by the physical eyes or ears; a spiritual phenomenon had to take place.

If you desire the gifts of the Spirit to function in your life, you must be a person of action. You must say, "I am ready for the battlefield. I am ready for God's weapons to function in my life."

The charismatic move of God today is the hope of the church. It is absolutely necessary to God's plan for the world.

There was a great outcry several years ago, proclaiming, "God is dead!" The move of God today is His answer to that statement. God is very much alive, and He is alive within us! He is alive right now, doing just as much for the church today as ever before.

We can receive the same gifts today that the infant church received in the first century. We can visualize that New Testament army of God as it moved across the world, and we can expect God to do the same in His church today.

4
Two Foundation Stones

Perhaps the greatest thing about the gifts of the Spirit is the two foundation stones on which they are laid: unity and love. If the gifts of the Spirit are to function in any church body, these two elements must be present.

The apostle Paul explained the need for unity and love in his first epistle to the Corinthian church.

The twelfth chapter deals with unity in the body of Christ. It takes an entire chapter to reveal how important it is for you to have not just a nose, but a nose and an ear; not just an arm, but an arm and a leg. The body of Christ is one complete structure, and there must be unity. I am not better than you; you are not better than I. We are one together in the Lord Jesus Christ.

The thirteenth chapter drives home the most important point of all: There must be love, pure love. Without it, the spiritual gifts cannot function.

In studying the nine spiritual gifts from 1 Corinthians, chapters 12–14, it would be best to ignore the chapter divisions. Paul wrote this epistle as a continuous letter. There were no chapters. If you would read it with that in mind, you would see that what we view as chapter 13 is not specifically a dissertation on love, but an amplification of the gifts of the Spirit.

Unity

There must be unity in the body of Christ.

The gifts of the Spirit will not function long without unity. On the day of Pentecost—the day the church was born—the people were all together in one place and in one accord, not divided or separated. The church was born in unity, and the church can only be great in unity.

In years past, there have been celebrity evangelists who possessed certain spiritual gifts, but they seemed to function and operate as separate entities. Thirty or forty years ago there were some great manifestations of the gifts of the Spirit in America, but I am ashamed to say that the people through whom these gifts functioned pulled away from the body. Some began to call themselves by such names as "God's man of the hour." The gifts then were not identified with the body of Christ, but only with a person. That cannot be.

I am discovering more each day that God is "body-conscious." By that, I mean He sees us continually as one body—the body of Christ. You and I, as members of that body, must learn to flow together. I am not one thing and you another; we are one together. For the gifts of the Spirit to flow as they should, it must be through the body, which is the church.

God is ready for these gifts to function through the total body, without a great emphasis upon any one individual. Each of us should feel that we are chosen by God. No one who is being used by the Holy Spirit is unique in himself; he is only unique in that he is permitted to be a part of the body. All of us are part of Christ's glorious body! Today we are entering that time of unity, and I am so thankful for it. We are becoming the same size, where there are no little ones or big ones—just everyone flowing together in the gifts of the Holy Spirit.

In 1 Corinthians, chapter 12, we see this unity of the Body described:

Now concerning spiritual gifts, brethren, I would not have you ignorant....Now there are diversities of gifts, but the same Spirit. And there are differences of administrations, but the same Lord. And there are diversities of operations, but it is the same God which worketh all in all. (1 Cor. 12:1, 4–6)

The Gifts and Ministries of the Holy Spirit

Diversities of Gifts

Within the nine gifts of the Spirit, there are three groups: revelation, power, and inspiration. There are diversities of gifts, but all three groups flow from only one Source: the Holy Spirit of God.

Differences of Administrations

What does this mean? Let me give you an example.

It may cost Dr. Billy Graham $50 million to run his evangelistic association for a whole year, while a little country preacher may not pay more than $500 a year. What is the difference? Their administrations are not the same. Billy Graham reaches out to millions of people. A little country preacher may not reach more than fifty people during an entire year.

There may be differences of administrations, but always remember, it is the same Lord. That means we should neither look down on anybody nor look up to anybody. All of us are functioning for the same reason under the guidance and direction of the same Lord.

We are not to exalt persons, no matter who they are. We are to exalt Jesus. No matter what size the administration might be, there is only one Lord—the same Lord who does both the little things and the big things. We must not despise one and praise another. We must say, "Thanks be unto the Lord for all the wonderful works He does on the face of this earth!"

Diversities of Operations

Different ministries go about their tasks in different ways. Some reach out via television; others, via radio; still others, via the printed page. Some are involved in all three. Yet many others confine themselves to direct personal contact with the people, face-to-face and eye-to-eye.

Again, you must never forget: No matter what type of operation is being used, *"it is the same God which worketh all in all."*

You may say, "The Lord must not be with me. I'm not doing much." If you have brought even one soul to Jesus, that is worth the whole world.

We must stop exalting or debasing, looking up or looking down. We must look forward by the power of the Holy Spirit into the great harvest fields. Then God can use us and bless us. These gifts of the Spirit will not function until we form the right attitude in our souls. There are diversities of operations, big and little, but it is the same God who works in all of them.

The Gifts Bring Profit

"But the manifestation of the Spirit is given to every man to profit withal" (1 Cor. 12:7).

To manifest means "to show." This flowing out of these gifts of the Spirit is given to every man. Some people have developed a philosophy that in every church body there should be only one or two people who operate in spiritual gifts. That cannot be found in the Bible. God wants each of us to have the gifts of the Spirit functioning in our lives.

"The manifestation of the Spirit is given to every man to profit withal." When God gives you something, it is a good thing. It is a plus, not a minus, and there is profit behind it.

No church body ever decreased when the gifts of the Spirit were in operation there.

No person ever became weaker when the gifts of the Spirit held a dominant role in his life. These gifts always bring a profit. Your assets are better when you get the gifts of the Spirit working. God wants the gifts of the Spirit to function in your life. He wants you to profit and He wants the body of Christ to profit.

First Corinthians 12:8–10 lists the nine gifts of the Spirit:

For to one is given by the Spirit the word of wisdom; to another the word of knowledge by the same Spirit; to another faith by the same Spirit; to another the gifts of healing by the same Spirit; to another the working of miracles; to another prophecy; to another discerning of spirits; to another divers kinds of tongues; to another the interpretation of tongues.

153

The Gifts and Ministries of the Holy Spirit

Then in verse 11 we again see the thought that was conveyed in verse 7:

But all these worketh that one and the selfsame Spirit, dividing to every man severally as he will.

To every man—God said it twice in just these few verses, *"dividing to every man severally."* That means you need not stop with one or two; you can receive several of them.

Then there is a small qualification: *"as he will."* The Holy Spirit has something to do with it. He knows your capacity. He knows how you would use the gifts. Therefore, He gives them as He wills.

One Body Together

In verse 12 there is another admonition for unity: *"For as the body* [human body] *is one, and hath many members* [collectively], *and all the members of that one body, being many, are one body: so also is Christ."*

The Lord is pleading through the apostle Paul for unity in the body of Christ. For many hundreds of years it has grieved the Lord and made the devil laugh whenever we as children of the Lord fight among ourselves. I pray the Lord will never permit me to fight with another Christian as long as I live. When I discern a fight in the works, I seek with all my heart to back off.

God's people should not fight with one another over doctrines and denominational differences. We are bound together neither by denominations nor by doctrines, but by the shed blood of the Lord Jesus Christ. We are blood brothers, born again of His spirit and by His blood. Any person who has been born again is your brother or sister, no matter what their denominational tag may be. If a person belongs to Jesus, he belongs to you, too. Both of you are the body of Christ. If he draws a circle and leaves you out, you should draw a bigger one and take him in!

Strength in Unity

"For by one Spirit [the Holy Spirit] *are we all baptized into one body, whether we be Jews* [the religious people] *or Gentiles* [the non-religious people], *whether we be bond or free; and have been all made to drink into one Spirit"* (1 Cor. 12:13).

There is a strength and a force in unity that will not be found any other place. The unity of the body of Christ is like none other.

Once the church of Jesus Christ comes together and flows as one colossal body, the power and love of God will spread throughout the whole world.

> For the body is not one member, but many. If the foot shall say, Because I am not the hand, I am not of the body; is it therefore not of the body? And if the ear shall say, Because I am not the eye, I am not of the body; is it therefore not of the body? If the whole body were an eye, where were the hearing? If the whole were hearing, where were the smelling? But now hath God set the members every one of them in the body, as it hath pleased him.   (1 Cor. 12:14–18)

You may not like being an ear and may want to be a nose; but if God made you an ear, be a good one. Keep yourself open to hear.

If God has made you a toe, walk well. Be a support for the foot, because that is what God has called you to do.

Chosen by God

I believe the Lord chooses just the right place for each of us to fill in the body. God needs all kinds of people to appeal to all kinds of people. We must recognize the total body and determine to flow together in Him. I think perhaps there is nothing more dynamic in the world than to be placed in the body of Christ by Him.

When I started off to go around the world as a missionary at 20 years of age, I had only $12 in my pocket. As I began to weep,

The Gifts and Ministries of the Holy Spirit

the Lord said, "Read John 15:16." So I turned to it: *"Ye have not chosen me, but I have chosen you."* Then I realized a great truth: It was not my decision to be a missionary and travel around the world. The Lord had made the decision for me. All I had to do was agree to do what God had asked of me. What a relief!

How beautiful it is when God sets us in the body! If God has called you to be a businessman, stay right where you are and be a good one. You are needed in that position. God put you there for a purpose. If you are a housewife, be the greatest there is. If God has planted you in the ministry, then be an effective minister, in Jesus' name!

Wherever God has put you, just be strong. You have no idea how many lives you will touch and bless and strengthen in the place God has put you. You are what you are because God made you that way. It was not by accident.

There Must Be Unity

And if they were all one member, where were the body? But now are they many members, yet but one body. And the eye cannot say unto the hand, I have no need of thee: nor again the head to the feet, I have no need of you. Nay, much more those members of the body, which seem to be more feeble, are necessary. (1 Cor. 19–22)

Why would God use language like this to speak of the gifts of the Spirit? To show us with clarity the need for unity. In order for these nine spiritual gifts to function in the body, there must be unity.

If you are contrary to the unity of the body, you cannot expect these gifts to operate in your life. The beginning of the knowledge of these gifts is knowing they are in the body in the unity of the Spirit. We will see this flow as we honor one another, appreciate one another, and lift up one another.

You are a candidate for these mighty gifts of the Holy Spirit to function in your heart and in your life. God wants His people to operate in His power. Nothing is so powerful as an idea whose time has come, and I believe the time has come now for these gifts to flow. That is why it is so necessary for the body of Christ to have teaching in this area. We must not go astray. We must not misuse what God has provided. As long as we keep the gifts in the place God wants them, they will function today just as they did in the Acts of the Apostles.

Nay, much more those members of the body, which seem to be more feeble, are necessary: and those members of the body, which we think to be less honourable, upon these we bestow more abundant honour; and our uncomely parts have more abundant comeliness. For our comely parts have no need: but God hath tempered the body together, having given more abundant honour to that part which lacked: that there should be no schism in the body; but that the members should have the same care one for another. And whether one member suffer, all the members suffer with it; or one member be honoured, all the members rejoice with it. (1 Cor. 12:22–26)

The word *"schism"* (v. 25) is important. It means a division or separation. God does not want a schism in the church. He does not want us fighting with one another. When a person comes to you grumbling or finding fault with another person, don't even argue with him. The best way to put a stop to it is by saying, "Why don't we pray about that situation? God will take care of it for you."

It is the beginning of the moving of God's power among us when we start caring one for another, really caring. There should be a real spiritual relationship among God's people.

It is so easy to become selfish and isolated, to separate ourselves when God wants us to flow in the body. You cannot see yourself as a separate entity. You cannot go off into a corner and say, "Look at me. I'm really great!" No, you are not great. *God* is great; *Jesus* is great; *the Holy Spirit* is great! You are what you are because of what God did for you through Jesus.

Now ye are the body of Christ, and members in particular. And God hath set some in the church, first apostles, secondarily prophets, thirdly teachers, after that miracles, then gifts of healings, helps, governments, diversities of tongues. Are all apostles? are all prophets?

are all teachers? are all workers of miracles? Have all the gifts of healing? do all speak with tongues? do all interpret?   (1 Cor. 2:27-30)

The answer to each of these questions is a very definite, "NO!"

The key verse in this entire passage of Scripture is verse 31: *"But covet earnestly the best gifts."*

The word *"covet"* is a strong word. When used in the carnal sense, it is wrong; we are not to covet our neighbor's goods. (See Exodus 20:17.) But coveting between you and God is different.

You will not receive the gifts of the Spirit by accident. You will receive the gifts of the Spirit only because your desire is so intense that you must have them; then you will receive them.

"But covet earnestly the best gifts: and yet show I unto you a more excellent way" (v. 31). This *"more excellent way"* is the second foundation stone on which the operation of the gifts of the Spirit is based: love.

Love

The goal of the New Testament church is to sweep the world with the power of God, but it cannot be done without love. Love is the key that unlocks the door to all God has for us today.

Let's look at what the apostle Paul has to say about love in 1 Corinthians, chapter 13. In the first three verses, various spiritual gifts are enumerated. However, we are told that without love, these gifts will add up to nothing.

Though I speak with the tongues of men and of angels, and have not charity, I am become as sounding brass, or a tinkling cymbal. And though I have the gift of prophecy, and understand all mysteries, and all knowledge; and though I have all faith, so that I could remove mountains, and have not charity, I am nothing. And though I bestow all my goods to feed the poor, and though I give my body to be burned, and have not charity, it profiteth me nothing.   (1 Cor. 13:1-3)

Paul is saying here that without love, you cannot produce the gifts of the Spirit. You cannot produce them in an atmosphere of selfishness and jealousy; they just will not function.

You may have a million-dollar cathedral, but without love you are nothing.

Your minister may be the finest orator in the world, but without love he is nothing.

Your choir may be the finest choir anywhere on earth, but without love it is nothing.

Your congregation may include the finest, most respectable people in the city, but without love they are nothing.

You may be able to raise the dead in your ministry, but without love you are nothing.

Then in verses 4–8 we are told what love is:

Love is that force within you that suffers a long time and is kind and gracious.

Love is that force within you that does not envy. Another person may have more than you have, but it doesn't matter. His car may be nicer than your car, his home nicer than your home, but you are not envious.

Love does not promote itself.

Love is not puffed up, making a big "I" and a little "u."

Love does not behave itself unseemly or inappropriately. It always acts the right way.

Love does not seek her own, is not easily provoked, and thinks no evil.

Love does not rejoice in iniquity, but rejoices in the truth.

Love bears all things, believes all things, hopes in all things, and endures all things.

Love never fails!

Then verse 13 says: *"And now abide faith, hope, love, these three; but the greatest of these is love"* (NKJV).

5
Weapons of Our Warfare

I make the following statement without qualification because I believe it with all my heart: The greatest unused energy in the world today cannot be found under the ground with the oil and coal resources; that latent power is within the church of the Lord Jesus Christ.

The power of God is invincible, and the gifts of the Spirit have been given to the church as the weapons of our warfare. However, the church today is going into battle without a true knowledge of those weapons. Any time you go to battle without your weapons properly functioning, you cannot expect to win the fight.

It is my true desire that through this study of the gifts of the Spirit, you will recognize the true greatness of these spiritual gifts and allow them to become a vital part of your life.

When our Lord Jesus came to this earth to conquer it and redeem it, He functioned only within the framework of the gifts of the Spirit. His total ministry on earth was not as God, but as a man, functioning in the gifts of the Spirit. All the "miracles" Jesus performed were the result of a gift of the Spirit functioning at that time.

Do you believe that Jesus always told the truth? He did! Then let me remind you of what He said in John 14:12: *"He that believeth on me, the works that I do shall he do also; and greater works than these shall he do; because I go unto my Father."* The ministry Jesus performed on this earth was directed, guided, and energized by the Holy Spirit—the same Holy Spirit that you and I have today. We can expect to do the same works Jesus did if we will follow, line upon line and precept upon precept, everything the Word of God teaches.

Each one of us has a right to every gift of the Holy Spirit, without exception. Each believer in Christ has the right to any and every gift of the Spirit. When we leave ourselves out, it is through unbelief. We say, "That is for someone else. It can't be for me." But the gifts are for you! They are provided for the total body of Christ, and you as a believer are a part of His body.

It is time to cry out, O church of the Lord Jesus Christ! Put on the whole armor of God! Clothe yourself in the gifts of the Spirit! Go out against the enemy and destroy him! Bring to the king-dom of God glory and majesty because He is the King of Kings and the Lord of Lords! You and I should see victories every day, and never know defeat!

Jesus said that if you wish to take a prey, you must first bind the strong man. (See Matthew 12:29.) When we seek to take a prey in a pagan land, such as Tibet or India, it is imperative that we use the weapons of our warfare. Not to do so is to suffer humiliating defeat at the hands of witchcraft, superstition, and heathen religion. Only when that pagan darkness is pushed back can we know true victory.

Zechariah 4:6 says it is *"not by might* [or organization], *nor by power* [or a decision of a board], *but by my spirit, saith the* LORD *of hosts."*

We can reach out today to save the world in which we live, but it will never be done by organizational strength or even by the strength of numbers. God can win a mighty battle with just a few people. By using only Gideon and his faithful 300, God took care of tens of thousands of the enemy. (See Judges 7 and 8.)

God does not need a host of men to win a battle; He just needs sincere and dedicated people, whose hearts are fully turned to Him. In this case, to win a total victory He needs those who have received the endowment of the gifts of the Spirit to function in their lives and ministries.

The body of Christ is an advancing army; we do not retreat. We have total victory; we do not know defeat. Our warfare is not carnal; it is spiritual. We are not fighting doctrines or people or denominations. We are warring in the spirit, and the gifts of the Spirit are a necessary part of our fighting gear, both defensive and offensive, but especially offensive. It is the power of God flowing from our spirits that convinces people.

I believe we are living in a prophetic moment. Jesus Christ will soon be returning for His church, and He does not want to come back for a church that is sick and sad and defeated. He wants to come back for a church that is glorious—winning victory after victory and setting men free by the power of God.

6
God's Gifts to the Church

The gifts of the Spirit cannot be earned. They are called "gifts" to reveal that there is only one way to obtain them: They are given to the church by God. However, this by no means minimizes their importance.

These gifts are not optional. The people of the church have missed God in the past by deciding for themselves whether or not they would accept them. The gifts of the Spirit are not placed at the disposal of the church on a take-it-or-leave-it proposition. We either take them or lose what we have.

Categories of Gifts

The gifts of the Spirit are divine communications, transmitted from the Holy Trinity through the channel of the Holy Spirit, the third person of the Trinity, into the church—the body of the Lord Jesus Christ upon the earth.

The number of divine perfection is 3. Everything in the universe that is stamped with perfection is stamped with that 3.

There is the threefold nature of God: Father, Son, and Holy Spirit. *"For there are three that bear record in heaven, the Father, the Word, and the Holy Ghost: and these three are one"* (1 John 5:7).

There is the threefold nature of man: spirit, soul, and body. *"And the very God of peace sanctify you wholly; and I pray God your whole spirit and soul and body be preserved blameless unto the coming of our Lord Jesus Christ"* (1 Thess. 5:23).

The Gifts and Ministries of the Holy Spirit

You will notice as well the mark of divine perfection in the gifts of the Spirit. They divide themselves naturally and spiritually into 3 primary categories: revelation, power, and inspiration. Within each of the 3 categories, there are 3 subgroups.

So you have 3 + 3 + 3. Perfection x Perfection, or Perfection + Perfection + Perfection.

No matter how you choose to look at it, that is absolute perfection.

Each category is distinguished from the others by the work God is doing through it. In each category He is doing something separate and distinct from the others. It is through these three vast areas—revelation, power (or energy), and inspiration—that the church of Jesus Christ becomes an invincible force, stronger than any power known on the face of the earth.

Revelation Gifts

Through this prime category—the revelation gifts—the infinite God, Creator of the universe, is revealing His truth to man. There is a revelation from heaven of certain facts that man could not know by way of his physical senses. It would have to be a miracle; man would have no way of knowing except by divine revelation.

We see an example of this in Matthew 16:16–17: *"Simon Peter answered and said, Thou art the Christ, the Son of the living God. And Jesus answered and said unto him, Blessed art thou, Simon Barjona: for flesh and blood hath not revealed it unto thee, but my Father which is in heaven."*

Within this category there is the word of wisdom, the word of knowledge, and the discerning of spirits.

Power Gifts

In the second category of spiritual gifts—the power gifts— God imparts His own divine powers and abilities to man. The gifts of power involve a supernatural ability and energy that man does not naturally possess.

This category of power gifts includes the gift of faith, the gifts of healing, and the working of miracles. Within this group is found the only gift that has plurality: the gifts of healing. We will explain later why it is in the plural form.

Many of these gifts are like a chain. Each is linked together with others in such a way that when you pull one, you are pulling the whole load. Sometimes it is difficult to divide the links and distinguish between them because they are so interrelated. We see this especially in the gifts of power because both the gift of faith and the working of miracles are operating in the supernatural.

Inspiration Gifts

The third category of the gifts of the Spirit is inspiration. In the gifts of inspiration God brings His anointing and His blessing to the church.

This category includes the gift of prophecy, the gift of tongues, and the interpretation of tongues. These gifts have to do with corporate worship, not with personal worship.

First Corinthians 14:3 gives the total blessing of these gifts of inspiration: edification, exhortation, and comfort. These three gifts, which come to us through inspiration, are the three most needed ministries in the church of the Lord Jesus Christ.

Each Gift Defined

The nine gifts of the Spirit are as distinct as the seven lamps of the golden lampstand in the temple in Jerusalem and as individual as the nine fruit of the Spirit that blossom in our lives. Yet they are so linked and interlinked by the Holy Spirit that it is sometimes difficult to determine exactly which gift is in manifestation. At times there might be the working of miracles, at other times the gifts of healing.

For this reason I admonish you to avoid a heavy emphasis on definitions. Definitions can cause separation among the people. The devil would love to have us quarrel over definitions.

The Gifts and Ministries of the Holy Spirit

Arguments can arise between two people who actually believe the same thing but are defining it differently.

Let's be careful to be courteous and remain in love. How a person is healed—whether through the working of miracles, the gifts of healing, or the gift of faith—really is not the issue. The important thing is that he is healed!

The following are brief definitions of each gift of the Holy Spirit:

The word of wisdom is the revealing of the prophetic future under the anointing of God. In the Old Testament every seer and every prophet who foretold the future was endowed with this gift. A word of God's wisdom is just that: *a word*. When God gives you a word of His wisdom, He gives only a fragment. The same is true with the word of knowledge.

The word of knowledge is the revealing of a fact in existence that can only be supernaturally revealed. It cannot be seen or heard or known naturally.

This is the difference between the word of knowledge and the word of wisdom: The word of knowledge is a revelation of a fact that exists; the word of wisdom is a revelation of the future. Daniel was operating in the word of wisdom when he said there would be a Persian empire, a Grecian empire, and a Roman empire. At that time those empires had not been born.

The discerning of spirits has to do with the comprehending of the human spirit, supernaturally revealed by the Holy Spirit. It is not the discerning of demons, but the discerning of the human spirit—good and bad. With this gift, you can look straight through a person and know whether or not he is telling the truth.

The gift of faith is God's bringing to pass a supernatural change. No human effort is involved.

On the other hand, the gift of the *working of miracles* does work through a human instrument. It is a person doing a supernatural act by the divine energy of the Holy Spirit. An excellent example is Samson bare-handedly killing a lion. That was a miracle.

In the *gifts of healing* God supernaturally heals the sick through a ministry anointed by the Holy Spirit. A person is given a gift from the Spirit of God to pray for a particular kind of sickness or disease. Remember, there are many ways to be healed. This includes only a small portion of them. There might be as many gifts as there are diseases. This is why the term is in the plural form.

The gift of tongues is the ministry of proclaiming in a public meeting a message from God in a language not understood by the person giving it. Because he has not studied that language and does not know it, he does not give it from his mind, but from his spirit.

When a message in tongues has been given, then *the interpretation of tongues* goes into operation. Without any mental faculties being involved, the message that has been given in another language is interpreted supernaturally by the Holy Spirit through another person.

The gift of prophecy is the anointed speaking forth of words of edification, exhortation, and comfort—words supernaturally given to the church from God.

7

The Revelation Gifts

There are three gifts of revelation: the word of wisdom, the word of knowledge, and the discerning of spirits. In these three revelation gifts, God reveals information supernaturally to a man or woman—information that comes from outside the bounds of that person's natural processes; information that their minds did not conceive, their ears did not hear, and their eyes did not see.

The Word of Wisdom

The gift of the word of wisdom is a supernatural revelation of the divine purposes of God. It is a divine communication, a message to the church from God, given by the Holy Spirit through a believer.

In the gift of the word of God's wisdom, God gives forth a small segment or portion of information from His vast storehouse of wisdom. Wisdom has to do with that which is unborn, or of the future. When God gives a word of His wisdom, He is revealing something that has not yet come to pass. Every prophet in the Bible possessed this gift, and prophets who live today also possess it.

This gift unveils, in part, the purposes of God on the earth. The apostle Paul explains it this way: *"But we speak the wisdom of God in a mystery, even the hidden wisdom, which God ordained before the world unto our glory"* (1 Cor. 2:7). The word of wisdom involves speaking the hidden things—things we would not normally or naturally know.

Remember, this is not just the gift of wisdom; it is the *word* of wisdom. It is a fragment of the total wisdom of God, just as a word is a fragment of a sentence. The word of wisdom is a part or portion of the great omniscience of God.

It is very difficult for us as human beings to realize that God is all-wise—that He knows the total past, the total present, and the total future, all at one time. When He conveys to the church through one of His servants a word of wisdom, He has made that person wise in that one matter, but not wise concerning all things. When a person receives the gift of the word of wisdom, he does not suddenly become a "know-it-all." The word of wisdom has no relation to a person's natural knowledge. Whether a person has achieved brilliant academic success has nothing to do with this gift. A person with very little education can operate it just as well.

This gift of the word of wisdom can transform the world in which we live today. It can fascinate this world. The devil has a counterfeit for everything God has. These people who claim to read the future are counterfeiting what God wants to do through His people in the earth. God wants you to know the future. It is time for this gift to function in a way that it has never functioned before in the history of the world.

If the church was moving in the spiritual gifts of revelation—the word of wisdom, the word of knowledge, and the discerning of spirits—there would be no need for fortune-tellers, crystal-ball gazers, Ouija boards, tea-leaf readers, palm readers, and all the other paraphernalia that the devil uses to deceive the people of our generation. We are engulfed in the greatest wave of black magic and witchcraft this country has ever known. One reason for this is that the church has not properly operated in the gifts of the Spirit. We have not used the weapons of our warfare to stop the devil's counterfeits.

I challenge you to seek God for these major gifts. As 1 Corinthians 12:31 says, we are to *"covet earnestly the best gifts."* If we will do that—and seek them with all our hearts—we will find that they are available to us.

The Gifts and Ministries of the Holy Spirit

Through the gift of the word of God's wisdom, God makes you wise to the future and you know what is going to take place. Rather than worry about it or work at making it come to pass, you merely let it function, and it happens exactly as God has told you.

In the Acts of the Apostles, we see these gifts functioning time and time again. If they functioned in the early church, they should function in today's church; and they will function today if we will desire it. God wants us to have it.

Revelation Gifts in the Old Testament

There are some very remarkable men in the Old Testament who had the gifts of the Spirit functioning in their lives. The power that motivated these remarkable Old Testament ministries—men like Noah, Ezekiel, Daniel, David, Joel, and Isaiah—is the same power that motivates us today: the power of the Holy Spirit.

God is not doing something special through the operation of spiritual gifts today. He has always worked this way, and He always will. By harnessing these powers and utilizing them as God desires, we can change the world in which we live.

God wants to motivate us by the same gifts of the Spirit that He used to motivate all those men of the Old Testament. They were not just select individuals—special people in whose footsteps no ordinary Christian could hope to follow. All that they did—the works that are recorded in the divine record—is available to us today. We should expect the gifts of the Spirit to function in our lives just as they did during Old Testament times.

Word of Wisdom in the Old Testament

All the prophets of the Bible were endowed with the spiritual gift of wisdom. They were seers of the future, making known God's wisdom about what would come to pass. Here are some examples:

Noah

In Genesis 6:12–13 God revealed to Noah the coming of the Flood:

> *And God looked upon the earth, and, behold, it was corrupt; for all flesh had corrupted his way upon the earth. And God said unto Noah, The end of all flesh is come before me; for the earth is filled with violence through them; and, behold, I will destroy them with the earth.*

Noah knew for a hundred and twenty years that God would destroy the earth. This is the gift of the word of God's wisdom functioning in Noah. He received only a word of what God was going to do.

Daniel

The prophet Daniel had great visions. He saw empires leap into existence and perform on the stage of human history. Before they were ever born, he named the very nature these empires would have: lions and bears and leopards and beasts. It was the gift of the word of wisdom in operation that caused him to know these things.

Ezekiel

The prophet Ezekiel very dramatically foretold the whole future, as we see it in Ezekiel 38–39. This demonstrates how God reveals the future. Every day we got nearer to the fulfillment of that word of God's wisdom.

He said that from the north there would come an army against the country of unwalled villages. In Ezekiel's day there was no such thing as an unwalled village; they did not exist. The towns needed walls for protection against wild animals and enemies. Today there is not one village in Israel with a wall around it. Also, there had never been a real threat to Israel from the northern parts before Russia took her place there as a world empire.

That is a word of God's wisdom. God told Ezekiel exactly what would happen. When we see these things coming to pass, we should rejoice. These are the words of God's wisdom being fulfilled before our very eyes.

David

David revealed through the Psalms how the Messiah would come and how He would die. It was a revelation of the future as seen, for example, in Psalm 2 and 22.

Joel

When the prophet Joel prophesied that in the last days God's Spirit would be poured out upon all flesh, he was revealing the future. A word of God's wisdom was being brought forth.

Isaiah

Chapter 53 of Isaiah is one of the greatest prophecies in the Bible. The great prophet Isaiah described the nature of the Messiah. He described the way He would die, what kind of person He would be, and what His death would mean to us. He even wrote that by His stripes we would be healed. In Isaiah's day stripes were not known as a form of punishment. This was the word of God's wisdom functioning through Isaiah.

Word of Wisdom in the New Testament

Foremost among those demonstrating the word of wisdom in the New Testament was the ministry of the Lord Jesus Christ.

In Matthew 24, Luke 21, and Mark 13, Christ foretold the destruction of the temple in Jerusalem, which came a few years later, and the signs that would accompany His return to earth for His church. Many of these things are coming to pass in our generation. Some of them have yet to come to pass. All of this is what the word of God's wisdom is—a revelation of the future.

The New Testament is filled with instances of the gift of the word of wisdom being manifested. In several epistles to the church, the apostle Paul revealed things that would come to pass in the last days. The apostle Peter was very emphatic about signs that would come to pass before the Lord Jesus returned. The word of wisdom functioned through these men just as it did through the Old Testament prophets.

An example of this gift functioning for the apostle Paul is related in Acts 23, when Paul almost lost his life at the hands of an angry Jewish mob. When it looked as if he would die, the Lord spoke to him by the word of wisdom and said: *"Be of good cheer, Paul: for as thou hast testified of me in Jerusalem, so must thou bear witness also at Rome"* (Acts 23:11). Paul had no way of knowing he would ever speak for God in Rome, but God revealed the future to him. That was the word of God's wisdom.

How Wisdom Is Manifested

The Holy Spirit can convey the word of wisdom in many ways.

To Joseph it was the *interpreting of a dream* of the future. When Joseph was 17 years old, God showed him his whole life—that he would be a great leader and even his own brothers would bow down before him. No one believed it, but it came to pass.

Daniel received wisdom by *a night vision*. It was the word of wisdom projected into the future.

Ezekiel was *caught away into the Spirit* for a revelation.

The apostle John was *caught up in the Spirit* on the Lord's day, and the entire book of Revelation flashed before him.

God has no set way of dealing with the problems of this world. He unveils hidden mysteries and the wisdom to execute His counsels in the way He considers best at that time.

Many times we think Jesus can do things only one way, but that is not true. The same is true with the word of wisdom. It does not have to function the same way each time. It can function as a dream or a vision. You could even be caught up into the third heaven as Paul was. God has many ways to do things. He can work with you in a unique way—a way He has not operated before. He can do whatever He wants to do.

Prophecy versus Word of Wisdom

A clear distinction must be formed in our minds regarding the simple inspirational gift of prophecy in the New Testament and the word of wisdom.

First Corinthians 14:3 gives the full measure of the blessings of prophecy. There is no element of revelation associated with it. *"He that prophesieth speaketh unto men to edification, and exhortation, and comfort."*

Any person who speaks out in church, foretelling the future, has left this simple gift of prophecy—the least of the gifts—and has moved into the greatest and foremost revelation gift—the word of wisdom—whereby he foresees the future. The prophet of either the Old Testament or the New Testament is a seer. He sees into the future and possesses the gift of the word of God's wisdom to tell the future.

The Word of Knowledge

The second gift in the category of revelation is the word of knowledge. We could add an extra word and call it a gift of the word of God's knowledge. Then there would be no mistaking it for man's knowledge.

The word *knowledge* is related to fact. If a thing is knowledge, then it is not mystery. The gift of the word of knowledge deals with what exists, whether it is in the past or in the present. In the gift of the word of knowledge God reveals to one of His servants something that now exists or did exist on the earth. This must be something that that servant could not know naturally—something his eyes have not seen and his ears have not heard. Normally it would have to do with the meeting of an emergency. God would not reveal such a thing if there were no real purpose for doing so.

Word of Knowledge in the Old Testament

Here are some examples of the gift of the word of knowledge operating in the Old Testament:

Elijah

In 1 Kings, chapter 19, Elijah is speaking. Beginning in verse 14, he said,

> And he said, I have been very jealous for the LORD God of hosts: because the children of Israel have forsaken thy covenant, thrown down thine altars, and slain thy prophets with the sword; and I, even I only, am left; and they seek my life, to take it away.

I would say that Elijah was a little discouraged. He thought he was the only one left. Have you ever thought you were the only one left? That's just how Elijah felt.

> And the LORD said unto him, Go, return on thy way to the wilderness of Damascus: and when thou comest, anoint Hazael to be king over Syria: and Jehu the son of Nimshi shalt thou anoint to be king over Israel: and Elisha the son of Shaphat of Abelmeholah shalt thou anoint to be prophet in thy room. And it shall come to pass, that him that escapeth the sword of Hazael shall Jehu slay: and him that escapeth from the sword of Jehu shall Elisha slay. (v. 15–17)

Now notice verse 18:

> Yet I have left me seven thousand in Israel, all the knees which have not bowed unto Baal, and every mouth which hath not kissed him.

So here we find a prophet named Elijah, who of his own knowledge said, "You know, there is not another good man living except me." This is a strong statement to make, especially when you are talking to God. Elijah said, "All the preachers are gone. I'm the only preacher left."

But then God revealed to Elijah a word of knowledge. God said to him, "You said there wasn't one except you. I'm now revealing to you that there are 7,000 more, and not one of them has bowed his knee to Baal, not one of them has reached over and kissed this idol. Every one of them is free from idol worship. Why don't you just do what I tell you to do? Get busy. Go and anoint Jehu as king and Elisha as prophet."

There have been times when I have spent so much time answering letters and dealing with problems that I began to feel as if I were part of the problem. So I just stood up, walked out of my office, got in my car, drove to the hospital, and began to pray for people. I stepped out from behind my desk and got out there where the needs were. Instantly, something was revived inside me. I felt brand new!

Elijah had been out of connection. He had been out on his own and did not realize that God had an army. God revealed through a word of His knowledge that at that moment there were 7,000 men in Israel who had not bowed their knees to Baal. They had stood up straight, refusing to have any part in idol worship. They were God's wonderful servants for that hour, and He knew their names, their addresses, and their abilities.

Elijah knew nothing about it, so God had to reveal it to him supernaturally. That is what is meant by a word of God's knowledge. God reveals something that you do not know naturally.

Elisha

A very remarkable incident is found in 2 Kings 5:20–27. It is the story of Elisha and Gehazi. Elisha had succeeded the prophet Elijah who had gone on to heaven.

Naaman, a very wealthy Syrian general, had come to Elisha and received a remarkable healing from leprosy. After being healed, Naaman turned to the prophet and said, "I want to give you a gift."

But Elisha said, "I don't want any gifts. You are healed. Just thank God for it and go on home." Naaman had already promised to quit worshipping idols.

Gehazi, Elisha's servant, decided to take the offering that Elisha turned down, so he ran after Naaman's chariot. When

Naaman stopped, Gehazi said to him, "Since you were there, two men have come from a great distance, and they need some money and some clothes." So Naaman gave him what he asked for. When Gehazi took the offering, he had no intention of telling the prophet.

When Gehazi returned home, Elisha spoke to him and said, "Did my spirit not go right along with you? Did I not see the whole thing that happened?" The gift of the word of God's knowledge was operating through Elisha. He watched in the spirit realm as Gehazi took the money from Naaman.

This man Elisha had a most remarkable manifestation of this gift. The word of knowledge functioned more times through him than anyone else in the Old Testament.

In 2 Kings, chapter 6, when the alien armies of Syria were coming against his country, Elisha sent word to his king and said, "They are at the southeast corner tonight, and they are hiding. Just go get them." So the king went out and won the battle.

A few days later, Elisha said, "They have come back again. They are on that northwest corner in hiding. They are behind those certain bushes and trees. Go get them."

Finally the Syrian king said, "Somebody among us is a spy and is telling the king of Israel where our army is."

They said, "No, no, King, there is no spy among us. We are all true. They've got a prophet among them named Elisha, and he knows everything. He knows where we are and what we are doing."

Again, we see the functioning of the word of God's knowledge. God made Elisha know where those armies were, so that he could communicate it to his king.

Samuel

In 1 Samuel, chapter 10, we find a very interesting example. The prophet Samuel wanted Saul to become king of the country of Israel. The people of Israel were going to have a great celebration and inauguration of Saul as king over their country; but

Saul was reticent. He did not want to be part of it. Though Saul was a big man, standing head and shoulders above anyone else in the land, he hid himself in a haystack on the day of the inauguration.

Nobody could find him until the prophet Samuel arrived. Samuel prayed to the Lord, and the Lord gave him the answer. Samuel received a word of God's knowledge. He knew what his eyes had not seen and his ears had not heard. Through the Holy Spirit, God told Samuel exactly where Saul was. Samuel said, *"Behold, he hath hid himself among the stuff"* (v. 22). The people then found Saul and made him king.

This gift was manifested in other instances as well. One time when Saul had lost some donkeys, Samuel said, "I can tell you where they are." And he did.

In the Old Testament we have some very vivid operations of the omniscience of God, how He revealed certain things through a word of His knowledge and showed the people how they could supernaturally understand the knowledge He had.

Other Old Testament examples can be found. In 2 Kings 6:12 the king's servant said of Elisha, *"The prophet that is in Israel, telleth the king of Israel the words that thou speakest in thy bedchamber."*

I suggest that you research and study these Old Testament stories until you become familiar with them. Then find other examples where God revealed His knowledge supernaturally to the people.

Word of Knowledge in the New Testament

In the New Testament our Lord Jesus exercised this gift, and He exercised it with divine authority.

In John's gospel, chapter 4, we see the story of Jesus and the woman at the well. Jesus came to a well in Sychar, a town north of Jerusalem. As He was sitting there by the well at about the sixth hour (about noon), a woman came to draw water. This was most unusual because that was not the normal time people drew water. At noon the sun is hot and the jug heavy, so they usually drew water early in the morning or in the evening.

At noon Jesus was seated by the well, no doubt thirsty, when the woman walked up. He said to her, "Would you give me a drink of water, please?" It was a deep well, and He needed her to use her rope to lower her jar into the water.

She looked at Him and said, "You are a Jew; I'm a Samaritan. We don't have any fellowship. What do you mean asking me for water? We don't get along at all."

Then Jesus rebuffed her by saying, "If you would have asked of Me, I would have given you living water and you would never have thirsted again."

Immediately she said, "Do you mean you are greater than our father Jacob who dug this well and that you have water that would keep me from ever being thirsty again? Give me some of this water."

Then Jesus said, "Call your husband."

"I'm not married."

He said, "You told the truth then. You've had five husbands already, and the fellow you are living with now isn't your husband."

She got so excited that she left her jug and went running back into the city. She said to the men, "Come and see a man who told me everything I have done!"

Here we have the functioning of the word of God's knowledge. Jesus knew fact after fact after fact. When He revealed these facts to that Samaritan woman, she was startled. When she came back and told the people, the whole city received a surge of God.

I have found that if you will permit the gifts of the Spirit to function, you will have a movement of souls that will come to you like never before. When the gifts function, souls are saved every time. Just let the gifts of the Spirit begin to function and people will pour into the kingdom of God!

Peter and Cornelius

In the Acts of the Apostles, chapter 10, we see the story of Peter and a vision he received while at Joppa. After he saw the vision and was thinking about it, the Spirit of God spoke to him and said, *"Behold, three men seek thee"* (v. 19).

Those men were sent by a man named Cornelius who was at Caesarea. Caesarea is a town located on the coast a number of miles north of Joppa. Peter was in Joppa, and Cornelius was in Caesarea. The Bible says that as Cornelius was praying, the Lord spoke to him and said, "In Joppa, at the house of Simon the tanner, is a fellow named Peter. Tell him to come up here, and he'll give you the words of truth."

That was a word of God's knowledge. God supernaturally gave Cornelius knowledge of Peter's whereabouts. So Cornelius sent three men south to Joppa to find Peter. When these three messengers came to inquire at the house of Simon the tanner, we find that God had already spoken to Peter and given him the word of knowledge, saying, "Standing down at the gate are three men, and I want you to go with them." Peter knew supernaturally by a word of God's knowledge that these men were at the gate.

So here we see from the New Testament how a word of God's knowledge functioned through His people. Peter and Cornelius knew facts they could never have known otherwise. Because of it in this instance, the whole Gentile world was opened to the Gospel of Jesus Christ. These were the first Gentiles to move in the word of knowledge from God.

Word of Knowledge in Operation

A few years ago while I was conducting a revival meeting in Tulsa, Oklahoma, a lady invited me to dinner. After dinner, she had me sit in a rocking chair; then she looked at me and said, "Brother Sumrall, some of the people at our church think I'm a witch." She then related the following story to me:

One morning as she was sitting in that rocking chair, reading her Bible, the thought came to her that her son, daughter-in-law, and grandchildren were going fishing. She saw them hitch the boat trailer to their car, drive to a lake about fifty miles outside of Tulsa, and park under a tree at the end of the lake. She saw them back up the car, put the trailer into the water, release the boat, put all their fishing gear into the boat, and push away from shore. Then she saw her son reach over to one of the children and cause the boat to capsize. Immediately, she knew that all five of them had drowned.

Nothing like that had ever happened to her before. She grabbed the phone and dialed her son's number, but there was no answer. Then she called the fire department and told them the story. At first they thought she was crazy, but because of her persistence, they agreed to check out her story. They went to the lake and found the place she described. A car was parked there with a boat trailer in the water, and away from shore a boat was floating upside down. After dragging that area of the lake, the firemen recovered the five bodies.

She said, "Brother Sumrall, am I a witch?"

I said, "No, you had one of the gifts of the Spirit functioning in you. God showed you through the word of knowledge exactly where they were and what had happened. Otherwise, they might have been there for a long time before anybody found them."

You may ask, "Why didn't God stop it?" I cannot say. I have no idea if they were saved and if they had any relationship with God at all. I only know that as a godly, Spirit-filled mother was reading her Bible, God opened her spirit and gave her the gift of the word of knowledge.

The Discerning of Spirits

The third gift of revelation is the discerning of spirits.

What It Is Not

The discerning of spirits has no relationship to that which is natural. It is not some kind of metaphysical operation. It is not thought reading. It is not psychoanalysis or projection of extra-sensory perception. It has nothing to do with the realm of the mind. Some people claim to have "the gift of discernment," but there is no such gift. It is not a discernment of things; it is the discernment of spirits.

There are three areas in which this gift can operate: the divine, the demonic, and the human or natural. I must emphatically state that this gift is not primarily a discerning of devils, though some people hold that view. It is divinely comprehending and understanding a human spirit—the kind of spirit a person possesses.

This gift is not a clash of human personalities. Sometimes when a wife has had a fight with her husband, she may think he is possessed by the devil.

The discerning of spirits certainly is not the gift of suspicion—suspecting a person of being a certain way when he is not that way at all.

What It Is and What It Does

The discerning of spirits is the divine ability to see the presence and activity of a spirit that motivates a human being, whether good or bad. This revelation comes to the church through the functioning of the Holy Spirit.

The discerning of spirits gives members of the body of Christ insight into the spirit world, a realm that their five physical senses—feeling, hearing, seeing, smelling, tasting—cannot enter. The telescope can reveal the amazing stars in space. The microscope can bring to light the intricate mysteries of microscopic life. But it takes the gift of discerning of spirits to penetrate to the dividing of soul and spirit within a person.

This discerning of spirits can bring tremendous inspiration to a church body. It can produce a real spirit of security against false doctrines, lies, and all kinds of things that are unreal. It can enable a church to choose the proper men and women to fulfill their ministries within the church.

Bible Examples of Discerning of Spirits

Let's look into the Word of God and see some of the remarkable instances of discerning of spirits.

Simon, the Soothsayer

In Acts, chapter 8, a man named Simon looked on with wonder as Peter and John laid their hands on people to receive the gift of the Holy Spirit.

This man, who was a soothsayer, thought in his heart: "If only I had such power. It would make me a big man among the people. Every man has a price; I'll persuade these men to sell this power to me." So he went to the apostles and said, "I'd like to give you money for that power" (Acts 8:18–19).

Peter looked at him and said:

> *Thy money perish with thee, because thou hast thought that the gift of God may be purchased with money. Thou hast neither part nor lot in this matter: for thy heart is not right in the sight of God. Repent therefore of this thy wickedness, and pray God, if perhaps the thought of thine heart may be forgiven thee. For I perceive that thou art in the gall of bitterness, and in the bond of iniquity.* (vv. 20–23)

Here was a man in the church fellowship who, when he saw this supernatural manifestation, said: "I'm going to grab that. I'm going to buy it and use it and make money with it."

Until it was revealed by the Holy Spirit, the others did not understand. But Peter was seeing something that could not be seen with the physical eye and he said, "You are in the gall of bitterness, the bond of iniquity." We cannot make merchandise out of the works of God.

Dozens of times people have come to me for prayer and tried to leave money. I say to them: "If you want to give money, go to church and give it. Don't give it to me when I have prayed a prayer of faith for your deliverance. You can't pay for the blessings of God."

Elymas, the Sorcerer

In Acts 13:6–12 we find Paul discerning the evil tendencies of Elymas, the sorcerer:

The Gifts and Ministries of the Holy Spirit

Then Saul, (who also is called Paul,) filled with the Holy Ghost, set his eyes on him, and said, O full of all subtlety and all mischief, thou child of the devil, thou enemy of all righteousness, wilt thou not cease to pervert the right ways of the Lord? (vv. 9–10)

Elymas may have looked as normal and natural as anybody, but Paul by the discerning of spirits looked straight through him and told his whole life story.

Ananias and Sapphira

In the Acts of the Apostles, chapter 5, we read about a certain couple in the church, Ananias and Sapphira. In their church fellowship there was a man who become very popular. The apostles named him Barnabas, which means "the son of consolation." He got that name by selling all his property and giving the money to the church.

Ananias and Sapphira decided they, too, wanted to be popular in the church, so they sold their property. But when they hold that big bag of money, they thought, "This is too much to give the church. Let's keep back part of it. No one will ever know." (But the Bible says in Numbers 32:23, *"Be sure your sin will find you out."*)

Ananias wanted to take the money down to the church right then, so he got his bag of money and went running down to the church. The people said, "Here comes Ananias. Look at the big bag of money he has. He sold his property and is going to give it all to the church!"

When Ananias stood before Peter with his bag of gold, he said, "Peter, you know how Barnabas sold his property there in Cyprus and became such a wonderful person in the church? We sold our property, too, so we're going to give all of our money to the church!"

Peter looked at him and said, "All of it?"

"Oh, yes, all of it."

Peter was a good ballplayer; he wanted to give Ananias three strikes before calling him out. He said, "Now, Ananias, you are speaking before the body and you are speaking before God. Is this all of it?"

"All of it." Strike one!

"Ananias, that is a large bag of money. It must have been beautiful property. Is all of it in there?"

"It's all in there." Strike two!

"Ananias, did God tell you to sell your property and give the money to the church?"

"Yes, God told me to. All of the money is in the bag." Strike three—you're out! Ananias dropped dead right there in church! Some young men in the church took up his body and buried it.

About three hours later Sapphira walked in, expecting to get a lot of praise that day. After all, they had given a bag of gold to the church! When she saw Peter, she said, "Oh, Peter, aren't you proud of us? We sold our property and gave all the money to the church."

"All?"

"Yes, sir. Hasn't Ananias told you about it?"

He said, "Sapphira, do you know how much you sold it for?"

"Yes. It was all in that bag."

"Sapphira, I'm going to ask you one more time: When your husband left the house to come down here to the church, was all the money in that bag?"

"Oh, yes!" She fell down dead!

When Peter saw Ananias, the gift of discerning of spirits came into manifestation. Peter knew immediately that Ananias was lying to God, and Ananias paid the price for it!

Discerning of Spirits at Work Today

A number of years ago, I was present in a small Wednesday-night prayer meeting. A beautiful young woman, a stranger, came into the auditorium and sat toward the back. When there was a pause in the meeting, she stood up and said, "I'm an evangelist, and God has told me to conduct a special revival campaign in this church. No one is to resist me because I am God's servant and the revival must begin tonight. The Lord has sent me here to bless you and to preach to you."

Her words brought a strange coldness over the meeting. There was a moment of quietness. To one side of the auditorium sat a little lady with head bowed. Suddenly, she stood to her feet and, with her face raised to heaven, said, "You are a harlot from St. Louis, Missouri. (The woman had said she was from another city.) You are in this town living with a man to whom you are not married. You have boasted to him that you could come to this church, deceive these people, preach to them, and collect an offering without their knowing you are a harlot. If you do not repent, you will die before you leave this building."

God's power fell heavily on the church and all of us fell to our knees in prayer. When we lifted our heads, the woman was gone. The discerning of spirits had revealed the truth and she fled from it.

My Experience in Java

In Java as I was walking down the church aisle, a woman caught me by my sleeve. When I turned to see what she wanted, she said, "You have a black angel in you, and I have a white angel in me."

As I turned around, God spoke through my lips and said, "I have a white angel in me, not black; but you do have a black angel in you; and I command you now to come out of her!"

The woman was set free at that moment. Her eyes, which had been glassy, were instantly made clear. Her face changed its appearance. She had been under the power of that demonic spirit for fifteen years!

Through the discerning of spirits, I immediately knew that there was a foul spirit within her, a spirit of evil. That was knowledge I would not have received any other way. She looked as normal as the other people in that congregation. Had you asked me to walk among them and pick out such a person, I would not have been able to do it. God had to reveal it to me. When the spirit within her moved, I was able to identify it and cast it out in Jesus' name through the gift of the Spirit that oper-ated in me.

A Gift to Cleanse the Churches

The gift of discerning of spirits is an excellent instrument to clean out the pulpits and pews of America. Many pastors and church leaders today are engaged in activities that are not right and honest and true. Church members as well are living in sin, doing things totally opposed to the will of God for their lives. Through the discerning of spirits, we can have a holy church without spot or wrinkle. (See Ephesians 5:27.)

But are we willing for this gift of the Spirit to function? That is the place we must reach, where we are ready and willing for the gifts of the Spirit to function in their fullness among us.

The discerning of spirits is a gift that enables one to appraise motives. But more than this, it gives the believer power to see what others do not see. As Howard Carter has stated, "The discerning of spirits is a gift of the Holy Spirit by which the possessor is enabled to see into the spirit world. By this insight he can discern the similitude of God, the risen Christ, the Holy Spirit, cherubim and seraphim, the archangels and the host of angels, or Satan and his legions."

8
The Power Gifts

The second category of spiritual gifts is actually an artillery of gifts known as the gifts of power: the gift of faith, the gifts of healing, and the working of miracles. These gifts are second in appreciation and second in greatness, the revelation gifts being the greatest God can give.

The Gift of Faith

We must recognize, first of all, that there are many kinds of faith. Sometimes the gift of faith is mistaken for the simple faith it takes for salvation. But the two are not the same.

Everyone has faith, the Bible says so: *"God hath dealt to every man the measure of faith"* (Rom. 12:3). This type of universal faith has no relation to the supernatural sign gift of the Holy Spirit we are studying about here. There is a difference between the measure of faith, which the Bible says is given to every believer, and the gift of faith.

Natural Faith

There is a natural faith that human beings have—the kind of faith a farmer has when he sows seed. He plants a seed of corn, believing that it will die, burst open, come up out of the ground as a simple little blade, and grow into a healthy stalk that will produce more corn. The farmer has faith for that; otherwise, rather than planting the corn seed, he would eat it. That is an example of natural faith.

A fisherman has this same kind of natural faith. He believes that if he goes out on a lake and casts his net in the right spot at the right time in the right way, he will catch fish. And he is generally successful in his belief.

Saving Faith

In the spiritual realm there is a kind of faith we call "saving faith." A person hears the Gospel of Jesus Christ, believes it, accepts Jesus into his heart, and is saved. That is saving faith.

Every redeemed person in the world has this saving faith, but not every person has the gift of faith. The thief on the cross next to Jesus had saving faith. (See Luke 23:42–43.) He just believed on Jesus and received his salvation as he hung there on that cross. He had no time to receive the gift of faith from the Spirit.

The Philippian jailer had saving faith. He fell at the feet of Paul and Silas and asked, *"Sirs, what must I do to be saved? And they said, Believe on the Lord Jesus Christ, and thou shalt be saved"* (Acts 16:30–31). He believed and was converted.

We need this kind of faith to become converted and we need it to receive healing. We say, "Lord, I bring my disease to You. I believe that by Your stripes I am healed. I accept it, thank You for it, and confess that I've got it now."

The Gift of Faith Is Special

The gift of faith is different from other types of faith. It is a special faith that supernaturally achieves what is impossible through human instruments. We observe the gift of faith in operation when God, through the power of the Holy Spirit, performs supernatural exploits that cannot be humanly explained. These exploits cannot be what is done ordinarily; otherwise, they would have no relation to the supernatural gifts of the Holy Spirit.

This kind of miracle has to be something that a human being could not do normally. There is no human strength involved in it. This fact must be clearly understood: The gift of faith has to do with the functioning of God in you and through you, but with no human strength involved on your part. You do nothing. In this gift, God does something supernaturally on your behalf.

The gift of faith can operate in areas of divine protection and divine provision. But in whatever area it works, it works independent of you. You do nothing about it; God does it all for you. It is the power of faith functioning gloriously and amazingly on your behalf, just as it functioned through Jesus. He spoke mighty words to the tempest, and immediately it was calmed. That was faith functioning through Him. He did nothing but speak words of faith, and it was done.

Most Christians probably do not believe they drink from the same fountain Jesus drank from, but they do. We have the same kind of power flowing through us that flowed through Jesus.

This truth came dramatically to me. I was not taught as a boy that we could be anything like Jesus. I thought men like Moses and the apostle Paul had a special inroad with God that I would never be able to experience. It was exciting when I discovered that I was a participant in the same strength, the same power, the same vitality, the same wisdom, and the same knowledge that Jesus had.

Unlimited Faith

The gift of faith has been manifested by many of God's servants. It is evidenced when a supernatural event occurs with no human effort.

Faith permits God to perform on your behalf. This gift of faith is unlimited for the simple reason that God, not man, is the door. God is the source of its energy. If this were not the case, then the gift of faith would have to be limited, as are some of the other spiritual gifts. (The gifts of healing are limited, as we will discover later.)

The gift of faith deals with *"more than conquerors"* (Rom. 8:37). A conqueror is a person who meets another person of equal strength and knocks him out. A person who is more than a conqueror just stands and says, "Fall," and down goes that other person!

The gift of faith functions in all those who are more than conquerors. God does something while your hands are closed. That means you are more than a conqueror. He does the fighting; you do the rejoicing! In the gift of faith, God does all the work. I do not mean to imply that you are lazy. You simply have the anointing and the power of God within you. You speak it, and God does it.

If you say, "It can't be done," you are right—it can't, in your life. You cannot function in God without faith. That is why you should read the Bible every day. *"Faith cometh by hearing, and hearing by the word of God"* (Rom. 10:17).

The Gift of Faith Illustrated

The gift of faith functions on behalf of the believer to bring about what otherwise would not be possible through that person's efforts.

Let's illustrate this gift of faith with some examples from the Word of God.

Moses

Moses, according to the Word of God, took his staff and dropped it at the feet of the greatest king of his day, Pharaoh of Egypt. Pharaoh was the strongest monarch upon the face of the earth at that time. His was the kingdom of strength on earth.

When Moses laid down his shepherd's staff, it suddenly changed into a king cobra. So Pharaoh called in his magicians. When they threw down their staffs, they, too, became serpents— but Moses' serpent devoured theirs! When Moses reached down and took up the cobra, it became a staff again. (See Exodus 7:10–13.)

Here was a functioning of sovereign power on Moses' behalf. Moses had nothing to do with what happened. He was just an observer of what God did, and it was a miracle, very convincing to the monarch. Pharaoh finally let the children of Israel leave the land of Egypt because of the mighty miraculous signs that Moses called into being. Moses called the miracles into being and God performed them. The great power of God was demonstrated without Moses even lifting a finger; he just folded his hands.

Elijah

This gift of faith is beautifully shown to us in the life of Elijah, God's prophet. In 1 Kings, chapter 17, Elijah was hidden away in the wilderness with nothing to eat (and there were no bakeries or shops close by!). The Lord caused the ravens to bring meat and bread to Elijah. It was a miracle that the ravens did not eat the food before it reached Elijah, because that is their natural way of doing things. But God is able to take what ordinarily happens and change it to suit His purposes.

Elijah did nothing to get his meals. There was no labor on his part, none whatsoever. He just said, "Lord, I thank You for supplying my needs."

Here we find that, not only did God supply Elijah his bread and meat there, but also when the brook dried up, God told Elijah, *"Arise, get thee to Zarephath…behold, I have commanded a widow woman there to sustain thee"* (1 Kings 17:9). When Elijah reached Zarephath, he found that the widow also was about to die.

He asked her for some bread and water, and she told him, *"I have not a cake, but an handful of meal in a barrel, and a little oil in a cruse: and, behold, I am gathering two sticks, that I may go in and dress it for me and my son, that we may eat it, and die"* (v. 12).

In response, Elijah spoke words of faith and comfort to her. He said, *"Fear not; go and do as thou hast said: but make me thereof a little cake first, and bring it unto me, and after make for thee and for thy son"* (v. 13).

Elijah told her to make him a little cake first. You know, when we pay our tithes to God first, we are going to get first treatment from Him. God will treat us that way, and I want first-class treatment from God, don't you?

So the woman prepared the cake and gave it to Elijah first, and through the command of this prophet of God, *"she, and he, and her house, did eat many days. And the barrel of meal wasted not, neither did the cruse of oil fail, according to the word of the LORD, which he spake by Elijah"* (vv. 15–16). The woman was supernaturally fed through three years of famine because of the word spoken by God's man, Elijah. That was a gift of faith to Elijah.

Elisha

Another example of the gift of faith in operation is in 2 Kings, chapter 6. Elisha had his Bible school boys out cutting down some trees. When one of the students hit a tree with an ax, the ax head flew off and fell into the Jordan River, *"and he cried, and said, Alas, master! for it was borrowed. And the man of God said, Where fell it? And he showed him the place. And he cut down a stick, and cast it in thither; and the iron did swim"* (vv. 5–6).

The man of God, Elisha, acted in the gift of faith, illustrating the power of that gift.

Seven of the nine gifts of the Spirit functioned in the Old Testament. (The only two of the nine gifts that began with the New Testament are tongues and the interpretation of tongues.) These seven gifts in the Old Testament did not function in the same way as in the New Testament. They came upon men only at special times in special situations.

Elisha was one of the most remarkable of these men. Read 2 Kings, chapters 2–13, and notice how many times Elisha demonstrated the word of knowledge. He functioned in the word of knowledge more than anyone of his day. Read beginning with the time Elijah called him into service until his death and see how many times he supernaturally understood things from a distance. It is a very enlightening study.

Daniel

Daniel was a remarkable man of faith. Having been brought from his homeland of Israel into Babylon, he was a refugee; but more than that, Daniel was a prisoner of war. He was such a handsome, clever fellow that he was put into training with the other young men. He was so clever, in fact, that he soon rose to the top and, with some of his friends, was actually ruling Babylon.

The Babylonians became jealous of Daniel because of his remarkable wisdom, which was actually coming from God. He had a Source of information, a Source of blessing, that the Babylonians knew nothing about.

Out of jealousy, these men spied on Daniel to find something for which they could accuse him before the king. When they found him praying three times a day to Jehovah, they managed to trick the king into passing a law, proclaiming that prayer could be offered to no one except the king of Babylon. They made their king into a god, not because they loved him, but because they hated Daniel. The penalty for anyone disobeying this law was to be thrown into a special den of lions.

Daniel knew about the law, but his faith was so strong that he would not stop praying to his God. He prayed with his windows wide open for all to hear and see. Eventually he was arrested and brought before the king. When the king realized what had happened, he was very sorry about the situation, but had no choice except to condemn Daniel and command that he be cast into the den of lions.

The king must have had faith in Daniel's faith, though, because he told him, *"Thy God whom thou servest continually, he will deliver thee"* (Dan. 6:16). And the next morning he hurried to check on Daniel. He must have had faith or he would not have done that. He simply would have sent out servants to pick up Daniel's bones. When he reached the den, he found Daniel safe and sound, ready to go back to work. How did that happen? By the power of faith!

When Daniel was placed in the den of lions, he was immediately the master of the situation. He did not hurt the beasts; he did not ask God for power to tear them to pieces. He simply radiated a force that caused the lions to lie down in perfect peace as he slept among them. Daniel personally did nothing; it was

God who performed the amazing miracle. The gift of faith was in action!

Daniel told the king, *"My God hath sent his angel, and hath shut the lions' mouths, that they have not hurt me"* (v. 22).

The Three Hebrew Children

As we see in Daniel's case, the gift of faith is the opposite of fear. There is no sense of fear or apprehension or uncertainty involved in faith. If there is, then it is not faith. Faith only functions in serenity, confidence, and peace.

One of the choicest illustrations of this faith action, I believe, is that of the three Hebrew children in the book of Daniel, chapter 3. These three young men—Shadrach, Meshach, and Abednego—refused to bow down and worship the golden image of Nebuchadnezzar, the king of Babylon. When Nebuchadnezzar heard of this, he commanded that they be placed in a fiery furnace that had been heated seven times hotter than usual. (See Daniel 3:19–20.)

When they were cast into the furnace, Shadrach, Meshach, and Abednego made no effort to fight the flames. They did not resist, nor did they complain.

When the king looked in, he said in shock, *"Did not we cast three men bound into the midst of the fire?"* (v. 24).

His men answered, "Yes."

"He answered and said, Lo, I see four men loose, walking in the midst of the fire, and they have no hurt; and the form of the fourth is like the Son of God" (v. 25).

And it was! Jesus was walking among them. When those three Hebrew children walked out of that furnace, not a hair of their heads was singed and not even the smell of fire was about them! (See verse 27.)

Here we find in operation the dynamic gift of faith. These men, thrown into a furnace, had no way to exercise their own strength or power. Yet they walked out of that furnace without having resisted or fought it in any way. That is faith! It was the gift of faith, a supernatural faith, an instance in which supernatural things take place because people believe.

The Gifts and Ministries of the Holy Spirit

If those men had not believed, they would have died in that fire. If they had been fearful, they would have died. But they stepped into the furnace with courage and with honor, and they came marching out unscathed! They had an element with them called faith and it functioned in their total being. That is the gift of faith.

The Gift of Faith in My Life

I entered into the ministry with a kind of faith that perhaps many young men of my time did not possess. The day I walked out the front door of my father's house to become a preacher, I had just a few coins in my pocket, but I was not concerned. I knew only one thing: I was called by God to preach the Gospel of the Lord Jesus Christ.

Many people would never enter into fulltime ministry with no resources at all; but to me it seemed the only thing to do, and I had no problem doing it. I had no negative thought about it; I just did it.

Three years later, I was in San Francisco, ready to set out around the world as a missionary. For three nights before boarding the ship, I preached in a very large church for which I received no offering. I had to look to God as my Source.

When the pastor of that church took me to the boat, he proceeded to tell me how I would starve to death in China. In response, I said that if I did, I wanted him to send a little tombstone to China that read, "Here lies Lester Sumrall, who starved to death trusting Jesus."

He said, "I won't do it!"

I said, "I won't need it!"

Those were my last words on mainland America. I boarded ship and sailed away, headed for Australia and New Zealand to start preaching around the world.

Throughout my journey, God provided for me locally. I had no contacts in America, no churches contributing to my support. God supernaturally provided for my every need. I lived in a constant state of having to believe God for my next day's transportation.

Sometimes when traveling long distances, such as across Siberia and Russia, we had to pay in advance. I always had the necessary money at the proper time.

For our trip to Tibet, which took three months on muleback, we had to hire a cook, an interpreter, and 17 pack animals. A few nights before we were to leave, I had no funds to pay for the trip. The Lord provided the whole amount through one Chinese woman, a general's wife, to whom I had ministered healing from our Lord Jesus.

In the function and operation of faith, you do not scream and cry, "What am I going to do?" You must rely on God to meet your need. We just rejoiced in the Lord, and it came to pass!

The Gift of Faith in Smith Wigglesworth

I was very well acquainted with Smith Wigglesworth, having visited in his home many times before he passed away. He was certainly a dynamic man of faith.

Smith Wigglesworth and his wife met and were married in the Salvation Army. Though a plumber by trade, he worked with his wife in a local mission. He was slow of speech, so he handed out songbooks and took up the offering, while his wife did the preaching.

But there was something big inside Smith Wigglesworth. When he prayed for people, things happened. He demonstrated some amazing feats of faith in his life.

One day, when he came home from work, he was met at the door with news that his wife had died—that she had been dead for two hours.

To that, Wigglesworth replied, "No, she's not dead." He dropped his lunch bucket and tools, walked into the bedroom, pulled her out of bed, stood her against the wall, called her by her first name, and said, "I command you to come to me now!" Then he backed off, and here she came! She lived a number of years after that.

Faith was a primary strength in the life and ministry of Smith Wigglesworth. He knew what it was to have the gift of faith.

The Gifts and Ministries of the Holy Spirit

The Gift of Faith in Howard Carter

Many beautiful operations of this special gift of faith occurred in the life of Howard Carter.

At one time, Rev. Carter made arrangements to purchase by faith a church for a local congregation in London, England. He was given sixty days to pay the note. At the time he was president of Hampstead Bible School. As the days and weeks went by and no money came in, the faculty and students became very concerned. They were so nervous in fact that the last day or two they found it difficult to eat—everyone, that is, except Rev. Carter. His appetite was as good as usual.

The night before the day of foreclosure on the property, there still were no funds; but Rev. Carter was a man of faith. He said very simply, "God has assured me that I will have the full payment on schedule. I don't have the money now, but I don't need it until tomorrow."

The last mail delivery in London is 9:00 P.M. As Rev. Carter picked up the mail from the box, there was a large brown envelope. As he himself told me, "I picked up the envelope and laid it on the mantle with the other mail. I was going to leave it there until the next morning. Usually when I get a large brown package like that, it is a load of clippings that someone has sent for me to read."

But the Lord spoke to his heart and said, "Open it tonight."

He argued for a while, but finally surrendered to that urging within his spirit. When he tore open the package, he found a bundle of new pound notes from the bank—exactly the amount he needed to purchase the church.

There was no name or return address on the envelope. The gift was anonymous. God oftentimes provides for His servants that way.

Anyone else would have jumped up and down, shouted with excitement, and run upstairs to tell everybody what had happened. Not Rev. Carter. He very calmly placed the envelope on the shelf where it had been and went to bed.

The next morning at breakfast, he told the students and faculty about their blessing. Then he passed around the brown envelope for all to see. While everybody went wild with joy and excitement, Rev. Carter hardly wrinkled his face. He said, "I knew it two months ago and I was sure of it two months ago. I told the Lord I wasn't nervous about when He would send it. I didn't need it until 11 A.M. that certain day, so any time before that would be fine."

Another great demonstration of the gift of faith occurred when Rev. Carter was in prison during World War I, serving time as a conscientious objector. He was placed in a cell so narrow that he could not move around. The concrete roof above him leaked, and the dripping of water on his head was extremely aggravating.

Finally, one night he said, "Lord, stop that leak."

The Lord answered, "No, I won't stop it. You stop it."

"But, Lord, how can I stop it?"

"Speak to it."

That is when Howard Carter discovered his power with God. Lying on a cot in a prison cell, iron bars on each side, a concrete roof above him, water peppering down on his head, Rev. Carter spoke to the water. He commanded it to flow the other way. At that moment, the leak stopped and not another drop of water came through during the war! It was a dynamic act of the gift of faith.

Howard Carter was a man of solid truth. I lived with him for many years and never knew him to exaggerate. Whatever he told was absolute truth.

The Gifts of Healing

The gifts of healing may possibly be the most controversial of the nine gifts of the Spirit. It is the only gift of the nine that is in the plural form, the only gift that has to do with more than one aspect, which would lead to the question: How many gifts of healing are there?

It has been suggested that there are possibly as many categories of disease in the world as there were stripes placed upon Jesus' back. He received thirty-nine stripes and, according to Isaiah 53:5, *"With his stripes we are healed."*

The Gifts and Ministries of the Holy Spirit

Jesus was very careful to differentiate between the various kinds of sicknesses and diseases He came up against. For example, in Matthew 17 He dealt with a little boy who would throw himself into the fire and into the water. Of this, He said, *"Howbeit this kind goeth not out but by prayer and fasting"* (v. 21). The Lord was showing that special attention had to be given to someone who is being relieved of satanic oppressions—that there had to be special preparation—a cleansing of the one who was to deliver the healing.

A Limited Gift

Why is "the gifts of healing" the only gift that is actually limited? Why cannot one minister have all nine gifts of the Spirit?

The Lord Jesus is the only person who possessed consistent, perfect gifts of healing in His ministry. He never failed to heal. The apostle Paul could not heal everyone. He even left behind a certain member of his own evangelistic party for the simple reason, the Bible says, that he was sick. (See 2 Timothy 4:20.) Even Simon Peter had to call upon Jesus to heal his mother-in-law. (See Matthew 8:14.)

There is a divine purpose for this: If all nine gifts of the Spirit functioned through one channel, that person would then be like God. If he healed all people that were sick whenever he wanted to, he would be accepted by the world as God. If one human being had the ability to heal every disease among men, he would be unable to withstand the praise, honor, and riches that would be lavished upon him. I have seen it happen in the last forty years, both in England and in America.

Here are some examples of healing ministries that have risen during the twentieth century:

Alexander Dowie

Probably no ministry in modern times had more amazing miracles of healing than that of Dr. John Alexander Dowie. With Chicago as his home base, Dowie developed a ministry in the power of God that brought him worldwide fame. In 1900, he purchased a 6,000-acre tract of land north of Chicago where he built the city of Zion. Within two years this new city had grown to a population of 10,000.

The public acclaim and adoration that Dowie received was more than he could withstand. As the result of "divine revelations," he began to see himself as "Elijah the prophet" and the "first apostle" of the church. His personal proclamations, plus financial irresponsibility, caused Dowie's followers to revolt against his tyrannical control.

Though he experienced tremendous miracles of healing during the years of his ministry, Alexander Dowie died a broken man in 1907.

Stephen Jeffreys

Another great healing minister was Stephen Jeffreys, a Welshman. Through Jeffreys' ministry, hundreds of people were healed of various ailments; but there was a particular anointing in his life for the healing of rheumatoid arthritis. Howard Carter said that in Brother Jeffreys' great crusades in England, some people in wheelchairs were so crippled with rheumatoid arthritis that their faces could not be seen.

One night during a crusade, Brother Jeffreys started laughing in the spirit. Then he jumped off the platform, went over to a man, and lifted him from the wheelchair. Within three minutes, that man was running up and down the aisles, pushing his wheelchair! Without a doubt, the gifts of healing operated in Jeffreys' ministry.

When the sick are healed, people want to lavish gifts upon the minister who was God's instrument in their healing. As a result, Stephen Jeffreys became a wealthy man. According to Howard Carter, Jeffreys stood on a platform in South Africa, where thousands of amazing miracles of healing had taken place, and spoke these words before a mass of people: "Ladies and gentlemen, the world is at my feet."

Not long after that, the man who had ministered healing to literally thousands of people became ill. In Jeffreys' weakest moment, when he was weary physically and boasting pridefully that the whole world was at his feet, Satan struck him down.

While in England, I decided to visit Stephen Jeffreys, so I went to his house in a little town in Wales. When his wife opened the door, I introduced myself and she invited me in. There in a wheelchair sat a twisted, knotted form, head pulled down and feet drawn up. It was Stephen Jeffreys. To see his face, I had to kneel down before him.

Having ministered healing and deliverance to thousands, Stephen Jeffreys died of rheumatoid arthritis. When he said the world was at his feet, he was sorely mistaken. The world is at Jesus' feet.

Fred Squire

Of course many stayed humble before God. While serving as song leader for Stephen Jeffreys, Fred Squire received an anointing to minister healing. He was especially blessed in ministering to the blind. There were over 400 people whose eyes were opened in his meetings. Whenever a blind person was in one of his meetings, Fred Squire was joyous, knowing beyond doubt that he would be healed. This is one of the gifts of healing.

Jack Coe

In the early 1950s Jack Coe, an evangelist with the Assemblies of God, conducted a remarkable ministry of divine healing. I attended one of his meetings in New York City where a tent, holding over ten thousand people, was packed to capacity. That night while seated on the platform with Coe, I witnessed tremendous demonstrations of the gifts of healing. At least a dozen people rose from their wheelchairs and cots.

No doubt Jack Coe's ministry was one of the most outstanding, but he began to exalt himself. No matter how glorious his ministry was, he tried to make himself more glorious in the eyes of the people, and his life was cut short. In late 1956 while preaching in Hot Springs, Arkansas, Coe became critically ill and was later diagnosed as suffering from polio. He died early in 1957. He told Gordon Lindsay that God was removing him from the ministry.

William Branham

Another minister of almost unbelievable miracles was William Branham. Wherever he conducted meetings in the world, phenomenal miracles took place. Not only did he possess the gifts of power, but the gifts of revelation functioned through him in a most remarkable way.

When people are gifted by the Holy Spirit in ministry, it is sometimes difficult for them to remain humble and unselfish before God. Eventually, Branham developed some doctrines that were removed from the truth. By the 1960s he was regarded as an extremely controversial teacher. In 1963 he received a "revelation" that he was one of the witnesses in Revelation, chapter 11.

In December, 1965, Branham was driving cross-country to Arizona when his car was struck head-on by a drunken driver. He lay in a coma for several days until his death on Christmas Eve. For several days thereafter, some of his followers believed he would rise from the dead. One group, who believed Branham to be God, born of a virgin, was even expecting his resurrection on Easter Sunday, 1966.

Smith Wigglesworth

Smith Wigglesworth was especially blessed with a ministry to people who suffered from seizures of various kinds. When people with epilepsy were brought to his meetings, Wigglesworth knew there would be a revival because they were nearly always healed.

A number of times when people had epileptic seizures during his meetings, Wigglesworth would stop his sermon, leave the platform, minister deliverance to them, return to the platform, and continue preaching. He had no doubt that when he touched them, they would be set free—and they were!

Ways to Be Healed

Now we come to the most important aspect of this subject: the ways a person can be healed. We must always remember that there are many ways to be healed.

The greatest way to be healed is to *pray for yourself.* More people are healed by praying for themselves than all the other ways combined.

The second way is to *have a family member pray for you.* Millions of healings have been the result of mothers and fathers praying for their children. If families would develop this truth, they would not stop with their own family, but would reach out in prayer to their entire neighborhood.

Another way is to *call for the minister and elders of your church.* This biblical way is set out in James 5:14–15: *"Is any sick among you? let him call for the elders of the church; and let them pray over him, anointing him with oil in the name of the Lord: and the prayer of faith shall save the sick, and the Lord shall raise him up; and if he have committed sins, they shall be forgiven him."* You are to call for the elders in the body—spiritual leaders among your fellowship who are full of faith and full of the Word. As they lay hands on you and anoint you with oil, you will be healed.

Then there is a sign gift ministry—*the gifts of healing*—which, as we have already discussed, is a remarkable way to be healed. Through this ministry the Lord endows His servants with special gifts to pray for specific diseases. A minister does not always have to seek a certain sign gift of healing. Many times it will be bestowed upon him in the line of ministry, and as his understanding increases, that ministry gift will also grow and increase.

The Working of Miracles

In the category of power gifts, there is the gift of the working of miracles. Regarding this gift, we must realize one thing: We are dealing with God, and it is a miracle only as far as man is concerned. Since God is omnipotent—having all power—He does not recognize a certain event as a miracle. What we consider to be a miracle is only an act of God; it is only the voice of God speaking, causing something to come to pass. What might be a very small thing in God's sight is a miracle to man because he is unable to perform it in his own natural strength.

A supernatural occurrence is called a miracle because it is beyond our natural comprehension. When we receive our glorified bodies, the acts we consider to be miracles at the present time will no longer be miracles; they will be perfectly normal.

The Lord Jesus Christ spoke to a fig tree and said, "Die." (See Mark 11:12–14.) The disciples were shocked to see it withered up just the next morning. (See verses 20–26.) To the Lord Jesus that was a very simple thing. To the disciples it was an enormous situation, an unbelievable thing, simply because it was outside their regular operating forces and strength.

The Greek words for "working of miracles" are *energema* and *dunamis*. From the word *energema* we derive our word "energy"; from the word *dunamis* we derive our word "dynamite." Dunamis is the same word translated "power" in Acts 1:8. Jesus said to His disciples, *"Ye shall receive power, after that the Holy Ghost is come upon you."* Thus, we can see that this gift of energy, or dynamite, is God's doing something of an explosive nature.

The gift of the working of miracles means a supernatural intervention by God in the ordinary course of nature. It is God working through a person, an animal, or some other instrument, to do something that could not be done normally.

In the first power gift—the gift of faith—God is working in our behalf, but independent of us. We do nothing. In the gift of faith God does something sovereignly, dramatically, and gloriously, while we just watch and marvel. God does the work for us, not through us.

In the gift of the working of miracles the exact opposite is true. God is entrusting us with a strength, with an energy, that we do not normally have. It is the power of the Spirit of God surging through us, through our hands, our feet, our minds—causing us to do or be something that is not normal or natural to our behavior. We call this the gift of the working of miracles.

The Gifts and Ministries of the Holy Spirit

A Dumb Animal Spoke

By the working of miracles, very often the laws of nature are altered or suspended, and what is abnormal to our natural reasoning becomes effective around us. This gift has functioned in the Bible, even through an animal, as we see in the Book of Numbers, chapter 22.

This is a very unusual story. The prophet Balaam was weak and wavering in respect to God's express will and was being tempted by the enemies of God's people.

> *And Balaam rose up in the morning, and saddled his ass, and went with the princes of Moab. And God's anger was kindled because he went: and the angel of the LORD stood in the way for an adversary against him. Now he was riding upon his ass, and his two servants were with him. And the ass saw the angel of the LORD standing in the way, and his sword drawn in his hand: and the ass turned aside out of the way, and went into the field: and Balaam smote the ass, to turn her into the way.* (Num. 22:21–23)

When Balaam's donkey saw the angel of the Lord standing in the way, it turned aside into a field. Then it crushed Balaam against a wall and finally laid down under him. Each time Balaam punished the donkey, *"Balaam's anger was kindled, and he smote the ass with a staff"* (v. 27).

Then the Lord spoke through the animal and said, *"What have I done unto thee, that thou hast smitten me these three times?"* (v. 28).

Balaam said, *"Because thou hast mocked me: I would there were a sword in mine hand, for now would I kill thee"* (v. 29).

Again God spoke through the animal to Balaam, *"Am not I thine ass, upon which thou hast ridden ever since I was thine unto this day? was I ever wont to do so unto thee?"* (v. 30).

Then God opened Balaam's eyes and he saw the angel standing in front of him with sword drawn. It was only the animal that had kept Balaam from being killed. If the animal had not held back, Balaam would have died when he ran into the two-edged sword of that angel. The animal could see it, but the prophet could not. Then God gave that animal the voice of a human. To us that is a miracle.

On this occasion the miracle that took place was not a small affair. God would not have His people cursed. Finally, out of this strange prophet's lips came these words: *"How shall I curse, whom God hath not cursed? or how shall I defy, whom the* Lord *hath not defied?"* (Num. 23:8).

Balaam was unable to compromise with the enemy, even though he was offered great treasures to do it.

Elijah

The gift of miracles is remarkably demonstrated through the prophet Elijah in 2 Kings 2:8. *"And Elijah took his mantle* [which is an ordinary coat], *and wrapped it together, and smote the waters, and they were divided hither and thither, so that they two* [Elijah and Elisha] *went over on dry ground."*

When both were on the other side, the waters again flowed normally. Because Elijah used a material object—his coat—this act must be classified, not as an act of faith, but as the working of a miracle.

David

King David operated in the working of miracles. In 1 Samuel, chapter 17, he tells how he slew a lion and a bear with his naked hands:

> *And David said unto Saul, Thy servant kept his father's sheep, and there came a lion, and a bear, and took a lamb out of the flock: and I went out after him, and smote him, and delivered it out of his mouth: and when he arose against me, I caught him by his beard, and smote him, and slew him.* (vv. 34–35)

Then David proceeded to face Goliath, a Philistine who stood ten feet tell. Armed with only a stone and a sling, David slew the giant, for he had said, *"The* Lord *that delivered me out of the paw of the lion, and out of the paw of the bear, he will deliver me out of the hand of this Philistine"* (v. 37).

These acts would have to be classed as the working of miracles because David was involved in their completion. He could not kill a lion or a bear with his bare hands. For him to wrestle with a lion and win took a power that he normally did not have.

This is different from the story of Daniel in the lions' den. Daniel functioned in the gift of faith. He did not touch a lion; he trusted God. It was an angel that came and closed the jaws of the lions.

Samson

Another illustration of the working of miracles can be seen in the life of Samson. Samson was a very unusual person. Before he was born, his mother gave him to God and proclaimed him a Nazarite, which meant that he would never touch dead flesh, or drink wine, or clip his hair. (See Judges 13:5.)

The Bible says that as Samson became a young man, the Spirit of God moved upon him. (See Judges 13:25.)

> *And, behold, a young lion roared against him. And the spirit of the LORD came mightily upon him, and he rent him as he would have rent a kid, and he had nothing in his hand.* (Judg. 14:5-6)

When three thousand men came against him, he slew a thousand men with only the jawbone of an ass. (See Judges 15:14–15.)

Then, as his final act, Samson dislocated the two middle pillars of a great temple, where thousands of pagans were worshipping their god. (See Judges 16:29–30). By pushing those pillars out of place, he destroyed more of the enemies of God at one time than he had destroyed in his whole life.

Samson possessed the gift of the working of miracles.

Jesus and the Working of Miracles

At the wedding feast in Cana of Galilee Jesus turned water into wine. (See John 2:1–11.) Through the working of miracles, the laws of nature were affected: the fermenting stage was accelerated.

In Matthew 14, when Jesus broke the bread and the fishes to feed the multitude, every break was a miracle of multiplication. He took each loaf and each fish and with His natural hands kept breaking them until the disciples had enough to feed thousands of people. With little, Jesus fed many, and there were twelve baskets of leftovers! His disciples were amazed. This is the functioning of the gift of the working of miracles.

9
The Gifts of Inspiration

The third group of spiritual gifts consists of the gifts of inspiration: prophecy, tongues, and the interpretation of tongues.

Unlike the first two groups—the gifts of power and the gifts of revelation—these three gifts of inspiration are not the kind that change the world. The gifts of inspiration are strictly for the benefit of the church. They have a threefold ministry: edification, exhortation, and comfort.

God wants His people to be strong and mature in spiritual matters. He wants a church that is alive and powerful. These three gifts of inspiration were designed for that purpose.

The Gift of Prophecy

Prophecy is the greatest of the three gifts of inspiration. In 1 Corinthians, chapters 11–14, the gift of prophecy is referred to a total of 22 times, which seems to reveal its importance.

What Prophecy Is Not

The gift of prophecy is not foretelling the future. Prophecy in the New Testament is different from a prophet who foretells the future. God specifically limits this gift to three beautiful exercises—edification, exhortation, and comfort—and none of these have to do with the gifts of power or the gifts of revelation.

According to Ephesians 4:8–12, the prophet is one of the five ministry gifts given to the church. He is a person, not a vocal gift. He holds the office of prophet. Acts 21:9 tells of Philip's four daughters *"which did prophesy."* They were not prophets, but they prophesied. They had a ministry of edifying the church, but they did not foretell the future.

The prophetic office always predicts the future; the gift of prophecy never predicts the future.

The gift of prophecy is not to be used for guidance. This is one of the major ways in which people have misused this gift. Guidance is not one of the three blessings of prophecy.

The gift of prophecy is not preaching. To preach means to proclaim and pronounce the Good News—the Gospel of Jesus Christ. Preaching comes from the natural mind; prophecy is the mind of the Holy Spirit speaking to us in a supernatural utterance. Preaching can be inspired or anointed, but it is not supernatural; prophecy is always supernatural. Prophecy is a supernatural utterance that comes from a person who is anointed to speak the treasures of God to the body of Christ.

The gift of prophecy is not rebuke. There is no element of rebuke in prophecy; there is always encouragement. In the New Testament, correction comes, not from prophecy, but from preaching the Word with doctrine. Paul dealt with excesses as a teacher, a pastor, and an apostle, but never through the gift of prophecy.

The gift of prophecy is not a ministry of criticism. Prophecy is not one person's opinion against another. It is a divine operation under the anointing of God, designed to warn men and women of sin or shortcomings so that they might be ready when Jesus comes. The gift of prophecy can lift a Christian out of his depression, his negligence, and his lukewarmness, and put him back into the mainstream of the thrust of God.

Threefold Purpose of Prophecy

The gift of prophecy is for three reasons: edification, exhortation, and comfort.

Edification

To edify means to build up. This gift of prophecy will build up the church of Jesus Christ. If a man is weak spiritually, it will build him up. If a woman is afraid, it will remove the fear. This gift of prophecy in its root meaning signifies "to erect, to strengthen, to build up." There are multitudes of Christians today who are in great need of having their spiritual lives built up and strengthened. This is why the gifts of inspiration were given to the church by the Holy Spirit.

In 1 Corinthians 14:18, Paul wrote, *"I thank my God, I speak with tongues more than ye all."* No doubt, the reason Paul spoke in tongues more than the entire Corinthian church fellowship was his desire to be built up. This is one of the secrets of his amazing spiritual strength.

Exhortation

In exhortation we have a call to encouragement. Many times I have heard a word of prophecy that will exhort a church fellowship to holiness, consecration, and separation from the world. Many times when the devil discourages us, this gift of prophecy will encourage us. It can bring an exhortation: "Jesus is coming soon. Don't stop here. Don't let the world come in like a flood. Keep moving with God." It exhorts us to keep ourselves built up and strong in God.

There have been times when a word of exhortation has changed my life. I could feel the Holy Spirit speaking such forceful words through a person.

Comfort

The Greek word for comfort is *consolation,* which would include the healing of distress, of sorrow, of persecution, and of suffering.

We live in a world of broken lives, broken homes, and broken ambitions. People today do not necessarily need sympathy or pity; they need comfort. The church needs divine comfort from the Holy Spirit to bring heaven's healing into their hearts. It is our duty and our privilege to come to church and say, "Lord, we want the tenderest of the gifts to function. We want prophecy to function."

Some people who come to our churches are so sad; they don't know what to do. Some of them are actually contemplating suicide. If there is anything we should give these people, it is comfort—healing of the inner person, healing of the memories, healing of sadness and depression. We can do it through the praises of God and through sincere fellowship with our brothers and sisters in the body. We can bring comfort when we shake hands with one another and embrace one another. We can say, "The Lord comfort you and bless you."

These three ministries of prophecy—edification, exhortation, and comfort—should be functioning in every prayer group and church fellowship. If prophecy is the most tender of all the gifts, how much should it function in all our lives!

This gift is available, not to just a few, but to the total church. Begin now by saying, "Lord, I want these gifts to function in my life." If you are sincere, God will cause these gifts to function in and through you. He wants you to be an instrument He can use to edify, exhort, and comfort His people.

Controlling the Gift of Prophecy

According to 1 Corinthians 14:32, the possessor of the gift of prophecy can control that gift: *"The spirits of the prophets are subject to the prophets."* Whenever a person says of their utterances, "I can't stop doing this," you can be sure that an alien spirit is involved. At no time is a person bound by the manifestation of a spiritual gift.

This is the difference between being controlled by the devil and being controlled by God. You can stop God and grieve the Holy Spirit at any time. You are not under bondage to the Holy Spirit. You work with Him and flow with Him because you want to. You have to keep flowing in the Spirit if you expect the gifts to operate in and through you.

First Corinthians 14:29 tells how the gift of prophecy is regulated: *"Let the prophets speak two or three, and let the other judge."* There should be at the most only three messages of prophecy in one meeting. Even if you should feel a thrust to prophesy, you should control it if God has already spoken three times. The Word says that is enough for one service.

Verse 33 tells how this gift can be safeguarded and protected: *"God is not the author of confusion, but of peace."*

In 1 Thessalonians 5:20 we are told plainly: *"Despise not prophesyings."* Some pastors and ministers do not want the gift of prophecy to function in their churches because they cannot personally control it. When dealing with the supernatural, there is a certain element of danger involved, which is true with so many things. Driving an automobile or flying an airplane can be dangerous. Anything worth very much can be somewhat dangerous.

When the gifts of the Spirit are not functioning properly, they can be dangerous to the church. You can have a fire in the basement of a building; but as long as the fire is inside the furnace, there is no problem. Should that fire be outside the furnace and in the center of the room, you would have trouble. Though it is the same fire, it is in the wrong place.

The gifts of the Spirit have a proper place and a proper time. To function best, they should function at that place and time.

Romans 12:6 says, *"Let us prophesy according to the proportion of faith."* If a person prophesies things that do not come to pass, he is speaking beyond his faith and he should stop. The apostle Paul wrote these words to Timothy: *"Stir up the gift of God, which is in thee"* (2 Tim. 1:6). No doubt the gift he was speaking of was the gift of prophecy.

Diverse Kinds of Tongues

Diverse kinds of tongues is a gift used for public ministry. It is a sign gift from God, a distinguishing gift that does something very particular.

"Wherefore tongues are for a sign, not to them that believe, but to them that believe not: but prophesying serveth not for them that believe

not, but for them which believe" (1 Cor. 14:22). Tongues is for a sign to the unbeliever, to stir him inside.

Speaking with tongues as the Holy Spirit gives utterance is a unique ministry that has not been used in other dispensations. It is identified only with the church age, the age we are living in today.

The phenomenon of speaking in tongues began on the day of Pentecost—the day the New Testament church was born in Jerusalem. This gift of tongues has been identified with the church since its inception and it has not left the church since that day. None of the nine gifts have left the church.

This sign gift of diverse kinds of tongues is a supernatural utterance, which comes from God through the person of the Holy Spirit. This remarkable gift is directed through man's spirit and manifests as a spirit language, a divine and spiritual communication that is different from his native tongue.

Tongues is the most misunderstood of all the spiritual gifts. There is no gift in the entire world that receives so explosive a reaction as the gift of tongues. Because the devil is afraid of it, he gets everybody fighting over it. If tongues did not cause him trouble, he would ignore it, but speaking in tongues is dynamic. It will change a person's life, so Satan fights it with every force he can muster.

We need to understand it better, so we can use it more. If we are going to use the sword, we must use it with dexterity. If we are going to use this gift of tongues, we must use it mightily as unto the Lord.

What Tongues Is Not

The sign gift of tongues is not the prayer language of tongues that comes with the infilling of the Holy Spirit. It is not the receiving of the Spirit at baptism when one is "filled with the Spirit," as in Acts 2:4: *"And they were all filled with the Holy Ghost, and began to speak with other tongues, as the Spirit gave them utterance."*

The gift of tongues is not the learning of languages. Tongues has positively no relationship to the thinking abilities of man. When a person speaks in tongues, he has no understanding of what he is saying. The apostle Paul wrote, *"For if I pray in an unknown tongue, my spirit prayeth, but my understanding is unfruitful"* (1 Cor. 14:14). His spirit is speaking to God. *"He that speaketh in an unknown tongue speaketh not unto men, but unto God"* (v. 2). Tongues is speech to God—a vocal miracle. What a joy it is to speak personally and directly to the Most High God!

This means there is an element of faith and an element of courage related to this gift. You must be able to say in faith, "Lord, I believe this is You." You must be able to say with courage, "I don't care what men think; I'm going to let the blessing of God flow through me."

God wants it to flow through each one of us. The gift of tongues is a special challenge and a sign to those, the Bible says, who are uninformed.

Who Can Have the Gift of Tongues?

Only Spirit-filled, or Spirit-baptized, believers are candidates for this gift. The infilling of the Holy Spirit is the door to the operation of spiritual gifts in your life. You must pass through that door to reach all the "goodies" on the inside. Many people want these mighty gifts of the Spirit to function in their lives, but are unwilling to step through that door.

Before a person can operate this church gift, he must first experience Acts 2:4; he must speak with tongues. In 1 Corinthians 14:5 Paul said, *"I would that ye all spake with tongues."* None of us have the right to say, "Let somebody else do it. I won't do it."

Tongues is a part of the Great Commission to the church—the Lord Jesus Christ's last words on earth before He was taken up into heaven. He said,

> *And he said unto them, Go ye into all the world, and preach the gospel to every creature. He that believeth and is baptized shall be saved; but he that believeth not shall be damned. And these signs shall follow them that believe; in my name shall they cast out devils; they shall speak with new tongues.* (Mark 16:15–17)

This gift was prophesied even by such a great prophet as the Lord Jesus Christ. There is no doubt or ambiguity about what Jesus said. He said exactly what He meant and meant exactly what He said! It is available to each of us.

Where Does This Gift Operate?

Tongues is a gift for the body. First Corinthians 14:23 refers to tongues operating when the whole church has come together into one place. Verse 26 says, *"When ye come together, every one of you hath a psalm, hath a doctrine, hath a tongue, hath a revelation, hath an interpretation."*

"When ye come together." The gift of tongues is a come-together gift. It operates when we assemble ourselves together. However, when you use your own private prayer language, there is no need for anyone else. It is a beautiful experience you can enjoy alone. When I am speaking in my prayer language, I am alone most of the time. I get more inspiration walking around by myself or driving alone in my car, talking to the Lord. It is a beautiful experience for the spiritual man or woman.

Tongues Edify

God specifically says the vocal gifts of inspiration are designated to edify or build up the total church of the Lord Jesus Christ. When we understand this, then every time we meet together, we can say without reservation, "Let the gifts function."

"He that speaketh in an unknown tongue edifieth himself" (1 Cor. 14:4). When this beautiful gift of tongues is in manifestation, it causes a building up and a strengthening within the speaker.

This gift can function in two ways: by speaking and by singing. Colossians 3:16 says, *"Let the word of Christ dwell in you richly in all wisdom; teaching and admonishing one another in psalms and hymns and spiritual songs, singing with grace in your hearts to the Lord."*

This is such a beautiful verse. We are to teach and admonish one another in psalms, hymns, and spiritual songs. Have you ever thought of songs as being for teaching and admonishing? Ephesians 5:19 says, *"Speaking to yourselves in psalms and hymns and spiritual songs, singing and making melody in your heart to the Lord."*

So here we find tremendous evidence of how this gift of tongues can function to the edifying and building up of the body.

Tongues Is for Everyone

Church leaders must not forbid the use of this gift. In 1 Corinthians 14:39 Paul wrote, *"Brethren, covet to prophesy, and forbid not to speak with tongues."* If the Word says, *"Forbid not,"* I think we should be careful about what we forbid. In some areas of our world today we would be forbidden to practice this gift. Thank God, we are living in a new atmosphere in this country. Almost every denomination in America today has within it a certain segment that has been filled with the Holy Spirit.

Paul had previously stated, *"I would that ye all spake with tongues"* (1 Cor. 14:5). If the Word of God says all of us should have this gift, then without exception all of us should have it.

The gift of tongues should not be neglected, but it can be. It can lie dormant within us. In 1 Timothy 4:14 the apostle Paul wrote to young Timothy, *"Neglect not the gift that is in thee, which was given thee by prophecy, with the laying on of the hands of the presbytery."*

Will Tongues Cease?

Some have said that tongues will cease. *"Charity never faileth: but whether there be prophecies, they shall fail; whether there be tongues, they shall cease; whether there be knowledge, it shall vanish away"* (1 Cor. 13:8).

When will tongues cease? The Holy Spirit is particularly identified with the church. Has the church age ended? No. There is no Bible intimation of a change to be made in church law or policy or construction from the day the church was born until it is raptured and taken to be with Jesus. Tongues will cease, but it will not occur until the end of this age. At the same time the other gifts will cease. When the church is with God, the gifts of the Spirit will no longer be needed.

Why Will Tongues Cease?

In heaven we will no longer need the Holy Spirit to guide us into all truth. We will speak the same language as Jesus, so the gift of tongues will not be necessary at that time.

One purpose of tongues is as a sign to the unbeliever, but there will be no unbelievers in heaven. We will no longer need unknown tongues to glorify God in heaven; there will be only one language—heaven's language—and all of us will be speaking it.

We will no longer need tongues to edify ourselves. We will be edified by being in God's presence forever, jubilant throughout all eternity!

Why Speak in Tongues?

Here are a number of reasons why Christians should speak in tongues:

1. *Tongues is evidence of the infilling of the Holy Spirit.* This is shown three times in the Acts of the Apostles: in chapter 2, on the day the church was born; in chapter 10, about ten years later when Peter ministered to the Gentiles; in chapter 19, about twenty years later when Paul laid hands on the believers in Ephesus. In each of these passages, the Bible specifically says the people spoke with tongues.

2. *Tongues is your prayer language.* As we find in 1 Corinthians 14:2, when you speak in tongues, you are speaking supernaturally to God. Your spirit prays, but your mind does not understand. Your spirit is the real you—your inner man—and it is that inner person (the real you) who is talking to God.

3. *With tongues, you magnify God.* To magnify God is to make Him great. *"They heard them speak with tongues, and magnify God"* (Acts 10:46).

4. *Tongues edifies.* First Corinthians 14:4 says, *"He that speaketh in an unknown tongue edifieth himself."* When you edify yourself, you are building up spiritual strength within yourself.

5. *Tongues brings gladness in singing.* In 1 Corinthians 14:15 Paul wrote, *"I will sing with the spirit, and I will sing with the understanding also."* Singing with the spirit becomes a source of gladness in singing unto the Lord.

6. *Tongues is a source of intercessory prayer.* Intercessory prayer is one of the greatest spiritual undertakings. Romans 8:26 says, *"Likewise the Spirit also helpeth our infirmities: for we know not what we should pray for as we ought: but the Spirit itself maketh intercession for us with groanings which cannot be uttered."* This is a different level of prayer. In the forty or fifty years of my ministry, I have experienced this type of in-depth intercessory prayer only five or six times.

7. *Tongues is a source of spiritual refreshing.* Isaiah 28:11–12 says, *"For with stammering lips and another tongue will he speak to this people....This is the rest wherewith ye may cause the weary to rest; and this is the refreshing."* Tongues provides a spiritual stamina that comes only from God.

8. *Speaking and ministering to the Lord in tongues is somewhat like a repository of profit.* As is stated in 1 Corinthians 12:7, *"But the manifestation of the Spirit is given to every man to profit withal."* Through tongues, God can bring into your life an enrichment and a spiritual blessing you have never known before as you realize and experience a new nearness to God.

The Interpretation of Tongues

The third gift of inspiration is the interpretation of tongues—the supernatural verbalization of the meaning of a message just delivered to the church by a member of the body of Christ in a language he does not understand.

The purpose of this gift is to interpret and render a message intelligible that was given forth in an unintelligible tongue. One person gives a message in a language he does not know, and another person interprets it. This reveals the presence of God in that place. God has brought to those people a very special message, calling for action.

The person who operates in the gift of tongues should seek the gift of interpretation. *"Wherefore let him that speaketh in an unknown tongue pray that he may interpret"* (1 Cor. 14:13). If you possess the gift of tongues and happen to be in a gathering where there is no interpreter, you should be able to interpret.

The ministry of this gift is to edify and build up the church. When the gift of interpretation functions with its sister gift, the gift of tongues, it equals prophecy, which according to 1 Corinthians 14:4 does edify the church.

Tongues and interpretation is the functioning of a miracle that can easily be observed by the unbeliever, causing consternation when it is witnessed, just as on the day of Pentecost when the church was born.

The interpretation of tongues is not a translation. If one person gives forth a message in tongues and two different people have the interpretation, each interpretation will be different. The essence of the message, the deep root of it, will be similar; but the phrasing of it will be different because it is not a word-for-word translation. A translation is an exact rendering from one language to another in precise grammatical terms; an interpretation reveals what God wants us to know. This explains how at times a message in tongues might be long while the interpretation is short.

On some of my trips to foreign countries, there were times when I thought my interpreter was preaching his own sermon. It seemed that way because he was interpreting my message, not translating it.

The interpretation of tongues is not an operation of the human mind. It is the functioning of the Holy Spirit through the mind. The interpreter does not understand the language or the tongue that he is interpreting. His mental faculties are not a part of the message, so he has no thought in his mind as to what the Spirit is going to say. If he does, he is not interpreting by the Spirit.

I have been in foreign countries and heard a person speak. Though I did not know the language, I knew supernaturally that it was a message in tongues, so I stood up and interpreted it in English. Since no one present understood English, my interpreter had to interpret what I said into their native language. If I had not interpreted the message, it would have been lost.

When a message is given in tongues and no interpretation follows, there are two possible reasons:

1. No one present has the gift of interpretation.

2. The speaker was simply magnifying God and no public interpretation of the message was necessary.

The interpretation of tongues can come in two ways: The interpreter speaks the words inspirationally, or he sees what he is speaking about in the form of a vision.

The interpretation of tongues requires a measure of faith. The interpreter normally receives only one or two words at a time; he does not receive the complete message at once. By faith, he must give those words; and by giving those words, God gives him the next words. As he speaks, the message will continue to come a few words at a time until he is finished. Even if the message lasts thirty minutes, the interpreter gets only a few words at a time.

This Gift Illustrated

A tremendous illustration of the fruit of this gift took place when I preached in Washington, D.C. After my sermon, one brother gave a message and another interpreted. When they had finished, a young man walked to the front and spoke in a foreign language to the one who had given the message.

The brother answered, "I'm sorry, sir, but I don't understand any other language."

The man replied, "But you spoke my language beautifully. I am Persian. You spoke my language and told me that I must get right with God, that I must find God right now."

The brother answered, "No, it was the Spirit who spoke to you. It was God talking to you, not me."

Much to that young man's surprise, neither of the two men—the one who gave the message in tongues and the one who interpreted it—spoke or understood his language. He stood there, trembling, then knelt down and gave his heart to the Lord Jesus Christ.

That night the gifts of tongues and interpretation were magnificently fulfilled. Just as the Bible says, it was a sign to the unbeliever. God spoke to that man in the Persian language through two men when neither of them understood a foreign tongue. One man was a real estate agent; the other was a car salesman.

Tongues and Interpretation—Rules of Operation

Tongues and interpretation of tongues are regulated by the Scriptures. If a fellowship of believers does not function properly in the gifts of the Spirit, those gifts will cease to function. If believers try to operate the gifts outside the bounds of the Word, they will cease. There are literally thousands of churches in our generation that at one time possessed the gifts of the Spirit to some extent; but because the people did not understand them correctly, the gifts ceased.

Tongues without interpretation is forbidden in the church.

The apostle Paul wrote,

I thank my God, I speak with tongues more than ye all: yet in the church I had rather speak five words with my understanding, that by my voice I might teach others also, than ten thousand words in an unknown tongue. (1 Cor. 14:18–19)

From five words to ten thousand words is quite a jump! Paul is simply showing how meaningless it is for a person to speak out during a church service in a tongue that is not interpreted. He would rather speak only five words that had meaning than rattle off ten thousand words and not say anything that anyone could understand. He is showing the rationale of performing the gifts of the Spirit as God wants them to be performed.

The Gifts and Ministries of the Holy Spirit

The gift of tongues is limited in its use.

How is it then, brethren? when ye come together, every one of you hath a psalm, hath a doctrine, hath a tongue, hath a revelation, hath an interpretation. Let all things be done unto edifying. If any man speak in an unknown tongue, let it be by two, or at the most by three, and that by course; and let one interpret. (1 Cor. 14:26–27)

As previously stated, in any service there should be a maximum of three messages given forth in an unknown tongue with an interpretation each time. I have always thought that, since heaven does things so precisely, surely the Holy Spirit can say all that needs to be said in three messages.

The reason for this is found in 1 Corinthians 14:33, which says, *"For God is not the author of confusion, but of peace, as in all churches of the saints."* These gifts are regulated, not by God, but by the church.

Again verse 27 says, *"If any man speak in an unknown tongue, let it be by two, or at the most by three, and that by course; and let one interpret."* In some churches I have visited, there have been two different messages in tongues and two different people giving the interpretations. The Word of God says, *"Let one interpret."* Normally in a service only one person should interpret.

In Great Britain the gifts of the Spirit have been in much greater evidence than in the United States. At a conference there, the moderator will stand at the opening session and announce who will interpret during the convention. No matter who gives a message in tongues, that same person will interpret each time. Though there may be many interpreters in a church, the Bible says the same one should interpret during each individual service.

First Corinthians 14:28 says, *"But if there be no interpreter, let him keep silence in the church; and let him speak to himself, and to God."* This is one of the clearest manifestations of church order you will find. If there is no interpreter and the speaker does not possess the gift of interpretation, then he should keep silence in the church and speak only to himself and to God.

This proves that when we are operating in spiritual gifts, we have control over the situation. We are not controlled by an extraneous power. According to the Bible, the Holy Spirit is a true gentleman. He will never force a person to do anything. He offers the opportunity; whether or not we take it is our choice.

In 1 Corinthians 14:29–32 we read:

Let the prophets speak two or three, and let the other judge. If any thing be revealed to another that sitteth by, let the first hold his peace. For ye may all prophesy one by one, that all may learn, and all may be comforted. And the spirits of the prophets are subject to the prophets.

When anyone says, "I'm uncontrollable," he is not under the power of the Holy Spirit, but under the devil's power.

God will not force a person to go to heaven; neither will He force a person to live right. He did not force Lucifer, the archangel, to live right when Lucifer rebelled against Him. He did not try to make Adam live right after he had sinned in the Garden of Eden. Nowhere in the Bible does God force anyone to live right.

You have to want to live right, and you have to want the gifts of the Spirit. God will not force them on you. When you do receive them, have respect for them. Learn what God has said about them; then you will have great wisdom in the operation of these gifts and they will remain with you. There is no reason for the gifts to ever leave your life.

Prophecy versus Tongues

Having studied the three inspirational gifts—prophecy, tongues, and interpretation of tongues—we will now see how these gifts function together in the body of Christ. The apostle Paul wrote in 1 Corinthians 14:1–2:

Follow after charity, and desire spiritual gifts, but rather that ye may prophesy. For he that speaketh in an unknown tongue speaketh not unto men, but unto God: for no man understandeth him; howbeit in the spirit he speaketh mysteries.

The Gifts and Ministries of the Holy Spirit

Paul is showing here the difference between the gift of prophecy and the gift of tongues. Together, the sister gifts of tongues and interpretation have the same message, anointing, power, and abiding presence as prophecy. They are simply two ways God has of doing the same thing. Prophecy speaks to the people; a message in tongues speaks to God and to the sinner.

When a person speaks in tongues, we cannot understand what is being said; in prophecy we can.

Paul continued in 1 Corinthians 14:3–4 to say:

> *He that prophesieth speaketh unto men to edification, and exhortation, and comfort. He that speaketh in an unknown tongue edifieth himself; but he that prophesieth edifieth the church.*

This is the basic difference in these two ministries in the body: Tongues edifies and builds up the speaker; prophecy builds up the church.

In verse 5 Paul wrote, *"I would that ye all spake with tongues, but rather that ye prophesied: for greater is he that prophesieth than he that speaketh with tongues, except he interpret, that the church may receive edifying."* Prophecy and tongues are different unless there is someone present to interpret the tongues; then they become the same.

> *Wherefore tongues are for a sign, not to them that believe, but to them that believe not: but prophesying serveth not for them that believe not, but for them which believe.* (1 Cor. 14:22)

Tongues is a sign, not to the believer, but to the unbeliever. It will do amazing things for sinners. I have seen tongues and interpretation strike terror in the hearts of sinners.

Prophecy is for the church; the edification, exhortation, and comfort of prophecy belong to God's people.

> *If therefore the whole church be come together into one place, and all speak with tongues, and there come in those that are unlearned, or unbelievers, will they not say that ye are mad? But if all prophesy [or speak out in a language all can understand], and there come in*

one that believeth not, or one unlearned, he is convinced of all, he is judged of all: and thus are the secrets of his heart made manifest; and so falling down on his face he will worship God, and report that God is in you of a truth.   (1 Cor. 14:23–35)

When an unbeliever comes into a group and hears these mighty words of inspiration flowing forth, he will recognize that God is present and among those people. The words they are speaking are supernatural words, not coming forth from the natural flow of their minds. The sinner will know that, and he will identify the power of God in their midst.

10
The Gifts in Jesus' Ministry

Jesus Christ came to this world for one reason: to redeem it from sin. *"God so loved the world, that he gave his only begotten Son, that whosoever believeth in him should not perish, but have everlasting life"* (John 3:16).

Christ came to conquer this world, to snatch it out of the hands of the devil and save us from hell. When Jesus appeared to the apostle John on the Isle of Patmos, He proclaimed that the keys of death and hell were in His hand (Rev. 1:18). Just after His resurrection, He told His disciples, *"All power is given unto me in heaven and in earth"* (Matt. 28:18). That means there is total victory for the body of Christ. As a sideline to this, we have been given the gifts of the Spirit as an aid in winning the world to the Lord Jesus Christ.

Our Example in the Gifts

Some people have the idea that everything Jesus did was because He was God, but they are 100 percent wrong! The amazing ministry of Jesus Christ is a perfect example of a ministry that functioned within the framework of the gifts of the Spirit. If Jesus had performed His earthly ministry because He was God, then you and I could not follow His example because we are not God. But the remarkable thing is that He confined His ministry within the framework of the gifts of the Spirit.

I use the word "confined" because, as the Son of God, Jesus was not required to operate in this framework. He did not have to function through the gifts of the Holy Spirit. He could have chosen another way. As God, He could have spoken worlds into existence as was done in the beginning. (See Genesis 1.) But He deliberately confined Himself to minister within the limits of the gifts of the Spirit, and He did so for one purpose: that He might be a perfect example to you and me.

If what Jesus did, He did because He was the Son of Man and used the Holy Spirit to do it, then you and I can do it, too. If the ministry of Jesus was directed, guided, and energized by the Holy Spirit, then we can have the same kind of ministry because we have the same Holy Spirit.

We can do the same works Jesus did. Jesus said in John 14:12, *"He that believeth on me, the works that I do shall he do also; and greater works than these shall he do; because I go unto my Father."* That is hard to believe, but Jesus said it. These *"greater works"* cannot be greater in quality; they can only be greater in quantity.

He was saying to His disciples, "You will do greater works than these because I am only one person; you are twelve." And He sent them out to do the same works He did. You and I today are part of these *"greater works."*

It should give you courage and strength to know that you are part of the great things God wants to do in the earth. We are a blessed people to be alive during this time. I am so glad that God permitted me to live and minister today.

Jesus functioned under the nine gifts that are in the New Testament—so can we. These gifts of the Holy Spirit are the weapons of our warfare—the instruments we fight and win with. They are our victory instruments. Had Christ performed His ministry as God, being the Son of God, all of us would have been eliminated because we are not God.

If these gifts of the Spirit were for Paul, Peter, Moses, David, Elijah, and Daniel—but not for us today—I would not have the courage to share these things with you. But I have the courage because I know beyond the shadow of a doubt that we can have what Moses and Elijah had; we can do what Peter and Paul did. If these men had done those works because they were specially selected by God to do them, then no ordinary Christian could hope to follow such a pattern. Their stories would be only a divine record that we could read and marvel about. But the same power that was in them is available to you and me. The works that they did, we can do today.

In our generation we can do the same works as Moses, as David, as Daniel—and as Jesus. Why? Because we have the same power of God and the same anointing of the Holy Spirit motivating us that motivated them. This is the purpose of this book. I know that He who was is. I know that He who is will be. There are no yesterdays and there are no tomorrows, because He is the mighty I AM!

Greater Works Than These Shall Ye Do

Let me give you an example to illustrate my point.

When I was in the Philippines, God gave us a phenomenal revival. The superintendent of the Methodist church, Rubin Candalaria, came and asked if he could help me. As superintendent of the churches in the Manila area, he could gain entrance into every church, so we were able to minister in fifty different churches. There may never have been a city so ready for revival as Manila was. Night after night we went into churches of all denominations.

The move of the Spirit was so grand and so beautiful. Such remarkable things took place. The first night in the great Knox Memorial church, the oldest Protestant church in the country, the entire deacon board knelt at the altar and accepted Jesus Christ as their Lord and Savior.

When I could not keep an appointment at a certain church, I said to Rubin Candalaria, "You go in my place."

He turned pale and said, "I can't do that!"

"But you have to do it. The meeting is announced and the people can't be disappointed."

He kept saying, "I can't."

"Why can't you?"

"I have been with you all these months. After every service you lay hands on everyone who wants to be prayed for. I have witnessed hundreds of miracles take place. It would not be right for me to go before them. I don't have any power to help them."

I said, "If you knew you had the power of God to do it, would you do it?"

He said, "Yes." Before you could count to three, I grabbed him and prayed the anointing of the Holy Spirit on him. Then I said, "Go quickly!" He went, and has been going ever since! You can do the same!

The Gifts as They Functioned in Jesus

We would expect the gifts of the Spirit to be manifested in the ministry of Jesus. Our only problem would be in identifying them and describing how they functioned in His life. Let's identify some of them now.

The Word of Wisdom

In Matthew's gospel, chapter 24, Jesus predicted the future. He said that false Christs and false Messiahs would come; that there would be wars and rumors of wars; that there would be famines, pestilences, and earthquakes (vv. 5–7). He said there would be great tribulation such as the world has never seen (vv. 21–22). He said the sun would be darkened and the moon would not give her light (v. 29). He said the Son of Man would return just as He had gone away (v. 30).

Jesus was projecting the future, functioning not as God, but as a Spirit-anointed man through the gift of the word of wisdom.

Most of these events have not yet come to pass. After 2,000 years they are standing as the words of eternal life because of the word of God's wisdom.

The Word of Knowledge

An example of the gift of the word of knowledge operating in the ministry of the Lord Jesus Christ can be seen in John

The Gifts and Ministries of the Holy Spirit

1:45–50. When Jesus saw Nathanael walking toward Him, He said, *"Behold an Israelite indeed, in whom is no guile!"* (v. 47).

Nathanael responded, *"Whence knowest thou me?"* (v. 48). (In other words, "How can you call me a good man? How do you know me?")

> *Jesus answered and said unto him, Before that Philip called thee, when thou wast under the fig tree, I saw thee.* (v. 48)

He knew who Nathanael was and where he was. He identified him through the word of God's knowledge. Supernaturally, the Lord Jesus Christ saw Nathanael the day before, sitting under a fig tree. This was a word of God's knowledge to Nathanael, and it made a believer out of him!

> *Nathanael answered and saith unto him, Rabbi, thou art the Son of God; thou art the King of Israel. Jesus answered and said unto him, Because I said unto thee, I saw thee under the fig tree, believest thou? thou shalt see greater things than these.* (v. 49–50)

The Discerning of Spirits

Again, we can use Nathanael as an example. When Jesus saw Nathanael, He said, *"Behold an Israelite indeed, in whom is no guile!"* He recognized a holy spirit within Nathanael, a man He had never before laid eyes on.

Many times Jesus discerned what was in the hearts of the people that were around Him. This was a functioning of the gift of the discerning of spirits.

In John 6:61 Jesus knew in himself that the disciples were murmuring. He knew the hearts of all men, which was the gift of discerning of spirits in operation. He knew the hearts of people because He discerned what was inside them. There are many evidences of this. In Luke 11 when a Pharisee invited Him to dinner, Jesus discerned what the man was thinking within himself regarding the fact that Jesus did not wash His hands before dinner.

The Gift of Faith

Jesus spoke to a fig tree and cursed it. He said, *"Let no fruit grow on thee henceforward for ever"* (Matt. 21:19). Then He went on His way. The next day as they passed by, the disciples saw that the fig tree had died.

We often ask, "Why did the Lord do this?" Because that particular type of tree always bore fruit before it had leaves. When Jesus said that it had leaves but no fruit, He saw it as a hypocrite, so He cursed it. This only reveals to us how much the Lord Jesus Christ despises hypocrisy.

Here we see the functioning of the gift of faith. Jesus never touched the tree with His hands; He merely spoke a word. By the next day, the tree had died, withered up from the roots. The gift of faith—a faith that was pungent, powerful, and demanding—said, "Die!" and that is exactly what happened.

We also see this gift demonstrated in Jesus during storms at sea. (See Mark 4:37–41; Luke 8:23–25.) The Lord spoke one word to the tempestuous waves, to the thunderings in the heavens, and to the blowing winds. One word is all He needed: Peace! He did not say to His disciples, "Get your oars, boys, and let's see if we can equalize this thing." He said, *"Peace, be still"* (Mark 4:40), and at His words all those billowing waves suddenly became like a glassy sea.

Again the disciples were amazed: *"What manner of man is this, that even the wind and the sea obey him?"* (v. 41). He did all of this with no strength pouring forth from His natural being. It was the force and pungency of a gift called faith.

The Working of Miracles

We can see the working of miracles function many times in the Lord Jesus Christ. When He laid His hands on blind eyes, something flowed through Him into that person and those eyes were opened. He raised up cripples with a hand. He took bread from a little boy, broke it, and began to fill enough baskets to feed thousands of people.

The Gifts and Ministries of the Holy Spirit

The Gifts of Healing

Christ began His ministry by demonstrating the gifts of healing. According to Matthew's gospel, His first healing was the healing of a leper:

And, behold, there came a leper and worshipped him, saying, Lord, if thou wilt, thou canst make me clean. And Jesus put forth his hand, and touched him, saying, I will; be thou clean. And immediately his leprosy was cleansed. (Matt. 8:2-3)

In the same chapter Jesus continues His ministry by healing Peter's wife's mother of an incurable fever (vv. 14–15). Then they brought to Him *"many that were possessed with devils: and he cast out the spirits with his word, and healed all that were sick"* (v. 16).

During the ministry of Jesus Christ, healing was a top priority. His total life was dedicated to alleviating misery and hurt and pain from the human race. I believe that healing is also the ministry of the body of Christ today. Every Christian should be praying for somebody every day. Jesus had compassion on the sick; and you can have compassion, too. Just pray for everybody you find who is sick.

The Gift of Prophecy

In the life of the Lord Jesus Christ, the gift of prophecy can be seen in the Sermon on the Mount from Matthew's Gospel, chapters 5-7. The words poured from Him with such magnificence. Many of His utterances were purely a result of the gift of prophecy.

Tongues and Interpretation of Tongues

The gift of tongues and the gift of interpretation of tongues were actually born with the church. It was not yet time for their function and operation during Jesus' ministry.

11
The Gifts in the Early Church

Thus far in this study on the gifts of the Holy Spirit, we have dealt with the doctrine of the gifts. We have defined each gift in simple terms and discussed how each works. Now we come to one of the most exciting portions of the entire study: the gifts of the Spirit as they operated in the early church.

The Lord Jesus Christ said to His disciples:

> *Nevertheless I tell you the truth; It is expedient for you that I go away: for if I go not away, the Comforter will not come unto you; but if I depart, I will send him unto you....Howbeit when he, the Spirit of truth, is come, he will guide you into all truth: for he shall not speak of himself; but whatsoever he shall hear, that shall he speak: and he will show you things to come. He shall glorify me: for he shall receive of mine, and shall show it unto you. All things that the Father hath are mine: therefore said I, that he shall take of mine, and shall show it unto you.* (John 16:7, 13–15)

This was magnificently demonstrated in the Old Testament when Abraham (a model of our heavenly Father) desired a bride for his only son, Isaac. Abraham sent Eliezer, the chief steward of his house (a model of the Holy Spirit), into a far land to get a bride for Isaac. When Rebekah, the bride, was brought back by Eliezer, she was decorated with gifts.

As the New Testament church—the bride of Christ—we have been presented with gifts by the Holy Spirit. We must exercise these gifts to the very fullest.

The Gifts and Ministries of the Holy Spirit

In Acts 1:8 the Lord Jesus said, *"But ye shall receive power, after that the Holy Ghost is come upon you."* Power has to do with two elements: authority and energy. We sometimes see power only as energy, but this is not fully true. Power is also authority. When God spoke the worlds into existence, He did not use energy; He used authority—the authority of His Word. He spoke and worlds came into being. (See Hebrews 11:3.)

By the significance of a spoken word we, too, can speak things into existence. That is power! The source of this power is the Holy Spirit, and you receive that power when the Holy Spirit comes to rest upon you.

In Matthew's gospel, chapter 16, the Lord Jesus was talking with His disciples—the first buds of the great church to be born on the day of Pentecost. In verse 15 Jesus asked, *"Whom say ye that I am?"*

"Simon Peter answered and said, Thou art the Christ, the Son of the living God" (v. 16).

Then Jesus said to Peter, *"Blessed art thou, Simon Barjona: for flesh and blood hath not revealed it unto thee, but my Father which is in heaven....Thou art Peter, and upon this rock I will build my church; and the gates of hell shall not prevail against it"* (vv. 17–18).

If we are going to win a tremendous battle, we must have weapons and armor. The gifts of the Holy Spirit are the weapons of our warfare, which the gates of hell cannot prevail against. We can break down nations through the gifts of the Holy Spirit.

As was previously stated, the ministry of the Lord Jesus Christ was the embodiment of these gifts. The power of His ministry did not stem from the fact that He was the Son of God; it was because the Holy Spirit rested upon Him.

Again I quote Jesus' words in John 14:12: *"He that believeth on me, the works that I do shall he do also; and greater works than these shall he do; because I go unto my Father."* Jesus could not have spoken these words in sincerity had such gifts not been made available to you and me. We draw our power from the same Source as the Lord Jesus: the Holy Spirit of God. We can have the same Source of strength He had. We can deliver to the people the same kind of authority and blessing He did.

Jesus said that even the gates of hell—the greatest force the devil has—cannot hold up against the power of the church. We can take the weapons of our warfare and give the devil a good beating with them!

The Acts of the Apostles records the actual history of the infant Christian church. It presents the early church as it progressed for one generation, its first 33 years. If you have any question concerning the early church, the first thing you should do is read the Acts of the Apostles. God may have put the answer to your question within those pages.

The New Testament church began with only eleven disciples. (Of the original twelve, one was lost: Judas Iscariot.) By the day of Pentecost, there were 120. From that moment there began the greatest spiritual upheaval ever recorded by man. History has never known a period of time like those years following the day of Pentecost. Of the early Christian church, it was written, *"These that have turned the world upside down are come hither also"* (Acts 17:6). Any people who have gained that kind of publicity and notoriety deserve to be studied at length.

How did they do it? Did they start a Bible school? Did they get a good advertising scheme? Did they hire a good public relations man? We can see how people are trying to do it today; let's see how they did it then—how the Gospel grew from an infant on the day of Pentecost to a church that encompassed the world in only one generation.

There have been great revivals and great spiritual leaders. Martin Luther changed a continent by the force and strength of one Bible truth: *"The just shall live by faith"* (Rom. 1:17). John Wesley moved not only the continent of Europe, but the United States as well. John Knox moved the country of Scotland to God as he created what is known today as the Presbyterian Church.

But for the greatest spiritual revolution in history, we cannot speak of those times; we must return to the day of Pentecost when the power of God was demonstrated with fire and with wind. The beginning of the Christian church was more dramatic than any revival ever held on the face of this earth. It circumnavigated the then-known world.

We need to know how it was done. Was there a specific pattern that we could follow—a pattern in the Word of God that perhaps has been hidden from us through the traditions of denominationalism? What makes the Acts of the Apostles—that fifth book of the New Testament—so outstanding? What makes it one of the most exciting books on the face of the earth?

In the city of Manila, I bought 10,000 copies of the Acts of the Apostles just to give away in my local crusade. I wanted so much for those people to read the Acts of the infant church. I purchased these from the Bible Society in Manila. Never before in the history of the Bible Society had anyone purchased 10,000 copies of the Acts of the Apostles. I took them to my meetings and gave them away. It was a joy!

The Infant Church

The infant church, born in Jerusalem, went forth to challenge and defy the entire Roman Empire with all its paganism, sensualism, witchcraft, and military might. Rome fell, but that little church marches on!

The infant church defied atheistic Athens with all its philosophical might, where the mighty brains of the Grecian Empire wrote their scripts. Standing on Mars Hill, the apostle Paul boldly proclaimed the existence of a true and living God, who changed the lives of men. (See Acts 17:22–31.)

The infant church emerged to convert the untutored barbarian, living in a primitive hut and held in the clutches of the awful forces of witchcraft. To him, the church said, "We will change you, transform you, make you a person you have never been before."

The infant church had turned the world upside down. They were world-changers, but they did not change the world through intellectualism or by military might. They changed the world with the gifts of the Holy Spirit. The early church knew what a battle was. It knew the issues of the battle and used only the weapons that would bring victory—the gifts of the Spirit.

The Gifts in the Church

I believe that the divine pattern for spiritual growth and direction is found in the Acts of the Apostles. In this one little book there are over fifty instances of the gifts of the Spirit in operation.

When the book of Acts was written, there were no chapter divisions. It was one continuous letter, filled with the function and operation of the Holy Spirit, giving a true picture of the church as it is supposed to be—a church filled with love.

The gifts of the Spirit never function selfishly. They always function for the benefit of the body of the Lord Jesus Christ. They function to bless others. As they operate through you, you will receive a blessing, but most of the blessing will belong to those around you.

Prophetically speaking, we are living at the very end of this dispensation, and it will terminate like it began—with a glorious outburst of the mighty power of God; and the gifts of the Spirit will be in full manifestation, just as they were in the early church. If you will follow what God has placed in the book of Acts, you will know how to handle the gifts of the Holy Spirit like a veteran.

The gifts of the Spirit functioned through the Lord Jesus Christ in Acts, chapter 1. He spoke the word of wisdom to His disciples in these two instances:

> *And, being assembled together with them, [Jesus] commanded them that they should not depart from Jerusalem, but wait for the promise of the Father, which, saith he, ye have heard of me. For John truly baptized with water; but ye shall be baptized with the Holy Ghost not many days hence.*
> (Acts 1:4–5)

> *But ye shall receive power, after that the Holy Ghost is come upon you: and ye shall be witnesses unto me both in Jerusalem, and in all Judaea, and in Samaria, and unto the uttermost part of the earth.*
> (Acts 1:8)

The promise of the Holy Spirit being poured out in the city of Jerusalem at Pentecost was a prediction of what was to come:

The Gifts and Ministries of the Holy Spirit

The gifts of the Holy Spirit would be poured out and the church would be born by the power of the Holy Spirit. This was a word of God's divine wisdom, and it functioned through our Lord and Savior, Jesus Christ.

In Acts 1:11 the gift of wisdom functioned through an angel. After Jesus was taken up to heaven in a cloud, an angel appeared to the disciples and said:

> *Ye men of Galilee, why stand ye gazing up into heaven? this same Jesus, which is taken up from you into heaven, shall so come in like manner as ye have seen him go into heaven.*

This was a word of God's wisdom. The angel was speaking of the future, an event that had not yet come to pass. It still stands as one of the gifts of the word of God's wisdom that projects the future.

In Acts 2:4 the gift of tongues functioned at least through the 120 disciples that are identified, and possibly through the whole 3,000 souls who joined the church that day (v. 41).

In Acts 2:39 the word of wisdom functioned through the apostle Peter: *"For the promise is unto you, and to your children, and to all that are afar off, even as many as the Lord our God shall call."*

Acts 2:43 says, *"And many wonders and signs were done by the apostles."* This must have involved prophecy, healing, and miracles, though it could have included all nine gifts of the Spirit.

In Acts, chapter 3, we see the functioning of the gifts of healing through the apostle Peter as a lame man was healed at the gate of the temple:

> *And Peter, fastening his eyes upon him with John, said, Look on us. And he gave heed unto them, expecting to receive something of them. Then Peter said, Silver and gold have I none; but such as I have give I thee: In the name of Jesus Christ of Nazareth rise up and walk. And he took him by the right hand, and lifted him up: and immediately his feet and ankle bones received strength. And he leaping up stood, and walked, and entered with them into the temple, walking, and leaping, and praising God.* (Acts 3:4–8)

In Acts, chapter 4, the gift of faith functioned through the body of believers as they lifted up their voice to God with one accord and prayed: *"That with all boldness they may speak thy word, by stretching forth thine hand to heal; and that signs and wonders may be done by the name of thy holy child Jesus"* (vv. 29–30). When they finished praying, *"the place was shaken where they were assembled together; and they were all filled with the Holy Ghost, and they spake the word of God with boldness"* (v. 31).

In Acts, chapter 5, the gift of discerning of spirits functioned through Peter as Ananias and his wife Sapphira tried to deceive the apostles. When Ananias and Sapphira came to the apostles, the gift of discerning of spirits functioned and Peter knew all the secrets of their hearts. Peter said, *"Ananias, why hath Satan filled thine heart to lie to the Holy Ghost, and to keep back part of the price of the land?...why hast thou conceived this thing in thine heart? thou hast not lied unto men, but unto God. And Ananias hearing these words fell down, and gave up the ghost"* (vv. 3–5).

In Acts 5:12 we read, *"And by the hands of the apostles were many signs and wonders wrought among the people; (and they were all with one accord in Solomon's porch.)"* The gift of the working of miracles was functioning and all the apostles were taking part.

In Acts 5:15–16 the gifts of healing were in operation through Peter: *"They brought forth the sick into the streets, and laid them on beds and couches, that at the least the shadow of Peter passing by might overshadow some of them. There came also a multitude out of the cities round about unto Jerusalem, bringing sick folks, and them which were vexed with unclean spirits: and they were healed every one."*

In Acts 5:17–20 the gift of the working of miracles functioned through an angel. When the apostles were thrown in jail, the angel of the Lord by night opened the prison doors, and brought them forth (v. 19).

Both the working of miracles and the gifts of healing functioned through Stephen: *"And Stephen, full of faith and power, did great wonders and miracles among the people"* (Acts 6:8). A vital point here is that Stephen was not an apostle, but a deacon in the church.

Acts 8:6–7 shows how the gifts of healing and the working of miracles were demonstrated in the life of Philip, another deacon of the church: *"And the people with one accord gave heed unto those things which Philip spake, hearing and seeing the miracles which he did. For unclean spirits, crying with loud voice, came out of many that were possessed with them: and many taken with palsies, and that were lame, were healed."*

Verse 13 also refers to the working of miracles through Philip: *"Then Simon himself believed also: and when he was baptized, he continued with Philip, and wondered, beholding the miracles and signs which were done."*

In verse 39 the working of miracles again operated in Philip's behalf: *"And when they were come up out of the water, the Spirit of the Lord caught away Philip, that the eunuch saw him no more: and he went on his way rejoicing."*

In Acts 9:1–9 the working of miracles took place as Jesus appeared to Saul of Tarsus on the road to Damascus. In verse 6 Jesus spoke a word of wisdom to Saul: *"Arise, and go into the city, and it shall be told thee what thou must do."*

Acts 9:17–18 demonstrates the gifts of healing through a disciple named Ananias, who laid hands on Saul of Tarsus that he might receive his sight.

In verse 34 Peter operated in the gifts of healing as a man sick of the palsy was raised up, and in verse 40 he ministered healing to a disciple in Joppa who had died.

In Acts 10:1–8 the gift of the word of knowledge operated through an angel. Then in verses 19–20 the word of knowledge came through Peter: *"While Peter thought on the vision, the Spirit said unto him, Behold, three men seek thee. Arise therefore, and get thee down, and go with them, doubting nothing: for I have sent them."*

Verses 44–46 tell how the gift of tongues manifested after Peter had spoken the Gospel to a group of Gentiles.

In Acts 12:5, 7 the gift of faith operated for the believers by the power and strength of an angel as Peter was set free from prison: *"Peter therefore was kept in prison: but prayer was made without ceasing of the church unto God for him....And, behold, the angel of the Lord came upon him, and a light shined in the prison: and he smote Peter on the side, and raised him up, saying, Arise up quickly. And his chains fell off from his hands."*

We see the gift of prophecy functioning in Acts 13:1–3 as the prophets and teachers in Antioch ministered to the Lord and fasted. *"As they ministered to the Lord, and fasted, the Holy Ghost said, Separate me Barnabas and Saul for the work whereunto I have called them"* (v. 2).

In verses 9–11 there was the gift of the working of miracles by Paul as Elymas the Sorcerer was struck blind for standing against the Gospel.

We see the gift of the working of miracles by the apostle Paul in Acts 14:8–10: *"And there sat a certain man at Lystra, impotent in his feet, being a cripple from his mother's womb, who never had walked: the same heard Paul speak: who stedfastly beholding him, and perceiving that he had faith to be healed, said with a loud voice, Stand upright on thy feet. And he leaped and walked."*

In verses 19–20 we see the gift of the working of miracles by the disciples after Paul had been stoned and left for dead outside the city. *"Howbeit, as the disciples stood round about him, he rose up, and came into the city: and the next day he departed with Barnabas to Derbe"* (v. 20).

Acts, chapter 16, shows the gift of discerning of spirits through the power and anointing of the Holy Spirit when Paul was forbidden by the Holy Spirit to preach the word in Asia (v. 6).

Verse 9 is the word of wisdom to Paul: *"And a vision appeared to Paul in the night; There stood a man of Macedonia, and prayed him, saying, Come over into Macedonia, and help us."*

Verse 18 shows the gift of discerning of spirits by Paul: *"But Paul, being grieved, turned and said to the spirit, I command thee in the name of Jesus Christ to come out of her. And he came out the same hour."*

In verses 25–26 the gift of faith and the working of miracles was demonstrated by Paul and Silas: *"And at midnight Paul and Silas prayed, and sang praises unto God: and the prisoners heard them. And suddenly there was a great earthquake, so that the foundations of the prison were shaken: and immediately all the doors were opened, and every one's bands were loosed."*

In Acts 18:9–10 we see the gift of the word of knowledge to Paul from the Lord Jesus: *"Then spake the Lord to Paul in the night by a vision, Be not afraid, but speak, and hold not thy peace: for I am with thee, and no man shall set on thee to hurt thee: for I have much people in this city."*

In Acts 19:1–7 there is the demonstration of tongues and prophecy as the Holy Spirit functioned through twelve disciples in the city of Ephesus.

Verses 11–12 tell of the gifts of healing through the hands of the apostle Paul: *"And God wrought special miracles by the hands of Paul: so that from his body were brought unto the sick handkerchiefs or aprons, and the diseases departed from them, and the evil spirits went out of them."*

The gift of the working of miracles operated through Paul in Acts 20:7–12 as a young man was raised from the dead after falling from a third-story window.

Verse 22 shows the gift of the word of wisdom being activated in Paul when he said, *"And now, behold, I go bound in the spirit unto Jerusalem, not knowing the things that shall befall me there."*

In Acts 21:8–9 we see the gift of prophecy through the four daughters of Philip: *"And we entered into the house of Philip the evangelist....And the same man had four daughters, virgins, which did prophesy."*

In verse 11 a prophet called Agabus spoke a word of wisdom: *"And when he was come unto us, he took Paul's girdle, and bound his own hands and feet, and said, Thus saith the Holy Ghost, So shall the Jews at Jerusalem bind the man that owneth this girdle, and shall deliver him into the hands of the Gentiles."*

Paul received a word of wisdom through the Lord Jesus in Acts 22:17–21. Verse 18 says, *"Make haste, and get thee quickly out of Jerusalem: for they will not receive thy testimony concerning me."*

In Acts 23:11 the word of wisdom came again to Paul through the Lord, revealing the future: *"Be of good cheer, Paul: for as thou hast testified of me in Jerusalem, so must thou bear witness also at Rome."* Did it come to pass? It did! From all natural evidence, it seemed certain that Paul would die in Jerusalem, but he was delivered.

Again the gift of the word of wisdom was manifest through Paul in Acts 27:21–22: *"But after long abstinence Paul stood forth in the midst of them, and said, Sirs, ye should have hearkened unto me, and not have loosed from Crete, and to have gained this harm and loss. And now I exhort you to be of good cheer: for there shall be no loss of any man's life among you, but of the ship."*

In Acts 28:3-6 there is the gift of the working of miracles through the apostle Paul:

> *And when Paul had gathered a bundle of sticks, and laid them on the fire, there came a viper out of the heat, and fastened on his hand. And when the barbarians saw the venomous beast hang on his hand, they said among themselves, No doubt this man is a murderer, whom, though he hath escaped the sea, yet vengeance suffereth not to live. And he shook off the beast into the fire, and felt no harm. Howbeit they looked when he should have swollen, or fallen down dead suddenly: but after they had looked a great while, and saw no harm come to him, they changed their minds, and said that he was a god.*

The apostle Paul operated in the gifts of healing in Acts 28:7-9. *"And it came to pass, that the father of Publius lay sick of a fever and of a bloody flux: to whom Paul entered in, and prayed, and laid his hands on him, and healed him. So when this was done, others also, which had diseases in the island, came, and were healed"* (vv. 8-9).

If we could add one more to this list, it would be found in Acts, chapter 29; but there is no twenty-ninth chapter of Acts in the Bible. I am referring to your Acts—you are part of Acts 29. The Acts of the Apostles is a book with no termination, no conclusion. It is still being written today.

In the Acts of the Apostles we have truth. In the Acts of the Apostles we see the church being born, springing full-grown upon the stage of human events. With the Great Commission before her, she went forth to conquer the world, to revolutionize Caesar's empire, to fight against the mighty philosophies of Greece. Finally, of her, those grand words were spoken: *"These that have turned the world upside down are come hither also"* (Acts 17:6). It was not that a visitor had come or that a creed had come; it was a people who had turned the world upside down!

The gifts of the Spirit met human needs in the early church. Wherever there were people, these gifts helped resolve their needs.

It was the power of the Holy Spirit that changed Peter from a backslider to an aggressive witness for the Lord Jesus Christ. Until he received the gift of the Holy Spirit, Peter was vacillating, shifting from one side to the other. But on the day of Pentecost, he stood before the people and boldly proclaimed the truth of the Gospel.

It was the Holy Spirit who changed Thomas from an unbelieving, doubting person to a person who was strong with living faith.

It was the Holy Spirit who changed James and John from power seekers, who wanted a throne on each side of Jesus, to humble and anointed men. (See Mark 10:35–37.)

It was the power of the Holy Spirit that drove Jesus' disciples to the ends of the earth, witnessing for their Lord and Savior.

In Acts 24 Paul was given wisdom to answer the infidels in Caesar's diplomatic court. In Acts 17 he was given wisdom to answer the Stoic and Epicurean philosophers in Athens to whom everything was god. They had even erected an altar for the worship of "The Unknown God."

The strongest forces of that day, forged by the evil of the devil, could not stand before the church. The ingenious minds of perverted men could not control its power. Armies could not destroy it. Parliaments could not enforce laws against it. Legislators could not pass edicts to stop it. The world was facing a power it could not deal with: the power of Almighty God!

A Gift Unrecalled

The Lord Jesus Christ wants His church to receive the maximum of His love and of His gifts. There is no record in the Acts of the Apostles where the gifts of the Holy Spirit went out of commission. According to Peter's speech on the day of Pentecost, *"the promise* [the gift of the Holy Spirit] *is unto you, and to your children, and to all that are afar off, even as many as the Lord our God shall call"* (Acts 2:39). The call of God is the call to repentance, the call to salvation, so as long as God is saving people, He is still giving them the gifts of the Holy Spirit.

The church today is right on schedule in the divine pattern to get the gifts of the Spirit functioning in their fullness. That last unfinished chapter of Acts is still being written.

12
The Gifts in the Apostle Paul

The apostle Paul very definitely possessed and demonstrated the gifts of the Spirit in his ministry. It was Paul who brought to the church the amazing revelation of these gifts. Perhaps it was during the three years he spent in Arabia that he delved so deeply into the mysteries of God.

This was true of Howard Carter, who often said that had he not spent World War I in prison as a conscientious objector, the world would never have had the truth of the doctrine we know today as the gifts of the Holy Spirit.

Until that time the whole church accepted them only as natural gifts. They never said "gift of the word of wisdom," only "gift of wisdom." Instead of "word of knowledge," they said only "knowledge." To them, knowledge was a human accumulation of facts; therefore, a man who knew much had the gift of knowledge. It was Mr. Carter who established these as supernatural sign gifts.

It was Paul who numbered the gifts at nine, which was a sign of their divinity and perfection. Everything God does is branded with a three. Not only did Paul number the gifts, he named them as well. Then in 1 Corinthians, chapter 14, he laid down laws regulating them. He also told us how we should seek after them. The principle in truth is reaching to receive them.

Paul was not just a teacher, a preacher, or a writer; he was a possessor of great truth. Because of this, we should expect to observe the manifestation of these gifts of the Holy Spirit in his personal ministry. How could he have the doctrine of the gifts without having the fruit of them? Let's look at some of these gifts and see how they functioned for him.

The Word of Wisdom

We can see the word of wisdom functioning many times in Paul's life. In Acts 27:10, 22 he forecast the wreckage of the ship upon which he was riding, but he also forecast that no one aboard the ship would be lost. To say such things on a bright sunshiny day is one thing. To say it in a storm when the ship is falling to pieces is another thing entirely. Paul was operating the gift of the word of wisdom.

In his writings to Timothy and to the Thessalonian church, Paul related the signs of the times—events that would come to pass in the last days. In 1 Timothy 4:1 he said, *"Now the Spirit speaketh expressly, that in the latter times some shall depart from the faith, giving heed to seducing spirits, and doctrines of devils."* He said this would happen, not in his time, but in latter times. Today we are living in those latter times. Multitudes have left the faith and given heed to seducing spirits and doctrines of devils.

Just recently while I was in the St. Louis airport, a very handsome young man approached me, held out a book, and said, "May I give you this?" Immediately, I saw that it was Hinduism, a religion that originates in demon worship. This was a very fine-looking man, not special in any way; yet he was seeking to convert us to paganism in our own country. Paul told us these things would take place: that many would forsake the faith and give heed to seducing spirits and doctrines of devils.

The Discerning of Spirits

In Acts, chapter 16, we see Paul manifesting the gift of discerning of spirits:

And it came to pass, as we went to prayer, a certain damsel possessed with a spirit of divination met us, which brought her masters

> *much gain by soothsaying: the same followed Paul and us, and cried,*
> *saying, These men are the servants of the most high God, which show*
> *unto us the way of salvation.* (vv. 16–17)

But Paul looked inside her and saw an evil spirit. Finally, he turned and said to that spirit, *"I command thee in the name of Jesus Christ to come out of her. And he came out the same hour"* (v. 18).

In the same chapter, Acts 16, we read, *"And a vision appeared to Paul in the night; There stood a man of Macedonia, and prayed him, saying, Come over into Macedonia, and help us"* (v. 9). Paul discerned in his spirit that someone in Macedonia was open to the Gospel, so he immediately went there to find that open door. God gave him abundant entrance into Europe. Macedonia became Greece, so the Gospel began there and spread across to Rome.

Acts 18:19 says of Paul: *"He came to Ephesus, and left them there: but he himself entered into the synagogue, and reasoned with the Jews."* Paul knew exactly what those people needed, and he poured out God's truth to them. They were amazed that out of this man was coming forth such knowledge of them. He knew their needs, their problems, and their sorrows; but he also know what to do about it. That knowledge and discernment was pouring forth from his innermost being.

Acts 13 gives the exciting story of Elymas the Sorcerer who withstood Paul and sought to turn away the deputy from the faith. Paul said to him:

> *O full of all subtlety and all mischief, thou child of the devil, thou*
> *enemy of all righteousness, wilt thou not cease to pervert the right*
> *ways of the Lord? And now, behold, the hand of the Lord is upon thee,*
> *and thou shalt be blind, not seeing the sun for a season. And immedi-*
> *ately there fell on him a mist and a darkness; and he went about seek-*
> *ing some to lead him by the hand.* (vv. 10–11)

Through the discerning of spirits, Paul recognized that Elymas was a sorcerer, full of evil.

In Acts 19, there were vagabond Jews, who thought they could call out the name of Jesus over people and cause evil spirits to leave. They would say, *"We adjure you by Jesus whom Paul* preacheth" (v. 13). Paul knew and understood that these people were evil by the power of the Lord Jesus Christ.

The Gifts of Healing

The healing power of God flowed from this man, Paul. He demonstrated the gifts of healing in Acts 14:8–10: *"And there sat a certain man at Lystra, impotent in his feet, being a cripple from his mother's womb, who never had walked"* (v. 8). With a loud voice, Paul said to the man, *"Stand upright on thy feet"* (v. 10). Immediately, the man leaped and walked.

Paul's own testimony says, *"I will not dare to speak of any of those things which Christ hath not wrought by me, to make the Gentiles obedient, by word and deed"* (Rom. 15:18). The Gentiles, which includes all nations except the Jews, must be made obedient "by word and by deed." These must always go together. Paul goes on to explain why:

> *Through mighty signs and wonders, by the power of the Spirit of God; so that from Jerusalem, and round about unto Illyricum, I have fully preached the gospel of Christ. Yea, so have I strived to preach the gospel, not where Christ was named, lest I should build upon another man's foundation.* (vv. 19–20)

Paul said without doubt that he saw signs and wonders in his ministry. He was bold to declare that he did not come second to Peter or any of the other disciples, but that he had the gifts of the Spirit flowing through him just as they had.

The Gift of Faith

We can see the gift of faith demonstrated through Paul in Acts, chapter 16, when Paul and Silas are in prison, hands and feet bound with iron. They had been beaten with stripes and the blood was running down their, backs, itching and burning. There was no way they could help themselves. They could have cried and complained, but what did they do? The Bible says that at midnight they sang praises to God! (See Acts 16:25.)

The gift of faith began to function! That old jail began to shake; their bonds dropped off; the doors were flung open; and that Philippian jailer fell to his knees, wanting to know what he could do to be saved. That same night the jailer and his whole house were saved and baptized. That's fast movement! And it all happened because of the faith that God had planted within their hearts.

Again, we see the gift of faith through Paul in Acts, chapter 28: *"And when Paul had gathered a bundle of sticks, and laid them on the fire, there came a viper out of the heat, and fastened on his hand.... And he shook off the beast into the fire, and felt no harm"* (vv. 3, 5).

When the viper had attached itself to Paul's hand, he did not react in fear. He just shook it off into the fire. The faith flowing through him surged out and he *"felt no harm."*

The Working of Miracles

Two examples of the gift of the working of miracles through Paul can be seen in Acts 19 and 20. In Acts 19 there were miracles of healing: *"And God wrought special miracles by the hands of Paul: So that from his body were brought unto the sick handkerchiefs or aprons, and the diseases departed from them, and the evil spirits went out of them"* (vv. 11–12). Healing was an area in which Paul had full blessing. In Acts 20:7–12 Paul raised the dead:

> *And upon the first day of the week, when the disciples came together to break bread, Paul preached unto them, ready to depart on the morrow; and continued his speech until midnight. And there were many lights in the upper chamber, where they were gathered together. And there sat in a window a certain young man named Eutychus, being fallen into a deep sleep: and as Paul was long preaching, he sunk down with sleep, and fell down from the third loft, and was taken up dead. And Paul went down, and fell on him, and embracing him said, Trouble not yourselves; for his life is in him. When he therefore was come up again, and had broken bread, and eaten, and talked a long while, even till break of day, so he departed. And they brought the young man alive, and were not a little comforted.*

In this incident the word of knowledge also was demonstrated. Paul knew that life was in that young man, but he could not know it by looking at him or by feeling him. There was no physical evidence of life. Paul knew that life was in him because of the gift of the Holy Spirit.

The Gift of Prophecy

In 1 Corinthians 14:3 Paul speaks about the gift of prophecy: *"He that prophesieth speaketh unto men to edification, and exhortation, and comfort."* These are the three vital categories of blessing within the gift of prophecy. Whenever a person prophesies in church, it should always accomplish at least one of these three blessings: to edify, or build up; to exhort, or encourage; and to comfort, or bring healing to the inner man.

The apostle Paul possessed the gift of prophecy. It functioned through him to bless multitudes.

The Gift of Tongues

We know Paul possessed the gift of tongues because in 1 Corinthians 14:18 he wrote, *"I thank my God, I speak with tongues more than ye all."* He went on in the next verse to say, *"Yet in the church I had rather speak five words with my understanding, that by my voice I might teach others also, than ten thousand words in an unknown tongue."*

The gift of tongues is the elementary gift—the first gift you receive. Tongues is the open door to the other gifts, the starting place, because it is communication with God. *"He that speaketh in an unknown tongue edifieth himself"* (1 Cor. 14:4). Through tongues, you edify yourself, or build up yourself on the inside. It is your spirit communicating directly with the Father in heaven.

The Interpretation of Tongues

Paul said many things about the gift of the interpretation of tongues. One thing that seems to be neglected by some church bodies is found in 1 Corinthians 14:27: *"If any man speak in an unknown tongue, let it be by two, or at the most by three, and that by course; and let one interpret."* When one person gives forth a message in an unknown tongue, another should interpret. If the same person does both the speaking and the interpreting, he is limiting Jesus. The gift functions best when two people are involved rather than one.

Paul wrote, *"Having then gifts differing according to the grace that is given to us, whether prophecy, let us prophesy according to the proportion of faith"* (Rom. 12:6). Every gift of the Spirit functions by faith.

A Possessor of the Gifts

The apostle Paul led the way in the gifts of the Spirit. He witnessed mighty deeds and glorious deliverances. In 1 Corinthians 7:7 he wrote, *"For I would that all men were even as I myself. But every man hath his proper gift of God, one after this manner, and another after that."*

Not only did Paul teach us and present the broad scope of all these beautiful gifts, but he also allowed them to function in his own life. We have merely touched upon them. An in-depth study of Paul's writings would reveal a wealth of information as to how the gifts functioned in his life and ministry.

I thank God that Paul was not only a teacher, but also a possessor, which is how we should wish to be. We should not be satisfied with being taught about the gifts of the Holy Spirit, but should want to possess them, so that in these last days the gifts pour forth through us in a mighty way.

13
How You Can Receive the Gifts

In order to receive things from God, you must first have knowledge. God cannot bless ignorance. Matthew's gospel, chapter 4, describes Jesus' ministry: *"And Jesus went about all Galilee, teaching in their synagogues, and preaching the gospel of the kingdom, and healing all manner of sickness and all manner of disease among the people"* (v. 23). Jesus was first a teacher, then a preacher, then a healer.

Teaching is so important. Without it, there would be no depth of the Word to hold onto after salvation. If you teach a man about the Gospel, then give him the good news that he can have it, there will be something he can hold onto and the miracles will begin to flow.

In this final chapter on the gifts of the Spirit, I want to share how you personally can receive the gifts of the Holy Spirit. Definitions and identifications relating to the gifts of the Spirit are not sufficient. You must also know how you can receive these gifts in your own life.

Let me emphasize one point: If you are trying to drink water out of an empty well, you will get only dirt. If you are seeking your source of strength at a church that has no blessing in it, you will be unable to function in the gifts of the Holy Spirit. To function in the Spirit, you must go where the Spirit functions.

How can you receive the gifts of the Spirit?

Here are some of the ways:

The Gifts and Ministries of the Holy Spirit

By receiving the promise.

On the day of Pentecost, Simon Peter said, *"Repent, and be baptized every one of you in the name of Jesus Christ for the remission of sins, and ye shall receive the gift of the Holy Ghost. For the promise is unto you, and to your children, and to all that are afar off, even as many as the Lord our God shall call"* (Acts 2:38–39).

When God makes a promise, He keeps it. You can begin seeking the gifts of the Spirit because the Lord said you could have them. They are for you, for your children, and for every believer. The first way to receive the gifts of the Spirit in your life is by saying, "The promises are mine."

By divine revelation.

The apostle Paul received the gifts of the Spirit through divine revelation from God. In Galatians 1:17–18 he wrote, *"Neither went I up to Jerusalem to them which were apostles before me; but I went into Arabia, and returned again unto Damascus. Then after three years I went up to Jerusalem to see Peter, and abode with him fifteen days."* Paul went to Jerusalem to show Peter all the gifts and revelation he had received. No human being taught Paul; he was instructed by the Holy Spirit.

In Matthew 16:16 Peter said to Jesus, *"Thou art the Christ, the Son of the living God."* Jesus answered with these words: *"Blessed art thou, Simon Barjona: for flesh and blood hath not revealed it unto thee, but my Father which is in heaven"* (v. 17). Peter did not learn this from any earthly source. The Father in heaven revealed it to him.

We can receive these gifts directly by revelation from God. I have met people in many countries who received the gifts of the Spirit, having never heard one word about them from any human. God can do things sovereignly.

By the laying on of hands.

Timothy received the gifts of the Spirit through the laying on of hands. We see this in 1 Timothy 4:14: *"Neglect not the gift* [the

How You Can Receive the Gifts

gift of the Holy Spirit] *that is in thee, which was given thee by prophecy, with the laying on of the hands of the presbytery."* Strong men of God—Paul, Barnabas, and Silas—laid their hands on Timothy and instantly the gifts of the Spirit began to function in this young man's life.

By desiring them.

There are several scriptures that show that you will not receive these gifts until you intelligently seek after them. They will not become a part of your life accidentally or casually.

Paul tells us to *"covet earnestly the best gifts"* and to *"desire spiritual gifts"* (1 Cor. 12:31; 14:1). The word *"covet"* is a strong word. If you do not intensely desire these gifts and seek God with your total heart, you will never get them. The gifts of the Spirit are not delivered to complacent people. They are not rocking chair gifts; they are battlefront gifts. Spiritual power does not come easy. If you expect a great move of God in your life, you must consecrate yourself.

That desire for spiritual gifts must come from within you. It is a craving coming up out of you like liquid fire, so that you say with determination, "I will receive."

Then in 1 Corinthians 14:12, Paul said, *"Even so ye, forasmuch as ye are zealous of spiritual gifts, seek that ye may excel to the edifying of the church."* There are two words in this verse that need special emphasis: zealous and seek. We are to be zealous of spiritual gifts and seek to excel in them. To seek a fortune requires effort. You have to go out after it, not just sit in the house all day. To excel in spiritual gifts, you have to keep moving. You cannot receive the full manifestation of any gift of the Spirit by stopping to rest on a spiritual plateau.

How I Received the Gifts

Witnessing the lives and ministries of men like Howard Carter and Smith Wigglesworth stirred a desire deep within me to be a part of God's movement on the earth. As I observed these men, both publicly and privately, I experienced the kind of burning within me that the disciples must have known while walking with the Lord Jesus.

The gifts of the Spirit began to function through me as I was a missionary on the foreign field. The first gift to manifest was the discerning of spirits. I was ministering for just one night in a Full Gospel church in Java. During the service a little girl left her seat and began to writhe like a snake. The pastor and elders did not react, but within my spirit I heard God say, "That is a devil." I had never before seen anything like it—a human being so abused by the devil.

When I took the pulpit, I said to her, "Get up and sit on that pew!" Though she did not understand English and I could not speak her language, she instantly returned to her seat. As I preached the sermon, she just sat there, gazing up at me.

When I had finished my sermon, I leaned over and said, "Now come out of her!" Instantly she was delivered and the power of God hit that vast audience. Hundreds of people received salvation that night. Before I could give an invitation for them to get saved, they began streaming to the altar to give their hearts to God.

14

The Devil's Counterfeit

One thing we must guard against spiritually is the devil's counterfeiting of these supernatural gifts of the Holy Spirit. Satan is a deceiver. The Bible says he sometimes appears as *"an angel of light"*—a counterfeit angel (2 Cor. 11:14). There will even be a counterfeit Christ called the Antichrist. In all of history, anything that was of value has almost invariably had some form of counterfeit. Naturally, then, we can expect the devil to counterfeit the nine gifts of the Spirit.

Some people cannot see the real for the counterfeit, but I believe the Spirit of God within us will reveal to us whether or not something is real. No one should ever be confused about what is real and what is counterfeit. God wants us to know these things.

The Word of Wisdom

The gift of the word of God's wisdom is the ability to know and understand future events. Every great prophet of the Old and New Testaments functioned in this gift, and today there are men and women who supernaturally know things that will come to pass. We sincerely feel that we have come to that place in history when this gift is going to be tremendously increased, whether it is called the prophetic ministry or the gift of the word of wisdom.

God has always wanted to show His people the future. He sent an angel to inform Abraham in advance that He was going

259

to destroy the cities of Sodom and Gomorrah because of their terrible wickedness. God does not want to hide from us the things He is going to do.

In 1 Corinthians 12:8–10 God gives us an outline of the true gifts of the Holy Spirit: *"For to one is given by the Spirit the word of wisdom"* (v. 8).

Has the devil sought to counterfeit the word of wisdom? Yes, and not just from the beginning of the church, but from the beginning of time. These counterfeits are called witches.

A witch is a person who seeks to know from supernatural sources other than God things not known normally or naturally. His or her supernatural source is the devil. No wonder the Bible says in many places that the land should be free of witches. Why? Because they try to assume the place of God. They lead people to worship the wrong entity. You cannot worship both the living God and the devil at the same time.

Anyone who follows the satanic counterfeits of the gifts of the Spirit will never see heaven or God. We oppose these counterfeiters, not only because they are worthless, but also because they lead to destruction. If one is going to dabble in the occult to try to know the future, he will only know damnation and sorrow. He will not find that which his heart desires. He will not know truth, only deception.

The devil has no relationship with truth. Jesus said of the devil: *"There is no truth in him....For he is a liar, and the father of it"* (John 8:44). He was a liar from the beginning, and he always will be. If you believe him, you will be deceived.

Witches, soothsayers, and magicians seek to know the future and the unknown by satanic powers. God says we should not be part of these people. In 2 Corinthians 11:13 such are called *"false apostles, deceitful workers, transforming themselves into the apostles of Christ."* Verse 14 says, *"Satan himself is transformed into an angel of light."* It is no marvel then that his ministers are also transformed into false ministers of righteousness, *"whose end shall be according to their works"* (v. 15).

Above all, God wants us to live in truth. If there is a problem ahead, we need to know about it. Whether it is a problem in our ministry, our home, or our church, we need to be aware so we can deal with it. God wants us to know.

Some ministers say, "Don't talk about the devil. You are eulogizing him." Closing our eyes to Satan and his devices does not take them away. Whenever I talk about the devil, he is not eulogized. He is greatly offended, greatly hurt, and greatly defeated!

The devil does have counterfeits, and the Word of God warns us that they pose as apostles and prophets. We must be on guard against them. How can we recognize such people? You will know every man by his fruits (Matt. 12:33). You will know every person by the spirit that is within him. God will reveal these things to us through prayer and listening to His still, small voice as the Spirit speaks to us.

I must say emphatically regarding the word of wisdom that if anyone stands and offers himself as a prophet of God to tell you the future, just check one thing: Does it come to pass? If it does not, then he is to be branded for what he is: a false prophet. He should be put out of the church. The church of Jesus Christ is no place for imposters!

In our church fellowship we permit no foolishness within the body of the Lord Jesus Christ. If anyone wishes to prophesy about the future, we say, "Go ahead, but it had better come to pass!" We permit no false prophets to function in our midst. God knows what He is doing; and if someone says something that is wrong, then we have no need to hear from him again. We want to hear from the Holy Spirit. We want the gifts of the Spirit to function, but they can function only through the body of Christ—holy and pure and clean.

God's people do not need witches or soothsayers or magicians to know what God is going to do in the future. I feel very sorry for people who always want to know what is going to happen tomorrow. What is going to happen, will happen. Why should we worry? If we walk with Jesus, it is going to be good! All you have to do is to live for Him—love Him and serve Him—and everything will be good! If you are going to walk by faith, let Him hold the future. Just say, "Lord Jesus, You hold the future, so I know it will be good. I'm satisfied."

The Word of Knowledge

The second of the gifts of the Spirit that the devil would love to counterfeit is the gift of the word of God's knowledge. While the word of wisdom concerns the future, the word of knowledge deals with that which already exists. Knowledge is a fact—something that exists now, not in the future.

The word of knowledge is that gift given by God that allows a person to know something he cannot learn through his natural senses. God reveals it to his spirit. The devil, of course, would love to have people do that, too; only he uses false knowledge. The devil will "reveal" things, but his purpose is to trick you, to deceive you, to lead you into a trap.

There are people who go to palm readers and mediums seeking knowledge supernaturally. Sometimes when a person has lost something, he will consult a medium to find out where the lost article is. If you do this, I have just one thing to tell you: It will follow you home and eventually cause you grief, because you are dealing with an evil spirit.

If you go to a séance and become involved in the occult, you open yourself to satanic influence. Whenever you become involved in this type of activity—in these things that belong to Satan—it is not just a onetime deal. You are entering into a relationship that could carry you right to your grave. This is dangerous business!

You have to recognize that you have an enemy. The devil will do all in his power to rob you of the use of the spiritual gifts that you possess, because without the gifts functioning in the church, we cannot win the battle of these last days.

Once a couple had planned to fly to one of our meetings to bring their mentally afflicted son for healing. These parents later told us that, though they had not even told the boy about it, the night before they were to leave, he ran away. He was acting on knowledge that the devil had put in him. The parents had made preparations to bring the boy for deliverance from that demon within him, and the demon tried to interfere.

There are thousands of people who need to be set free, just like this boy, but the devil is keeping them in bondage. He does not want God's people to have the power and authority to set others free. But this is a glorious hour, a victory hour. We must press hard to identify the devil and his schemes to counterfeit God's great and precious gifts.

Discerning of Spirits

There is a great attempt in our country today to "get inside" people through some potentially dangerous forms of psychology and psychiatry. ESP is terribly dangerous. If you try to reach beyond the human mind to gain information supernaturally, the only force you will contact is the devil. God cannot be reached through this type of manifestation.

In our world today we have mind readers and gurus with all sorts of philosophies. We have people who are trained to discern the inner man; but all of it is a counterfeit, belonging only to the devil. It has no relationship to reality and God does not want us to take part in such things.

The mind is a very precious commodity. Be careful not to loan it to a stranger. Give it only to Jesus.

The Gift of Faith

I can assure you that the devil would love to simulate this precious gift. The gift of faith is a remarkable gift. There is no human energy exercised in this gift; it comes purely from the power of God flowing through a person.

The devil would have us to believe that the things we desire will come simply by believing for them—which is a form of witchcraft. In fact, curses come about this way, especially in places where black magic is a common practice. In Indonesia if a woman wanted to destroy her husband, she could pay a visit to the witch doctor. He would take a little doll, which represents the husband, start putting pins into it, and say incantations. The husband is supposed to get sick and die. They claim that it works—that he would die without their touching him.

If we were talking about the things of God, we would call that an instrument of faith—believing something to happen.

The Working of Miracles

Once while in Java we went to a village in which everyone, including the mayor, was a Christian. We found that it was a city of refuge. If a person was persecuted in some other village, he could go there to live in peace and security. In fact, most of the people living there were refugees who had come seeking escape from persecution.

It had all begun with a Dutch girl, who very innocently had gone to this place to preach. After a few days of listening to her preach, the witch doctor came to her and told her to leave. When she refused to go, he explained why he wanted her out of the village. He said, "I am the witch doctor here, and I was here first. It is not proper for two of us to be in the same territory."

The girl told him, "No, I'm not leaving. And I'm not into witchcraft as you are. I serve the living God who is in heaven above."

"I know nothing about that," the man answered. "I have heard you talking about miracles, and I am in charge of such things here. That is my job, so you will have to go!"

When the young lady refused, the witch doctor challenged her to a public contest with the understanding that the loser must pack up and leave. The girl agreed, not really knowing what she was getting into.

A public contest between the two was set to take place three days later. The girl did not know that the witch doctor was planning to spend those three days in fasting and prayer to the devil, which he did. She went about her usual business without much thought of what she was facing.

They met together for the contest on a platform before the whole village: the witch doctor versus the lady missionary. The witch doctor announced to the crowd that they were about to have a showdown to decide who was to stay and who was to leave. The village would belong to the strongest power.

The girl agreed, still not really knowing what the witch doctor had in mind.

He asked her, "Do you want to go first?"

"No," she answered, "you go ahead." That was a mistake.

He lay down on the wood floor and within one minute his whole body became as stiff as death. Then it gravitated, floating about ankle high. When it reached knee high, it just rested there. His eyes were closed; his body was straight as a board.

Needless to say, the girl was scared! There she was—a simple missionary girl, talking about Jesus—and here was a witch doctor, floating knee high from the ground. She thought, "Well, Lord, it looks as if I may be leaving town."

As she was standing there dumbfounded, looking at the man, she prayed, "Lord, what should I do? I came here to preach."

The Lord answered, "Get him down."

"But, Lord, how can I do that?"

"Knock him down."

"Lord, how should I knock him down?"

"Put your foot on him."

So that little woman walked over to the floating witch doctor, placed her foot on his stomach, and pushed him to the floor. Then the Lord said, "Tell that unclean spirit to come out."

She screamed, "Come out of him, you unclean spirit!"

The witch doctor went into a convulsion, then woke up. The first thing he said was, "Where am I?" He had become so full of the devil that he had no idea where he was or how he got there.

The missionary said to him, "All these people came to see who was the most powerful. Now, are you ready to receive Jesus as Lord?"

"Yes," he answered. She led him in the sinner's prayer, and he gave his heart to Jesus. Then she asked him, "Do you want the Holy Spirit?"

He said, "I want everything you have." She laid hands on him and he received the infilling of the Holy Spirit right there before that group of people.

After the meeting he said, "I don't want you to leave," so she said, "All right. Let's have our own city."

He told her, "You be the top administrator and I will be the mayor." Together they chose the rest of the organization for the city. Our party stayed there for several days, and it was one of the happiest communities I have ever seen.

That witch doctor had the power to float, but it was not God's power. It was a counterfeit, and God's power superceded it.

We see the same in Exodus, chapter 7, when Moses and Aaron stood before the Pharaoh of Egypt. Pharaoh demanded Moses to show him a miracle, so Aaron threw down his rod and it became a serpent. Immediately, Pharaoh called his sorcerers and they did the same thing. They threw down their rods, and they also became snakes, *"but Aaron's rod swallowed up their rods"* (v. 12).

There will be times of contests like this for the church. We must know what is spiritual. If we do not, the devil will defeat us. There are thousands of people in our country today who have been deceived by the devil's power. But as God's people, we must not be among those who have been deceived.

The Gifts of Healing

This may be the biggest counterfeit of all. Healing cults have existed almost from the beginning of time. Recently my wife was telling me about a cult in the Philippines that performs surgery without a knife, with just their fingers. Swarms of people from England, Canada, Australia, the United States, and Sweden were traveling to the Philippines for this "miracle healing." I knew about it when we lived there in the Philippines, but no one was coming then.

Now literally thousands of people have been deceived by it.

I know of a doctor there whose brother claimed to have experienced one of those "miracle surgeries." He claimed that his gallstones had been removed without an incision, without leaving a scar. When the doctor persuaded his brother to be examined, the X rays clearly showed that the gallstones were still there. Not only had the man been deceived about his health, he had also been cheated out of the money he had spent for his "miracle."

Some people think that when they are "healed," it is only temporary. Healing cults will say things like that. But that is only the devil. When God heals, it is permanent!

I was healed of tuberculosis by God's power. At the time nobody was praying for me. No one was in the room except my parents and me. I had a tubercular fever and was spitting up blood. The doctor said I would die that night, but God healed me. There was no "hocus-pocus" and no burning of incense.

God's healings are always clean, pure, and above reproach, undeniable. The devil's "healings" are always mystical and shrouded in a cloud.

The Gift of Prophecy

And when they [Paul and Barnabus] *had gone through the isle unto Paphos, they found a certain sorcerer, a false prophet, a Jew, whose name was Barjesus: which was with the deputy of the country, Sergius Paulus, a prudent man; who called for Barnabas and Saul, and desired to hear the word of God. But Elymas the sorcerer (for so is his name by interpretation) withstood them, seeking to turn away the deputy from the faith. Then Saul, (who also is called Paul,) filled with the Holy Ghost, set his eyes on him, and said, O full of all subtlety and all mischief, thou child of the devil, thou enemy of all righteousness, wilt thou not cease to pervert the right ways of the Lord? And now, behold, the hand of the Lord is upon thee, and thou shalt be blind, not seeing the sun for a season. And immediately there fell on him a mist and a darkness; and he went about seeking some to lead him by the hand. Then the deputy, when he saw what was done, believed, being astonished at the doctrine of the Lord.* (Acts 13:6–12)

I feel from the depths of my spirit that there are going to be people just like this man Elymas—deceivers, deceiving government leaders. Washington is full of them. There are more people in Washington practicing black magic and divination than probably any other city in America. In the city of Philadelphia there are 3,000 registered witches.

We are living in the last days, and in these last days God wants to pour out His Spirit upon all flesh. You and I are those receivers of God's power, just like the apostle Paul. We are to rebuke that which is evil and to keep our nation clean by the power of God. There is no other way for this nation to stay clean spiritually except by the power of God working through His church—and it will work today as it worked in the early church.

Speaking in Tongues

Another of these counterfeits of Satan may seem strange to us, but I believe the devil seeks to counterfeit the gift of speaking in tongues. I have seen dozens and dozens of people uttering things that could not be understood either by the other native people in the meeting or by me as a foreign visitor. They were merely stammering out words under demonic power.

Anything that God does—no matter what it is—the devil will try to counterfeit. We, as the children of the Most High God, must learn to recognize these counterfeits. We are to stand in the truth always, and to stand strong. If we do, God will give us the victory. No devil in hell—no evil, no lie, no counterfeit—can stand against us.

If we stand in truth, we also stand in power, knowing that we will win every time. God did not send us out into the world unequipped for the job. We are to invade the devil's territory, tear him to pieces, and destroy him, as well as any manifestation he has on the gifts of the Holy Spirit.

In the high mountains of Luzon in the Philippines, among very primitive people, I built a little church of metal and concrete blocks. I went there to dedicate this little church without knowing that the chief witch in the area had said she would come and close the meeting. I knew nothing about it, nor did any of the members of that congregation.

Just as I started to speak, a woman in the back stood up and began to say unintelligible words. Later the people said they had never heard anything like it and had no idea what she was saying. Since I was a foreigner, I did not know if she was speaking the native language of the people, but inside I knew something was wrong. My spirit knew it was a demonic manifestation. So I leaned over and said to her, "Shut up and sit down!" And she did!

God gave us a great meeting that night. Many people were saved. News spread the next day that the woman still was unable to speak. God had locked her jaws!

When I commanded her, in Jesus' name, to shut up and sit down, fear came upon those heathen people and they thought, "We had better serve the living God and leave this witchcraft alone."

This will happen. If we will speak the truth and resist evil, many people will be brought to God.

The devil will try to counterfeit the gifts of tongues and interpretation of tongues, so we must be on guard against his deceptions.

The Antichrist

Now let's look at a very important type of deception—the Antichrist, who will come upon the face of the earth and deceive the world through counterfeit gifts of the Spirit.

Revelation 13:15 says that the False Prophet will have power to give life unto the image of the Beast (the Antichrist). This same chapter speaks of three spirits who came out of the river. One of them entered into the dragon, that is, the devil.

There are going to be *three demonic deceptions* in the last days:

First, there will be a *moral deception*. Satan's deception from the Garden of Eden until now has never changed; it is a moral deception. Look how he deceived Eve and how he tried to deceive Jesus. He will be doing the same thing in these last days. He has not learned one new thing in these 6,000 years. He is still doing the same thing in the same way; there have been no alterations, no changes.

Second, there will be a *political deception*. I assure you that in the near future there will be politicians on the world scene who will speak words so amazing that the world will follow them. They will have promises so astounding that the whole world will say, "Let's follow after this person." This is the spirit of anti-christ.

Third, there will be a *religious deception*. This will be the False Prophet, which is the religious spirit.

The devil will deceive by miracles. Revelation 13:14 states that *"he deceiveth them that dwell on the earth by the means of those miracles which he had power to do in the sight of the beast."* These miracles will be performed in the sight of the man who is the Antichrist, just as the Egyptian sorcerers had the power to do false miracles in the eyes of Pharaoh. But Moses put an end to all of that. What a sinner sees and what God's servant sees are two entirely different things. They may believe a lie, but we will not.

The devil will deceive people, *"saying to them that dwell on the earth, that they should make an image to the beast, which had the wound by a sword, and did live"* (v. 14). Here we see the healing of a deadly wound, so that the people believe that he is God. There are many false healers making the rounds today, deceiving many.

> *I beheld another beast coming up out of the earth; and he had two horns like a lamb* [this is the False Prophet], *and he spake as a dragon. And he exerciseth all the power of the first beast before him* [the Antichrist], *and causeth the earth and them which dwell therein to worship the first beast, whose deadly wound was healed.*
>
> (Rev. 13:11–12)

So we find that this beast could do things that to the people were completely supernatural. We know these things are not honest and true; they are counterfeit. But the Bible says the whole world will go after it. Jesus said, *"I am come in my Father's name, and ye receive me not: if another shall come in his own name, him ye will receive"* (John 5:43).

We live in a strange world today. There are people who will pass up the truth in order to grab a lie. This world would love to have the benefit and blessing of healing without having to get right with God. Then they could go on living in sin and still get their miracle free of charge. But that is not how it works. Jesus told the man who had been healed at the Pool of Bethesda, *"Behold, thou art made whole: sin no more, lest a worse thing come unto thee"* (John 5:14).

Revelation 13:13 says, *"And he doeth great wonders, so that he maketh fire come down from heaven on the earth in the sight of men."* Notice that this deception is done in the sight of men. It is a magician's trick, a counterfeit.

The Bible tells us that when the Antichrist comes, it will be through a great system of deception; so it is obvious that the way before him will already be prepared. When he comes, it will be easy because the people will already be conditioned for him.

Today our world is conditioned for a lie. Almost every television program you see shows a superman. The Antichrist will be that superman, and this gullible world will say, "Who is like him? We must all follow him."

The climax of it all will be the Antichrist, in whom a counterfeit of all nine gifts will be manifested. Those who have refused the gifts from us will accept the counterfeit gifts from him. Isn't that sorrowful? Tens of thousands of people who do not accept healing from the stripes of the Lord Jesus Christ will accept it from spiritism, or from some pseudo-science that has no blood sacrifice attached to it.

I urge you to commit yourself to stand against the counterfeits that Satan will bring into the world. Say, "God, I am against these counterfeits of Satan, and I am going to fight them. I will recognize them when they rise up, expose them for what they are, and resist them, in Jesus' name. I will be on Jesus' side every time."

Part II
Ministries of the Holy Spirit

Introduction

In addition to the nine separate and distinct gifts of the Holy Spirit, there are nine offices of ministry that were given to the church after the resurrection of the Lord Jesus Christ. We could call them "resurrection gifts," because they were given to the body of Christ after the Resurrection and will belong to us until the Lord Jesus returns for His church. In the book of Ephesians, chapter 4, we read about these nine ministry gifts.

> But unto every one of us is given grace [that is, our salvation] according to the measure of the gift of Christ.　　(Eph. 4:7)

We are given the gift of God according to the measure of the gift of Christ. Christ freely and abundantly gave His total life, reserving nothing; so we receive, in like manner, the gifts of God—in fullness and total capacity. God is not stingy with His giving. He gives abundantly, so we should receive abundantly.

> Wherefore he saith, When he [Christ] ascended up on high, he led captivity captive, and gave gifts unto men.　　(Eph. 4:8)

The Lord Jesus Christ, through the instrument of the Holy Spirit, gives two types of gifts:
1. The gifts of the Holy Spirit—the nine gifts of the Spirit.
2. Men and women as gifts to the body.
These "gifts to the body" are listed in verse 11: "And he gave some, apostles; and some, prophets; and some, evangelists; and some, pastors and teachers."

The Gifts and Ministries of the Holy Spirit

In 1 Corinthians 12:28 we find two other groups—*"helps"* and *"governments"*—and in 1 Timothy 3 are mentioned the offices of bishop, or elder, and deacon.

We will examine each of these nine ministries further in our study, but first let's consider the ninefold purpose of these ministries.

15
The Ninefold Purpose of Ministry Gifts

God never gives anything without a purpose. In Ephesians 4:12–16 after listing the five major ministry gifts to the body of Christ, the apostle Paul states the ninefold purpose of these ministries to the church:

> *For the perfecting of the saints, for the work of the ministry, for the edifying of the body of Christ: till we all come in the unity of the faith, and of the knowledge of the Son of God, unto a perfect man, unto the measure of the stature of the fulness of Christ: that we henceforth be no more children, tossed to and fro, and carried about with every wind of doctrine, by the sleight of men, and cunning craftiness, whereby they lie in wait to deceive; but speaking the truth in love, may grow up into him in all things, which is the head, even Christ: from whom the whole body fitly joined together and compacted by that which every joint supplieth, according to the effectual working in the measure of every part, maketh increase of the body unto the edifying of itself in love.*

1. For the perfecting of the saints.

When God calls an apostle, a prophet, an evangelist, a pastor, or a teacher, it is for one purpose: the perfecting of the saints. This person is to give himself. No gift that God gives is ever for self. When we say, "Lord, bless me," God can't hear that prayer. He wants us to bless others. When He gives us something, it is to share with someone else.

A little boy handed his lunch of fish and bread to the Lord Jesus and said, "This is all I have," then he stood back to see what would happen. The Lord Jesus began to break it and hand it to His disciples not for them to eat or to shove into their pockets for tomorrow's lunch, but for them to pass out to others.

When Jesus handed out the bread and fish to His disciples, it was for one purpose: to meet people's needs. It is not God's purpose just to enrich us, but to make us into people who can enrich others. If we fail to share our gifts with others, these gifts will soon fade away.

Christianity is a unique institution. If we take it and put it in a golden box, it will die. Christianity does not fit in a box. It was made for only one purpose: to be given to the world—to all those on the highways and byways, the fugitives, the outcasts, both the down-and-outers and the up-and-outers. If you take the Gospel of Christ and keep it inside the four walls of a church, it will perish. It was made to be shared—to be spread to all those people outside the church who have never met the Lord Jesus. And so it is with these ministries: they were created for action. If you are given one of these ministries, it is to be used, first of all, to perfect the saints.

2. For the work of the ministry.

The ministry of the Lord Jesus Christ requires work. There is much work to be done—apostolic, prophetic, evangelistic, pastoral, and teaching work of the ministry. Laborers are needed in the fields to bring in the harvest.

3. For the edifying of the body of Christ.

These ministry gifts are for the edifying, or building up, of the body of Christ. None of them have to do with inward and selfish motives. Each has to do with the life of Jesus pouring out of those who possess them—giving of ourselves, blessing others, and helping others. The whole structure of Christianity is built upon the concept of blessing others. That is what Jesus and the salvation message are all about.

4. Till we all come in the unity of the faith...

It hurts to see Christians divided one against the other, denomination against denomination. If all the churches in America were to suddenly start working together, the devil would have to pack up and leave this country! But as long as we are divided and fighting against each other, he has the advantage over us. He will lose that advantage when we all come into the unity of the faith.

5. ...And of the knowledge of the Son of God...

It is easy to have knowledge about so many things except Jesus. We are to come into a true knowledge of the Son of God—who He is, what He is, what He has done, and what He can do. What a tremendous thing it will be when all of us really and truly know the totality of what Jesus Christ can do for us. He is not a has-been God; He is the living God. Anything He has ever done, He can still do! Anything He *can* do, He *will* do!

6. ...Unto a perfect man...

God is shooting for high stakes. He is not looking for imperfection; He is not looking for defeat. He intends to have these ministries and gifts in the body of Christ until we become a perfect man!

7. ...Unto the measure of the stature of the fulness of Christ...

What a magnificent thing! We are going to keep these ministries active until we bring the total body *"unto the measure of the stature of the fulness of Christ."* Look at Christ standing tall—with faith, with no fear of any kind—before demons, demoniacs, and raging storms. It didn't matter! There was no fear! We are to bring our people up to that same measure—as tall and strong and confident as Jesus Christ. That is our goal.

6. ...That we henceforth be no more children...

It amazes me sometimes how a person can be a Christian for years and still act like they are about three months old, screaming about everything that doesn't suit them. God says that henceforth we are to *"be no more children, tossed to and fro, and carried about with every wind of doctrine, by the sleight of men."* Some people will believe anything they hear, but we are to stick to the great principles of divine truth in the Word of God. This is one of the functions of the ministry gifts: to instruct us and to keep us from being led astray into false doctrines by deceitful men.

9. ...But speaking the truth in love...

Now to me it is a great commission to speak the truth in love. We are to speak God's truth not in anger, but only in love. Why? That all of us might grow up in Christ:

> *Speaking the truth in love, [you] may grow up into him in all things, which is the head, even Christ: from whom the whole body fitly joined together and compacted by that which every joint supplieth, according to the effectual working in the measure of every part, maketh increase of the body unto the edifying of itself in love.*

The Lord Jesus Christ is the Head; and from Him, the whole body is fitly joined together. You are what you are—and what you are going to be—because Christ has joined you there. Don't worry about what you will be. He will get you there; He never fails.

We are fitly joined together as a body by Him; and we are compacted together in strength, so that every joint—each of us—is a part of the body.

This is the ninefold purpose of the ministry gifts that are given unto the body of the Lord Jesus Christ. Now we will view each gift individually in the light of God's Word.

16
The Fivefold Ministry Gifts

And he gave some, apostles; and some, prophets; and some, evangelists; and some, pastors and teachers; for the perfecting of the saints, for the work of the ministry, for the edifying of the body of Christ.
–Ephesians 4:11

The Office of Apostle

The first position of church leadership we will give attention to is the office of apostle. There are those who say there are no more apostles in the world—that all the apostles died out with the original Twelve—but as we will see, apostleship was not confined to the original twelve disciples. There are at least twenty-four apostles mentioned in the New Testament alone, and I believe there are apostles in the church today. As long as there is a church, there will be apostles.

I know men today with apostolic ministries—men around the world who are doing the work of an apostle at this very moment—and I believe there will be many more. In these last days the greatest ministries are going to become tremendously accelerated, along with the operation and functions of the Holy Spirit.

The office of apostle is the foremost ministry in the church of the Lord Jesus Christ. An apostle is not appointed by men. The Bible says the Holy Spirit is the One who establishes these ministries in the church.

Let's look at the word *apostle*. There are several translations in the New Testament of the Greek word referring to the apostles.

The Gifts and Ministries of the Holy Spirit

One of these translations is *apostolos,* meaning "a delegate; one sent with full power of attorney to act for another." An apostle is a divine delegate—one who has come to the people of the world, representing the Trinity in heaven. The apostle does not act on his own behalf; he is anointed by the Holy Spirit to act on behalf of the body of Christ, the church of the Lord Jesus Christ. In other words, an apostle is one delegated with the power of attorney to act on behalf of the Lord Jesus Christ, sent by the power of the Holy Spirit to you.

This word *apostolos* appears many times in the New Testament. It is translated *messenger* twice:

> *Whether any do inquire of Titus, he is my partner and fellowhelper concerning you: or our brethren be inquired of, they are the messengers of the churches, and the glory of Christ.* (2 Cor. 8:23)

> *Yet I supposed it necessary to send to you Epaphroditus, my brother, and companion in labour, and fellowsoldier, but your messenger.*
> (Phil. 2:25)

Seventy-eight times the word *apostle* means "sent one." In John 13:16 Jesus said, *"Verily, verily, I say unto you, The servant is not greater than his lord; neither he that is sent greater than he that sent him."* When an apostle goes forth, he is not greater than the One who sent him; he is a representative of the One who sent him. In other words, an apostle is one with delegated authority. He does not act on his own and do as he pleases; he is one sent forth from God with a message from God for the people. Now, that is a humbling situation.

The position of apostle, as the very word implies, means a person who is sent forth to do a work for God. Such a person is not greater than his Lord, not greater than the One who sent him. The Lord Jesus Christ is always the Great One.

When an apostle comes into our midst, he is a gift of the Holy Spirit to us as a person. He did not become an apostle by studying or working hard; apostleship does not come that way. He was made an apostle by God. Apostles are born through the power of the Holy Spirit.

The apostle is different from the other four offices in that he has the ability to perform those other functions. This is what makes an apostle and why the Bible always lists the apostle first. Some people think the prophet should be first, but the apostle is above the prophet. Any person—man or woman—with an apostolic calling has the ability, the authority, and the anointing to raise up a church without any outside help. Paul had this amazing ability. He could enter a town, walk into the marketplace, and have a church formed before nightfall. He could stir up the devil and divide a city within only a few hours. Not only could he raise up a church—establish it and found it—but he also had the power and ability to remain there as pastor. He could teach the people in that church, then start a school and send out workers to other places.

The apostle is a combination of the other four church ministries. He can be whatever is needed—pastor, evangelist, teacher, or prophet. In addition, the apostle can set church government in order. He can establish deacon boards and elderships, develop the ministry of helps within a church body, and place governments in a church so the body will function properly.

People today seem so reluctant to recognize the ministry of an apostle. We have no problem with the offices of pastor and evangelist, but we are almost afraid to call a man an apostle. We fear that pride could enter in and cause that person to be lifted up. But if a person is truly an apostle, he will never be prideful. When Moses' face shown with the glory of God, he was the last to realize it. A person with the true power of God oftentimes hardly recognizes it himself.

As long as we realize these gifts and ministerial abilities as spiritual qualities that God has placed within us, then there is no need for pride. If it is a gift of God, what do we have to be proud of? We did nothing to earn it; it was a gift from God.

If a minister fills all five offices of ministry to the body of Christ, then he is an apostle.

The Gifts and Ministries of the Holy Spirit

New Testament Apostles

As mentioned above, there are at least twenty-four apostles listed in the New Testament. Let's examine some of them. You may be surprised at the first one: **the Lord Jesus Christ**. Hebrews 3:1 says,

> *Wherefore, holy brethren, partakers of the heavenly calling, consider the Apostle and High Priest of our profession, Christ Jesus.*

Heaven sent Jesus: *"God so loved the world, that he gave* [sent, delegated] *his only begotten Son* [the Lord Jesus Christ]*"* (John 3:16).

It is not difficult to understand that the Lord Jesus Christ was an apostle. The office of apostle involves the total ministry of God, and Christ had a total ministry. He was perhaps the only full-fledged, complete apostle the world has ever known—the total embodiment of what it means to be a "sent one"—delegated, as He often said, to do what He was told to do.

The apostle Paul. In Galatians 1:1 we read,

> *Paul, an apostle, (not of men, neither by man, but by Jesus Christ, and God the Father, who raised him from the dead).*

Here Paul is defining apostleship and his relationship with the body, which you can either accept or reject. If Paul was appointed to this job by the Holy Spirit, he is speaking by the anointing of the Holy Spirit and what he says must be totally true. He is saying, "I am Paul, an apostle."

If a person has a ministry ability, he should not hide it. It is nothing to be ashamed of. Paul was not hesitant at all about speaking of his relationship with God and of his calling by God. He says boldly, "I am *'an apostle (not of men, neither by man, but by Jesus Christ, and God the Father, who raised him from the dead).'*"

Then a little further in Galatians we read what Paul wrote about Peter: *"For he that wrought effectually in Peter to the apostleship of the circumcision, the same was mighty in me toward the Gentiles"*

(Gal. 2:8). Paul was showing how Peter had become an apostle to a certain group, the circumcision (the Jews).

I have seen this demonstrated many times. Great men of God had tremendously effective ministries in one area or to one group of people, but they failed when attempting to minister in other places or to other groups. An apostle of God has an ability and a ministry, but he must be directed where God wants him. Not only does God have the right to make you something, He also has the right to tell you where to function. And if you think it will work wherever you please, just try it!

The First Twelve. Matthew 10:2–4 lists the first twelve apostles who walked with Jesus:

> *Now the names of the twelve apostles are these; The first, Simon, who is called Peter, and Andrew his brother; James the son of Zebedee, and John his brother; Philip, and Bartholomew; Thomas, and Matthew the publican; James the son of Alphaeus, and Lebbaeus, whose surname was Thaddaeus; Simon the Canaanite, and Judas Iscariot, who also betrayed him.*

Jesus chose these men, set them aside, and anointed them— that they might be "sent ones," the cornerstones of the church. These men were "super persons." Almost all of them died a martyr's death, giving their blood for the church.

Matthias. After Judas betrayed the Lord Jesus and killed himself, the remaining eleven decided to choose another to take his place. We read in Acts 1:26:

> *And they gave forth their lots; and the lot fell upon Matthias; and he was numbered with the eleven apostles.*

Barnabas. In 1 Corinthians 9:5–6 we read,

> *Have we not power to lead about a sister, a wife, as well as other apostles, and as the brethren of the Lord, and Cephas? Or I only and Barnabas, have not we power to forbear working?*

Here Paul specifically stated that Barnabas bore all the marks of apostleship, that he possessed all the abilities and ministries of apostleship. As far as Paul could determine, Barnabas was one of God's "sent ones."

Then there are some names that we know very little about: **Andronicus and Junia.** In Romans 16:7 Paul wrote,

Salute Andronicus and Junia, my kinsmen, and my fellowprisoners, who are of note among the apostles, who also were in Christ before me.

Paul was not the first person in his family to find Christ. He may have been fighting against his own family, even putting some of them in jail. He said here that his own kinsmen—Andronicus and Junia—were in Christ before he was, and that they were of note among the apostles.

Apollos. First Corinthians 4:6, 9 says,

And these things, brethren, I have in a figure transferred to myself and to Apollos for your sakes; that ye might learn in us not to think of men above that which is written....For I think that God hath set forth us the apostles last.

Paul clearly stated here that Apollos was an apostle.
James, the Lord's brother. Galatians 1:19 says,

But other of the apostles saw I none, save James the Lord's brother.

James 1:1 reads,

James, a servant of God and of the Lord Jesus Christ, to the twelve tribes which are scattered abroad, greeting.

Silas and Timothy. In 1 Thessalonians 1:1 Paul began his letter,

Paul, and Silvanus [Silas], *and Timotheus* [Timothy], *unto the church of the Thessalonians.*

In 1 Thessalonians 2:6 he wrote,

Nor of men sought we glory, neither of you, nor yet of others, when we might have been burdensome, as the apostles of Christ.

We see here that Paul referred to Silas and Timothy as apostles of the Lord Jesus Christ.

Titus. In 2 Corinthians 8:23 we read,

Whether any do inquire of Titus, he is my partner and fellowhelper concerning you: or our brethren be inquired of, they are the messengers ["apostolos"] of the churches, and the glory of Christ.

Here we see that Titus was an apostle, or a "sent one."

Epaphroditus. Philippians 2:25 says,

Yet I supposed it necessary to send to you Epaphroditus, my brother, and companion in labour, and fellowsoldier, but your messenger ["apostolos"], and he that ministered to my wants.

So we find in the New Testament that there were not just twelve apostles, nor did this office of ministry cease to exist when those twelve were gone from the earth.

The seventy that Jesus sent out were also men with an apostolic ministry. They were a follow-up group, who ministered the same as the original twelve. (See Luke 10:1.)

Ministry of an Apostle

Apostleship is a ministry for the church as long as the church is upon the face of this earth. They are the divine leaders God has commissioned to lead His church.

An apostle is one who can pioneer, who can construct and begin a work with no problem. But not only can he conceive and bring into being a body of believers, he can remain behind to found that church and put it on a solid rock of truth. He can organize it, set it in order, and teach it with great fluency and accuracy.

A Price to Pay

All those who have a place of leadership in Christ Jesus will suffer persecution. The bigger the job, the dirtier the devil wants to get you. But don't let that deter you. If you want leadership, reach for it. In Jesus' name, be what God wants you to be!

As a young man, I decided strongly that I would never permit the joy that had grown in my heart to be dependent on other people's opinions. If one person says I am great while another says I am nothing, neither of them affect me. Other people's opinions are no basis for our security; our security is in Jesus Christ. We are what we are by the power of God—and no other way.

At one time in my life, I was envious of people who were wealthy or important, but no more. I have learned that the person at the top may not always have it so good. Again I quote the apostle Paul in 1 Corinthians 4:9: *"For I think that God hath set forth us the apostles last, as it were appointed to death: for we are made a spectacle unto the world, and to angels, and to men."*

If you are seeking greatness in God, you may not achieve greatness with humans. You may have to endure many unpleasant things.

The Office of Prophet

As we have already seen, the office of apostle is the highest ministry of the church. The second ministerial office is that of the prophet. The office of prophet cannot be filled through a democratic election. A prophet is called of God and set apart by God. The person God picks to fill this office is not chosen on the basis of personality, education, or public standing. When God appoints a prophet in the land, the people there have nothing to do with it.

Old Testament Prophets

In the Old Testament, the position of a prophet was one of divine guide. He was sent by God to lead the people of Israel. The prophet at that time was also called a seer:

Beforetime in Israel, when a man went to inquire of God, thus he spake, Come, and let us go to the seer: for he that is now called a Prophet was beforetime called a Seer. (1 Sam. 9:9)

The Hebrew word *ra'ah*—to see or to perceive—tells us what the ministry of the prophet is all about. Also, the word *chozeh*—beholder of visions—is used as that of a seer or a prophet.

The Bible lists seventy-eight prophets and prophetesses. That would be sufficient for us to exhaust any area of knowledge relative to the prophets, if we were to study them in an in-depth way from Genesis to Revelation.

Adam

It is usually agreed that Adam was the first prophet.

And out of the ground the LORD *God formed every beast of the field, and every fowl of the air; and brought them unto Adam to see what he would call them: and whatsoever Adam called every living creature, that was the name thereof.* (Gen. 2:19)

Adam moved in a spiritual sphere at that moment. He had some foreknowledge of what each animal would be like, so he named them according to the relationship they had with the rest of creation. This was a prophetic definition.

Enoch

A very remarkable prophet of the Old Testament is Enoch. Genesis 5:21 says, *"And Enoch lived sixty and five years, and begat Methuselah."* The word *Methuselah* means "at his death the sending forth of waters."* Enoch was caught up with God when he was 365 years old, but his son Methuselah lived 969 years. Comparing the day Methuselah was born with the date of the Great Flood, you will discover that he died the year of the Flood.

Marked Reference Bible, Edited by J. Gilchrist Lawson, Zondervan Publishing House, Grand Rapids, Michigan.

I believe he died the hour that the Flood began since his name means "at his death the sending forth of waters."

More of Enoch's prophecy is found in the book of Jude, verses 14–15:

And Enoch also, the seventh from Adam, prophesied of these, saying, Behold, the Lord cometh with ten thousands of his saints, to execute judgment upon all, and to convince all that are ungodly among them of all their ungodly deeds which they have ungodly committed, and of all their hard speeches which ungodly sinners have spoken against him.

This has not yet come to pass, so Enoch not only prophesied relative to his own son and the judgment that would come at his death 969 years later, but he said that God (in Jesus Christ) would one day come with ten thousand of his saints. Enoch was only the seventh man from Adam, yet imagine his knowing that Jesus was going to come back with many thousands of His saints. What a tremendous source of strength for seeing the future and predicting that which his mind had no capacity to know! This had to be a prophetic vision.

So prophets are not new and they are dramatic in their foretelling of what will come to pass. They have no earthly means of knowing what they foretell. Enoch made no calculations by the moon or stars or with the soothsayers. Only God told him. And he was such a godly man that he did not even see death, but was translated to heaven miraculously when he was 365 years old.

Noah

Another prophet of this magnitude is Noah. Genesis 6:8–9 says, *"But Noah found grace in the eyes of the LORD. These are the generations of Noah: Noah was a just man and perfect in his generations, and Noah walked with God."*

For over a hundred years Noah said there would be a flood of water that would cover the earth. He was a walking prophet, but he had to wait over a hundred years before his prophecy came to pass.

If you were a prophet or prophetess, a hundred years would be a long time to hang around with your prophecy not coming true. There would be plenty of people laughing at you and mocking you, saying it was all nonsense. It would be very discouraging.

But Noah walked with God. He believed what God had said for over a hundred years. (Some say it might have been as long as 120 years.) Then one day the clouds began to frown, the lightning began to flash, the thunder rolled, and the Flood came upon the face of the earth. This prophet of God said it would happen, and it did come to pass. That is what is meant by biblical prophet.

Anything that a true prophet foretells will come to pass because the Holy Spirit, who told it to him, cannot lie. The Bible says that God cannot lie. *"God is not a man, that he should lie; neither the son of man, that he should repent: hath he said, and shall he not do it? or hath he spoken, and shall he not make it good?"* (Num. 23:19). So when one of God's prophets—a person who is anointed of God—speaks, it will come to pass.

Abraham

Abraham was another great prophet of God. In Genesis 24:6-7 we read about the time Abraham sent his servant to his home country to find a wife for his son Isaac:

> *And Abraham said unto him* [the servant], *Beware thou that thou bring not my son thither again. The* LORD *God of heaven, which took me from my father's house, and from the land of my kindred, and which spake unto me, and that sware unto me, saying, Unto thy seed will I give this land; he shall send his angel before thee, and thou shalt take a wife unto my son from thence.*

Abraham said of God, "He shall do it." Now that is prophesying. He spoke to his servant and said, "Go back to my father's people—because God wants to keep this bloodstream pure—and there you will find a young woman who will be the bride for my son. She will be there and you will bring her back."

That is prophesying. Then when the beautiful young girl was brought back, Isaac was out in the field looking for her, which shows that he had faith in the prophecy made by his father. Isaac knew that what Abraham had prophesied would most certainly come to pass.

Jacob

Then there is Jacob. Genesis 49:1 says, *"Jacob called unto his sons, and said, Gather yourselves together, that I may tell you that which shall befall you in the last days."* He continued then to tell them what kind of tribes they would head and what kind of lives they would lead. They are living almost that same disposition this very day.

Jacob told his sons that they would leave the land they were in and possess the land that belonged to them. He also told them just what kind of people they would be one to the other. Jacob was most definitely a prophet.

Joseph

Of Joseph, Genesis 41:15–16 says,

And Pharaoh said unto Joseph, I have dreamed a dream, and there is none that can interpret it: and I have heard say of thee, that thou canst understand a dream to interpret it. And Joseph answered Pharaoh, saying, It is not in me: God shall give Pharaoh an answer of peace.

This dream was God's way of telling Pharaoh what He was about to do—that there would be seven years of plenty, followed by seven years of famine; and that if they did not prepare, all of them would die. And it came to pass just as Joseph had said it would.

Moses

Moses, we discover, wrote 475 verses of prophecy, which was quite a bit of prophesying. In Exodus 11:4–5 Moses said,

Thus saith the LORD, About midnight will I go out into the midst of Egypt: and all the firstborn in the land of Egypt shall die, from the firstborn of Pharaoh that sitteth upon his throne, even unto the first-born of the maidservant that is behind the mill; and all the firstborn of beasts.

It took courage for Moses to make a statement like that. Not only did he foretell what would happen, he even gave the exact hour it would take place. If there had been no dead first-born children the next morning, Moses would have been a false prophet.

And there shall be a great cry throughout all the land of Egypt, such as there was none like it, nor shall be like it any more. But against any of the children of Israel shall not a dog move his tongue, against man or beast: that ye may know how that the LORD doth put a difference between the Egyptians and Israel. And all these thy servants shall come down unto me, and bow down themselves unto me, saying, Get thee out, and all the people that follow thee: and after that I will go out. And he went out from Pharaoh in a great anger.

(Exod. 11:6–8)

Moses was not a superman; he was just like you and me. He was a man, yielded to God and willing for those words to flow out of his mouth.

In Exodus 12:29–51 all this was completely, gloriously, mightily, and wonderfully fulfilled; so we would have to say that one of the greatest prophets of all times was this man called Moses.

Elijah

Elijah was well known in his day as a prophet of God. He was a seer; he saw the future and foretold what would come to pass before it happened.

In 1 Kings 17:1, Elijah had said to Ahab, *"As the LORD God of Israel liveth, before whom I stand, there shall not be dew nor rain these years, but according to my word."* In other words, Elijah was saying, "It will not rain unless I tell it to."

How would you like to make a statement today saying it would not rain again until you told it to?

In 1 Kings 18:41 we read, *"Elijah said unto Ahab, Get thee up, eat and drink; for there is a sound of abundance of rain."* There had been no rain for over three years, but Elijah heard the sound of rain. There was no rain in the sky. Where was that sound? It was in Elijah's spirit. Verse 45 says, *"And it came to pass in the mean while, that the heaven was black with clouds and wind, and there was a great rain."*

Isaiah

In his writings Isaiah reveals one of the greatest prophecies ever to come through the heart and lips of a human being: *"Therefore the Lord himself shall give you a sign; Behold, a virgin shall conceive, and bear a son, and shall call his name Immanuel"* (Isa. 7:14).

Further in his writings, Isaiah tells how this One would come and die:

He is despised and rejected of men; a man of sorrows, and acquainted with grief: and we hid as it were our faces from him; he was despised, and we esteemed him not. Surely he hath borne our griefs, and carried our sorrows: yet we did esteem him stricken, smitten of God, and afflicted. But he was wounded for our transgressions, he was bruised for our iniquities: the chastisement of our peace was upon him; and with his stripes we are healed. All we like sheep have gone astray; we have turned every one to his own way; and the LORD hath laid on him the iniquity of us all. He was oppressed, and he was afflicted, yet he opened not his mouth: he is brought as a lamb to the slaughter, and as a sheep before her shearers is dumb, so he openeth not his mouth. He was taken from prison and from judgment: and who shall declare his generation? for he was cut off out of the land of the living: for the transgression of my people was he stricken. And he made his grave with the wicked, and with the rich in his death; because he had done no violence, neither was any deceit in his mouth. Yet it pleased the LORD to bruise him; he hath put him to grief: when thou shalt make his soul an offering for sin, he shall see his seed, he shall prolong his days, and the pleasure of the LORD shall prosper in his hand. He shall see of the travail of his soul, and shall be satisfied: by his knowledge

shall my righteous servant justify many; for he shall bear their iniqui-
ties. Therefore will I divide him a portion with the great, and he shall
divide the spoil with the strong; because he hath poured out his soul
unto death: and he was numbered with the transgressors; and he bare
the sin of many, and made intercession for the transgressors.

(Isa. 53:3–12)

The prophet Isaiah was telling of the ministry and sacrifice of Jesus 700 years before He was born, and every word was perfectly fulfilled.

David

Although we tend to think of David as a shepherd boy, a warrior, a poet, or a king, he is called a prophet in the New Testament. (See Acts 1:16.) David wrote 385 verses of prophecy—385 verses related to the future.

In Psalm 22:18 we read, *"They part my garments among them, and cast lots upon my vesture."* Imagine David's seeing Calvary and knowing what was going to take place there—how at Calvary they would divide Christ's raiment and gamble over it with lots. Imagine his seeing this scene in his spirit and knowing what was going to come to pass so far in the future.

Jeremiah

The last of the individual prophets we will consider is the great prophet, Jeremiah. In his book he spoke 985 verses of prophecy, beautifully foretelling future events—some of which were not good news. He foretold the Babylonian captivity of Judah, the things that would happen to them while in Babylon, and how a remnant would return one day. He told their whole story before it came to pass. His people were so angry with him that they threw him into a well to die. (Before you start praying to receive the ministry of a prophet, perhaps you should consider what the cost might be. You may not be cast into a well like Jeremiah was, but there are many other ways to be persecuted.)

The Gifts and Ministries of the Holy Spirit

One of the prophecies Jeremiah wrote is found in chapter 8, verse 11, *"For they have healed the hurt of the daughter of my people slightly, saying, Peace, peace; when there is no peace."* This prophecy is fulfilled in 1 Thessalonians 5:3 relative to the second coming of our Lord and Savior Jesus Christ.

Most of Jeremiah's prophecies were related to the people of Israel because of their forsaking God, turning away from Him, backsliding, and going into bondage. It came to pass just as he had spoken.

From Jeremiah to Malachi, there are fifteen prophets who recorded their prophecies, and the things they wrote came to pass. That is significant indeed.

Prophets in Groups

In this study relative to the prophets, we have considered them in the singular. Now we will deal with them, not as individuals, but in groups, beginning with the seventy elders of Israel.

The Seventy

> *And the LORD came down in a cloud, and spake unto him* [Moses], *and took of the spirit that was upon him, and gave it unto the seventy elders [the men around Moses who supported him]: and it came to pass, that, when the spirit rested upon them, they prophesied, and did not cease.* (Num. 11:25)

God took the great prophet Moses and through him—possibly through the laying on of hands—commissioned seventy others to become prophets.

A Company of Prophets

> *After that thou shalt come to the hill of God, where is the garrison of the Philistines: and it shall come to pass, when thou art come thither to the city, that thou shalt meet a company of prophets coming down from the high place with a psaltery, and a tabret, and a pipe, and a*

harp, before them; and they [a whole company] *shall prophesy: and the spirit of the LORD will come upon thee, and thou shalt prophesy with them, and shalt be turned into another man. And let it be, when these signs are come unto thee,…for God is with thee. And thou shalt go down before me to Gilgal; and, behold, I will come down unto thee, to offer burnt offerings, and to sacrifice sacrifices of peace offerings: seven days shalt thou tarry, till I come to thee, and show thee what thou shalt do. And it was so, that when he* [Saul] *had turned his back to go from Samuel, God gave him another heart: and all those signs came to pass that day. And when they came thither to the hill, behold, a company of prophets met him; and the spirit of God came upon him, and he prophesied among them.* (1 Sam. 10:5-10)

Here we find a company of men who prophesied the future as a group. They spoke to this young man who was to be the king of the land and told what would happen before it came to pass—and it happened just that way.

Sons of the Prophets

And Elijah said unto Elisha, Tarry here, I pray thee; for the LORD hath sent me to Bethel. And Elisha said unto him, As the LORD liveth, and as thy soul liveth, I will not leave thee. So they went down to Bethel. And the sons of the prophets that were at Bethel came forth to Elisha. (2 Kings 2:2-3)

This was a group called the *"sons of the prophets."* I suppose they had left their work (whatever it might have been) and had come to Bethel to a school that tutored in prophesying.

New Testament Writing Prophets

There were four New Testament writing prophets: Peter, Paul, James, and John.

Peter

On the day of Pentecost Peter preached to the people that they were seeing the fulfillment of that which was spoken by the prophet Joel (Acts 2:16). He also wrote many things relative to the signs and times of the coming of the Lord Jesus:

> *To an inheritance incorruptible, and undefiled, and that fadeth not away, reserved in heaven for you, who are kept by the power of God through faith unto salvation ready to be revealed in the last time. Wherein ye greatly rejoice, though now for a season, if need be, ye are in heaviness through manifold temptations: that the trial of your faith, being much more precious than of gold that perisheth, though it be tried with fire, might be found unto praise and honour and glory at the appearing of Jesus Christ.* (1 Pet. 1:4–7)

Paul

In his sermon to the Athenians on Mars Hill, Paul said,

> *Because he* [God] *hath appointed a day, in the which he will judge the world in righteousness by that man* [Jesus] *whom he hath ordained; whereof he hath given assurance unto all men, in that he hath raised him from the dead.* (Acts 17:31)

This was a prophecy. Paul wrote many other prophetic statements, such as 2 Corinthians 5:10, *"For we must all appear before the judgment seat of Christ."* Here he prophesied that the Lord Jesus Christ would be the One to judge the world.

James

James was another of the writing prophets of the New Testament. In his epistle he wrote,

> *Go to now, ye rich men, weep and howl for your miseries that shall come upon you. Your riches are corrupted, and your garments are motheaten. Your gold and silver is cankered; and the rust of them shall be a witness against you, and shall eat your flesh as it were fire. Ye have heaped treasure together for the last days. Behold, the hire of the labourers who have reaped down your fields, which is of you kept back by fraud, crieth: and the cries of them which have reaped are entered into the ears of the Lord of sabaoth* [the Lord of battles]. *Ye*

have lived in pleasure on the earth, and been wanton; ye have nour-
ished your hearts, as in a day of slaughter. Ye have condemned and
killed the just; and he doth not resist you. Be patient therefore, breth-
ren, unto the coming of the Lord. Behold, the husbandman waiteth for
the precious fruit of the earth, and hath long patience for it, until he
receive the early and latter rain.   (James 5:1-7)

We could write a whole chapter describing the prophecies of
James, a remarkable person through whom the Holy Spirit was
flowing.

John

The last of these four writing prophets of the New Testament
was John, the Beloved. He wrote,

And the world passeth away, and the lust thereof: but he that doeth
the will of God abideth for ever. Little children, it is the last time: and
as ye have heard that antichrist shall come, even now are there many
antichrists; whereby we know that it is the last time.
                                        (1 John 2:17-18)

Then in the Revelation we read:

The Revelation of Jesus Christ, which God gave unto him, to show
unto his servants things which must shortly come to pass; and he sent
and signified it by his angel unto his servant John.   (Rev. 1:1)

So these are the prophets who wrote in the New Testament—
Peter, Paul, James, and John—whose ministries are recorded and
remain with us until today.

New Testament Speaking Prophets

There were other New Testament prophets who did not
write, but who spoke prophetically.

First, there was John the Baptist. We have recorded instances
where this man prophesied and foretold events that were to
come to pass. In Matthew 3:11 as John was baptizing, he spoke
concerning the Messiah who was to come:

The Gifts and Ministries of the Holy Spirit

I indeed baptize you with water unto repentance: but he that cometh after me is mightier than I, whose shoes I am not worthy to bear: he shall baptize you with the Holy Ghost, and with fire.

In John 1:29, 32–34 we find this record:

The next day John seeth Jesus coming unto him, and saith, Behold the Lamb of God, which taketh away the sin of the world....And John bare record, saying, I saw the Spirit descending from heaven like a dove, and it abode upon him. And I knew him not: but he that sent me to baptize with water, the same said unto me, Upon whom thou shalt see the Spirit descending, and remaining on him, the same is he which baptizeth with the Holy Ghost. And I saw, and bare record that this is the Son of God.

Another New Testament prophet was Zacharias. In Luke 1:67–71 we read,

Zacharias was filled with the Holy Ghost, and prophesied, saying, Blessed be the Lord God of Israel; for he hath visited and redeemed his people, and hath raised up an horn of salvation for us in the house of his servant David; as he spake by the mouth of his holy prophets, which have been since the world began: that we should be saved from our enemies, and from the hand of all that hate us.

Simeon was another of these great old prophets. His prophecy at the temple to Joseph and Mary concerning the infant Jesus is recorded in Luke 2:25–35. God spoke through Simeon, telling what would certainly come to pass in the life of His Son.

These prophets mainly dealt with the life of Christ; but concerning the church in the New Testament, we find others such as Agabus. The Bible says very little about this man, except that he was a prophet:

And in these days came prophets from Jerusalem unto Antioch. And there stood up one of them named Agabus, and signified by the Spirit that there should be great dearth throughout all the world: which came to pass in the days of Claudius Caesar. (Acts 11:27–28)

Then in Acts 21:10–11 we read,

And as we tarried there many days, there came down from Judaea a certain prophet, named Agabus. And when he was come unto us, he took Paul's girdle, and bound his own hands and feet, and said, Thus saith the Holy Ghost, So shall the Jews at Jerusalem bind the man that owneth this girdle, and shall deliver him into the hands of the Gentiles.

Agabus made these two tremendous prophecies (he might have made hundreds, but these are the only two of which we have record), and both of them came to pass exactly as he predicted.

Also in the Acts of the Apostles we find an incident in which God spoke to Ananias and commanded him to go and minister to Saul of Tarsus:

The Lord said unto him [Ananias], Go thy way: for he [Saul] is a chosen vessel unto me, to bear my name before the Gentiles, and kings, and the children of Israel: for I will show him how great things he must suffer for my name's sake. (Acts 9:15–16)

Receiving this prophecy from God that Saul was not a killer, but rather a servant of God, Ananias obeyed God and did as he was commanded. God told him exactly where to find Saul and what to say:

And the Lord said unto him, Arise, and go into the street which is called Straight, and inquire in the house of Judas for one called Saul, of Tarsus: for, behold, he prayeth....And Ananias went his way, and entered into the house; and putting his hands on him said, Brother Saul, the Lord, even Jesus...hath sent me, that thou mightest receive thy sight, and be filled with the Holy Ghost. (Acts 9:11, 17)

We also notice in Acts 13:1–2 how the spirit of prophecy flowed through several people at one time:

Now there were in the church that was at Antioch certain prophets and teachers; as Barnabas, and Simeon that was called Niger, and

The Gifts and Ministries of the Holy Spirit

Lucius of Cyrene, and Manaen, which had been brought up with Herod the tetrarch, and Saul. As they ministered to the Lord, and fasted, the Holy Ghost said, Separate me Barnabas and Saul for the work whereunto I have called them.

Here the Bible says that in this particular church there were certain prophets—and it names them—who foretold the future. I assume that nearly all churches have deacons or elders; but how many churches today claim to have apostles or prophets? They should. Apostles and prophets are as much a ministry of the church as elders and deacons. I believe God is ready to bring them out and have His glorious power manifested on the face of this earth in a way that we have never known before.

Sometimes prophets speak only to individuals as in Acts, chapter 5, when Peter spoke to Ananias and Sapphira. At other times prophecy is directed to a group. For instance, in Revelation, chapter 2, one prophecy was directed to each one of the seven churches through the prophet John.

Sometimes prophecy is directed to an entire nation. Many times the whole nation of Israel received prophecies from God. It is possible for God to speak to our whole nation at one time and to say, "America, thus saith God to you...." A prophecy can be for one person, for a group, for a nation, or it can be for the whole world. God said to Jeremiah, *"Before I formed thee in the belly I knew thee; and before thou camest forth out of the womb I sanctified thee, and I ordained thee a prophet unto the nations"* (Jer. 1:5). Jeremiah was a prophet not just to Israel, but to the nations—and God ordained it so.

Prophetesses

There is very little that has not already been said about the subject of female involvement in the ministry. In many instances, I feel that God does not see male nor female; He sees into hearts and spirits, knowing the desires within a person.

Because my father was not converted until he was an elderly man, my mother was the spiritual force in our home. I learned to respect the spiritual power of a woman as I grew up.

When my grandfather suffered a stroke and was in a wheelchair, paralyzed, the preachers prayed for him, but nothing happened. Then my mother gathered a group of prayer ladies together around his chair and began to weep and travail before the Lord, and God healed him. My grandfather came out of that wheelchair completely healed and lived a good, strong, totally healthy life for the next forty years. The night he died at eighty-seven years of age, he ate a good dinner and went to bed about nine o'clock. When we heard a little noise in the bedroom and went in to check on him, he had already gone to be with the Lord. Anyone who says that God does not use women has not studied history or the Bible.

God wants us to judge ministries, not people. If the Spirit of the Lord and divine words are flowing from a person—man or woman—who are we to say it is wrong?

There have been a number of prophetesses in the Scriptures. God has used women in many ways, both conventional and unconventional.

Miriam

And Miriam the prophetess, the sister of Aaron, took a timbrel in her hand; and all the women went out after her with timbrels and with dances.　　　　　　　　　　　　　　　　　　　　　　(Exod. 15:20)

Here the Bible recognizes Miriam as a prophetess. A prophetess is only one thing—one who prophesies. Of that, there can be no doubt.

Deborah

Deborah, a prophetess, the wife of Lapidoth, she judged Israel at that time.　　　　　　　　　　　　　　　　　　　　　　　(Judg. 4:4)

Deborah was both a prophetess and a judge in the land of Israel. It might have been that God could find no one else to do it.

Huldah

> *So Hilkiah the priest, and Ahikam, and Achbor, and Shaphan, and Asahiah, went unto Huldah the prophetess…(now she dwelt in Jerusalem in the college;) and they communed with her.* (2 Kings 22:14)

Huldah is also mentioned in 2 Chronicles 34:22–23:

> *They that the king had appointed, went to Huldah the prophetess… and they spake to her to that effect. And she answered them, Thus saith the LORD God of Israel.*

All these men—the priests of God—went to Huldah, the prophetess, in order to hear from God.

False Prophetess

In Nehemiah 6:14 we read these words:

> *My God, think thou upon Tobiah and Sanballat according to these their works, and on the prophetess Noadiah, and the rest of the prophets, that would have put me in fear.*

Here we have a false prophetess, a prophetess of the devil, a woman who had given herself over to the devil.

Isaiah's Wife

Another very interesting fact is recorded by Isaiah. It seems that his wife was a prophetess. He wrote, *"And I went unto the prophetess; and she conceived, and bare a son. Then said the LORD to me, Call his name Mahershalalhashbaz"* (Isa. 8:3). (I'd have called him junior!)

Anna

In the New Testament we have a prophetess of the Lord named Anna:

And there was one Anna, a prophetess, the daughter of Phanuel, of the tribe of Aser: she was of a great age, and had lived with an husband seven years from her virginity; and she was a widow of about fourscore and four years, which departed not from the temple, but served God with fastings and prayers night and day. And she coming in that instant gave thanks likewise unto the Lord, and spake of him [the baby Jesus] to all them that looked for redemption in Jerusalem.
(Luke 2:36–38)

Prophets Today

We find in the Word that God has used men and women to be His prophets and prophetesses, and the God who produced this ministry throughout the Bible wants to do the same today in an even greater way. He wishes in these last days to breathe upon the total church of the Lord Jesus and speak to us through these submitted and dedicated vessels, that we might know things that will surely come to pass and that we might have direction.

The carnal mind does not know what it ought to do, but the spirit does. We are saying in our hearts, "Oh, God, send us prophets and prophetesses that we might better know what we should do for You in the days in which we live." I am sure our hearts are open for God to reveal unto us His chosen prophets and prophetesses.

And there *are* prophets today!

I lived for many years with Howard Carter, who fulfilled the office of prophet. At times it seemed somewhat frightening to live with such a man. He knew so many things about so many people. Never would he leave these prophecies to doubt. He would write them down and circulate them to make sure people knew what he was talking about. The accuracy with which he prophesied was astounding.

As I have already related in this book, Rev. Carter knew in advance how he would meet me and the exact words I would say when we met as strangers. He circulated that prophecy in England until there were probably twenty-five preachers carrying a prophetic record of how Howard Carter would meet a stranger from afar and the very words that stranger would speak when they met. Rev. Carter was not the least bit surprised when I walked up to him and spoke those words. On the other hand, I was shocked at my behavior. Here was a man I had never met and knew nothing about, yet I had just told him that God had sent me to work with him. And work together we did for many years, until Rev. Carter went home to heaven.

God does have prophets today. He is speaking to people, but much of the body of Christ is ignorant of this fact and not desirous of it. There are only a few things that can keep us from knowing the future. One is sin; another is unbelief.

Unbelief cuts off the miracle power of God. In churches where the people say God cannot act, He only shakes His head and says, "You're right. I can't act here." What we must do is say, "Lord, if You wish to give me one of these ministries in the body of Christ, I accept it." By doing this, you will see more of the power of God than ever before in your life.

Perhaps there is nothing so exciting as prophecy. In these last days we must have the prophet's ministry at work among us. All kinds of people will be reading the stars and predicting future events. The devil will be out to fool as many people as he can regarding the future, so God's people must take their place against him.

Don't be afraid of the future. No matter what happens, I guarantee you a greater move of the supernatural than you have ever seen before. Let's get ready for it. Let's seek it. Let's love it. I know that the God of heaven is going to bless us in it, and I am ready for His blessing! Let the ministry of the prophet be heard in the land!

The Office of Evangelist

The evangelist is a proclaimer of the Gospel. That is his purpose of ministry, and he does not deviate from it. He simply preaches the love and forgiveness of God and the salvation that is available to all through His Son Jesus Christ. When he preaches this simple Gospel message, people receive salvation.

An evangelist is a gift from God to the church. A person cannot go to Bible school and study to become an evangelist.

If you need an evangelist, call upon the Holy Spirit and He will send you one—Jesus said He would:

The harvest truly is plenteous, but the labourers are few; Pray ye therefore the Lord of the harvest, that he will send forth labourers into his harvest. (Matt. 9:37–38)

Philip

The church in Jerusalem had picked this man Philip, as one of the seven deacons who would serve the apostles and the other disciples. He was described as being *"of honest report, full of the Holy Ghost and wisdom"* (Acts 6:3). But God had some other plans for Philip. Though Philip had no training as an evangelist, that is the office God called him to fill, and a whole city came to God because of his evangelism:

Then Philip went down to the city of Samaria, and preached Christ unto them. And the people with one accord gave heed unto those things which Philip spake, hearing and seeing the miracles which he did. For unclean spirits, crying with loud voice, came out of many that were possessed with them: and many taken with palsies, and that were lame, were healed. And there was great joy in that city.
(Acts 8:5–8)

Later we see that Philip left Jerusalem and moved to the oceanside at Caesarea where he became known as God's evangelist:

And the next day we that were of Paul's company departed, and came unto Caesarea: and we entered into the house of Philip the evangelist, which was one of the seven; and abode with him. (Acts 21:8)

Timothy

In 2 Timothy 4:5 Paul wrote to the young preacher Timothy, *"Watch thou in all things, endure afflictions, do the work of an evangelist, make full proof of thy ministry."* This means Paul was very conscious of the fact that God had laid His hands upon that young man, Timothy, and had called him to save souls. So he admonished him to do the work of an evangelist. Paul was saying to him, "Now God has given you this ministry gift, and I want you to make full proof of it. Get out there and get those people saved!"

The Need for Evangelists

The number of evangelists today is not large. I believe we should pray for God to give us more. As an evangelist, nobody has to give you a place to preach. When God calls you to do something, just go out and start doing it.

The morning I left home to preach, I had no idea where I was going; we headed north toward the country. In the afternoon we stopped at a little country schoolhouse and started a revival meeting there. We stayed several weeks and baptized sixty-seven adults. A church was established. Two missionaries later went out to Africa from the crusade. Also, one pastor entered the ministry.

Evangelists get discouraged sometimes when they go to a church and fail to get many people saved. The reason is they are doing their evangelizing in the wrong place. You cannot expect to grow corn if you plant the seed around the church altar. Evangelists need to go out and plant their seed where the sinners are, and then they will reap a harvest. We need to pray that God will give us some great evangelists, and that could mean you.

The Office of Pastor

A pastor is a shepherd. The Greek word *poimen* occurs seventeen times in the New Testament. Only one time is it translated "pastor," which is in Ephesians 4:11. The other sixteen times, it is translated "shepherd." So in Ephesians 4:11 Paul is saying that the pastor is to be the shepherd of his flock, of his church.

Matthew 9:36 says, *"When he [Jesus] saw the multitudes, he was moved with compassion on them, because they fainted, and were scattered abroad, as sheep having no shepherd."* Jesus is the chief

Shepherd, the chief Pastor. He saw the multitudes and was moved with compassion.

This demonstrates the pastor's heart. There are some people who cannot see a multitude. All they see is a crowd, and they don't like crowds; they don't like being jostled and pushed. But Jesus did not see only a crowd of people; He saw a multitude in need, and He was moved by their needs. He saw that they fainted and were scattered, like sheep with no shepherd. They needed a pastor.

The Hebrew word *ra'ah* means "to tend sheep." In the Old Testament this word is translated "pastor" eight times, as in Jeremiah 2:8:

> *The priests said not, Where is the LORD? and they that handle the law knew me not: the pastors* [those who were supposed to be tending God's sheep] *also transgressed against me, and the prophets prophesied by Baal, and walked after things that do not profit.*

In Jeremiah 3:15 God said, *"And I will give you pastors according to mine heart, which shall feed you with knowledge and understanding."*

This is the ministry of a pastor: to feed the flock with knowledge and understanding, to feed the souls of all who come by the Spirit of God. And it need not be just a few. It can be 6, or 600, or 6,000. In fact, the more people there are, the more inspiration a pastor can get and the better he can feed them. It inspires that force and anointing within him and enables him to feed them well.

I have heard people comment that a particular church congregation is too large for the pastor to handle effectively. However, he can pastor only one person at a time. When he stands and speaks, he is speaking to one person. When he feeds a group of any size, he is feeding them only one at a time.

Think how it must have been in the first church in Jerusalem. There were 3,000 saved in one day and 5,000 saved another day. Acts 2:47 says, *"The Lord added to the church daily such as should be saved."* There must have been 50,000 members in that church!

A young man named Charles Spurgeon went to London when he was only seventeen years of age, and in a few months was pastoring a very large congregation. Within a year or two, it was the largest congregation in England. Spurgeon held that congregation in the Metropolitan Tabernacle in London until he died. He was a good shepherd; he had a pastor's heart. He wanted to feed people, to heal the wounded.

In addition to a shepherd, the Bible also speaks of hirelings— people who say they are pastors. In John's gospel, Jesus said,

> *I am the good shepherd: the good shepherd giveth his life for the sheep. But he that is an hireling, and not the shepherd, whose own the sheep are not, seeth the wolf coming, and leaveth the sheep, and fleeth: and the wolf catcheth them, and scattereth the sheep. The hireling fleeth, because he is an hireling, and careth not for the sheep.*
> (John 10:11-13)

There is a great difference between someone who has been hired and someone whom God has commissioned. A real pastor is commissioned by God to do his job, and he will pastor even if he never gets a dime. He will keep doing it, if he never gets any appreciation. Why? Because God told him to do it. A hireling, on the other hand, will quit if he does not get exactly what he wants.

The distinguishing mark is the pastor's heart. A shepherd's heart cannot be fabricated. It cannot be received at Bible school. A shepherd's heart comes only from God. Either you have it, or you do not.

The Office of Teacher

A teacher of the Word can be located in one place, or he can travel. The office of teacher carries a very special anointing for opening people's understanding of God's Word.

Howard Carter filled this ministerial office. There was nothing in the Bible that he could not simplify so that even a child could understand. For a number of years he and I lived and traveled together with great unity and blessing, and I was always amazed at his ability to teach. In our meetings, he would teach first; then I would operate as the evangelist. After he had finished teaching the saints, I would bring the Gospel message of salvation to those who were not yet Christians.

Rev. Carter was recognized as one of the great Bible teachers in the world; but if we had a houseful of sinners, he could not get even one of them saved. He was not called to be an evangelist. That is why God fit us together; we could work well together to edify His church. We made a great team! I had an ability for evangelism, not an ability I had learned, but one that God had put in my heart—the ability to have compassion on the lost, to bring them in, and to give them to Him; Howard Carter, on the other hand, had been given the gift of teaching.

You might be surprised at the number of great Bible teachers who are almost illiterate. If you ask them a question about philosophy or some other subject, they are at a loss; but they can open a Bible and simply amaze you with their knowledge and understanding. As they give an exposition on the Word of God, it is truth pouring forth from them. Though they have little or no education, they are anointed to teach the Word of God. On the other hand, you may meet a learned professor who cannot understand a single page in the whole Bible.

All the education in the world will not make a teacher of God's Word. A teacher is a person who has been set in the body of Christ by God for one specific purpose: to teach the Word.

17
Elders, Deacons, Helps, and Governments

H aving studied the fivefold ministry gifts—apostles, prophets, evangelists, pastors, and teachers—we now come to the portion of laborers in the body of Christ who are set aside by these spiritual leaders.

The Office of Elder

The first we will deal with is the elder, or bishop. First Timothy 3:1 states, *"This is a true saying, If a man desire the office of a bishop* [or elder], *he desireth a good work."* It is good to desire the office of elder—not the title, but the ministry it involves.

First Timothy 5:17–19 reveals how the elder is to function in the body of Christ:

> *Let the elders that rule well be counted worthy of double honour, especially they who labour in the word and doctrine. For the scripture saith, Thou shalt not muzzle the ox that treadeth out the corn. And, the labourer is worthy of his reward. Against an elder receive not an accusation, but before two or three witnesses.*

In Acts 20:17 we read, *"And from Miletus he* [Paul] *sent to Ephesus, and called the elders of the church."* Paul called them together for a consultation about their ministry—what they should do and how they should work in the church.

In James 5:14–15 we read,

Is any sick among you? let him call for the elders of the church; and let them pray over him, anointing him with oil in the name of the Lord: and the prayer of faith shall save the sick, and the Lord shall raise him up.

Acts 14:23 states, *"And when they had ordained them elders in every church, and had prayed with fasting, they commended them to the Lord, on whom they believed."*

These elders were men of the church who were mature, both physically and spiritually. Such men were ordained or anointed and set aside for service by the laying on of hands.

In Titus 1:5–6 Paul wrote,

For this cause left I thee in Crete, that thou shouldest set in order the things that are wanting, and ordain elders in every city, as I had appointed thee: if any be blameless, the husband of one wife, having faithful children not accused of riot or unruly.

Here Paul was showing us the responsibilities and qualifications of these elders. It is good to obey the Lord in everything, especially when it concerns elders, because they are the ones who function in the spiritual part of the church.

In our church there are about fifty elders, who visit church members each week. When a member of our church is ill, the elders will go quickly and joyfully to minister to them. We receive good reports of how God heals and blesses through the work of our elders.

Verses 7–9 continue,

For a bishop [or elder] *must be blameless, as the steward of God; not selfwilled, not soon angry, not given to wine, no striker, not given to filthy lucre* [that is, not a lover of money]; *but a lover of hospitality* [one who invites people into his home and ministers to them], *a lover of good men* [associates with good people], *sober, just, holy, temperate; holding fast the faithful word as he hath been taught, that he may be able by sound doctrine both to exhort and to convince the gainsayers.*

Notice this last phrase: *"as he hath been taught."* The apostle, prophet, evangelist, pastor, or teacher whom God has set in the church takes those in the church and teaches them. As verse 9 continues, an elder is taught *"that he may be able by sound doctrine* [as he has been taught] *both to exhort and to convince the gainsayers* [those who come against the body]." This is the role of the elder: a spiritual overseer in the church, involved in blessing the people spiritually.

The Office of Deacon

Next we have the office of deacon. The first deacons were chosen in Acts, chapter 6:

And in those days, when the number of the disciples was multiplied, there arose a murmuring of the Grecians against the Hebrews, because their widows were neglected in the daily ministration....Wherefore, brethren, look ye out among you seven men of honest report, full of the Holy Ghost and wisdom, whom we may appoint over this business. But we will give ourselves continually to prayer, and to the ministry of the word. (vv. 1, 3–4)

You probably know the rest of the story. They chose seven men to be deacons, *"and when they had prayed, they laid their hands on them"* (v. 6). As deacons, these men were given jobs to do in the church.

In 1 Timothy 3:8–12 we read,

Likewise must the deacons be grave, not doubletongued, not given to much wine, not greedy of filthy lucre; holding the mystery of the faith in a pure conscience. And let these also first be proved [not novices]; then let them use the office of a deacon, being found blameless. Even so must their wives be grave, not slanderers, sober, faithful in all things. Let the deacons be the husbands of one wife, ruling their children and their own houses well.

As qualifications for both the eldership and the deaconship, God said these men should be capable of ruling their own house. Americans have been taught very little about this subject, and it grieves me.

Once I was preaching in what was then the largest Full Gospel church in the world—an enormous church in Stockholm, Sweden. While I was there, the pastor told me a very exciting story. Shortly before I arrived, he had resigned the church, though he was its founder. One day he stood before the congregation and said very simply, "I resign." When the board asked, "Why?" he answered, "One of my children [he had eleven] is not living for God. I will resign and stay at home in prayer until he is saved."

Immediately, that church body set themselves as one to pray for his son. What was that boy to do when 6,000 church members started praying? He got saved in a hurry!

Here was a man who ruled his house well, which is how a deacon is to be.

My wife and I witnessed a very interesting occurrence in Puerto Rico. As we were preaching there, a missionary came by the church to visit. He stood during the service and, rather than preaching, gave his life's testimony. He said, "I was called to be a missionary in India. While there my wife fell in love with another man and left me. Now I am alone as I go out preaching the Word. I've come down here because I love you and I'm going to preach the Word to you. How glad I am to be with you."

The pastor of that church stopped him and said, "Sit back down. A man who can't control one little woman is surely not going to preach to my people. You can just go back to America." (Those people are called "natives," but they know how to operate their church.)

The Bible says that a deacon must be faithful in all things, the husband of one wife, ruling his children and his house well. *"For they that have used the office of a deacon well purchase to themselves a good degree, and great boldness in the faith which is in Christ Jesus"* (1 Tim. 3:13). Deaconship is a good work. The Lord expects a deacon to be an example to the people in his church.

The Ministry of Helps

Now we come to the ministry of helps. There has been much confusion about this subject since very little has been taught about it.

The Gifts and Ministries of the Holy Spirit

The New Testament is filled with examples of helps in action. The word *helps* in Acts 27:17 speaks of the ropelike cable that sailors used to wrap around the ship during a storm: *"They used helps, undergirding the ship."* The ministry of helps is what God wraps around us to hold us together in our stormy times.

The Bible mentions seven people who ministered in this area of helps. For example, there is Phebe. In Romans 16:1–2 Paul said, *"I commend unto you Phebe our sister, which is a servant of the church…that ye receive her in the Lord…for she hath been a succourer* [helper] *of many, and of myself also."* Phebe was a helper. She carried the book of Romans to Rome for Paul at his request. Though she was not a preacher, Phebe helped spread the Word.

Lydia was another helper who supported Paul. We find in Acts 16:14–15 how she provided lodging in her home in Philippi for Paul and his group.

In the Old Testament there were two men who held up the arms of Moses during a battle. (See Exodus 17:8–12.) As long as Moses held up his hands, there was victory for the children of Israel; but when he became weary and let them fall, they began to lose. So Aaron and Hur held up Moses' fired arms and helped win the victory. They were helpers; Moses could not function without them.

No man of God can function without helpers. I am surrounded with helpers; and when we get to heaven, they may get a bigger reward than I. That will be God's business, not mine.

You may ask, "Why would they get a larger reward?" Because they may have been more faithful in their helping than I have been in my ministering.

It was the Lord Jesus who said that if you give even a drink of water to a prophet, you shall receive a prophet's reward for helping. (See Matthew 10:41–42.) There are big stakes involved for being a helper.

The secretaries in my office are helpers. The person who runs our printing press is a helper. Without these helpers, I would be unable to minister.

All those who supported Paul's ministry, financially or otherwise, were helpers.

When King David went out to defeat the enemy, there went before him a standard-bearer who carried his shield. That person was a helper. He may not have been a strong man, but all he was required to do was to carry that shield. He was a helper, and that ministry is important.

Though God has appointed only a few apostles and prophets, he has thousands of helpers. These helpers are very important to God, and they have their reward in heaven. There are many bricks in a brick wall, and we cannot tell which is the most important. Each brick contributes to the strength of the whole wall. That is the function of a helper.

Through our television outreach, one lesson will be broadcast to perhaps several million people. It could not be done without the help of the cameramen and all the technicians. They are helpers.

The work of the Lord must have helpers. Any time we downgrade such helps, we are in danger of failure. Helps is a ministry that was placed in the church by God. As you study the whole of the Bible, you will see that all these helps are necessary. You can even go a step further and say that the giving of the tithe is a help. All of us are helpers in one way or another. Though the widow gives only three or four dollars and the businessman gives a hundred dollars, both are helpers—one is just as important as the other.

There is one particular family in our church that is always asking for names of people they can visit in the hospital. They are helpers, and God loves helpers. God has placed helpers in the church, and we must keep them there.

Governments

In 1 Corinthians 12:28 the Greek word for governments is *kubernesis*, meaning "to steer or to guide." This word *governments* means the steering committee; it has no reference to power or to ruling. Those who possess knowledge to steer a church and guide it around its problems become the governments of that church.

Within a church, there are many kinds of operations, all kinds of groups and committees. To build a new building, you choose a building committee. This is an example of church government.

You may ask, "Why does God want all of this?" Because He wants order. For everything to run smoothly, there must be organization. God wants church government to be well oiled with the Holy Spirit. This means that mature men and women can bless the church by being set aside to do certain things within the church, to operate the church in the way it ought to be operated.

Each Has a Place

These nine offices of ministry that God has set in the church have a purpose. All are necessary for a well-ordered church, and in these last days each of us has a place in the church. We should ask ourselves every day, "What can I do to fit more perfectly into the divine pattern that God has planned for the church of the Lord Jesus Christ?"

Each of us has a place in God's church, a job to fulfill. The Lord is waiting for us to move into our niche and do our best for Him.

18
Combinations of Ministries

When God gives ministerial gifts to the body of Christ, He may give more than one gift to the same person. For example, some people may fill a dual ministry, such as pastor and teacher. They can pastor a church magnificently, then proceed to a Bible college and open the Word of God to the student body in a splendid fashion. Others serve as both pastor and evangelist. They pastor their churches on Sunday; then go out on Monday, hold revival meetings, and cause hundreds of people to receive the Lord Jesus Christ.

This combination of ministries occurs, not because a person seeks these gifts, but because God has bestowed them upon him. He obtains them without struggling, without trying; they just flow from him under the anointing of the Holy Spirit.

In the church at Antioch, there were both prophets and teachers. Again I cite Acts 13:1–2 as an example:

> *Now there were in the church that was at Antioch certain prophets and teachers; as Barnabas, and Simeon that was called Niger, and Lucius of Cyrene, and Manaen, which had been brought up with Herod the tetrarch, and Saul. As they ministered to the Lord, and fasted, the Holy Ghost said, Separate me Barnabas and Saul for the work whereunto I have called them.*

God was calling out Barnabas and Saul (or Paul) that they might go as a pair to proclaim the Gospel of the Lord Jesus Christ. Paul was an apostle, and very likely Barnabas was also; but they were endowed with teaching abilities, so that wherever they went, they taught the truth of God. You will notice in Paul's writings that he was a tremendous teacher. Read Ephesians or Romans or Galatians, and you will see that Paul was a master teacher. Yet he was an evangelist, taking the Gospel throughout the then-known world; and he was a pastor, establishing churches and seeing them developed. (He stayed in one church for two years.)

As an apostle, Paul was a combination of all these ministries—performing every ministry in the church with excellence.

One combination of ministries that is particularly interesting involved deaconship. There are two examples of ministry I wish to share with you: Stephen and Philip.

In Acts 6:5 the church chose Stephen, *"a man full of faith and of the Holy Ghost,"* to be one of the original seven deacons. Then verse 8 says, *"And Stephen, full of faith and power, did great wonders and miracles among the people."* Though Stephen had been chosen and set apart as a deacon by the apostleship of the church, God had something more for him. The church leaders looked at Stephen and saw a good waiter; God looked at him and saw much more. He saw a man who would lay hands on the sick, cast out devils, and do miracles.

In Acts 6:9–10 we read,

> *Then there arose certain of the synagogue, which is called the synagogue of the Libertines, and Cyrenians, and Alexandrians, and of them of Cilicia and of Asia, disputing with Stephen* [not with the apostles, but with Stephen]. *And they were not able to resist the wisdom and the spirit by which he spake.*

We find that this man Stephen had much more going for him than just deaconship.

Philip also had been chosen as one of the original seven deacons, but God did something more with him: He made Philip into a tremendous evangelist. We read in Acts 8:5–8 how Philip moved a whole city at one time:

> *Then Philip went down to the city of Samaria, and preached Christ unto them. And the people with one accord gave heed unto those things which Philip spake, hearing and seeing the miracles which he*

did. For unclean spirits, crying with loud voice, came out of many that were possessed with them: and many taken with palsies, and that were lame, were healed. And there was great joy in that city.

Man said to Philip, "You wait on tables," but Philip did more than that. He performed the ministry of an evangelist. What a tremendous difference!

Men may select us for one thing, but the final selection is up to God—and when God selects us for a job, it is good. I believe, too, that God can enlarge the ministry within us. We begin at one level of ministry; and after we have proven ourselves at that, God adds to the anointing in our lives.

The opposite is true regarding a person who attempts to fill an office of ministry to which God has not called him. Again, I use Smith Wigglesworth as an illustration.

Wigglesworth was never called to pastor; he was called as an evangelist. When he had a church in England, he only stood in the back and handed out song books; his wife did all the preaching. Yet he could travel to South Africa or Switzerland or Scandinavia and minister to thousands of people with an anointing that just poured from him.

After his wife died, Wigglesworth gave up his pastorate; but he never surrendered his call to evangelism. When God places a ministry in an anointed vessel, it is normally there for life. Even while in his eighties, Wigglesworth could still preach for only three minutes and get people saved.

Pastoring and preaching are two entirely different aspects of ministry. Not every great pastor is a great preacher. In one of the largest churches where I have preached, the pastor was not a preacher. Anyone on the front row could have preached better than he. All he did was stand in the pulpit and minister love to his congregation. He was a true shepherd to his church flock. A pastor's love cannot be fabricated; and unless God gives you a shepherd's heart, you will never be able to fill that office.

You may ask, "How can I know the office of ministry that God has called me to fill?"

This is a common question and one that is very simple to answer. If a person has a ministry, his ministry will flow out of him and produce the proper fruit. Ministry is evidence, and it just makes a way and a place for itself.

A pear tree does not ask what it is; it just grows pears. There is no doubt about it: It is not a banana tree; its leaves are not the same and its fruit is not the same. People will know what you are by the fruit you produce. As you seek the Lord, pray in the Spirit, and study God's Word, the ministry gift that God has placed in you will surface without your having to force it out.

Start Where You Are

Let me close this study with some simple words of counsel. Many times we want to begin our ministry with something very big; but very seldom will it come about that way. A person does not conduct the Boston Symphony Orchestra the very first day he is handed a baton. A little preparatory work is required first.

I admonish you that as you are reaching out to minister for God, begin by doing everything your hand finds to do. If you feel in your heart that God is going to use you in a great way, do something close by. If you feel the call to be a pastor or teacher, start by teaching a Sunday school class. You will find out right away if you have the ability. If that little class falls to pieces, I suggest that you not try to pastor a church because you failed the elementary pastoring session.

Do you feel a call to evangelism? Then go out into your own neighborhood, to your neighbors and friends, and get somebody saved. Go across town to someone you have never seen before and see if you can lead him or her to Jesus. Go into the nursing homes and talk to the people there, or into the jail and preach to them.

The first place I preached was in a prison. I never knew whether I was worth anything to the kingdom; I was just struggling to do my best. I preached in prison a few times, preached in a ladies' prayer meeting, then went up into the country to a little country schoolhouse and preached there.

From there I moved on to another little country schoolhouse, then another, and another. It looked as if I was going to get educated at a country schoolhouse. I seldom preached in a church. Nobody invited me. I just preached in front of a school-house.

In one place the next day after I preached, the farmer where I was staying asked, "Did you enjoy your bed?"

I said, "Yes."

"Did you enjoy your food?"

"Yes."

"Then go feed my pigs."

I said, "But I'm the preacher."

"I know that; but around here if you don't work, you don't eat. If you want to come back to the table again, you'll have to go feed my hogs."

I was born in New Orleans and reared in Mobile, Alabama, and Panama City, Florida. I knew what ham was, but that was about all I knew about pigs!

The farmer showed me the slop bucket. (I almost got sick just at the name of it!) The bucket they used was just an old oilcan with a piece of wire across the top for a handle. The food for the pigs was so heavy that it slopped over the top and onto my clothes. (I guess that's why they were called slop buckets.) I had only two pairs of pants—one on and one off! It was very embarrassing to have to wash my clothes before I could change. Finally, I lay down in a cornfield and cried. I said, "Now I know I'm the prodigal son. I've got all the evidence of it. I'm in the pigpen, and I'd like to get out."

The Lord spoke up in my heart and said, "If you'll be faithful, I'll bless you."

Sometimes our beginnings are not easy. I preached for a whole week and the total offering I received amounted to 26 cents! There were no nickels, just 26 pennies.

You have to start where you are. Before you try to trust God for a seven-tier cake, trust Him for a doughnut. It gets easier as you get higher. But start where you are. Don't wait for the doors to open, or you will die of old age while you are waiting! Create doors all around you. There is so much that needs to be done, so get started!

Appendix
The Charisma through the Centuries

C urrent history is better understood in the perspective of the related past. The gifts of the Spirit, including speaking in tongues, have appeared and reappeared in the Christian church from its conception, having been a witness in every branch of Christendom.

In History

1. Dr. Philip Schaff, the well-known church historian, in his *History of the Christian Church*, Volume 1, writes:

> The speaking with tongues, however, was not confined to the Day of Pentecost. Together with the other extraordinary spiritual gifts which distinguished this age above the succeeding periods of more quiet and natural development, this gift also, though to be sure in a modified form, perpetuated itself in the apostolic church. We find traces of it still in the second and third centuries.

2. Irenaeus (A.D. 115–202) was a pupil of Polycarp, who was a disciple of the apostle John. In *Against Heresies*, Book V, he wrote:

> In like manner do we also hear many brethren in the church who possess prophetic gifts and who through the Spirit speak all kinds of languages, and bring mysteries of God, whom also the apostles term spiritual.

3. "The Latin church father, Tertullian (A.D. 160–20), writing against Marcion, said:

> Let Marcion then exhibit, as gifts of his god, some proph-ets, such as have not spoken by human sense, but with the Spirit of God, such as have predicted things to come, and have made manifest the secrets of the heart; let him produce a psalm, a vision, a prayer—only let it be by the spirit, in an ecstasy, that is, in a rapture, whenever an interpretation of tongues has occurred to him. Now all these signs (or spiritual gifts) are forthcoming from my side without any difficulty, and they agree, too, with the rules, and the dispensations, and the instructions of the Creator. (*Dr. William Smith's Dictionary of the Bible,* vol. 4, p. 3310).

4. "St. Pachomius (A.D. 292–346), the Egyptian founder of the first Christian monastery, is said to have enjoyed the use of the Greek and Latin languages which he sometimes miraculously spoke, having never learned them. This gift was given to him at times after special prayer for the power to meet an immediate need" (*Lives of the Saints,* Alban Butler, 1756).

5. "The history of the Waldenses in the 12th and 13th centu-ries reveals not only a devotion of the Bible reading and a desire to follow the primitive purity of the New Testament church, but also that both healing and speaking in unknown languages were experienced from time to time in their midst" (*Gift of Tongues,* Alexandria Mockie, p. 27).

6. John Calvin (1509–1564) wrote in his *Commentary on the Epistles of Paul the Apostle to the Corinthians,* Volume 1, p. 437:

> There are at present great theologians, who declaim against them with furious zeal. As it is certain that the Holy Spirit has here honored the use of tongues with never-dying praise, we may very readily gather, what is the kind of spirit that actuates those reformers, who level as many reproaches as they can against the pursuit of them.

This particular comment is in reference to Paul's statement in 1 Corinthians 14:5: *"I would that ye all spake with tongues."*

7. In *Souer's History of the Christian Church,* Volume 3, p. 206, the following statement is found:

> Dr. Martin Luther was a prophet, evangelist, speaker in tongues and interpreter, in one person, endowed with all the gifts of the Holy Spirit.

8. Regarding Dwight L. Moody, here are a few quotations from *Trails and Triumphs of Faith,* 1875 Edition, p. 402, by the Reverend R. Boyd. D.D. Rev. Boyd of the Baptist faith was a very intimate friend of the famous evangelist. He wrote:

> When I got to the rooms of the Young Men's Christian Association [Victoria Hall, London], I found the meeting on fire. The young men were speaking with tongues, prophesying. What on earth did it mean? Only that Moody has been addressing them that afternoon! What manner of man is this? I cannot describe Moody's great meeting: I can only say that the people of Sunderland warmly supported the movement, in spite of their local spiritual advisers.

9. At the dawn of the 20th century, the Holy Spirit outpoured in abundance. It centered in the metropolis of Los Angeles and soon spread around the entire earth.

Angels to Help You

Contents

Introduction

Never before in history has there been so much interest in supernatural phenomena. Many newspapers, magazines, and radio and television programs carry occasional items dealing with the occult, astrology, spiritism, exorcism, UFO's, and extrasensory perception. The film industry has found those subjects to be sure box-office hits.

Because of much misinformation and blatant falsehood presented about those topics, however, Christians have tended to shy away from anything supernatural. In doing so, they have ignored a vital area that God wants us to know about—the reality and ministry of angels.

There is a tremendous and exciting world of angelic existence, a world God has been pleased to reveal to us in the Bible, the only accurate sourcebook of information we have or need. I have made an exhaustive study of the nearly three hundred references to angels in the pages of the Old and New Testaments. In this book I present the results in a way I pray will be a rich blessing to you. May your spiritual eyes be opened wider by reading it.

1
The Reality of Angels

One morning during the Great Depression, while my father was away at work, someone knocked on the back door of our home. I opened it and saw a cleanly dressed individual standing there.

"I'm not a beggar," he said, "but I am hungry. Will you feed me?"

"Yes," replied my mother as she came to the door. "Come in."

While the meal was being prepared, the stranger sat at our table and talked about the wonderful truths in the Bible. He asked God's blessing on the food before he began to eat and after he had finished. Then he arose, looked at us for a few seconds, and walked out the door, closing it behind him.

My mother was the first to speak after he left. "Children, I have a very strange feeling about that visitor," she said.

Quickly, she opened the door and we all went out, but the stranger was nowhere to be seen. We looked into the street and all around the house. We searched fast; we searched diligently. But we could not find him.

As I think now about that incident from my boyhood years, I recall the words of Hebrews 13:2: *"Be not forgetful to entertain strangers: for thereby some have entertained angels unawares."*

Could that have been an angelic visitor to our home? I can't be sure, of course, but I do know that the Bible establishes beyond all doubt the reality of angels.

When we examine the Old Testament, for example, we find that angels are mentioned 108 times. Angels intervened in the lives of the patriarchs Abraham and Jacob, as the book of Genesis indicates. (See chapters 18, 19, 28, and 32.) Moses also knew the ministry of angels in his life, both in his call to return to Egypt (see Exodus 3:2) and during the wilderness wanderings. (See Exodus 14:19.) In all, the word *angel* or *angels* appears in the books of the Law, the writings of Moses, a total of thirty-two times.

Turn to the books of history and read of angelic activity in Joshua, Judges, 1 and 2 Samuel, 2 Kings, and in 1 and 2 Chronicles. Some thirty-seven references to the work and ministry of angels relate to the development of the kingdom of Israel.

Those who wrote the books of poetry continued to unfold the existence of angels. The oldest book of the Bible, Job, speaks of angels. (See, for example, Job 4:18.) Frequently the Psalms describe angels as protecting and delivering God's people from all kinds of danger. (See Psalm 34:7; 91:11.) With the exception of Jeremiah, all the major prophets alluded to the ministry of angels. The writer Daniel gave us the names of two angels, Gabriel (see Daniel 9:20–27) and Michael. (See Daniel 10:13.) Of the minor prophets, Hosea and Zechariah speak of angels.

The Old Testament writers did not feel it necessary to offer formal proof of angels or argue for their reality. Instead, the angels are assumed to exist, just as God is assumed to exist.

The Old Testament alone would be sufficient to establish the fact of angels, but the New Testament continues to enlarge our knowledge of angelic beings. In fact, although the New Testament is far shorter than the Old, angels are mentioned there even more often—a total of 165 times. The Gospels are filled with references to them, and six times in the book of Acts, angels ministered to the Lord's people. (See Acts 5:18–20.)

The writer of half the epistles, Paul, spoke of angels in many of the books that bear his name. James and Peter spoke of them in their letters, too.

The last division of the New Testament, the Revelation, refers to angels no fewer than sixty-five times. (Later, we will consider those references in detail.)

Surely, all these mentions of the reality and ministry of angels are convincing, but there is also the testimony of the Lord Jesus Christ. It was He, of course, who created angels in the beginning, so it comes as no surprise that He believed in and taught the existence of angels. (See Matthew 13:39–41.)

Angels are real. We know that with absolute certainty from the Bible and from the Son of God.

What are angels? Who are angels? Let's define them this way: Angels are created, spirit beings. We know angels are created from reading Psalm 148:2, 5: *"Praise ye him, all his angels: praise ye him, all his hosts....Let them praise the name of the* LORD: *for he commanded, and they were created."* We know angels are spirit beings because of passages like Hebrews 1:14: *"Are they not all ministering spirits, sent forth to minister for them who shall be heirs of salvation?"*

Another helpful definition of angels comes through the Greek and Hebrew words for them. *Angel* literally means "messenger." Angels are the heavenly messengers of God, often delivering His messages to men and women.

Now that we have looked at the reality of angels and have defined their name, let me give you a general overview of angels by making a number of "angels are" statements.

No Dying, No Death

First, angels are immortal. Some Sadducees once came to Jesus, trying to trap Him on the subject of the resurrection, an idea that they rejected. They wanted to know, so they said, about the case of a woman who had seven husbands in succession. Whose wife would she be in the resurrection? (See Luke 20:27–33.)

Jesus replied that, in heaven, people neither marry nor are given in marriage. Then He added, *"Neither can they die any more: for they are equal unto the angels"* (Luke 20:36).

Angels never get sick, never go to the hospital, and never die. You'll never read an obituary for an angel. You'll never go to an angel's funeral. God created angels to live forever.

Outranking Man

Angels are of a high order. Do you remember from your school days how you learned to rank things in their proper order? A comes before B. One comes before two. Life comes in order: human, animal, plant. You can cite many examples.

Where do angels rank in the created order of God? The Bible tells us that angels constitute a higher form than man. Psalm 8:5 declares, *"For thou hast made him* [man] *a little lower than the angels, and hast crowned him with glory and honour."* And in 2 Peter 2:11 we read that angels are greater in power and might than human beings.

Even so, angels rank far below God Himself. Lucifer, you will remember, was one of the angels who aspired to rise above God, as Isaiah 14 relates, but he failed. He didn't have that power.

Sometimes when a child learns about angels, he may say, "I'd like to be one!"' No, God has something far better for those who believe in Jesus Christ. In fact, one day, in our exalted, heavenly state, we will judge the angels. (See 1 Corinthians 6:3.)

Keen-minded

Angels are intelligent. Recently a young man was interviewed on television and was said to have an I.Q. of 206. That's simply amazing. But he wouldn't fare too well in a one-to-one confrontation with an angel. Angels have great intelligence. In 2 Samuel 14:20 we read about being wise *"according to the wisdom of an angel of God, to know all things that are in the earth."*

There are some things, of course, that angels don't know, such as the hour of our Lord's return from heaven. (See Matthew 24:36.) But angels want to know all they can about what God is doing. For example, they are trying to understand God's great plan of salvation for mankind. (See 1 Peter 1:12.) I've never heard the expression "smart as an angel," but perhaps we should coin it.

No Sin, No Stain

Angels are holy. When we consider that angels constantly dwell in the presence of God, we can well understand that they, too, must be holy. Mark 8:38 speaks specifically of angels as being holy. That's the way God created them.

Have you ever seen drawings of angels done by various artists? They are always pictured as being clothed in white, representing their purity as revealed in Scripture.

Count Them if You Can

Angels are innumerable. Men and women have often wondered how many angels there are. We are told that during the Middle Ages some people used to stand around debating how many angels could stand on the head of a pin. That would be nothing but vain speculation, of course, but still our minds wonder how many angels God created.

Once again, Scripture gives us a little information. Hebrews 12:22 speaks of those who *"are come unto mount Sion, and unto the city of the living God, the heavenly Jerusalem, and to an innumerable company of angels."* The word *innumerable* means one thing: You cannot count them. The group is so vast that numbers cannot be assigned.

The book of Job gives us the same idea in this reference to God's angelic armies: *"Is there any number of his armies?"* (Job 25:3).

The shepherds were given an incredible view of the angelic multitudes on the night our Savior was born. *"And suddenly there was with the angel a multitude of the heavenly host praising God, and saying, Glory to God in the highest, and on earth peace, good will toward men"* (Luke 2:13–14). How many angels came to take part in that announcement and call to worship, we do not know. Perhaps the entire sky as far as the shepherds could see was filled with the heavenly messengers. What a sight!

No Need for Workouts

Angels are strong. Second Thessalonians 1:7 tells us of a coming day *"when the Lord Jesus shall be revealed from heaven with his mighty angels."* Why do they need to be strong? Because they will perform all the things for God that need to be done on the face of this earth. Perhaps Revelation 18:1 gives us one good example: *"And after these things I saw another angel come down from heaven, having great power; and the earth was lightened with his glory."* Imagine that angel of superhuman strength lighting up the darkness with his appearance.

Consider also Psalm 103:20, which teaches that angels *"excel in strength."* Outside the Godhead, there is no order of creation any stronger. Angels are able to act effectively, with power, because they were given that ability by God.

Out of Sight

Angels are invisible. Although men and women have seen angels many times, as recorded in the Bible, we must remember that angels are spirits and only take on forms visible to human beings on relatively rare occasions, when God has them do so for some specific reason. We see an example of how they do God's work even when invisible to man in Numbers 22:22–31.

Not Made for Marriage

Angels do not marry. We do not know why the Lord Jesus chose to tell us this, but in Matthew's gospel we are informed that angels do not marry. (See Matthew 22:30.) We are not told anywhere in Scripture whether there are even female angels, and it would be pointless to speculate about the matter. What we do know, simply, is that angels do not participate in the institution of marriage.

That fact does tell us a little about angelic service to God, however, especially in light of the apostle Paul's advice to Christians in 1 Corinthians 7. In that chapter, he explained that it is good, if one feels so led, to remain unmarried in order to devote full attention to serving and pleasing God. (See verses 32–34.) The married person must please his spouse as well as God, but the single person can concentrate exclusively on the Lord.

Therefore, since angels do not marry, they are free to give their full devotion to God. There are no distractions, no earthly companions whose pleasure they might seek above the Lord's. They can be single-minded in going about the purposes for which God created them.

Sing for Joy

Angels are joyful. Could angels possibly have long faces or be depressed? I think not because of Luke 15:10: *"Likewise, I say unto you, there is joy in the presence of the angels of God over one sinner that repenteth."* In this world there is somebody being saved every moment of the day. Somebody is finding God, somewhere. Thus, what a good time angels must have! They are constantly filled with joy because of sinners coming to know Jesus as their personal Savior. When we consider that angels dwell in heaven with God and serve Him in holiness, they have great cause, indeed, for joy.

No, Don't Do It

When we stop to consider how wonderful the angels are, we may feel that we ought to make a little statue and bow down to worship them. In a sense, that must have been the way the apostle John felt when he was given all the tremendous insights he recorded in the book of the Revelation. Read what he wrote:

> *And I John saw these things, and heard them. And when I had heard and seen, I fell down to worship before the feet of the angel which showed me these things. Then saith he unto me, See thou do it not: for I am thy fellowservant, and of thy brethren the prophets, and of them which keep the sayings of this book: worship God.* (Rev. 22:8–9)

So not only does the Bible say we must not worship angels, but it also says that angels do not want to be worshipped.

The apostle Paul also spoke to the matter of angel worship: *"Let no man beguile you of your reward in a voluntary humility and worshipping of angels, intruding into those things which he hath not seen"* (Col. 2:18). So if someone says to you, in effect, "We ought to worship angels," don't listen to him. He's wrong. His teaching is contrary to God's Word.

This has been a brief introduction to the great theme of angels. We've looked at just a few of the characteristics angels possess. Is this an important study? It is, indeed, particularly in the time in which we live. It is my earnest belief that in these last days we are going to see more angels, more of their work and power, than at any other time since that recorded in Revelation. There are going to be tremendous things happening in the very near future, and we don't want, through unbelief or unconcern, to be blinded to or to miss what God is doing in our time.

2
Categories of Angels — Their Names and Ranks

Whether you ever served in the armed forces or not, I'm sure you are acquainted with how the military ranks its enlisted men and officers. In the army, for example, we have generals at the top and then down through colonels, majors, captains, and lieutenants. And enlisted men also may be identified by different ranks and responsibilities.

Do you know that God also ranks angels? Our Lord even used a military term once in connection with angels. When Jesus was about to be taken in the Garden of Gethsemane, Peter took out a sword and tried to protect the One he had come to love and serve. Jesus said, *"Thinkest thou that I cannot now pray to my Father, and he shall presently give me more than twelve legions of angels?"* (Matt. 26:53). The word *legion* was a Roman military designation referring to about six thousand soldiers.

The Heavenly Host

In a general sense, probably the largest group of angels is what we might call the "ordinary" angels. Most of the time when angels are mentioned in the Bible, it is these otherwise unidentified angels who are being referred to. To speak of ordinary angels seems a contradiction in terms, however, for how could these extraordinary, created beings be considered just something routine? Yet in one sense, this designation is proper when we contrast them with the several special classes, or orders, of angels that the Bible mentions.

Cherubim

Judging from various Scripture references, I believe the cherubim rank at the very top of God's angelic creation, both in power and in beauty. They are, in fact, the first of the angelic order to appear in the Bible, right after Adam and Eve's fall from grace. Genesis 3 records the events in the Garden of Eden. Having violated God's command not to partake of the Tree of the Knowledge of Good and Evil, it would have been possible for Adam and Eve to reach out their hands and *"take also of the tree of life, and eat, and live for ever"* (v. 22). So they had to be expelled from their earthly paradise. *"Therefore the LORD God sent him forth from the garden of Eden, to till the ground from whence he was taken"* (v. 23).

But what would have prevented Adam from returning to the garden to disobey God once more? The next verse gives the answer: *"He* [God] *placed at the east of the garden of Eden Cherubims, and a flaming sword which turned every way, to keep the way of the tree of life"* (v. 24).

What a terrible thing it would have been if Adam had eaten of the Tree of Life and so had been forever confirmed in his fallen state! To prevent that, God sent a contingent of glorious and trusted cherubim to guard access to the tree. What Adam's reaction was to seeing for the first time in human history those glorious cherubim, we are not told. Awe, fright, wonder—perhaps Adam experienced all those emotions as the truth struck home that his act of sin had severed him from the fellowship and presence of a holy God.

Strangely enough, the next appearance of the cherubim in the Bible concerns regaining what was lost. In Exodus 25, Moses was given explicit and detailed instructions on how to make various articles of furniture that would be used in the tabernacle. The first described was the ark of the covenant and the mercy seat, where God promised to meet and commune with Moses.

What did God wish placed on top of, or over, the mercy seat? He chose representations of the cherubim, in gold. Read the fascinating description God gave Moses:

> *And thou shalt make two cherubims of gold, of beaten work shalt thou make them, in the two ends of the mercy seat. And make one cherub on the one end, and the other cherub on the other end: even of the mercy seat shall ye make the cherubims on the two ends thereof. And the cherubims shall stretch forth their wings on high, covering the mercy seat with their wings, and their faces shall look one to another; toward the mercy seat shall the faces of the cherubims be.*   (Exod. 25:18–20)

What a great sight that must have been—the cherubim associated with the very presence of God.

From those two references in Scripture, it appears as though the cherubim's major responsibility may be to declare the sinfulness of man and protect the presence of God from sinful men. No doubt Adam never forgot the sight of the cherubim as he longed to return to the Garden of Eden, but they reminded him that he had transgressed the commandment of God. Once a year, the high priest of Israel would be permitted into the Holy of Holies; there he could look upon the mercy seat. I'm sure he must have felt on each occasion, "I don't belong here in the holy presence of God, for I am a sinner."

Seraphim

Another group of specifically identified angels is the seraphim. In the Hebrew language, *seraphim* means "burning ones." Burning how? Why? I believe it refers to their burning devotion toward God from hearts that are on fire to serve Him.

Isaiah 6 tells us of the seraphim. Isaiah recorded his glorious vision in these words:

> *I saw also the Lord sitting upon a throne, high and lifted up, and his train filled the temple. Above it stood the seraphims: each one had six wings; with twain he covered his face, and with twain he covered his feet, and with twain he did fly.*   (vv. 1–2)

What were the seraphim doing? *"And one cried unto another, and said, Holy, holy, holy, is the* LORD *of hosts: the whole earth is full of his glory"* (v. 3).

The prophet recognized at once that he had no right to be in the holy presence of God, and he confessed as much. So one of the seraphim took a burning coal from the altar and touched Isaiah's lips to cleanse his iniquity and purge his sin (vv. 5–7).

So, seraphim have wings. They proclaim the holiness of God. They indicate to men their need to be cleansed from sin.

Living Creatures

A third special group of angels is called, in the King James Version, *"the four beasts,"* but a better translation would be "the four living creatures." These angels, like the seraphim, have six wings. Revelation 4:8 declares, *"And the four beasts* [living creatures] *had each of them six wings about him; and they were full of eyes within: and they rest not day and night, saying, Holy, holy, holy, Lord God Almighty, which was, and is, and is to come."*

Their special ministry, then, is to worship God and give Him glory throughout all time and eternity. We read of them again in Revelation 5, 7, and 19. In each instance they are depicted in an attitude of worship and praise. In Revelation 15, however, they participate in the pouring out of the wrath of God on unrepentant men.

It may be that the living creatures have other duties God has not revealed to us. But the brief insights given are intended, I believe, to draw us up short to a realization that God is holy and will not let sin go unpunished.

Michael

Another angelic rank, archangel, is held by only one angel in the biblical record. The word *arch* means "chief," so this angel is the most prominent of all the holy angels.

The archangel's name is Michael. That name asks a question: "Who is like God?" Probably many parents, both Jews and Gentiles, who call their boys Michael have no idea what the name conveys. That's unfortunate. It would be great if the minds and hearts of people were directed to God each time they heard the name. Often in Scripture, as we will see, men who received angelic visitations wanted to worship the creation rather than the Creator. So how appropriate it is that the name of Michael, the archangel, invites us to direct our attention to almighty God.

The prophet Daniel introduces us to Michael. It seems that he had been praying, and God had dispatched an answer by the hand of a messenger who was hindered on his journey until, he testified, *"Michael, one of the chief princes, came to help me"* (Dan. 10:13). So Michael had to fight for the free passage of God's Word.

It might be appropriate to give Michael the title of general, for each time we see him, it is in connection with some type of spiritual struggle. In his role as a fighter, Michael has a particular responsibility to Israel. In Daniel 10:21 and 12:1, he is said to be the prince of that nation. As we read ancient and modern history, I believe we see the hand of Michael defending Israel. As you know, that little nation has fought four wars with its Arab neighbors since gaining statehood in 1948. The Arabs have often expressed their determination to drive Israel into the sea, but they have never been able to accomplish that feat. Could it be because Michael is on the side of Israel, influencing strategy and insuring victory? I think that may well be the case.

In addition to the Old Testament references, we also find Michael mentioned in the New Testament. In the little book of Jude, the ninth verse specifically calls Michael an archangel and recounts his battle with Lucifer over the body of Moses. With the Lord's help, Michael won.

That wasn't the only conflict between Michael and Lucifer, for John tells us in the book of Revelation,

> *And there was war in heaven: Michael and his angels fought against the dragon; and the dragon fought and his angels, and prevailed not; neither was their place found any more in heaven. And the great dragon was cast out, that old serpent, called the Devil, and Satan,*

which deceiveth the whole world: he was cast out into the earth, and
his angels were cast out with him. (Rev. 12:7–9)

Here we see Michael serving as commanding officer of a large group of angels. Evidently, Michael is the chief warrior of God.

Gabriel

The only other angel whose name is given in Scripture (besides Lucifer) is Gabriel. The meaning of *Gabriel* is "mighty one of God." He lives up to his name, for he does, indeed, do mighty things. Rather than being a fighter like Michael, Gabriel serves God more as a messenger. He appears several times in the book of Daniel to give important revelations concerning future events, especially relating to God's kingdom. After one of Daniel's visions, for example, the prophet wondered about its meaning. Then suddenly, *"there stood before me as the appearance of a man. And I heard a man's voice between the banks of Ulai, which called, and said, Gabriel, make this man to understand the vision"* (Dan. 8:15–16). Gabriel did. We have something similar in Daniel 9, where, following Daniel's prayer of confession of sin on behalf of his people, Gabriel again came to him, *"being caused to fly swiftly"* (v. 21).

Thus, in the Old Testament, we see Gabriel's ministry in connection with the kingdom. In the New Testament, he is concerned with the King. In the first instance, Zacharias was waiting before the Lord in the Temple. Suddenly, *"there appeared unto him an angel of the Lord standing on the right side of the altar of incense"* (Luke 1:11). Gabriel identified himself to Zacharias, *"I am Gabriel, that stand in the presence of God; and am sent to speak unto thee, and to show thee these glad tidings"* (Luke 1:19). That good news concerned the coming birth of John the Baptist, who would be the forerunner of the Lord Jesus, ruler of Israel and the world.

It was this same Gabriel whom God sent one day to the city of Nazareth *"to a virgin espoused to a man whose name was Joseph, of the house of David; and the virgin's name was Mary"* (Luke 1:27). What a great announcement Gabriel had to give to that young lady: *"Thou shalt conceive in thy womb, and bring forth a son, and shalt call his name JESUS. He shall be great, and shall be called the Son of the Highest: and the Lord God shall give unto him the throne of his father David"* (vv. 31–32).

Gabriel, then, is the one who bore the message of God concerning the coming kingdom and the King. God gave this specific angel that tremendous privilege and responsibility.

Lucifer

We learn the original name of the angel Satan in Isaiah 14:12. That verse not only names him but also tells us something vital about him: *"How art thou fallen from heaven, O Lucifer, son of the morning! how art thou cut down to the ground, which didst weaken the nations!"* Once, Lucifer was up there with God. But not any longer. Why? He was cast down because of his pride and ambition:

> For thou hast said in thine heart, I will ascend into heaven, I will exalt my throne above the stars of God: I will sit also upon the mount of the congregation, in the sides of the north: I will ascend above the heights of the clouds; I will be like the most High. (Is. 14:13–14)

Because of his own ego, and because of his promotion of himself, Lucifer lost his lofty position in heaven. He fell from the Father's divine grace.

So where does he operate now? He is right here on earth. Two different times our Lord described Lucifer as being the prince of this world. (See John 12:31; 16:11.) This earth on which we live is under his authority.

While the angels Michael and Gabriel have only single names, as far as we know, Lucifer has many that indicate facets of his evil character. Many people are better acquainted with two of his other names, Satan and the devil. Jesus also called him the evil one. (See John 17:15.) The book of Revelation assigns him a virtual dictionary of names, including the old serpent, the great dragon, the destroyer, the accuser, and the deceiver. I often think of Lucifer by another of his names, that of tempter, for it was he who came to tempt Jesus during his stay in the wilderness. (See Matthew 4:1, 3.)

We will look more closely at Satan and his demons in chapter 8.

Holy Ones and Watchers

There are various minor categories of angels mentioned in the Bible, such as holy ones and watchers. Babylonian King Nebuchadnezzar reported, *"I saw in the visions of my head upon my bed, and, behold, a watcher and an holy one came down from heaven"* (Dan. 4:13). They announced judgment *"by the decree of the watchers, and the demand by the word of the holy ones"* (v. 17). Then, *"the king saw a watcher and an holy one coming down from heaven"* (v. 23).

Could these watchers and holy ones still be at work today? It's an interesting thought. Nebuchadnezzar was overthrown because of his sin. From time to time, we read of contemporary rulers being overthrown as well. It may be that these angels continue to decree the downfall of sinful nations.

Godly Thrones, Dominions, Principalities, Powers

There are two passages from the writings of the apostle Paul that seem very similar at first glance. Let me show you a difference. In Colossians 1:15–16, we read these words:

[Jesus] *is the image of the invisible God, the firstborn of every creature: for by him were all things created, that are in heaven, and that are in earth, visible and invisible, whether they be thrones, or dominions, or principalities, or powers: all things were created by him, and for him.*

Those classifications seem to refer to godly powers of angelic orders. We have very little information about them other than their names. In the book of Ephesians, Paul used similar words, but this time with a different reference. We are told to

> *put on the whole armour of God, that ye may be able to stand against the wiles of the devil. For we wrestle not against flesh and blood, but against principalities, against powers, against the rulers of the darkness of this world, against spiritual wickedness in high places.*
>
> (Eph. 6:11-12)

These are obviously evil angelic hosts.

God is in control of those wicked forces and even uses them for His purposes. For example, He used them to afflict the Egyptians prior to the Exodus: *"He cast upon them the fierceness of his anger, wrath, and indignation, and trouble, by sending evil angels among them"* (Ps. 78:49).

Those are some of the angelic ranks. God in His wisdom has not given us as much information about the names of angelic orders as we might like. He has simply lifted the curtain of heaven a bit so that we might catch a glimpse of those spiritual beings in their activity on behalf of God and man.

3
What Angels Do

D oes the company you work for have a job description for your position? Most firms do that sort of thing. The personnel office of almost every large business, and many smaller ones as well, draws up a list of tasks for which each employee is responsible. It may give the qualifications for each job, too, and indicate the persons to whom employees must report.

That's a good approach. That way, there is no misunderstanding on the part of the boss or the worker about what is expected. Everything is open and on the table.

In a very real sense, the Bible gives us a job description for angels. Yes, God has been pleased both by way of deliberate teaching and by way of example to show us at least some of what His marvelous angelic creation does. Not all angels do the same things, of course, for the Lord has made various assignments.

God's angels are active. In this chapter, I'd like to show you some of the important things angels do. Let's take as our general reference point an outstanding verse from the Bible: *"For he shall give his angels charge over thee, to keep thee in all thy ways"* (Ps. 91:11). This affirms that it is God who gives angels their responsibilities and that many of their activities are on our behalf.

Worship First

Before angels do anything for human beings, they first continue their ministry to God in praise and worship. Often my mind and heart return to that scene foretold in Revelation 7:11: *"And all the angels stood round about the throne, and about the elders and the four beasts, and fell before the throne on their faces, and worshipped God."*

The Bible gives us several such pictures of angels worshipping God. We have already seen the seraphim proclaiming God to be *"holy, holy, holy"* in Isaiah 6:3. And in Revelation 5:11–12 we read, *"And I beheld, and I heard the voice of many angels round about the throne and the beasts and the elders...saying with a loud voice, Worthy is the Lamb that was slain to receive power, and riches, and wisdom, and strength, and honour, and glory, and blessing."*

The angels provide a good pattern for us to follow. How often do we rush off to serve God or others, perhaps in some good and necessary way, and neglect to first worship God and adore Him. Of course we should give God and others our every effort in service. But before that, we need to spend time in His presence, getting our hearts tuned up.

Go This Way

Certainly it must have happened to you—getting lost as you searched for some unfamiliar address. Perhaps you became completely disoriented. That can be frightening. So you pull into a service station, if one is available and open, and ask for directions. Maybe you buy a map. Then how comforting it can be to get your bearings and head out confidently for your destination.

The need for clear direction in spiritual matters is very important. One great thing angels occasionally do is to direct believers.

Three men who were once very glad about the reality of angelic direction were Abraham, a servant, and a son. Abraham's son Isaac was unmarried, and Abraham wanted to find a wife for him. So the patriarch sent off the eldest of his servants on the extremely important mission of finding a wife for Isaac among his relatives in the land from which God had originally called him. (See Genesis 24.)

Perhaps the servant was fearful that he might make the wrong choice. Abraham said something to him that was reassuring, *"He*

[God] *shall send his angel before thee, and thou shalt take a wife unto my son from thence"* (Gen. 24:7).

That's exactly what took place. An angel led the servant directly to the beautiful, young Rebekah, and she readily agreed to leave her home and people to become the bride of Isaac.

For another example of angelic direction, jump ahead several hundred years in the history of God's people to the time of the judges. Under great oppression, the Israelites cried out to the Lord, and He determined to send them deliverance through the man Gideon. *"And the angel of the LORD appeared unto him, and said unto him, The LORD is with thee, thou mighty man of valour"* (Judg. 6:12). Then this angel went on to tell Gideon just how he was to go about the job of freeing God's people from their enemies. Gideon didn't have to guess what he was to do or how he was to do it. The Lord gave specific direction through His angel.

The New Testament gives us other fine examples of angelic leadership. It happened to Philip, one of the original seven deacons. The Lord wanted to direct him to a special evangelistic task. But how would that direction be given? *"And the angel of the Lord spake unto Philip, saying, Arise, and go toward the south unto the way that goeth down from Jerusalem unto Gaza, which is desert"* (Acts 8:26). Philip obeyed at once, and from that point on, the Holy Spirit guided him.

The man Cornelius needed to know about the salvation that could be found only in the Lord Jesus Christ. So he was directed by an angel to send for Peter. (See Acts 10:3–5.)

Do angels perform this same service today, this ministry of providing direction for God's people? I'm confident they do, though, of course, it can't be proven one way or the other. I have often felt when I have gone to do something or to reach somebody that God's angel directed me and had gone on before. Isn't that beautiful?

You're Safe!

Angels also protect believers. We have many instances of such protection recorded in the Bible. The apostle Paul could tell you about that. Remember the time his ship was caught in a terrible storm as he went to Rome? It seemed certain that the vessel would be lost and all on board would drown. The sailors did everything they possibly could, but they recognized they were facing death. (See Acts 27:14–20.)

Then Paul went to them and told them to be of good cheer. How could he say that? How did he know? What inside information did he have? He told them:

> *There shall be no loss of any man's life among you, but of the ship. For there stood by me this night the angel of God, whose I am, and whom I serve, saying, Fear not, Paul; thou must be brought before Caesar: and, lo, God hath given thee all them that sail with thee.*
>
> (Acts 27:22–24)

With that angelic assurance of protection, no wonder Paul could encourage them to cheer up.

God's Word gives us other examples of how angels protect His people. An angel shut the mouths of lions as Daniel spent the night in their den. (See Daniel 6:16–23.) Three young Hebrew men—Shadrach, Meshach, and Abednego—seemed certain to burn to death after being cast into the furnace heated seven times hotter than it ought to have been. God's angel kept them from harm. (See Daniel 3:1–28.)

Think back on your life, my friend. Perhaps you were spared from some horrible accident that could have seriously injured you or even killed you. You came through without a scratch. Could an angel have been on duty to save you in your moment of peril? Don't be surprised to learn some day in heaven that that is what took place.

Information, Please

One of the main ministries of angels to human beings is to convey information from God to us. We have already looked at a few cases in which angels served as God's messengers: when angels spoke to the pagan King Nebuchadnezzar in a dream, and when Gabriel prophesied the births of John the Baptist and the Lord Jesus.

There have been many times when men have needed messages from God and angels have delivered them. Consider, for example, the enormous burden that rested on the shoulders of Moses as he undertook the leadership of God's people. They needed commandments, for one thing, so that they would know how to live lives pleasing to God. Angels had some part in that—exactly what we don't know—for we read that the nation Israel *"received the law by the disposition of angels"* (Acts 7:53).

Prophets such as Daniel and Zechariah were given visions that they could not interpret by their own wisdom. So God used angels to explain. (See Daniel 7:15-27; 8:13-26; Zechariah 4:1; 5:5; 6:5.)

In the Christmas story we all know so well, the shepherds were informed by angels of the time and place of the birth of God's Son. (See Luke 2:8-14.) Later, an angel warned Joseph to flee with Mary and the infant Jesus to Egypt because Herod wanted to kill Jesus. (See Matthew 2:13.)

An angel also had the joyous responsibility of announcing Jesus' resurrection to the women who came to His tomb on the first Easter morning. (See Matthew 28:5-7.) Imagine how those women felt as they received this news from such a marvelous being! (See Matthew 28:3.)

As God has relayed information through angels in these and many other cases in the past, so He could provide information to you at some time of special need in the future. We don't know, of course, when God will choose to use that extraordinary means of communication, and we can find principles in the Bible to give general guidance to every decision and action. God still can supply information through angels, and He could speak to you that way some day.

"Coming for to Carry Me Home"

In recent years, popular books by medical doctors and psychologists have attempted to establish the fact of life after death. Often they include the case histories of people who have died, at least from a clinical standpoint. Those individuals try to tell us what it is like to leave their bodies behind on hospital beds and venture into the unknown. Yet I find such mystic accounts unsatisfying and sometimes contradictory.

How much better it is to turn to the authoritative Word of God. In Luke 16, our Lord Himself related what happened at the deaths of a rich man and Lazarus, a beggar. *"And it came to pass, that the beggar died, and was carried by the angels into Abraham's bosom"* (v. 22). I love that. When my dear mother died, I believe that she, too, was escorted right into the very presence of God and the saints who went before her by an angel.

It is difficult and even dangerous to make a general statement from just one passage of Scripture, but I like to think that all believers who die do receive that angelic service. If that's true, you, too, when you leave this earth in death—if the Lord delays His return—won't have to grope to find your way. You won't have to wonder who is going to introduce you. An angel will take care of those things for you. With great joy he will take your soul from here to there.

Angels Bring Judgment

We have examples in the Bible of times in which God used and will use angels to send judgment. One of these took place during the kingship of David, and it's frightening. *"And Satan stood up against Israel, and provoked David to number Israel"* (1 Chron. 21:1). Apparently, David wanted to find out just how strong he was militarily, and that showed a lack of trust in God. So God had to send terrible punishment.

> So the LORD sent pestilence upon Israel: and there fell of Israel seventy thousand men. And God sent an angel unto Jerusalem to destroy it: and as he was destroying, the LORD beheld, and he repented him of the evil, and said to the angel that destroyed, It is enough, stay now thine hand. (1 Chron. 21:14–15)

Even earlier in Israel's history, God used an angel to execute judgment on Egypt for the Pharaoh's hardness of heart in refusing to allow Israel to leave. As the culmination of the various plagues God had brought on Egypt, He sent an angel of death, *"the destroyer"* (Exod. 12:23), to kill all the firstborn in every Egyptian household.

> And it came to pass, that at midnight the LORD smote all the firstborn in the land of Egypt, from the firstborn of Pharaoh that sat on his throne unto the firstborn of the captive that was in the dungeon; and all the firstborn of cattle. And Pharaoh rose up in the night, he, and all his servants, and all the Egyptians; and there was a great cry in Egypt; for there was not a house where there was not one dead.
> (Exod. 12:29–30)

In the New Testament, we have the account of King Herod's speech that caused his audience to declare him a god, a declaration he did nothing to discourage. (See Acts 12:21–22.) In response to that blasphemy, *"immediately the angel of the Lord smote him, because he gave not God the glory: and he was eaten of worms, and gave up the ghost"* (Acts 12:23).

We also know that angels will be instruments of God's judgment on sinful humanity in the end times. In His parable of the wheat and tares in Matthew 13, Jesus said, *"The field is the world; the good seed are the children of the kingdom; but the tares are the children of the wicked one; the enemy that sowed them is the devil; the harvest is the end of the world; and the reapers are the angels"* (vv. 38–39).

That time of the Great Tribulation will be the grimmest hour the world has ever known. Jesus continued, *"The Son of man shall send forth his angels, and they shall gather out of his kingdom all things that offend, and them which do iniquity; and shall cast them into a furnace of fire: there shall be wailing and gnashing of teeth"* (vv. 41–42).

There are also scenes of angels dispensing God's end-time judgments throughout the book of Revelation.

Helpers of the Great Physician?

We know God heals. Is it possible that angels are somehow involved in His work of healing? That suggestion comes to us from reading about a miracle of healing performed by our Lord Jesus. He restored a man who had been sick for thirty-eight years. And in that account, the Bible tells us that poor man had sought healing with many others at a pool called Bethesda.

> *In these lay a great multitude of impotent folk, of blind, halt, withered, waiting for the moving of the water. For an angel went down at a certain season into the pool, and troubled the water: whosoever then first after the troubling of the water stepped in was made whole of whatsoever disease he had.* (John 5:3–4)

Providing Food and Water

As we read through the Bible, we see a number of instances in which God used angels to provide the physical necessities of food and drink when they were not normally available. The first of those is found in Genesis 21, which records the conclusion of the story of Hagar. Abraham had to send her and her son away, yet he loved her and the lad Ishmael. So he gave them bread and a bottle of water before they left to go out into the desert.

Soon, however, those provisions were depleted. Hagar was sure they were going to die. She and Ishmael cried out to God and wept.

> *And God heard the voice of the lad; and the angel of God called to Hagar out of heaven, and said unto her, What aileth thee, Hagar? fear not; for God hath heard the voice of the lad where he is....And God opened her eyes, and she saw a well of water; and she went, and filled the bottle with water, and gave the lad drink.* (Gen. 21:17, 19)

What a touching story! What a gracious God!

There is a similar story in the life of Elijah. Immediately after his well-known confrontation with and victory over the prophets of Baal, his life was threatened by Jezebel. Elijah lost all his courage and took off like a scared rabbit, running for many miles. Finally he sat down under a tree and gave up. *"O LORD,"* he prayed, *"take away my life; for I am not better than my fathers"* (1 Kings 19:4).

God's ministry for Elijah, however, was not over. How would He intervene in this situation? The following verses tell us: *"An angel touched him, and said unto him, Arise and eat. And he looked, and, behold, there was a cake baken on the coals, and a cruse of water at his head. And he did eat and drink"* (vv. 5–6). That was a private, personal miracle extended by God through an angel to His servant Elijah, but God wasn't finished. God repeated the provision, and the prophet received so much strength and encouragement that he was able to go on traveling another forty days and continue his needed ministry. (See verses 7–8.)

If God would reach down and supply the needs of individuals like Hagar and Elijah, it should not surprise us to learn in the New Testament that He did the same for His beloved Son. After Jesus had fasted for forty days and nights, He was tempted by the devil. One of those temptations, you will recall, involved the turning of a stone into bread. (See Matthew 4:3.) Our Lord easily could have done it but that would have been using His power wrongfully to supply a personal need suggested by the tempter.

After the third temptation, the devil left Jesus, who was still hungry. What happened? *"Angels came and ministered unto him"* (Matt. 4:11). Although we are not told so specifically, it seems apparent that food and drink were provided, perhaps the same as that given to Elijah in his time of need.

Do angels minister to God's people in this manner in modern times? George Muller thought so. That great Englishman of the nineteenth century provided care for scores of orphans. Sometimes, he had nothing to place on the table before them, but somehow, unexpectedly, from some source, food would be provided and the children would not go hungry. Perhaps God used angels once again to give food and drink when human resources failed.

God's Warriors

God also uses angels as armies to fight for Him and His people. As we saw earlier when studying Michael the archangel, there was a war in heaven between Michael and his angels and Satan and his angels when Satan rebelled against God. (See Revelation 12.) The holy angels prevailed, and Satan and his angels were cast to the earth.

In 2 Kings 19, we see God sending an angel to fight for Israel in defense of Jerusalem. In verse 34, God promised to defend the city, and in verse 35 we read, *"And it came to pass that night, that the angel of the LORD went out, and smote in the camp of the Assyrians an hundred fourscore and five thousand: and when they arose early in the morning, behold, they were all dead corpses."*

Another good example of angels as warriors is given to us in 2 Kings 6. The king of Syria was waging war against Israel, but he could not capture the king of Israel, because the prophet Elisha was giving his king knowledge from God of the Syrians' plans. When the king of Syria was told that, he ascertained that Elisha was in Dothan and sent a large group of his soldiers and chariots there to capture Elisha.

Those soldiers arrived at night and encircled the city. *"And when the servant of the man of God was risen early, and gone forth, behold, an host compassed the city both with horses and chariots. And his servant said unto him, Alas, my master! how shall we do?"* (2 Kings 6:15).

Obviously, the servant thought he and Elisha were in a lot of trouble. We can well understand how frightened he must have been as he looked out over the enemy.

But Elisha knew that God was on his side and that awesome angelic forces were available to fight for him if need be. So he said, *"Fear not: for they that be with us are more than they that be with them"* (v. 16). Because he wanted the servant to be as confident of that as he was, *"Elisha prayed, and said, LORD, I pray thee, open his eyes, that he may see. And the LORD opened the eyes of the young man; and he saw: and, behold, the mountain was full of horses and chariots of fire round about Elisha"* (v. 17).

That fiery army, invisible to the Syrians, was made up of angelic powers sent by God.

Heavenly Encouragement

We all need encouragement on occasion, and sometimes when God's servants have been in special need, He has sent angels to provide it.

In Daniel 9:21, the angel Gabriel came to Daniel to give him an encouraging touch. Gabriel then told him a prophecy.

As we saw earlier, when Paul was on his way to Rome, the boat he was in got caught in a severe storm that threatened the lives of everyone aboard. But an angel came to Paul at night and encouraged him with God's promise that everyone would be saved. (See Acts 27:23–24.)

Our Lord Himself probably received angelic encouragement many times during His life on earth. The night of His greatest need was surely that night in the Garden of Gethsemane when He agonized over His impending death, the same night in which He was betrayed. In that time of great need, *"there appeared an angel unto him from heaven, strengthening him"* (Luke 22:43).

Look Carefully

What do angels do? They worship God. They direct men. They protect believers. Angels give information. Angels may be involved in carrying home the righteous when they die. Angels bring God's judgment on both the pagan and God's people. Angels may sometimes exercise a ministry of healing. God has used angels to provide the physical needs of His people. Angels do battle for God and His children. They strengthen and encourage His own.

Perhaps you think to yourself, *I wish I could see such great things for myself—to experience some of the things pointed out in the Bible.*

Yes, of course. But perhaps God has something different in store for you. He may want you on the giving end rather than on the receiving end. If an angel were to come to your door dressed in spectacular garments and radiating the glory of God, you would certainly invite him in and give gracious, loving service.

Suppose, however, that someone of low estate came to your home. How would you respond? Perhaps it would not be in the same way as if he were an angel. But remember Hebrews 13:2: *"Be not forgetful to entertain strangers: for thereby some have entertained angels unawares."*

So let's put this down as a final thing angels do: They may give you an unexpected opportunity to reach out with the love of God and become involved, personally, with one of this magnificent order of the Creator's handiwork.

4
What Angels Know

What a person does is based on what he knows. From time to time, for example, scientists warn of an epidemic that is expected to strike the country. The government makes the announcement in the electronic and print media and holds out encouragement with the development of a new vaccine. So millions of people go to their doctors or to clinics to protect themselves against what may cause them much sickness and pain.

Suppose you are in a hotel and someone shouts, "Fire!" You run for the nearest emergency exit, acting on what you know.

What is true of men is also true of angels. In the last chapter, we surveyed some things angels do. Why do they act? Presumably they act on the basis of what they know.

My mind immediately recalls 2 Samuel 14:20. A woman said to King Saul, *"My lord is wise, according to the wisdom of an angel of God, to know all things that are in the earth."* I'm not at all sure Saul was a wise man, based on some of the foolish things he did, but I am sure of the correctness of the woman's assessment of angels. Angels do indeed possess superhuman knowledge.

Where do angels get their knowledge? Directly from God Himself. He is the source of their intelligence. Their information comes directly from the throne of God, and that's the best of all wisdom in the universe.

Angels Know God Personally

Perhaps the chief thing angels know is God Himself. They know Him personally. They have a vital, intimate relationship with the Creator of all things. We have already seen time and again in this book that angels dwell in God's presence, surrounding His throne, worshipping Him.

When we consider further that true knowledge of God requires obedience to His commandments (see 1 John 2:3–5), we can better appreciate the ability of the holy angels to know God. Because they obey His commandments, they can more fully know Him. The mind of man was darkened by the Fall in the Garden of Eden, but those angels who remained loyal to God in the rebellion of Lucifer have had no such shades drawn over their understanding.

Angels Know the Reality of Demons

In addition to knowing God, angels also know the reality of demons. They know how Lucifer fell from heaven. They observed the many angels who elected to go with him and rebel against God, a subject we will consider in more depth in chapter 8. They know that spiritual warfare is still going on between the forces of God and the forces of Satan, a war that will continue until Satan and his followers are cast into hell for all eternity.

Now, what can we learn from this? I think angels are smarter than we are in regard to how to wage spiritual warfare. They know there is a war on, they are aware of it every day, and they are able to discern the devil's traps. A good place for us to start in our preparation for that struggle is Ephesians 6:10–18.

Angels Know Human Beings

Not only do angels know God and their demonic adversaries, but they also know mankind; they know human beings. The Bible tells us they were present at the creation of our physical universe (see Job 38:6–7), which logically implies that they had already been created at that point. So their knowledge of humanity began, I'm sure, with the very first pair to live on earth. I'm certain the angels observed Adam and Eve as they lived together in the Garden of Eden, tended the garden, and eventually sinned and had to be driven out of the garden. And we can be sure that those immortal creatures have been watching mankind ever since, often interacting with men and women at God's command.

Angels Knew of the Resurrection

As we study the biblical records, we observe that angels had to know of the resurrection. Certainly those angels who watched over the Lord during His earthly stay heard His repeated statements that He was going to be crucified and resurrected on the third day. (See Matthew 12:40; 16:21; 17:9, 22–23; 20:18–19.)

Not only did an angel announce the Lord's resurrection to the women who first came to the tomb (see Matthew 28:5–6), but he had already rolled the stone away from the door of the tomb. (See verses 2–3.) Even prior to that, you remember that back when the angel appeared to Joseph to tell him to go ahead and marry Mary even though she was pregnant, the reason the angel gave was that *"that which is conceived in her is of the Holy Ghost. And she shall bring forth a son, and thou shalt call his name Jesus: for he shall save his people from their sins"* (Matt. 1:20–21). The angel knew the Lord was coming to save us from our sins, and we can infer that the angel knew our Lord had to die and be resurrected in order to purchase our salvation. (See 1 Corinthians 15.)

When the Lord ascended into heaven some fifty days after the Resurrection, angels knew all about it. In fact, they had to nudge the apostles to tell them that, for the moment, their face-to-face encounter with Jesus was over. *"And while they* [the apostles] *looked stedfastly toward heaven as he went up, behold, two men stood by them in white apparel; which also said, Ye men of Galilee, why stand ye gazing up into heaven? this same Jesus, which is taken up from you into heaven, shall so come in like manner as ye have seen him go into heaven"* (Acts 1:10–11).

Angels Know the Purpose of God

The ultimate plan of God is to save men and women from their sins. To do that, He provided salvation through the Lord Jesus Christ, His Son. If you were asked to explain salvation to someone who had never heard of it, you probably could, given sufficient time.

Yet there are some things about salvation that are unexplainable because they are of such magnitude. Peter spoke of that fact in his first letter:

> *Of which salvation the prophets have inquired and searched diligently, who prophesied of the grace that should come unto you: searching what, or what manner of time the Spirit of Christ which was in them did signify, when it testified beforehand the sufferings of Christ, and the glory that should follow. Unto whom it was revealed, that not unto themselves, but unto us they did minister the things, which are now reported unto you by them that have preached the gospel unto you with the Holy Ghost sent down from heaven; which things the angels desire to look into.* (1 Pet. 1:10–12)

Angels, of course, transcend the times of the prophets. They have watched the unfolding of God's plan of salvation over the centuries, the millennia. They know it is the greatest possible theme of men or of angels. And although they know of salvation from an objective viewpoint (but not an experiential viewpoint, since angels don't need to be saved), they long to know it even more thoroughly.

Angels Know the Ministry of the Church

If we are not active participants in the churches we attend, we may not be aware of everything the church is or should be doing in its service to Christ. The angels of God, however, are well aware of the work and witness God ordained for the church. How do we know this? We know it from such passages as the one in Paul's first letter to Timothy. Paul there set forth the things that Timothy was to do as a minister of the gospel. Paul summed up that section with these words: *"I charge thee before God, and the Lord Jesus Christ, and the elect angels, that thou observe these things without preferring one before another, doing nothing by partiality"* (1 Tim. 5:21). That's a fascinating and even a somber thought—to recognize that angels view what is going on in the local church and how it follows or fails to follow the directives God has given it.

Angels Know the Certainty of Judgment

We live in an increasingly secular society. Lawmakers, jurists, and humanists have done a great deal over the past half-century to banish God from public acknowledgment and recognition. And we have by no means seen the end of this tragic movement.

If there is no God, there is no need to live responsibly as if there were one. Man is free to do his own thing, to live it up, to enjoy all the pleasures his body can stand or his pocketbook can afford. And so we are seeing a complete abandonment of moral values.

If man thinks of death at all, he conceives of it as a cessation of being, perhaps a final period. But there is no way we can get around the finality of Hebrews 9:27, which reads, *"It is appointed unto men once to die, but after this the judgment."*

Unsaved people and even liberal churchmen deny the truth that is taught there. It's unpopular and unsettling, but angels are persuaded of the fact and know, as we have seen in Revelation, that they will take part in God's judgment. Indeed, they know that the final destination of unrepentant men and women, hell, is a place prepared originally for their number who disobeyed God and joined Satan's rebellion. Jesus foretold to His disciples what He would one day say at the time of judgment: *"Then shall he say also unto them on the left hand, Depart from me, ye cursed, into everlasting fire, prepared for the devil and his angels"* (Matt. 25:41).

What must angels think as they look down on earth and observe people laughing and taking their pleasure while, unknowingly, they rush headlong down the path to eternal destruction?

5

Angels and Prophecy

One of the greatest human needs is that of self-revelation. John Donne's famous statement "No man is an island" is certainly true. We have a need to reveal ourselves to others. We need others to reveal themselves to us. Man is a social being and cannot find true happiness or fulfillment in himself alone.

God made us that way. In fact, God Himself seems to have a similar need, if we may speak of God as having needs. God is the original self-revelator. The term sounds strange, but it depicts accurately the fact that God has always been disclosing Himself. He did that, for example, in creating the natural world that, although marred by sin, contains such beauty. No wonder the psalmist exclaimed, *"The heavens declare the glory of God; and the firmament showeth his handiwork"* (Ps. 19:1).

God reveals Himself and His plans in many ways. In the past, He has talked directly with the leaders of His people and the prophets sent to them. Visions and dreams are other means God has used to communicate with men. We have already looked at a number of cases in which angels delivered prophetic messages to men and women. In this chapter, we want to look at a few more specific cases of that important angelic activity.

A Coming Destruction

The ultimate self-revelation, of course, came about in the person of God's Son, for as the writer of Hebrews stated it, God *"hath in these last days spoken unto us by his Son, whom he hath appointed heir of all things, by whom also he made the worlds"* (Heb. 1:2).

God's Son was active in history, however, long before He came to this earth as a babe in Bethlehem. Sometimes He came down from heaven in a pre-incarnate visit (called a "theophany" or, more specifically, a "Christophany"). We do not know if it was in the same body in which He would later appear as a man for His thirty-three years on earth, but perhaps that was the case.

Sometimes He came in the company of angels. That was true when one day He appeared while Abraham was seated in his tent door. *"And he* [Abraham] *lift up his eyes and looked, and, lo, three men stood by him"* (Gen. 18:2). One was the Lord Jesus, I believe, and the other two were angels.

Why had they come? For two reasons: The first was to reassure Sarah that she would become the mother of the long-promised son of Abraham.

We infer the second reason from Genesis 18:17–18: *"And the LORD said, Shall I hide from Abraham that thing which I do; seeing that Abraham shall surely become a great and mighty nation, and all the nations of the earth shall be blessed in him?"* Here was the Lord talking with angels about whether Abraham should be brought in on the coming destruction of Sodom. So it seems evident that those angels participated in this prophetic revelation to Abraham, giving him advance information that the wicked city in which Lot, his nephew, lived would be destroyed. That gave opportunity to Abraham to intercede for Sodom, but in vain. The angels left the Lord and Abraham on a hilltop, left them to go and rescue Lot and his family before God destroyed the city.

Angels Ascending and Descending

God also spoke directly to Abraham's grandson Jacob. Jacob, as you recall, was fleeing from home because he feared the wrath of his brother, Esau, for stealing the blessing of their father. Finally exhausted, Jacob lay down to sleep, cradling his head on a rock. *"And he dreamed, and behold a ladder set up on the earth, and the top of it reached to heaven: and behold the angels of God ascending and descending on it"* (Gen. 28:12).

It is hard to picture that dream in our own minds as God gave Jacob a special prophecy regarding the course of his life and what would happen to his descendants. Perhaps the angels stood by in solemn witness as God reminded Jacob of the Abrahamic covenant:

> *I am the LORD God of Abraham thy father, and the God of Isaac: the land whereon thou liest, to thee will I give it, and to thy seed....And, behold, I am with thee, and will keep thee in all places whither thou goest, and will bring thee again into this land; for I will not leave thee, until I have done that which I have spoken to thee of.*
> (Gen. 28:13–15)

In the many decades that he lived following that revelation, Jacob saw the fulfillment of the word God had spoken and to which the angels had been witness. And no doubt he reported the vision of God and the heavenly messengers to the sons God later gave him.

A Coming Mighty Man

After the death of Joshua, there was a time in the history of Israel when God used judges to guide His people. From time to time, angels, or, specifically, the angel of the Lord (perhaps a reference to the pre-incarnate Christ), were involved. The story of Manoah and his wife is a good example. One day this godly woman was visited by the angel, who said,

> *Behold now, thou art barren, and bearest not: but thou shalt conceive, and bear a son....and no razor shall come on his head: for the child shall be a Nazarite unto God from the womb: and he shall begin to deliver Israel out of the hand of the Philistines.* (Judg. 13:3, 5)

To whom was the angel of the Lord referring? It was none other than Samson, who became one of the most noted judges of

Israel and whose name even in secular society denotes super-human strength. Here we see the Lord encouraging His people by giving them hope that one would come to free them from their bondage.

Angel at His Side

Zechariah, who wrote the book called by his name, is known as one of the minor prophets—minor in that the prophecies he gave are confined to a few short chapters compared to the books of Jeremiah or Isaiah.

How did Zechariah get his knowledge of what would come to pass? The word *angel* appears some twenty times in the thir-teen short chapters Zechariah wrote. Often the heavenly mes-senger is described in the phrase, "the angel that talked with me." What a picturesque description—this man of God, asking questions about God's program, and receiving answers from "the angel that talked with me"!

Still Speaking Today?

It is easy to relegate all angelic activity with regard to proph-ecy to the ancient past. "But what of today?" you might ask. "Are angels still giving us revelations from God? Do they work with us in our service to the Lord Jesus?"

I believe they do. Although I can't prove that, let me give you a personal illustration that will help to explain my belief. Some years ago, I was flying from the Holy Land to New York City aboard a giant Boeing 747. I was using the time to study my Bible and prepare studies such as these.

A lady approached me, tapped me on the shoulder, and introduced herself. She was a widow, perhaps sixty years of age. "I was praying," she said, "and the Lord told me to tell you some-thing."

"Yes?" I replied.

"The Lord told me that He would send His angels and would clear and release the American airways from demon power and possession in order that Christian television could go through and allow you to preach the gospel of Christ to millions of people in these last days."

I thanked her and returned to my studies.

About thirty minutes later, she came back. "I was praying again," she said, "and the Lord said you didn't listen to me the first time."

Inwardly, I had to admit that had been the case. I had not listened with my full attention, either of head or of heart.

"Now listen to me," she continued. "The Lord wants me to impress upon you that angels are going to release and to clear the American airways from demon power and possession." She reiterated her previous communication about how it would be my privilege to use television to reach the lost with the message of salvation.

This time, her words got through to me. "I thank you. I thank you very much," I replied, "and I, too, will pray."

I bowed my head and began to talk to the Lord about that very wonderful thing that had been communicated to me through prophecy. My soul rejoiced because I believed that that very thing would come to pass.

Just a few days later, I received word from the government that the license I had been seeking had been granted. The Lord brought to my mind the words I had heard: "I have freed the airways so that you can use them." I have no doubt that angels are assisting in this work.

I find that tremendously exciting. Angels had something to do with that prophecy that came to me. And God allows the angels to clear the path of obstacles that may prevent us from doing the work of our heavenly Father.

Don't think that it could not be *your* privilege to work with angels in these last days.

Even if you do not have some personal experience with angels and prophecy, you need to know how God will use angels in the future, as given to us in the book of Revelation. I will talk about that in some detail in the next chapter.

6
Angels in the Life of Jesus

When we consider those events in human history that have changed the world, there are really very few. Chief among those that do rank in that category, however, is the coming and walking among us of God Himself in the person of Jesus Christ. Certainly those were the most remarkable thirty-three years of all time.

Given the extraordinary nature of the Incarnation and the importance of the mission Christ came to accomplish, it is not surprising that angels were very much in evidence in association with the birth, life, death, and resurrection of the Lord. If ever there was a life in which angels had cause to be involved, it was the life of the Lord Jesus.

In this chapter, we want to look specifically at how angels were involved in the earthly life of Christ. We have already mentioned most of the relevant Scripture passages in earlier chapters, but we want to bring them together here with a few others and focus in one place on the role of angels in the life of the most remarkable man in history, God in human form.

Telling of His Prophet

The story of angelic involvement in the life of Christ really has to start before we even look at Mary and Joseph, for God had ordained that a prophet would go before the Messiah, both to announce His coming and to prepare the hearts and minds of the people for Him. And in His wisdom and sovereignty, God decided that the birth of this prophet would itself be a miracle.

The parents chosen for the prophet were Zacharias, a priest, and his wife, Elisabeth. They had never had children because Elisabeth was barren, and now they were also beyond the childbearing years. (See Luke 1:7. Notice also how closely this account parallels the case of Abraham and Sarah in Genesis 18:11–12.) But God sent the angel Gabriel to Zacharias, as we saw earlier, to announce that not only would he and Elisabeth have a child, but also that their child would be the Messiah's forerunner, John the Baptist.

Later, when John the Baptist and Jesus were grown, John did indeed prepare the people for Christ, pointing out their sins and calling for repentance. And when Christ was ready to begin His public ministry and John's work was through, John said, *"Ye yourselves bear me witness, that I said, I am not the Christ, but that I am sent before him....He must increase, but I must decrease"* (John 3:28, 30).

Telling of His Coming

Angelic involvement in Christ's life continued before He was born, for His birth was to be a unique act, a new life conceived apart from the normal human process, without a man, in a virgin. Certainly the woman who was to bear the Christ child had to be told before the fact; she had to be prepared for an event that was impossible apart from the intervention of God. Also, even though the event was to be an act of the Holy Spirit, it might expose the young woman to the taunts and abuse of those among her family and neighbors who did not believe in the miraculous nature of the conception. Indeed, fornication, which would be the only normal way for an unmarried woman to become pregnant, was punishable by death under Mosaic Law. (See Leviticus 20:10.)

Therefore, God sent the angel Gabriel again, this time to tell the Virgin Mary what was about to happen. (See Luke 1:26–38.) When Gabriel gave her the news, Mary was understandably perplexed. Gabriel explained, however, that it was the power of God Himself who would cause it to happen.

Notice Mary's reaction, then, to the news: *"Behold the handmaid of the Lord; be it unto me according to thy word"* (Luke 1:38).

Next read Mary's beautiful Magnificat to see how thrilled she was to play such a part in God's eternal plan. (See Luke 1:46–55.) What a lesson she gives us of obedience and willingness to be used by God in whatever way He sees fit!

After Mary was found to be pregnant with the Christ child, Joseph, her betrothed husband, wanted to put her away secretly to protect her from shame. Surely Mary had told him how the pregnancy had come about, but apparently he was having trouble believing it. So an angel was sent to reassure Joseph of the miraculous, godly nature of Mary's pregnancy and to encourage him to take her as his wife. Joseph obeyed, giving us another example of gracious obedience to God. (See Matthew 1:18–23.)

Announcing His Birth

The next part in the story of angels in the life of Jesus is very familiar to all of us. When the Christ child was born in Bethlehem, God sent an angel to shepherds in a nearby field to announce His birth, *"good tidings of great joy"* (Luke 2:10) of the coming of a Savior. (See verses 10–12.)

As if that had not been enough to generate fear and awe in the hearts of the shepherds, after the angel told them where to locate the child, a multitude of angels appeared with the first angel, *"praising God and saying, Glory to God in the highest, and on earth peace, good will toward men"* (Luke 2:13–14).

Try to imagine yourself in that situation. Think what it must have looked and felt like. Then perhaps you can regain some of the wonder of that first Christmas. Think, too, of the overflowing joy and amazement the angels must have felt as they proclaimed that their Creator-God now lived among men as a tiny baby.

Protecting Him as a Baby

Jesus was born during the reign of King Herod, one of the family of Herods who ruled Palestine for several generations under Roman authority. When the three wise men came from the east to Jerusalem in search of the new King of the Jews, Herod called in the Jewish priests and scribes to ask where the Messiah was to be born. He then asked the three wise men when the star had appeared that had led them there. (See Matthew 2:4–7.)

Herod's motivations in asking those things, of course, were fear of a potential rival for the throne and a desire to eliminate that rival immediately. God knew that and understood that the life of the baby Jesus was in danger. So we read in Matthew 2:13 that when the wise men had left, *"the angel of the Lord appeareth to Joseph in a dream, saying, Arise, and take the young child and his mother, and flee into Egypt, and be thou there until I bring thee word: for Herod will seek the young child to destroy him."*

Joseph was again obedient to angelic instruction and took Mary and Jesus to Egypt. (See Matthew 2:14.) Then, as God had known would happen, Herod ordered the execution of every boy two years old and under in Bethlehem and the surrounding area. (See Matthew 2:16.) Herod figured that if he killed all the young boys, he would be sure to get the one whom he feared might overthrow him as king.

After Herod died and it was safe for Jesus and His family to return to Israel, *"an angel of the Lord appeareth in a dream to Joseph in Egypt, saying, Arise, and take the young child and his mother, and go into the land of Israel: for they are dead which sought the young child's life"* (Matt. 2:19–20). So we see that once again, angels were watching over this special child and protecting Him from those who would harm Him.

Sustaining Him in His Ministry

We are told very little in the Bible of the years when Jesus was growing into an adult. No mention is made of any angelic activity in His life after those events surrounding His birth, although it would not be at all surprising if we were to learn in heaven that they ministered to Him many times in those years.

We next see angels ministering to Him in the familiar story of His temptation in the wilderness, when He was beginning

His public ministry. He had been led into the wilderness by the Holy Spirit, and there He fasted forty days and forty nights. (See Matthew 4:1–2.) While He was there, Satan came and tempted Him, failing every time. When Satan finally gave up and left, *"angels came and ministered unto him* [Jesus]" (Matt. 4:11).

Later, when Christ was in terrible agony of soul in the Garden of Gethsemane, struggling with the fact of His impending death for the sins of humanity, *"there appeared an angel unto him from heaven, strengthening him"* (Luke 22:43). If ever someone needed such help, it was the holy Son of God at that moment as He faced the prospect of bearing the sins of the world and dying on a cross. And an angel was there to provide that help.

Later, when Jesus was being arrested, He gave us insight into the angelic forces that were at His disposal if He needed them. When the soldiers came to take Jesus, Peter had drawn a sword and cut off the ear of one of the high priest's servants who was with the soldiers. (See Matthew 26:51; also John 18:10.) Jesus, wanting to make clear to Peter that He was going to His death voluntarily, told him, *"Thinkest thou that I cannot now pray to my Father, and he shall presently give me more than twelve legions of angels?"* (Matt. 26:53). In other words, He was telling Peter, "It is not as though I am defenseless. All the angels I could possibly need to rescue Me are ready and waiting to do so if I so choose. I am being arrested of My own free will."

That statement from Jesus impresses upon us the fact that Christ truly did bear our sins willingly, demonstrating His love for us *"while we were yet sinners"* (Rom. 5:8). He had a choice; the angels were standing by to save Him; but He elected to die in our place.

Active in the Resurrection

The life and ministry of the Lord Jesus Christ did not end when He was crucified, for after death came the resurrection. The role of angels in His life continued as well.

When Jesus arose from the grave, *"there was a great earthquake: for the angel of the Lord descended from heaven, and came and rolled back the stone from the door, and sat upon it. His countenance was like lightning, and his raiment white as snow: and for fear of him the keepers did shake, and became as dead men"* (Matt. 28:2–4).

Picture yourself as one of those guards, and perhaps then you can appreciate a little better how they must have felt when that angel appeared and rolled the stone away from the mouth of the tomb.

After that, the angelic role continued, for angels next had the privilege of announcing Christ's resurrection to His disciples. All the Synoptic Gospels give us accounts of how the angels told the women who came to the tomb that Jesus was no longer there, that He had risen as He had said He would and as the Old Testament prophets had foretold. (See Matthew 28:5–7; Mark 16:5–7; Luke 24:3–7.) The gospel writers did not state it explicitly, but I am sure those angels must have been overflowing with joy as they gave the women that amazing, wonderful news.

Proclaiming and Participating in His Return

After forty days in His resurrected body, Jesus ascended into heaven, and again angels were involved. As Jesus' disciples watched Him ascend, two angels appeared beside them. (See Acts 1:9–10.) The angels prophesied, *"This same Jesus, which is taken up from you into heaven, shall so come in like manner as ye have seen him go into heaven"* (Acts 1:11).

What the angels did not say on that occasion, but which both Jesus and the apostle Paul affirmed, was that when Christ does indeed return to earth, the angels will come with Him. For example, Jesus said in Matthew 25:31, *"When the Son of man shall come in his glory, and all the holy angels with him, then shall he sit upon the throne of his glory."* (See also Mark 8:38; 2 Thessalonians 1:7.) So we see that even in Jesus' future glorification upon the earth, angels will be involved, just as they were with Him and ministered to Him during His incarnation.

7
Angels in the Revelation

I f you discover one word used seventy-two times in one book of the Bible, you can safely assume that God considers it very important. Open a concordance to the entries for "angel" and "angels," begin to count, and you may be amazed to discover that the last portion of the New Testament, the Revelation, has far more to say about angelic activity than any other portion of God's Word.

In one sense, angels are "bookends" for the Revelation, and you understand that I say that reverently. Look at chapter 1, verse 1: *"The Revelation of Jesus Christ, which God gave unto him, to show unto his servants things which must shortly come to pass; and he sent and signified it by his angel unto his servant John."*

When we turn to the final chapter, in the last section of verses, angels appear again, holding the Revelation in a single, tight unit. They are pointed out by our Lord Himself: *"I Jesus have sent mine angel to testify unto you these things in the churches"* (Rev. 22:16).

The book of Revelation is generally a chronological unfolding of future events, so let us look at angels in Revelation as their ministry progressively unfolds.

More than ten percent of the references to angels are found in connection with the letters to the seven churches in chapters 2 and 3. It's fascinating to consider that God might have detailed angels to carry messages to specific congregations. The meaning of "angel" in those references to the seven churches is not entirely clear, since "angel" literally means "messenger" and the word here could conceivably mean something like "pastor."

However, these references could also be to the spiritual beings we have been studying.

Up to the Throne

You will recall that on one occasion the apostle Paul was caught up into the third heaven. He testified that he *"heard unspeakable words, which it is not lawful for a man to utter"* (2 Cor. 12:4).

We must be very careful in any speculation about what Paul referred to there. But it's just possible that he was allowed to witness, in a prophetic vision, what is described in Revelation 7:11–12 concerning angels. *"And all the angels stood round about the throne...saying, Amen: Blessing, and glory, and wisdom, and thanksgiving, and honour, and power, and might, be unto our God for ever and ever. Amen."*

Did Paul see and hear the angels? I don't know, of course, but if he did, I think he would say it was simply indescribable in glory and majesty.

We have looked previously at the fact that one of the chief functions of angels is to worship God. We see in Revelation that they will have that privilege throughout eternity.

Executing Judgment

How disappointing it is to end our view of that heavenly scene and let our eyes again focus on things of earth. Here, instead of angels praising God, we see men and women blaspheming God and living in sin, with no sense of obligation to God.

Why is that? At least a partial answer is found in Ecclesiastes 8:11: *"Because sentence against an evil work is not executed speedily, therefore the heart of the sons of men is fully set in them to do evil."*

In this age of grace, all men benefit from the long-suffering and patience of God. He does not immediately punish sin, but there is coming a day when He will, and He will use angels as agents of His vengeance. In an earlier chapter, we had already looked briefly at angels as instruments of God's judgment. Let's focus now on their activity in that role in the book of Revelation.

Angelic Warnings, Angelic Reapings

The angelic job of warning people and then, if the warning is not heeded, bringing about the judgment of God will be especially in force during the end times in relationship to the Antichrist.

Let me begin to explain the above by quoting from Revelation 14.

And the third angel followed them, saying with a loud voice, If any man worship the beast and his image, and receive his mark in his forehead, or in his hand, the same shall drink of the wine of the wrath of God, which is poured out without mixture into the cup of his indignation; and he shall be tormented with fire and brimstone in the presence of the holy angels, and in the presence of the Lamb: and the smoke of their torment ascendeth up for ever and ever: and they have no rest day nor night, who worship the beast and his image, and whosoever receiveth the mark of his name. (vv. 9–11)

During his brief reign on earth, the Antichrist is going to control completely the economic life of everyone. No one will be able to buy or sell unless he has a mark on his forehead or his hand. So people will have to make a decision—to identify themselves with God's people and suffer death as the consequence, or to go along with the Antichrist. The great majority will make the wrong choice. They will say, "'I'm ready. Give me the mark.'"

Then, like a dam that is broken, the fury of God will spring forth. Notice how angels are involved:

And another angel came out of the temple, crying with a loud voice to him that sat on the cloud, Thrust in thy sickle, and reap: for the time is come for thee to reap; for the harvest of the earth is ripe. And he that sat on the cloud thrust in his sickle on the earth; and the earth was reaped. And another angel came out of the temple which is in heaven, he also having a sharp sickle. And another angel came out from the altar, which had power over fire; and cried with a loud cry to him that had the sharp sickle, saying, Thrust in thy sharp sickle, and gather the clusters of the vine of the earth; for her grapes are fully ripe. And the angel thrust in his sickle into the earth, and gathered the vine of the earth, and cast it into the great winepress of the wrath of God. And the winepress was trodden without the city, and blood came out of the winepress, even unto the horse bridles, by the space of a thousand and six hundred furlongs. (Rev. 14:15–20)

What a terrible picture that is of God's coming judgment, but one that is fully deserved. Now we think of angels as blessing the world and strengthening and guiding us down here. They do, but there is coming a time when angels will be dealing out the wrath of a righteous God. Where do you stand just now, under the present blessing of angels or under the coming judgment?

I pray that every reader of this book might come to know the Lord Jesus Christ as his or her personal savior. My words to you may not be effective, but will you receive warning from the Word of God? I urge you to get a Bible and read the sixteenth chapter of Revelation, which is too long for me to quote here. You will note how seven angels are used by God to execute His fierce wrath upon an unbelieving world. It's a terrible, terrible picture of things to come, and I would have you avoid it at all costs.

Babylon, Babylon

God is not only going to judge individuals during the Great Tribulation, but He is also going to bring judgment on world systems. Two Babylons are mentioned in Revelation, one in chapter 17 and one in chapter 18.

First to be judged is religious Babylon. We cannot be certain of its exact identity. But I want you to see how an angel was involved in giving John information. He wrote, *"And there came one of the seven angels which had the seven vials, and talked with me, saying unto me, Come hither; I will show unto thee the judgment of the great whore that sitteth upon many waters"* (Rev. 17:1). So an angel gave the apostle a preview of the judgment that is to come on that false religious system.

Even more striking is the angelic involvement with regard to the second, or economic, Babylon, described in Revelation 18.

> *And after these things I saw another angel come down from heaven, having great power; and the earth was lightened with his glory. And he cried mightily with a strong voice, saying, Babylon the great is fallen, is fallen, and is become the habitation of devils, and the hold of every foul spirit, and a cage of every unclean and hateful bird.*
>
> (vv. 1–2)

That is a remarkable prophecy having to do with the tribulation period. Nowhere else is an angel described quite like that. His mission is to judge economic Babylon. Some say it is New York City or the United Nations; we can't know for sure. But our point here is to emphasize the angelic involvement.

An Angel in the Sun

Artists often picture angels as having a bright countenance. Where do they get that idea? Perhaps from Revelation 19:17: *"And I saw an angel standing in the sun."* That seems to refer to a brilliance that shone from his face. What a sight that would be!

I don't think our eyes would remain on the angel for long, however, because this one, too, has a work of judgment to execute. The rest of Revelation 19 tells how the remains of a great army provide food for the fowls, and then how at last, the beast and the false prophet and those who worshipped his image are all cast into a lake of fire burning with brimstone.

The preceding have been just some highlights of angelic involvement in the judgments described in Revelation. You will want to read the entire book of Revelation for yourself to appreciate all that angels will be doing in the end times. Pay special attention to those passages that have not been discussed much in this study as they relate to judgment—for example, chapters 4–13, 20–22.

8
What Kind of People Receive Angelic Service?

Whenever you hear of something good coming your way, something desirable, you may ask yourself, "I wonder if I will receive it? I wonder if I am eligible?" Perhaps you have raised those questions in connection with our study on angels. So, we need to consider together who receives the services of angels.

As we begin this chapter, we need to keep in the front of our minds the sovereignty of God. He cannot be made to jump through a hoop, even if we think we have satisfied some list of requirements. He is God, not us; His understanding is perfect, not ours. And we know that with His perfect understanding of our lives and needs, He is causing all things to work together for our ultimate good. (See Romans 8:28.)

What we will be looking at in this chapter, then, are some general characteristics of people or situations for whom or in which God has provided angelic intervention in the past. There is no foolproof formula for getting angelic assistance. Even pagans, people who are anti-God, sometimes receive angelic aid. (Remember the warning given to Babylonian King Nebuchadnezzar?)

Given those cautions, let's look at a few examples of who receives angelic service. We have looked at some of these people and situations before, but now we want to look behind the scenes at motivations and causes.

Those Who Know and Serve God

Angels help those who know and serve God. That makes the scope very large. Do you have knowledge of God by virtue of being related to Him through His Son, Jesus Christ? If you do, you have been born again. You are on speaking terms with God, and the channels are open. God can now give you spiritual manifestations, such as the visitation of angels.

I began the first chapter of this book by relating a story from my boyhood years, and I will briefly refer to it again here. I told how a stranger once came to our door and asked to be fed. My mother agreed, provided the meal, and then sensed something unusual about him. Right after he left she opened the door, but he was nowhere in sight. Mother became aware that she may have been entertaining an angel, after the manner described in Hebrews 13:2.

That would not surprise me at all. My mother knew God—really knew Him. She knew and loved His Word. She knew and loved His Son. She was one of the most devoted women to prayer and to the reading of the Bible whom I have ever met.

Do you long for the things of God? Do you have a hunger to know Him better? Perhaps, for example, you hear the verse *"I was glad when they said unto me, Let us go into the house of the Lord"* (Ps. 122:1), and you reply, "Yes, let's go!" That's evidence that you are seeking God and all He has for you.

If you know God, you probably will serve Him as well. But suppose you were to learn, to your utter amazement and fear, that the government had just passed a law saying you could no longer pray to God? Would that change your prayer habits? You might excuse yourself by recalling the verse that speaks of going into a closet to pray. You might reason that if it were suddenly illegal to pray, it would be a good time for closet prayer. That is not true service to God, however.

Indeed, that very law was passed during the time of Daniel. The complete story is told in the sixth chapter of the book that bears his name. Did Daniel go to his walk-in closet and there pour out his petitions to God? *"Now when Daniel knew that the writing was signed, he went into his house; and his windows being open in his chamber toward Jerusalem, he kneeled upon his knees three times a day, and prayed, and gave thanks before his God, as he did aforetime"* (v. 10).

It is true that for breaking the king's law, Daniel was thrown into the den of lions. But he met an angel there and felt right at home, as we observed earlier. You see, Daniel served God devoutly all his life.

As you would expect, we find many similar examples in Scripture—accounts of God's servants who received angelic visitations. Mary, the human mother of our Lord, was such a person. She loved God; she truly loved Him. (Read of her love and reverence for God in the Magnificat in Luke 1:47–55.) God selected her among all the women of the world for all time to be the mother of the baby Jesus. That willingness on her part would bring her malicious talk, embarrassment—even the possible loss of her betrothed—but Mary was devout, and Mary saw an angel.

Ezekiel was another example of those who served God. Some people pass up reading his book because they don't feel it has anything to say to them. In reading it, however, we weep with the prophet over the sins of God's people, and at the same time we find our hearts warmed as they get in tune with his great love for God. And Ezekiel saw angels.

Do you remember the story of Cornelius? He was a Roman centurion stationed in Israel. What kind of man was he? The Bible says he was *"a devout man, and one that feared God with all his house, which gave much alms to the people, and prayed to God alway"* (Acts 10:2). Cornelius meant business with God. He wasn't just playing around, biding his time until he could get back to Rome and enjoy the good life. He knew that God was worthy of being sought with all his heart, and Cornelius saw an angel.

Those Who Need God's Special Help

People who have special needs have often received angelic service very beautifully, wonderfully, and dynamically. Think of Joshua. He found himself at the head of the Israelite army.

Although he had some military command experience under Moses, he had never before borne alone the entire load of leadership responsibility. He knew he needed help and that God was his only resource.

Does it surprise you that God came to Joshua's aid? Would you expect God to call down from heaven, "Sorry, but you're on your own"? No, of course not. Our heavenly Father wants to meet us at the point of our need, whatever that may be. Here, in Joshua's case, it was for military planning, and that's exactly what Joshua got.

How was that assistance and guidance given? Through the presence of an angel. (See Joshua 5:13–14.) No wonder Joshua was able to lead the people in a great victory!

Peter and the other apostles offer us another example. They found themselves in prison because they loved God and had been serving Him openly by preaching the Word faithfully. The Jewish religious leaders didn't like that. They had them cast into prison, but they were in for a shock. Why? Because

> the angel of the Lord by night opened the prison doors, and brought them forth....But when the officers came, and found them not in the prison, they returned, and told, saying, The prison truly found we shut with all safety, and the keepers standing without before the doors: but when we had opened, we found no man within.
> (Acts 5:19, 22–23)

Some people might say, "Well, that was a long time ago. I don't think God works like that today to deliver His saints."

Oh, but He does, my friend! The outstanding Indian evangelist Sadhu Sundar Singh was in jail in Tibet for preaching the gospel in that far-off country. The Lama had placed him in confinement, and to make sure he wouldn't go out, the Lama personally kept the key on his belt, but an angel came, and he didn't need the key. The next day, the Lama looked for his prisoner, but he was nowhere to be found. You see, Sundar Singh needed to get out, and God sent an angel to accomplish it.

Are you convinced that angels are aware of our needs and are fully commissioned by God, as He directs, to meet those needs? Many sick people have seen angels during their sickness and have regained health. At other times, people who have been preaching have seen angels at the pulpit. Angels come in times of great pressure, great need.

I want to leave you with the clear understanding that God has met and can meet special needs through angels. I also feel a need at this point, however, to remind you that God, with a higher purpose in mind, does not always work as we would expect. Peter, Sundar Singh, and others have been miraculously delivered from bondage, for example, but many other godly people have not. Read all the way through Hebrews 11 to see what I mean. Consider also the many Christians who are suffering for their faith, even as you read this, in parts of the world where there is no freedom of worship.

In all these situations, we need to have the attitude of the three Israelite young men who refused to worship Nebuchadnezzar's golden image and so faced the prospect of being thrown into the fiery furnace. They told Nebuchadnezzar that they knew God could deliver them and that they thought He would. (See Daniel 3:17.) Then they said, *"But if not, be it known unto thee, O king, that we will not serve thy gods, nor worship the golden image which thou hast set up"* (Dan. 3:18). You see, they were prepared for and ready to accept the possibility that God might choose not to deliver them; and even if that happened, they were not going to worship Nebuchadnezzar's idol.

Perhaps you have thought to yourself, *I know God. I serve Him with all my heart. From time to time, I have special needs.* If so, it seems evident that you, too, fit in with the people who received angelic help during the biblical era.

Just how or when or even if God may choose to send you angelic assistance, I cannot say. However, I know He can. I know He has in the past, and that's just one of many things that make the Christian life so exciting and adventurous.

9
The Rebel Angels

An entire volume could be devoted to the subject of Satan and his demonic angels. (I have, in fact, addressed this topic in my book *Demons: The Answer Book*.) But on these pages I would like to give you a brief overview of some things you should know, because God wants us to be informed about our adversaries.

Is He Real?

Many people question the reality of Satan. Some believe Satan is just a name for some sort of evil force in the universe that has no personality or individuality. Others think of Satan as just a character in stories who goes about in a red suit, carrying a pitchfork.

What does the Word of God say? It sets forth Satan as a person throughout the Old Testament. We run into this evil personage in the Garden of Eden (Gen. 3:1–15). We see him afflicting Job. (See Job 1:6–19; 2:1–7.) We detect his work among the heathen nations as described in many of the writers of prophecy.

What do we find in the New Testament? There he is again, in nineteen of the twenty-seven books that make up this portion of the Bible, and his existence is implied in the other books as well.

The Lord Jesus often spoke of the devil, and we could ask for no better authority.

As a person, you think, you feel, you act. Satan does the same. He gives every evidence of being a separate entity, as alive and as self-conscious as you are at this very moment.

Satan's Origin

It is only natural that you should ask where Satan came from. The Bible teaches us that *"by him [Christ] were all things created, that are in heaven, and that are in earth, visible and invisible"* (Col. 1:16). Satan is a created being.

Would our Lord make something evil, however, someone who has brought such curse and destruction on mankind? No. Satan developed into what he is today, but that's not the way he was in the beginning. Originally, Satan was an angel of great power and privilege. He was a perfect creature called *"Lucifer, son of the morning"* (Isa. 14:12). He lived in the presence of God.

And read what Ezekiel wrote of Satan:

> *Thou sealest up the sum, full of wisdom, and perfect in beauty. Thou hast been in Eden the garden of God....Thou art the anointed cherub that covereth; and I have set thee so: thou wast upon the holy mountain of God; thou hast walked up and down in the midst of the stones of fire. Thou wast perfect in thy ways from the day that thou wast created.* (Ezek. 28:12–15)

Satan's Fall

Then something happened. What was it? I broke off in the middle of the last verse quoted above. Let me finish it: *"...till iniquity was found in thee....Thine heart was lifted up because of thy beauty"* (vv. 15, 17). There is the answer. Satan was not content to remain as he was. He wanted to become "number one"—to replace God. This cherub who covered the throne of God, who protected the holiness of God, mounted a rebellion in paradise.

Can you picture in the eye of your mind that day in heaven so long ago when that event took place? The thought, the desire, and the determination came to Satan, and he said in his heart, once pure but now turned to wickedness, *"I will ascend into heaven, I will exalt my throne above the stars of God: I will sit also upon the mount of the congregation, in the sides of the north: I will ascend above the heights of the clouds; I will be like the most High"* (Isa. 14:13–14). What a decisive moment! What a great catastrophe!

Angelic Choice

Let me digress for a moment and draw your attention to a point that seems obvious and yet deserves a brief mention.

We just saw that Satan, in his original creation, was perfect, as man had been in his original creation. But then, like man, Satan chose to disobey God and go his own way.

The obvious and logical implication is that angels, like man, have a free will. They can choose to obey or disobey God. They are not machines programmed to respond in only one way. Those who have remained in heaven in God's service have chosen to obey Him; those who followed Satan chose disobedience.

Out—Now, Forever

As we noted in an earlier chapter, Satan's plan didn't work. God knew how to deal with his rebellion. Those two verses quoted above are preceded and followed by others that tell us what happened: *"How art thou fallen from heaven, O Lucifer, son of the morning! how art thou cut down to the ground, which didst weaken the nations!…Yet thou shalt be brought down to hell, to the sides of the pit"* (Is. 14:12, 15).

Satan made five "I will" statements as recorded above in Isaiah, but God made six "I will" statements as found in Ezekiel:

> *I will cast thee as profane out of the mountain of God: and I will destroy thee, O covering cherub, from the midst of the stones of fire….I will cast thee to the ground, I will lay thee before kings, that they may behold thee….Therefore will I bring forth a fire from the midst of thee, it shall devour thee, and I will bring thee to ashes upon the earth in the sight of all them that behold thee.* (Ezek. 28:16–18)

God always has the last word. He makes the final statement.

Satan's Allies

From time to time, we read in the papers or see on television accounts of people who have risen up to overthrow their governments. Almost always, a wide conspiracy is involved. An individual can't do it by himself. He has to have help. He needs co-plotters, coconspirators, co-revolutionaries.

Does it surprise you to learn, then, that when Satan was cast out of heaven, he didn't go alone? No, many of the angels joined Satan's cause. There is a suggestion of the number who did given in Revelation 12. We read there of a great red dragon, *"And his tail drew the third part of the stars of heaven, and did cast them to the earth"* (v. 4). So perhaps a third of all the angels God originally created decided to join Satan and were swept up in God's wrath and cast out of heaven.

It is those fallen angels who are now demons, or evil angels. Satan is their one and only leader. He is their commander in chief, their executive officer.

Satan's Work

Satan works in continual opposition to God's program and person, for he is the archenemy of God. He sets up counterfeit doctrine and religion. He doesn't mind, for example, that people go to church, so long as it is a church that doesn't preach, practice, or believe the gospel. Second Corinthians 4:3–4 teaches us that Satan blinds men to the truth that is in Christ.

As the great deceiver, Satan will misuse Scripture to try to get people to do wrong things while they think they're doing right, as he did when he tempted the Lord Jesus. (See Matthew 4:1–11.) He and his allies also disguise themselves as angels of light, or righteousness, in order to deceive and mislead people away from God. (See 2 Corinthians 11:13–15.) Jesus described him as the father of lies. (See John 8:44.)

Have you ever considered ways in which Satan may affect you? For one thing, he is the *"accuser of our brethren"* (Rev. 12:10). He reminds God when we fall and sin. But how wonderful it is that we have an answering *"advocate with the Father, Jesus Christ the righteous"* (1 John 2:1).

Whenever trials and difficulties come into your life, you wonder about the goodness of God. Satan may be responsible for those thoughts. Remember? That's how he got to Eve. (See Genesis 3:1–5.)

Satan is the great tempter. He tempts us to lie, to engage in immorality, and to kill.

Like Their Mentor

I'm sure you have heard the expression "Like father, like son." You might say sometimes that a certain boy acts or speaks just like Harry. And sure enough, you find out that he is Harry's son.

Those in the devil's camp also have a family resemblance. Jesus spoke of those who acted like their father, the devil (see John 8:44), and that generalization applies especially to those angelic beings who were dismissed from heaven at the same time as Satan.

Like their boss, evil angels are also personalities who talk, think, feel, and act. The Bible calls them spirits (see Matthew 8:16) and calls us to battle against their wicked organization. *"For we wrestle not against flesh and blood, but against principalities, against powers, against the rulers of the darkness of this world, against spiritual wickedness in high places"* (Eph. 6:12).

Those morally perverted beings are often described in the Bible as *"unclean spirits"* (Matt. 10:1; Luke 11:24). I'm sure even that designation fails to convey all their wickedness and depravity.

A Long List

What do those rebel angels do? As the emissaries of Satan, their major job, from our perspective, is to oppose the saints of God. It is no wonder that that outstanding passage in Ephesians 6 sounds such a strident call for us to arm ourselves with the whole armor of God so that we may stand against the wiles of the devil. Verses 13–17 tell us of the armor available to us through the provision of God. We need to read that passage frequently and obey its injunctions.

Demons want us to return to the old life with all its sins. They tempt us to go back to the things from which we were set free at the time of our conversion. I'm sorry to say that in many cases, they apparently succeed. How many people do you know, formerly strong Christians, who have slid back from what they once were in Christ? Perhaps they are still in the church, but on a routine, formalistic basis.

Some people may even be drawn away altogether from the faith. *"Now the Spirit speaketh expressly, that in the latter times some shall depart from the faith, giving heed to seducing spirits, and doctrines of devils; speaking lies in hypocrisy; having their conscience seared with a hot iron"* (1 Tim. 4:1–2).

We often read in the Old Testament of how evil messengers from Satan turned the people of God to idolatry. We read, for example, of those who *"offer their sacrifices unto devils, after whom they have gone a whoring"* (Lev. 17:7).

Do you see the hands of evil angels at work in the false religions of the world? Think of the hundreds of millions of people—like the Muslims, for example—who hold with such zeal to their false doctrine and are marching unknowingly on the road to hell.

You don't have to go off to the Middle East or India to gain evidence of demons working on the double. In the United States alone, we have scores of cults that blind people to the truth and keep them out of the kingdom of God. No doubt, much of this is due to the misleading of evil spirits. We need to underscore in our Bibles and in our thinking the words of John:

> *Beloved, believe not every spirit, but try the spirits whether they are of God: because many false prophets are gone out into the world. Hereby know ye the Spirit of God: Every spirit that confesseth that Jesus Christ is come in the flesh is of God: and every spirit that confesseth not that Jesus Christ is come in the flesh is not of God: and this*

is that spirit of antichrist, whereof ye have heard that it should come;
and even now already is it in the world. (1 John 4:1–3)

Afflicting the Body

Demons seem to have particular power to affect the human body. How often we see that during the earthly ministry of our Lord. Here is just one example from Matthew 12:22: *"Then was brought unto him one possessed with a devil, blind, and dumb: and he healed him, insomuch that the blind and dumb both spake and saw."*

Do you remember the case of the epileptic boy whose problem was caused by demonic activity? Jesus gave him healing, as recorded in Mark 9:17–27.

We have record in the Bible of a case of insanity that was caused by devils. Luke recorded the incident of the man who roamed among the tombs, naked and uncontrollable. At the command of Jesus, the demons announced their true identity, for there were many of them, so many that they could be called Legion. It's a frightening story given in Luke 8:26–40.

Please understand that I am not saying that all physical or mental illness is the result of demonic activity—by no means. But some is, and we should recognize that.

Demonic Possession

Unfortunately, the demonic activity mentioned in the Bible continues into present times. Demons can enter and take possession of people. I can give you a couple of illustrations from my own experience. Some of the most exciting moments of my life and ministry have been when the power of God has released those possessed with evil spirits.

In the city where I presently serve, a woman from a liberal church came on a Sunday night and asked for prayer. When I laid my hands on her, I was startled to hear what sounded like the barking of a dog coming from her mouth. I also heard growling and other animal sounds.

God set her free from that demonic possession. Then I asked her how she had gotten into that terrible situation. She confessed that she had been dabbling in spiritism and playing with a Ouija board. She had given herself to the occult, and the evil spirits had taken over. It took a confrontation between God and the evil things to release her from bondage.

One time during my missionary years in the Philippines, I was asked to go to prison and pray for a young woman who gave every evidence of being demon-possessed. Skeptics knew I had been invited, so there were some 125 people on hand to observe what transpired—prison officials, newspaper reporters, university professors, and key people from the medical world.

When I arrived, I found the woman twisting and turning and screaming under the power of the devil. As I laid hands on her to pray, she began to blaspheme all three members of the Trinity. "Come out of her!" I commanded on the authority of God's Word.

You can imagine the impact it had on those who had come to watch. Newspapers and magazines carried the complete story. As a result of that one instance, that one deliverance of a person bound by Satan, a revival broke out in the land. Many came to know the Lord, and rich blessings followed.

All that stemmed from believing what our Lord Jesus said in Mark 16:17: *"And these signs shall follow them that believe; In my name shall they cast out devils."* The book of Acts gives examples of this in biblical times, but I have seen the freeing of individuals in our time as well.

For You as Well

Every Christian has the power to exorcise evil spirits. Do you belong to Jesus Christ? He that is in you is greater than he that is in the world. (See 1 John 4:4). You have the right to pray for those ensnared and see the demons cast out. When you believe that and trust God for it, you may see it happen if God so chooses to use you.

Do not be foolhardy as you confront Satan, however. God is indeed infinitely more powerful than him, but that does not mean Satan is weak. Much to the contrary, everything we said earlier about the power and intelligence of angels applies to Satan and his demons as well. Remember that before his rebellion, Lucifer was one of the most glorious and powerful of God's angels. Remember also that the Bible portrays him *"as a roaring lion, walketh about, seeking whom he may devour"* (1 Pet. 5:8). He is not an adversary to be lightly regarded by anyone.

Victory Assured

At this point, you may wonder what is to be the fate of those rebel angels. The Word of God is very clear on that issue. We have many statements that indicate God has already decided the matter through the victorious life and death of the Lord Jesus. For example, *"For this purpose the Son of God was manifested, that he might destroy the works of the devil"* (1 John 3:8). And now it is our part to wait for the sentence against the evil one and his angels to be carried out completely.

Part of the devil's band may already have been apprehended. Note the words of 2 Peter 2:4: *"For if God spared not the angels that sinned, but cast them down to hell, and delivered them into chains of darkness, to be reserved unto judgment."* Jude 6 has something similar to say: *"And the angels which kept not their first estate, but left their own habitation, he hath reserved in everlasting chains under darkness unto the judgment of the great day."* So a portion of the evil angels—how many we do not know—may already be under lock and key, prevented from ravaging the world and the saints.

What about those that are loose and still active? Their time is limited, and their doom is equally certain. But before that day comes, we are going to see Satan especially at work concerning the person of the Antichrist. *"And then shall that Wicked be revealed, whom the Lord shall consume with the spirit of his mouth, and shall destroy with the brightness of his coming: even him, whose coming is after the working of Satan with all power and signs and lying wonders"* (2 Thess. 2:8–9).

391

The Final Defeat

The stage will then be set for the return of the Lord Jesus, and that event is marvelously described for us in Revelation 19.

> *And I saw heaven opened, and behold a white horse; and he that sat upon him was called Faithful and True, and in righteousness he doth judge and make war. His eyes were as a flame of fire, and on his head were many crowns; and he had a name written, that no man knew, but he himself. And he was clothed with a vesture dipped in blood: and his name is called The Word of God. And the armies which were in heaven followed him upon white horses, clothed in fine linen, white and clean.* (Rev. 19:11–14)

What a magnificent picture of our sovereign Lord and His own!

John went on to give us a picture of Satan's fate: *"And I saw an angel come down from heaven, having the key of the bottomless pit and a great chain in his hand. And he laid hold on the dragon, that old serpent, which is the Devil, and Satan, and bound him a thousand years"* (Rev. 20:1–2).

At the end of that temporary sentence, Satan will be loosed for a little while to resume his old activity of deceiving the nations. But then the end will come: *"And the devil that deceived them was cast into the lake of fire and brimstone, where the beast and the false prophet are, and shall be tormented day and night for ever and ever"* (Rev. 20:10).

I find that comforting and reassuring. Today Satan and his evil forces wreak their destruction on individuals, on homes, on nations. But the day is coming when it will all be over.

Our Lord is going to win. And we are going to win in Him. Meanwhile, let us be fully informed and draw closer to the One who gives us the victory.

10
Your Private Angel

Unless you are among the rich, you probably don't have enough money to buy services exclusively for yourself. But if you did, you might have a private chauffeur to drive you around town. You could have a private hair stylist to do everything possible to make you look your very best. You could hire a tutor to spend his time teaching you foreign languages or science. And in these days so filled with violent crime, you might want to get a personal bodyguard to protect your life.

I know something far better, however, that you can afford. In fact, you don't need money at all to enjoy fantastic personal services that God provides for you. The answer? Your private angel.

I cannot prove conclusively from Scripture the existence of private angels. There is no one passage of clear, unequivocal teaching on the subject. However, there are a few references that, taken together, seem to suggest strongly the reality of guardian angels. They are enough to convince me of the fact. Let's take a look at them. When we are finished, I think you will have an entirely new perspective that will make you eternally grateful to God.

For You Individually

I'm sure we often think of angels as being in general service to the entire body of Christ. Such a concept is not wrong. Angels do indeed minister to God's people as a whole. But they are also concerned for us as individuals.

When we look at Psalm 91:11, we begin to see the personal nature of angelic ministry: *"For he shall give his angels charge over thee, to keep thee in all thy ways."* Note that all those pronouns are singular. That is a first suggestion to me that each of us has a personal angel who watches over us. When we consider also that we who believe in Christ are indwelt by the Holy Spirit (see 1 Corinthians 3:16), we can be sure that God is always very much aware of our needs and concerns and is able to minister to them.

Another suggestion of personal angels comes to us in Genesis 48:16, where a dying Jacob (Israel) was blessing his grandchildren, Joseph's sons. In that blessing, he referred to *"the Angel which redeemed me from all evil."* Was that a guardian angel who had watched over Jacob throughout his lifetime? I like to think it was.

To the Rescue

Let me give you just one example of a time when God may have used my guardian angel to rescue me. Years ago, I was traveling with a group up near the border of Tibet. Somehow, I became lost—I mean absolutely lost. You know the feeling. I had been separated from my traveling companions from about 8:00 in the morning until about 4:30 that afternoon. There I was in a little Chinese village, all by myself, without knowing one word of the language. I was sad and tired, almost in tears.

Then I noticed a young man come riding through the gates of the village on a majestic horse. He rode right up to where I was, dismounted, and began to talk to me in perfect English.

"Where did you come from?" I asked. "How is it that you speak English so beautifully?"

He smiled and said to me, "I know the party you're looking for. I met them on the road. If you go out this gate and then go for about two hours, you'll find them ahead."

I took his advice. I got on my mule, headed out the gate, and, sure enough, before long I found the group I had been traveling with.

I inquired of them about the young man. They told me they had never seen him. They didn't know anything about him.

Could that have been my guardian angel? I believe it was.

Very Close

You might wonder just how far away your personal angel is when you need him. We have an answer in Psalm 34:7, which tells us, *"The angel of the* LORD *encampeth round about them that fear him, and delivereth them."* That means your angel puts up his tent around you. If you fear God, you have an angel by your side to give protection. You don't have to be afraid of leaving him behind when you board a jet to travel across the country, or when you jump into your car for a quick trip to the supermarket. No, he is always there, and that should be comforting.

Children, Too

We may ignore little children or think they are not very important. But God has a different perspective. It was our Lord Himself who said, *"Take heed that ye despise not one of these little ones; for I say unto you, That in heaven their angels do always behold the face of my Father which is in heaven"* (Matt. 18:10). That is perhaps the strongest biblical suggestion that each child (and, by inference, each person) has a guardian angel all his own.

Perhaps little children are in greater need of angelic protection than adults because they can't defend themselves as well. Do children need such protection? Just look through any metropolitan newspaper and you will get the sad answer. Child abuse is one of the greatest areas of social concern in this nation. It includes physical abuse, mental abuse, and even sexual abuse. Millions of children are the victims. It's something they can't easily shake off or forget. Whole lives may be ruined because of what happens in childhood.

God doesn't overlook what happens to children. His angels don't overlook it, and the day of accounting will most certainly come. I wonder if those who abuse or mislead children are aware of or believe God's promised judgment in Matthew 18:6: *"But whoso shall offend one of these little ones which believe in me, it were better for him that a millstone were hanged about his neck, and that he were drowned in the depth of the sea."*

More Than Enough

The concept of having a private angel might make you wonder whether there are enough angels to go around. It's perfectly proper to raise the question. Let me refer you to the book of Daniel and his vision of the Ancient of Days seated upon His throne, surrounded by angels: *"Thousand thousands ministered unto him, and ten thousand times ten thousand stood before him"* (Dan. 7:10). That second figure, taken literally, is 100 million. We don't know if Daniel was being literal there; perhaps he was speaking symbolically of a huge, uncountable number. Regardless, the point here is that there are undoubtedly vast legions of angels at God's command.

You might say, "There are more than four billion people on the earth, and the number is growing. Are there enough angels to help them all?" I can only say that if we are right in concluding that God does assign a personal guardian angel to every individual, there must be enough angels to do the job. Certainly there is no doubt that God was and is perfectly capable of creating all the angels He would ever want.

An Unequaled Record

I hope you feel on the victory side when you stop to consider that you have a personal angel. What an unparalleled record they have in their ministry to us. Angels never get too old to serve, too tired of the job, or too discouraged or sad to quit.

Never forget for even one moment your private angel or the intimate relationship with angels established by God to bless and help you. They come as friends and allies in the battle against Satan in your life.

11
Angels Forever

W hen I began to study angels prior to writing this book, I was guided by a theory that I refer to from time to time. I express it this way: God cannot bless ignorance. No, God wants us to be informed—to know what His Word says in every field of learning.

That theory needs to be applied in the study of angels. By and large, people are woefully ignorant. If you introduce the subject of angels, they may smile a little, recalling some incident involving angels in Old Testament times or perhaps in connection with the birth and later resurrection of our Lord. But they have no clear understanding of the role of angels in the past, in the present, or in the future.

I hope that ignorance is being dispelled by this book. I chose not to draw many illustrations from the outside, but to deliberately concentrate on expounding the Bible's teaching, convinced as I am that this is the best source of knowledge and great blessing.

Such a study of angels is going to stand us in good stead for eternity. Here on earth, we get caught up in transitory things. Our clothes wear out and have to be discarded. The washing machine breaks down or the car wears out, and they have to be replaced. Even books and information learned in school soon become outdated.

That's not the way it is when it comes to the angels. Angels are not short-term missionaries in God's eternal program. The time will never come when He will turn to them and say, "Sorry, I have no further use for you." Angels will most certainly continue their work of praising God and worshipping Him throughout eternity. They will always be standing by to serve God in any way He desires.

You Will See

Are you looking forward to seeing angels in heaven? I am! The Bible sometimes describes angels as being like lightning, or like the sun, or as having eyes like burning lamps. I want to see them in person and find out through my own observation, and I believe we'll be able to do that.

Meeting angels in heaven will, I believe, be one of our greatest sources of joy up there. I think we will know angels just as we presently know people. You see, I believe there will be no strangers in heaven. We won't have to walk up to someone, shake hands, and then ask, "Who are you? Where did you come from?" No, in heaven we will have perfect knowledge, and we will know people and angels instinctively.

Ask Adam

Our heavenly knowledge of others is going to open up tremendous experiences that will delight our hearts. For example, imagine seeing Adam in conversation with the cherubim God detailed for guard duty in the Garden of Eden. (See Genesis 3:24.) They will be friends up there, and so will we.

What will Adam and the angels talk about? Well, perhaps Adam will have some things he wants cleared up concerning the Tree of Life. Perhaps Adam will say, "Angels, if you hadn't been there with that flaming sword, I would have sneaked back in and eaten some of the fruit."

"I know," an angel may respond, "but that would have been a terrible thing for you and all who came after you, for you would have lived forever in your sinful state. God is so merciful and gracious that He couldn't allow that. He had a much better plan of salvation."

Do you think I am overdrawing what may happen? Perhaps you even wonder if Adam got to heaven. I like to think he did. Although he sinned in eating of the tree prohibited to him by God, I just can't believe he continued in his rebellion. I feel sure he got back into fellowship with God, that he walked with God, talked with Him, and offered sacrifices for his sins. I look forward to meeting Adam and finding out from him what it was like to be the first of the human race.

Jacob in the Corner

How magnificent it will be to talk with Jacob in some quiet place about the angel who wrestled with him during the night. I would like him to explain to me the details of that amazing struggle between a man of great strength and an angel of superhuman strength. "Jacob, did you expect the fight to go on as long as it did? Did you realize that would be a turning point in your life and result in a change of names?"

Perhaps you would rather ask Jacob about his vision of angels going up and down from heaven, as the Bible relates in the account of his vision. (See Genesis 28.) I'm sure he would be glad to elaborate. Maybe Jacob himself will want to turn to the angels involved in case he wishes some clarification.

Other Opportunities

One reason heaven is going to be heaven and eternity is going to be so wonderful is that we can discuss such tremendous things as long as we wish. I, for example, want to sit and talk with godly people who lived at the time of the Tower of Babel. What did they think on that day when God came down and confused human languages so that it would be impossible for the building task to continue? And maybe I'll have other questions after rereading the story in Genesis 11.

I want to converse with the people who were there in the Israelite camp when Moses was up on the mountain receiving the Ten Commandments. I want to ask what in the world they could have been thinking when they had Aaron make a golden calf for them to fall down before and worship. How did they feel when Moses returned to rebuke them? (See Exodus 32.) As you read the Scriptures, you probably come across many subjects on which you'd like more light. Well, in heaven, I think you will get it.

One after Another

On previous pages of this book, I have written about the role of angels in the lives of Joshua, Daniel, and the Three Hebrew Children. I will not take space here to go over those great happenings again, but perhaps in heaven you and I will be able to sit down with those famous personalities and receive from them more complete accounts than those given in Scripture. I don't think they will ever tire of telling the stories they lived, for in doing so they will bring glory to God.

Questions, Questions, Questions

Many things we will want to ask the angels directly. How did they feel when Jesus took on a human body and for a while was made lower than the angels? (See Hebrews 2:9.) And what were their emotions when Jesus returned to heaven, His work on earth accomplished?

I wonder why angels are always referred to in the masculine gender? Why are they considered not so much a race as *"an innumerable company"* (Heb. 12:22)? At times, angels have manifested themselves in human form as we have seen. Do all angels have the power to do that? I think we will find out in heaven.

What kinds of questions would you like to ask the angels? Perhaps you will be eager to find out why only Michael and Gabriel are named for us in the Bible, and just how extensive is Michael's authority as the archangel.

I think it will be interesting to inquire about how angels reacted when appearing to men. We know some men were afraid, some were awed, and some fell down to worship. But how did the angels feel about those reactions?

We know some angels have wings and some apparently don't. Why? In what other ways do they move about?

What did the good angels think when they witnessed the rebellion of Satan and watched as perhaps one-third of their number left heaven with him? Did they try to keep those foolish angels from taking that tragic step? Did they suspect something like that might happen when Lucifer began to boast about his beauty and position?

What did the angels feel when they watched the Lord Jesus being taken captive in the garden the night before His death, knowing that God's Son had but to speak a word and legions of their number would hurry to His aid?

Clarifying the Word

Something God said about angels has always fascinated me. God asked Job, *"Where wast thou when I laid the foundations of the earth? declare, if thou hast understanding....When the morning stars sang together, and all the sons of God shouted for joy"* (Job 38:4, 7). *"The morning stars"* and *"the sons of God"* are terms used to describe angels. So we know angels were present at the creation of the physical universe. How did they feel about observing that tremendous act of our God? I'd like to ask them, wouldn't you?

Then, there are eight little words Paul wrote almost as an aside when he was considering the matter of Corinthian Christians going to court before secular judges to resolve misunderstandings. Paul wrote, *"Know ye not that we shall judge angels?"* (1 Cor. 6:3). I believe that will take place in heaven, but why will we judge angels? When? By what standards? What will be the results of our judgment? How is it that God has seen fit to give us that responsibility? What do angels feel about it?

There are so very many facts about angels that we still don't know. In heaven we will surely have our questions answered, and I think we will be simply amazed at all we learn about those fantastic beings God has created.

Angels to Help You

What of the here and now? I hope I have been able on the preceding pages to demonstrate in some measure the reality and ministry of angels to God's people, you, today. As you make your pilgrim journey from this world to the next, let them reach out to you, touch you at your point of greatest need, and fill you with all the joy of heaven.

Demons: The Answer Book

Contents

Introduction

I t is a pity that in a great country like ours, with its freedom
of the press and millions of Bibles, books, and magazines,
people know less about demon power than citizens of Africa
or Tibet do. Possibly through gross neglect, the ministers of our
generation have not informed the people of the reality of demon
power.

There are three sources of power common to human understanding. (1) The *divine power,* or power that proceeds from the
omnipotence of God; (2) *satanic power,* or power coming from
Lucifer the fallen archangel (see Isaiah 14); and (3) *human power,*
or the power of man. This third power is a neutral force that can
be directed by the heavenly or demonic powers.

God has given man the authority and right to choose his lifestyle and destiny. He created man to rule and have dominion
over the total creation (Gen. 1:26–27).

The devil wishes to enslave man. On the subjection of Satan's
power, Jesus said that a woman whom the devil had bound
should be loosed (Luke 13:16). Christ sent his disciples to loose
the human race.

The purpose of this book is to reveal the actual powers operating in our world and our lives.

—Lester Sumrall

1
Bitten by Demons

Master, I have brought unto thee my son, which hath a dumb spirit;
and wheresoever he taketh him,
he teareth him.
—Mark 9:17–18

On May 12, 1953, the *Daily Mirror* in Manila carried a highly unusual story under the headline "Police Medic Explodes Biting Demons Yarn."

A city jail inmate puzzled police and medical examiners with her tale about two devils biting her....Sergeant Guillermo Abad, detailed with the city jail last night, said the girl claimed she was bitten twenty times, and she shouted every time she was hurt.

In the jail last night she talked and answered questions weakly, but sensibly, before a crowd of observers. Suddenly her facial expressions would change to anguish and horror as if she were confronted with "The Thing." She would look around wildly and then scream and struggle and hit her arms and shoulders....Then her strenuous resistance would cease and she would collapse into the arms of those holding her, weak and half-conscious.

After regaining her senses, she said that one of the devils was big and dark with curly hair on his head, chest, and arms. He had large, sharp eyes and two fangs. His voice was a deep-echoing sound. He was shrouded in black....

She was bitten for the last time on the right knee. That was the first bite on the lower part of her anatomy. Other bite marks appear on her neck, arms, and shoulders. Observers insist that they are within sight all the time.

The following day the *Manila Chronicle* reported further news of the young woman, Clarita Villanueva:

> At least twenty-five competent persons, including Manila's chief of police, Col. Cesar Lucero, say that it is a very realistic example of a horrified woman being bitten to insanity by "invisible persons." She displayed several bite marks all over her body, inflicted by nobody as far as the twenty-five witnesses could see. Villanueva writhed in pain, shouted and screamed in anguish whenever the "invisible demons" attacked her.
>
> Fr. Benito Vargas (Roman Catholic)...who witnessed Villanueva in her fits said it was not his to conclude any verdict. But he said the fact remains that "I saw her bitten three times."
>
> Villanueva was perfectly normal between fits. After talking for a while, she would shout, have convulsions and hysterics, all the time screaming, and her eyes flashing with fire. Then she would point to a part of her body being attacked, then fall almost senseless into the hands of investigators. Teeth marks, wet with saliva, marked the spots she pointed at.

At the time, I was founding a church in Manila. The newspaper accounts had not caught my attention, but a forty-five-minute radio program over station DZFM drew me into it personally. The radio announcer dramatically opened the broadcast: "Good evening, ladies and gentlemen. If you have a weak heart, please turn your radio off!"

I turned the volume of our radio higher. Instantly, I heard piercing screams followed by pandemonium. Doctors spoke out of the confusion: "This can all be explained!...Our records show that this phenomenon has been known before....This is epilepsy....It is extreme hysteria."

Others were excitedly saying, "Look, the marks of teeth appear!" Another said, "The girl is being choked by some unseen thing. She is blue in the face and there are marks on her neck." Then Clarita would scream again.

Listening to this in the comfort of our bedroom, I turned to my wife and said, "The girl is not sick and the doctors are helpless before such an enemy. Her cry is the cry of the damned and doomed; that girl is demon possessed."

It was impossible for me to sleep after listening to the program. I walked the floor, crying to God to deliver the poor girl in the city jail. But the longer I prayed, the heavier the load became upon my soul. I said, "Oh God, if the devil is in that girl, You can cast him out! Please do it!"

After praying until morning, God spoke to my heart: "If you will go to the jail and pray for her, I will deliver her."

But I didn't want to go. I found myself answering, "No, God. I can never go to that place. Scientists, professors, legal experts, and even spiritualists have been trying to help that girl. They all have had adverse publicity in the newspapers. I cannot go."

The Lord replied, "If you will go and pray for her, I will deliver her."

"No," was my reply.

But I found I could no longer pray for her. When I cried for her deliverance my conscience stopped me, saying, "You are not sincere, for you refuse to go and see her." Finally I decided to go to Bilibid prison and pray for the girl.

In a city of several million, and in a mammoth prison such as Bilibid, it would not be easy to get an interview with such a highly publicized person.

On my way to town the following morning I stopped at the home of the architect who had designed our church, Leopoldo Coronel, a personal friend of the Manila mayor. At my request, we visited Mayor Lacson and gained permission for me to pray for Clarita, but on one condition. Dr. Mariano Lara, chief medical adviser of the police department, must also grant permission. Mr. Coronel did not know Dr. Lara, but through another friend an interview was arranged.

Mr. Coronel and I arrived at Bilibid prison and were escorted to the morgue to see Dr. Lara. The surroundings were eerie. The first thing I noticed was a cadaver on the table. Another corpse lay wrapped in a blanket on a stretcher awaiting attention. On a table were a dozen or more jars of alcohol containing parts of human beings. We found out later that these were for student demonstrations.

Sitting on a bench in this drab place, Dr. Lara told us about himself. He was a professor and the head of pathology and legal medicine at the Manila Central University and professorial lecturer of legal medicine at the University of Santo Tomas. In his thirty-eight years of medical practice he had performed more than eight thousand autopsies, and he had never accepted the theory of a nonmaterial force existing in the universe.

Dr. Lara had not intended to be drawn into the Clarita Villanueva affair. On May 12, upon entering the office of one of his medical assistants, he first observed the young woman prisoner. Noticing the reddish, human-like bite impressions on her arms, both physicians believed Clarita had bitten herself. Considering her "abnormal," they agreed to recommend her for treatment in the national psychopathic hospital.

The following day, however, at the insistence of visitors who wanted to know Dr. Lara's medical opinion, he had her brought to the medical examiner's office in the police department. A class of interns was also there. According to the doctor, Clarita was unconscious when she was carried to the room. This is what he told me:

> Her arms lifted by me would fall without resistance. Pointed needles and pins touching her skin gave no response throughout her body surface. After several minutes in this condition, Clarita began to come out of this state of insensibility and trance.
>
> Meanwhile, I was like Sherlock Holmes of the detective stories, or Dr. Cyclops, the film character. Equipped with magnifying lens and with an unbelieving mind about this biting phenomenon, I scrutinized carefully the exposed parts of her body, the arms, hands, and neck to find out whether they had the biting impressions....She was still weak in her entire body and could not stand up by herself. One of my assistants, a cadaver technician, Alfonso by name, helped carry her to a bed for her to rest during this state of partial trance. Alfonso

got hold of her body and deposited her on the prepared bed, placing both her hands over her in order that they would not hang downward.

At that very instant, this girl in a semi-trance loudly screamed repeatedly the word "aruy" [a scream of pain in Tagalog], and when I removed Alfonso's hand from Clarita's I saw with my unbelieving eyes the clear marks or impressions of human-like teeth from both the upper and lower jaws. It was a little moist in the area bitten on the dorsal aspect of the left hand, and the teeth impressions were mostly from the form of the front or incisor teeth....

I could not understand or explain how the bites were produced, as her hand had all the time been held away from the reach of her mouth. The place where the bite impressions occurred, on the dorsal of the left hand, was the very place held by my assistant Alfonso. I knew she could not bite herself nor could Alfonso, who does not possess a single tooth, having recently had them extracted. And I am sure I did not bite the girl! Not finding any possible explanation insofar as my human experience in medical training is concerned, I kept my mouth shut, but not my mind.

Clarita kept on screaming for about fifteen minutes with this bite on her left hand, and she turned bluish in the face and legs as if being choked. There were also a few reddish whelps in the front of the neck....After about twenty minutes of this attack, accompanied by stiffness and screaming, her body became soft and in a trance-like condition—a repetition of the observation made when she was first brought into the room. After about ten minutes of this trance and softness of the entire body, she gradually recovered consciousness and, shortly thereafter, became normal again.

In this normal condition she sat on a chair and the group of interns talked with her. She answered all the questions they asked her sanely and intelligently, and she told us the following: She was born in Bacolod City in the province of Negros Occidental. She has several brothers but is not interested in them as they have been unkind to her. Her parents died several years ago.

I asked her who was causing her to suffer from the bites. She answered that there were two who were alternately biting her; one big, black, hairy human-like fellow, very tall and with two sharp eyes, two sharp canine teeth, a long beard like a Hindu, hairy extremities and chest, wearing a black garment, with a little whitish piece on the back resembling a hood. His feet were about three times the size of normal feet. The other fellow was a very small one about two or three feet tall, allegedly also black, hairy, and ugly.

This baffling Filipino girl had changed Dr. Lara's philosophy of life. He turned to me and said, "Reverend, I am humble enough to admit that I am a frightened man."

I realized that my first objective was to convince Dr. Lara that I knew what I was doing and that I knew how to help this girl. I began slowly.

"There are only three powers in the universe," I said. "There is the 'positive power,' or the power of a creative and benevolent God. There is the 'human power,' or the power of men here on the earth. And there is the 'negative power,' or the malevolent and sinister power of the devil. These powers are real and evident around us. Now, do you think Clarita is acting under God's power?"

He shook his head slowly and replied, "No, not God's power."

"Then do you feel that, with your experience with human beings, she is acting like any human being?"

"No, the actions of this girl are not related to human beings," he said.

"Then there is only one power left," I told him. "She must be acting under demon power."

Dr. Lara explained that his broad experiences as a medical man had not prepared him for an encounter with something that was beyond doubt "supernatural."

I continued, "Dr. Lara, if there is a negative force in the universe over which a positive force has no control, our universe would go to pieces. If there is an evil that no right can correct, then evil is mightier than right. This cannot be. If this girl has demon power in her, then Jesus Christ can deliver her from that power."

I turned to the Gospel of Mark and read, "*And these signs shall follow them that believe; In my name shall they cast out devils'* (Mark 16:17). Do you believe this?" I asked.

Dr. Lara looked at me and said, "I believe, but who will help us?" He thought spiritual assistance was out of the question. The Roman Catholic chaplain of Bilibid prison, the Catholic archbishop of the Philippines, and priests of the Roman Catholic healing center at Baclaran had all refused to pray for her.

I told him I would be glad to go and pray for the girl if he would permit it. He said I would be welcome. I requested that no medication be given to her during the time I would be praying for her and that no other groups be permitted to pray for her or offer assistance in any way. If Jesus healed her, He must have all the glory. He agreed, and an appointment was made for me to return the following morning. I fasted the rest of the day, spending the time in prayer and reading the Word of God.

Upon entering the dreary walls of Bilibid prison the following morning, I felt there was going to be a contest between the God of Elijah and the prophets of Baal. Ancient Bilibid, with its centuries of bloody history, was to witness a new kind of battle. Here the Spaniards had imprisoned their victims. Here the Japanese had conducted uncounted atrocities. Here American missionaries had almost starved until the day of liberation. And now there were hundreds of lawbreakers behind its stockades. It was an uninviting place to pray the prayer of deliverance.

On this first morning, Leopoldo Coronel accompanied me. We met Dr. Lara and a professor from the Far Eastern University and started walking toward the women's cellblock. Upon seeing the police officers, newspapermen, and photographers who were gathered, I could almost hear the devil whispering, "Just as I told you! Now you have made a fool of yourself!"

Following behind us was a motley crowd without the slightest idea of what they were going to see. By the time we had assembled in a small chapel for women prisoners, there must have been a hundred spectators, including prisoners.

At first I felt that my greatest battle would be with the spectators, but they were friendly and even sympathetic. Most of them had already seen the teeth bites on the girl. They had observed the failure of the doctors and psychiatrists and spiritualists. But they had never heard prayer for the diseased and demon possessed.

Steel bars covered the windows of the small chapel. A primitive Catholic altar stood at one end of the dreary room. The only other furnishings were a wooden bunk and a couple of small handmade chairs.

After we all gathered in the chapel, Dr. Lara asked that Clarita be brought in. She observed each person slowly and closely as she entered the room. When she came to me at the end of the line, her eyes widened, and she glared at me, saying, "I don't like you!"

These were the first words the devil spoke through her lips to me. The demons used her lips constantly to curse me, to curse God, and to curse the blood of Christ. She did this in English, yet after she was delivered I had to converse with her through an interpreter, as she could not speak English.

I had her sit on a wooden bench, and I drew up a chair in front of her.

"Clarita," I said, "I have come to deliver you from the power of these devils in the name of Jesus Christ, the Son of God."

Suddenly she went into a fit of rage, screaming, "No, no! They will kill me!" Her body became rigid and she became unconscious. This had baffled the doctors when they had tried to analyze her case, but I had dealt with devils before and understood some of their antics. Taking hold of her head with both hands I cried, "'Come out of her, you evil and wicked spirit of hell. Come out of her in Jesus' name!"

Immediately she began to rage again. This was the first time she had instantly come back from one of the trances. With tears flowing down her cheeks she begged me to leave her alone; she showed me terrible marks on her arms and neck where she had been bitten that moment. I was shocked. The teeth marks were so severe that some of the small blood vessels beneath the skin were broken. Rather than feeling like quitting, I simply forgot that I was surrounded with unbelievers and went into the greatest battle of my life.

The devils would curse God and I would demand them to quit and tell them God is holy. Then they would curse the blood of Jesus and I rebuked them, reminding them that he is the Master over every evil power and that His blood is holy. Then they cursed me in the vilest language. They declared they would never leave. It seemed that the powers of darkness and the powers of righteousness were in deadly conflict. I was just the mouthpiece for righteousness. Clarita was the mouthpiece of the devil. Undoubtedly the noise could be heard for some distance in the prison.

Finally it seemed that the girl was relieved. The devils refused to talk to me or to bite her. Some of those present thought she was delivered, but I told them she was not. It was nearly noon and I was soaked with perspiration and nearly exhausted. When I looked around I saw several of the people with tears in their eyes, moved by the things they had seen.

I told Dr. Lara that I desired to go home and fast and pray for another day, and then return the following morning. That day was spent in communion with God. It was precious. I could feel God's presence hovering over me, urging me not to be afraid.

However, I felt almost defeated because the evening newspapers had my picture on the front page, three columns wide, and a headline saying, "'The Thing' Defies Pastor." But God kept urging me to return.

That night, Rev. Arthur Ahlberg and Rev. Robert McAlister visited us at home and offered to go with me the following day. They would stand between me and the crowd and keep them from getting too close during prayer.

Upon our arrival at Bilibid the following morning, the captain of the prison said Clarita had not been bitten since the prayer. But I knew she was not yet delivered. This became evident as soon as the devils saw me. Through her lips they cried, "Go away! Go away."

I sat on the same small chair in front of her and spoke back with a thrilling feeling of authority. "No, I am not going away, but you are going away! This girl will be delivered today!"

Then I requested every person present to kneel—there were as many present as the day before, or more. Doctors, newspapermen, police officers, and professors humbly knelt as I prayed.

The battle began again. The devils realized it was their last struggle. They cursed and held on to their victim, begging permission to stay in her. Then they cursed her for not responding, but it was different on this day. The additional time of fasting and prayer had made a difference.

I felt the release and knew they had departed. Clarita relaxed. The demon look departed from her eyes. She smiled.

I looked around and noticed that reporters were weeping; there were tears in the eyes of doctors; hardboiled jailers were also weeping. I could now see how terrific the battle had been.

Softly I began to sing with brothers Ahlberg and McAlister:

> Oh, the blood of Jesus
> Oh, the blood of Jesus
> Oh, the blood of Jesus
> That washes white as snow![1]

On the second time around the Filipinos joined in. The atmosphere seemed clean inside that prison.

I asked Clarita if the devils were gone and she answered in her own language, "Yes."

"Where did they go?"

"Out that window," she replied.

We were ready to leave when suddenly, like a flash of lightning, the devils reappeared. The girl screamed and her eyes changed.

I said to them, "Why have you returned? You know you must go and not return."

Speaking in English through her lips they replied, "But she is unclean. We have a right to live in her."

I answered them in a determined voice. "Mary Magdalene was unclean with seven like you and Jesus came into her life and she became clean by His mighty power. Therefore, I command you now to depart, and Jesus will make her clean."

They had no power to resist. They left, and she became normal again. I explained to her what had happened and got her to pray with me for the forgiveness of her sins.

As we were preparing to leave, the same thing was repeated. The unconverted newspapermen could not understand what was happening. Again I questioned the demons why they had returned and they said, "She has not asked us to go. She wants us. It is only you who desires for us to leave."

Again I demanded that they leave her and again they left immediately. I explained to her why they had returned and demanded her to tell them to leave and not return. This she did. Then I taught her to pray and plead the blood of Jesus against them.

It was now about noon, and Clarita was weak from the ordeal. I told the prison officers to give her rest and, after that, food.

As I was leaving I told Clarita that I was sure these devils would return. "After I am gone," I said, "they will come. Then you must demand them to leave without my being present. You must say, 'Go, in Jesus' name,' and they will obey." With this I left the compound.

We asked the newsmen not to write about the morning's events, but they said they were obligated to. The story had run for two weeks and it must be concluded. Since the Methodist church is the oldest Protestant denomination in the islands, they presumed I was a Methodist, and it was in the papers that way. They did not know how to write of such an experience; therefore, some of what they said was not correct. But I feel mostly responsible for this, as I gave them no interview and left the city to get away from publicity.

The devils did return to attack Clarita, and a strange thing happened when she called on them to leave. She was engaged in a mortal struggle and went into a coma, her fists clenched. The doctor pried her hands open and to his astonishment, there lay some long, black, coarse hair. Dr. Lara placed this hair in an envelope and put it in a guarded place. Under the microscope he found that the hair was not from any part of the human body.

The doctor has no answer to this mystery—how an invisible being, presumably a devil, could have lost hair by a visible being pulling it out. This phenomenon we must leave unanswered at the present.

On May 28, a headline in the *Manila Chronicle* read: "Victim of 'The Thing' Says Torturer Has Disappeared."

> The Thing is dead! This every believer can now proclaim as Clarita Villanueva...claimed yesterday that "The Thing" has finally been exorcised.
>
> Clarita told of her deliverance from her attackers as she pleaded for mercy before Judge Natividad Almeda-Lopez, who was to have tried her on vagrancy and prostitution charges.
>
> The girl said the prayers of an American minister, Dr. Lester F. Sumrall, who purposely visited her to purge the devil, did it. Since Friday, May 22, when the minister prayed with her at the city jail chapel for women, "The Thing" had never appeared again, Clarita added.

Judge Almeda-Lopez placed Clarita in Welfareville, an institution for wayward girls, for observation. With Dr. Lara, I went to visit her twice and found her overjoyed at our coming. She rushed to us, saying she had feared she would never see us again. She hurried to bring us chairs and sat and talked with us at length. She did not seem like the same girl we had known in Bilibid prison, tormented by devils, her face distorted, screaming at the top of her voice. This was a perfectly normal Filipino girl who had recovered from the nightmare of demon possession.

Let the enemies of the Cross say what they will; Christ had conquered, and she who was bound was now set free!

Clarita was soon granted parole and placed in the home of a Christian family. After a time, in order to escape the curious people who wished to see her, she went to the north of Luzon and settled in a small town there.

It is not easy to give a detailed report of such a sensational story as this. In my travels in more than one hundred countries and more than one thousand cities of the world, I have not heard anything so amazing. The following facts are indisputable and unassailable: Clarita was bitten and choked by unseen adversaries. Her case could not be solved by medical or psychological science. She was delivered by the power of simple prayer to Christ. The glory and praise for this miracle we unreservedly give to God and the Lord Jesus Christ.

Notes

1. Source unknown.

2
Who Is the Devil and What Are Demons?

For still our ancient Foe
Doth seek to work us woe;
His craft and pow'r are great,
And, armed with cruel hate,
On earth is not his equal.

—Martin Luther,
"A Mighty Fortress Is Our God"

I feel very strongly that the devil is making his last attempt to capture the planet Earth. Reading about the final days of Howard Hughes, I was distressed to see how he died like an animal. He was so fearful that he wore gloves all the time so he would not contract disease. His private automobile was equipped with a germ-proof, air-filtering system that cost $15,000. He recycled the well water on his private golf course to be sure he would not be contaminated by germs when he played golf. All his money could not free him from his fears.

There are those in Hollywood, I am told, whose lives are so full of fear and torment that they live completely abnormal lives. Their predicament is caused by the devil. Fear is fostered by an evil spirit.

The late Pope Paul VI said, "Whole societies have fallen under the domination of the devil. Sex and narcotics provide openings for Satan's infiltration of mankind. One of the great needs of our time is a defense against that evil which we call the devil. We all are under an obscure domination. It is by Satan, the prince of this world, the number one enemy."

It was only a few years ago that those who took a stand against demons were criticized. They were not believed. Now that time is gone. Christians want information on how to discern demon power. They want to know how to exorcise demons and how to keep people free from satanic forces.

The devil's best defense has been his successful delusion of mankind into thinking he does not really exist. If we swallow that lie, we are simply proving how clever he is and how unbelievably naive we humans can be.

The Scriptures Are the Source of Information

In the Bible, Satan is directly mentioned more than two hundred times. Satan enters the realm of human activity in Genesis 3. In Job 1, he is an oppressor of good people. In Matthew 4, Satan audaciously tempts Jesus. His final incarceration and eternal confinement are described in Revelation 20.

We have the full story of the fall, the works, and the destiny of the devil in Ezekiel 28:12–19.

Son of man, take up a lamentation upon the king of Tyrus, and say unto him, Thus saith the Lord GOD; Thou sealest up the sum, full of wisdom, and perfect in beauty. Thou hast been in Eden the garden of God; every precious stone was thy covering, the sardius, topaz, and the diamond, the beryl, the onyx, and the jasper, the sapphire, the emerald, and the carbuncle, and gold: the workmanship of thy tabrets and of thy pipes was prepared in thee in the day that thou wast created. Thou art the anointed cherub that covereth; and I have set thee so: thou wast upon the holy mountain of God; thou hast walked up and down in the midst of the stones of fire. Thou wast perfect in thy ways from the day that thou wast created, till iniquity was found in thee. By the multitude of thy merchandise they have filled the midst of thee with violence, and thou hast sinned: therefore I will cast thee as profane out of the mountain of God: and I will destroy thee, O covering cherub, from the midst of the stones of fire. Thine heart was lifted up because of thy beauty, thou hast corrupted thy wisdom by reason of thy brightness: I will cast thee to the ground, I will lay thee before kings, that they may behold thee. Thou hast defiled thy sanctuaries by the multitude of thine iniquities, by the iniquity of thy traffic; therefore will I bring forth a fire from the midst of thee, it shall devour thee, and I will bring thee to ashes upon the earth in the sight of all them that behold thee. All they that know thee among the people shall be astonished at thee: thou shalt be a terror, and never shalt thou be any more.

Satan was created an archangel, one of the highest order of God's creation. This description in Ezekiel can only be applied to a superbeing, not a man who ruled Tyre.

The prophet Isaiah describes the devil's actual fall from his place of honor and glory as one of the archangels.

How art thou fallen from heaven, O Lucifer, son of the morning! how art thou cut down to the ground, which didst weaken the nations! For thou hast said in thine heart, I will ascend into heaven, I will exalt my throne above the stars of God: I will sit also upon the mount of the congregation, in the sides of the north: I will ascend above the heights of the clouds; I will be like the most High. (Isa. 14:12–14)

The apostle John supplies more description of Satan's fall:

And there was war in heaven: Michael and his angels fought against the dragon; and the dragon fought and his angels, and prevailed not; neither was their place found any more in heaven. And the great dragon was cast out, that old serpent, called the Devil, and Satan, which deceiveth the whole world: he was cast out into the earth, and his angels were cast out with him. And I heard a loud voice saying in heaven, Now is come salvation, and strength, and the kingdom of our God, and the power of his Christ: for the accuser of our brethren is cast down, which accused them before our God day and night....Therefore rejoice, ye heavens, and ye that dwell in them. Woe to the inhabiters of the earth and of the sea! for the devil is come down unto you, having great wrath, because he knoweth that he hath but a short time. (Rev. 12:7–10, 12)

Not content to be the beautiful, intelligent creature of God's creation and the highest order of angels, Satan aspired to a position of equality with God. His contest seems to have been most specifically with Jesus Christ, although the entire Godhead was challenged. This conflict has endured through the ages and will not be entirely consummated until Satan is cast into the lake of fire forever and ever.

Satan's Power

The devil's titles, abilities, and sphere of influence are clearly defined. In the tabernacle and temple in Jerusalem in Ezekiel 28:14, he is called *"the anointed cherub that covereth."* The cherubim were in the most holy place of worship during Old Testament days. Two golden-winged cherubim formed a part of the mercy seat or covering of the holy ark of the covenant, which was the symbol of Israel's holiest devotion to Jehovah. The anointed cherub had to do with the very holiness of God.

Satan Was Beautiful

He was perhaps the most gorgeous creature of all. His form was "covered" with gold and the most costly of stones. Ezekiel wrote that he was *"perfect in beauty"* (v. 12).

Melody and Music

Satan was evidently the first created being. The description in Ezekiel 28:13 includes a reference to musical instruments— "tabrets and pipes"—indicating that he had the ability to create lovely music. Some believe that before his fall he led musical praise to God. Certainly the devil today makes tremendous use of music.

From an Angel to a Devil

Satan fell first because of pride over his personal beauty (Ezek. 28:17). His greed and lust for physical and material things supplanted his spiritual service to Jehovah. He is spoken of as having a "multitude of iniquities" that led him to be full of violence. Perhaps this is a reference to his seeking after all things with no regard for whom he hurts in the quest.

These elements—pride and greed—have been major tools in tempting man to sin ever since. How many of us commit sin out of pride of possession and pride of physical beauty? If these could produce iniquity in the *"cherub that covereth,"* how easily will they produce iniquity in sinful flesh like ours!

Satan Is Still a Dignitary

In the Book of Jude, we read that the archangel Michael, an angel of great power and position in heaven, *"did not presume to pronounce a reviling judgment upon him* [Satan]" (v. 9, RSV) when disputing over Moses' body. Even in his fallen state, the devil is one of the most intelligent and keenest personalities created by God.

Lucifer, the Devil, Is a Real Person

The devil is not an influence or an idea or some abstract design. He is a person. Personal names and titles are given to him (Rev. 20:2). Personal acts and attributes are ascribed to him (Isa. 14:12–15). Jesus dealt with the devil as a person (Matt. 4:1–11) and waged war against him as against a person (Luke 13:16). Paul, in his Epistles, described the believer's battle with Satan as with a real person (Eph. 6:10–18). The devil is spoken of as possessing personal characteristics—heart, pride, speech, knowledge, power, desire, and lusts. (For a complete list of the names of the devil as used in Scripture, see Appendix.)

What Are Demons?

In several places Scripture speaks of angels that are aligned with the devil. In the famous passage about the kingdom of heaven, in Matthew 25:31–46, Jesus speaks of *"the everlasting fire, prepared for the devil and his angels"* (v. 41).

The most explicit description is in the book of Revelation. John is shown a vision of a *"wonder in heaven...a great red dragon"* (Rev. 12:3). The archangel Michael and his angels wage battle against this serpent. *"And the great dragon was cast out, that old serpent, called the Devil, and Satan, which deceiveth the whole world: he was cast out into the earth, and his angels were cast out with him"* (v. 9).

This same passage speaks of the dragon sweeping a third of the stars of heaven down with his tail (v. 4). Many commentators interpret stars as angels—that Satan caused a third of the heavenly hosts to rebel with him when he arrogantly tried to be like God. Since the angels are without number, *"ten thousand times ten thousand, and thousands of thousands"* (Rev. 5:11), the sheer number of Satan's angels is beyond our mind's grasp.

These angels are the demons or evil, unclean spirits the Bible speaks of. Their name comes from the Latin word *daemon,* meaning evil spirit, and from the Greek word *daimon,* a divinity.

Demons Are Ageless

From the Bible we understand that large numbers of demons roam the earth and the air. Since they do not die, they have been in the world since the beginning of time.

Demons Are Personalities

These demons are personalities without bodies, and they are highly organized. As fallen spirits they desire to dwell in a body in order to manifest themselves. They are angry with God because of their fallen state; their prime motive is to destroy what God loves or creates—chiefly, man.

In our travels we have heard of demon spirits who claimed to have been Napoleon, Alexander the Great, and other world leaders. They often state the names of people they have lived in previously. When someone who is possessed of a devil dies, that spirit immediately seeks a dwelling place in another person. He cannot walk into just any person's life; he must find one with an open door. If he is a spirit of lust, he seeks a lustful person. If he is a spirit of anger, he seeks to possess a person who has little control over his temper. A spirit of insanity will seek to enter a person's mind.

Paul Warned of Demon Power

That demons are highly organized can be seen from the concluding passage of the apostle Paul's letter to the Ephesians: *"For we wrestle not against flesh and blood, but against principalities, against powers, against the rulers of the darkness of this world, against spiritual wickedness in high places"* (Eph. 6:12). Satan and his demon-angels have their abode and base of operation in the high places.

Jesus Cast Out Demons

Jesus took for granted the existence of demons. He dealt with them constantly, casting them out of the people (Matt. 15:22, 28) and giving His disciples the power to set people free (Matt. 10:1; Luke 9:1; Mark 16:17).

The Apostles Believed in the Existence of Demons

The apostles believed firmly in the existence of demons. Matthew suggested their organization under Satan (Matt. 12:26) and spoke of their final doom (Matt. 25:41). Luke described their nature (Luke 4:33; 6:18), their expulsion from human beings (Luke 9:42), and their place of dwelling (Luke 8:27–33).

John also told of their dwelling place (Rev. 9:11), their activity (Rev. 16:14), and declared their existence (Rev. 9:20). Paul wrote to Timothy, warning him of *"doctrines of devils"* (1 Tim. 4:1).

Demons Name Themselves

Very often demons name themselves. The Bible denotes several examples. One told me he was "serpent spirit" and another said loudly, "I am the angel over blood." The spirits in the demon-possessed man of Gadara called themselves *"Legion"* (Mark 5:9).

Demons Are Liars

We must realize, however, that demons are liars and may not be telling the truth about their names, numbers, or strength. Evidently they vary in wickedness; some can be *"more wicked"* than others (Matt. 12:45).

Demons Vary in Power

They also vary in power (Mark 9:29) and they seem to know the names of those who rebuke them and exorcise them. In Acts 19:15 an evil spirit said, *"Jesus I know, and Paul I know; but who are ye?"*

Demons Believe and Tremble

Demons are not dead people any more than angels are glorified believers who have died and gone to heaven. Demons believe in God, and as James says, they *"tremble"* (James 2:19). Their belief is not one of faith and trust and commitment; it is rather one of knowledge.

Demons Have Willpower

Demons have willpower (Matt. 12:44); they oppose saints and have doctrines (Rom. 8:38, 1 Tim. 4:1); and they do not abide in the truth (John 8:44). But the chief thing we all need to remember is that they are subject to—they are under—the sovereignty of the Lord Jesus Christ. Peter reminded his first-century fellow believers of that when he wrote of Jesus: *"Who is gone into heaven, and is on the right hand of God; angels and authorities and powers being made subject unto him"* (1 Pet. 3:22).

3
How Jesus Dealt with the Devil

The devil is afraid of persisting,
because he shrinks from frequent defeat.

—Ambrose

Jesus said more about devils than He did about angels. He had
more to say about hell than heaven. On reading portions of
the Gospels, one quickly sees that much of Jesus' time was
taken up with encounters with evil spirits. They seemed to crop
up everywhere. In the opening chapter of Mark's gospel, Jesus
encounters no less than five situations involving Satan or evil
spirits. One third of chapter 3 deals with the commonplace manifestation of demons, and half of chapter 5 is used to describe the
classic case of the demoniac of the Gadarenes (also called Ger-
asenes). Throughout the book, "unclean" or evil spirits and their
chief ruler, Satan, lurk not far from the action wherever Jesus
goes.

No doubt this world is filled with devils, as Martin Luther
wrote. When the incarnate Son of God, filled with the Holy
Spirit, moved in righteous power through the countryside of
Galilee and Judea, the demons began to manifest themselves.
Without question, the Spirit is moving in greater power in our
day than He has for centuries, and the demons are again stirred
up. We can learn how to deal with these devils by observing
Jesus.

Jesus Encountered Demons Indirectly

The spiritual warfare that raged around Jesus was evident even before He was born. Matthew wrote of how King Herod became increasingly alarmed over reports that a new king was to be born in his realm. When the magi from the East came asking how they might find "Him who was born King of the Jews," Herod told them to keep him informed. He meant later to do away with this one he feared would take his throne. Upon discovering he had been tricked, that the wise men were not going to return to give him word, Herod ordered soldiers to fall upon Bethlehem and destroy all male infants two years of age and younger.

This extraordinary measure was not the action of a reasonable man! Far from it. Herod was inspired by the devil to commit such slaughter. Jesus was spared, of course, because an angel had warned Mary and Joseph to flee into Egypt for a time.

The conflict with Satan was further demonstrated in Nazareth where Jesus lived for thirty years. The townspeople had watched this son of Joseph grow into manhood. They had not heard Him blaspheme, curse, or hurt anyone. Yet when He returned to Nazareth and spoke in the temple (see Luke 4:16–32), they flew into a rage, seized Him and *"led him unto the brow of the hill whereon their city was built, that they might cast him down headlong"* (v. 29). Why would normal people attempt to kill a good, kind fellow citizen? It was abnormal. It was the devil seeking to destroy Him before His time.

We find this also with the "demoniac" of Gadara, the man who had a legion of devils in him. (See Mark 5.) According to the Bible, everyone was afraid of the man—they even feared to pass that way. Strangers and visitors took another road because of this wild man. When Jesus came by, this demoniac roared out against Him. He wanted to destroy Jesus. But Jesus stood before him and asked, *"What is thy name?"* (v. 9). When the spirits identified themselves as *"Legion: for we are many"* (v. 9), Jesus commanded them to come out.

Another indirect encounter with the prince of darkness happened when Jesus was asleep in the boat on the Sea of Galilee. A storm arose abnormally fast. The Scripture says it came up "suddenly." The devil has some control over the elements, as we learn from the book of Job, and while Jesus slept, Satan tried to dump the boat to the bottom of the sea. No doubt the devil thought if he could attack Jesus in an indirect way, he could destroy Him. But of course, his attempt failed; the disciples woke Jesus, He rebuked the storm, and a great calm came over the waters.

The devil also sought to destroy Jesus through the hatred and cunning of religious leaders. I do not believe those priests and Pharisees were normally men of hate. Something came upon them. It began with pride. They thought, "Now, if this Jesus stays around He is going to steal our prestige. We have to get rid of Him!"

The devil helped them right up to the point of murdering Jesus.

Satan also attacked Jesus indirectly through Judas, who betrayed our Lord. Luke records that *"then entered Satan into Judas"* (Luke 22:3). Judas was not Jesus' real enemy; the devil was using Judas. Avoiding a face-to-face confrontation, he chose rather to try to destroy Jesus by deceit.

The Direct Confrontations

The best example of direct conflict between Satan and Jesus is the wilderness temptation. Matthew and Luke both record this in detail. (See Matthew 4 and Luke 4.)

The devil came to Jesus when He was alone, preparing for His earthly ministry. For forty days He had prayed and fasted, and His body was weak. The devil thought this would be Jesus' weakest moment. He did not know that although a fasting person's flesh may lack strength, his spirit can be stronger than ever.

Satan first approached Jesus in the area of his fleshly appetite. "There is a stone," he said. "If you are God, turn it into bread."

Satan knew Jesus was God. After all, Jesus had made him. He knew Jesus was his Creator. But the devil is a deceiver and a liar. He said, "If you are the Son of God...."

Jesus answered, *"It is written, Man shall not live by bread alone, but by every word that proceedeth out of the mouth of God"* (Matt. 4:4). He stood upon the Word of God, quoting to the devil a passage from the Old Testament and thus setting a pattern and example for you and me. We must answer satanic attacks, not with our intelligence, nor our feelings, but with God's Word. Jesus won the first round of this temptation, and so will we when we use the Word of God.

Next, Satan tried to appeal to Jesus' soul. Taking Him to the highest point of the temple, he whispered in His ear, "Now, listen, You are trying to be an evangelist. But You haven't had Your name in the *Jerusalem Post* yet. Nobody has written a feature story about You. You are just a nobody. But now, jump off this temple right into the main street of Jerusalem and say 'I jumped seventy-two feet here and was not hurt!' Then everybody will praise You and the writers of the *Jerusalem Post* will run out and write a story about You. You need some publicity so that everybody will know about You."

Don't think the devil is not clever. He is. But Jesus answered immediately, *"It is written again, Thou shalt not tempt the Lord thy God"* (Matt. 4:7).

We must never believe the devil. We must not tempt God. What the devil said was true. (He was actually quoting Psalm 91:11–12 with a key phrase conveniently omitted!) If Jesus *had* fallen down, the angels *would* have taken care of Him. But Jesus said something greater: *"Thou shalt not tempt the Lord thy God."*

Occasionally a magazine or newspaper will carry a story about people who handle snakes as a part of their religion. I lived for a time in the jungle and deadly snakes were all around me. But I think it would have been tempting the devil for me to have taken one of them up in my arms. I have eaten things that were poisonous and God has healed me because I did not know they were poisonous. Jesus said, *"Thou shalt not tempt...."*

book

The devil had one more trick up his sleeve—his master stroke. He asked Jesus to simply bow down and worship him. Satan promised Him *"all the kingdoms of the world, and the glory of them"* (Matt. 4:8), but Jesus neither yielded nor bowed.

Jesus had come to earth for the very purpose of reclaiming mankind for His heavenly Father. But with this third temptation Satan didn't intend to grant what he was offering, and Jesus knew that. It was an attractive shortcut, another of the devil's lies. Jesus answered, *"Get thee hence, Satan: for it is written..."* (v. 10), and the devil left Him—for a time.

Satan's Three Appeals

Satan tempted Jesus along three lines, and he comes to us in these same three ways. His appeals seem attractive. They seem natural. They are pitched toward man's instinctive desire for self-preservation, self-adulation, and self-achievement. Watch out!

Jesus in Action

The Lord Jesus identified demon spirits. He recognized some as deaf spirits. He identified dumbness, infirmities, and wildness. Christ knew the number of demons a person had; He could bring out one or He could bring out a thousand. From Mary Magdalene He cast out seven demons. The number had no relationship to the deliverance. When He spoke the word, the demons had to go, and the people were set free.

It is worth particular notice that when He commanded Satan to leave, the devil obeyed. Satan had to bow to the greater authority. When you or I command the devil to go in the name of Jesus, he must obey us too. We have that authority.

From modern films and books on the occult and from rites within certain historic denominations, we might conclude that the exorcism of devils is something complex, and that it is for the select few. However, when we turn to the Bible, we see the opposite is true. Jesus rarely spent more than a few minutes setting a person free. Usually all He had to do was issue an authoritative command.

In Matthew 9:32–33, some men brought to Him a *"dumb man possessed with a devil"* (v. 32). The next verse says, *"And when the devil was cast out, the dumb spake"* (v. 33). On another day, *"Then was brought unto him one possessed with a devil, blind, and dumb"* (Matt. 12:22). Matthew simply says that Jesus healed him, restoring both the man's sight and speech.

Following the Transfiguration, Jesus returned to the foot of the mountain to find His disciples defeated and confused. They told Him that a man had brought them his son, *"a lunatic, and sore vexed"* (Matt. 17:15). They didn't have the faith to set him free. According to Matthew's account, Jesus immediately *"rebuked the devil; and he departed out of him: and the child was cured from that very hour"* (v. 18). True, Jesus did emphasize to them the extreme importance of prayer and fasting (v. 21), but the point is that He did not engage in lengthy analysis or ritual. He exercised His rightful dominion and set the boy free.

Our Example

This is an example to the church today. Jesus took authority, commanded demons to leave, and did not waste a lot of time doing it. We are to do the same. He commissioned the church, saying, *"And these signs shall follow them that believe; In my name shall they cast out devils"* (Mark 16:17). Certainly we must be clean vessels. Our hearts must be washed continually by obeying His Word. We must confess all known sin and constantly recognize our position as "under the blood of Jesus." And when we walk in this way, we need simply to command the evil spirits to come out by faith, and they will obey.

Jesus confronted demon power. He did not ignore it. He did not stand off from it. He was not afraid of it. Now we are the voice of Jesus upon this earth. We are the hands and feet of Jesus. We must be ready to carry on His ministry and cast out devils. There was never a time when it was needed so much as now.

Someone asks, "Where are the devils Jesus cast out?" They are not in prison or in hell, as some imagine. The demons Jesus cast out two thousand years ago are in the void of space, or some wilderness, or they are living in some person today. They seek to indwell human beings, as I found out when I first attempted missionary work in the island of Java, among unreached people dwelling in spiritual darkness. But these demons are not confined to the islands of the sea. Look around you and be convinced. Our work is cut out for us.

4
How I Learned to Cast Out Demons

Behold how many thousands still are lying,
Bound in the darksome prisonhouse of sin,
With none to tell them of the Savior's dying
Or of the life He died for them to win.

—Mary Ann Thomson, "O Zion, Haste"

Although I was raised in a Full Gospel church, I do not remember hearing much preaching on deliverance from demon power. I cannot remember ever hearing a whole sermon on the devil, his reality, and his works. If they talked about him they called him "Ol' Slewfoot" and said he had horns and a tail. And if they rebuked the devil they demanded he go back to hell, when in fact he is not in hell and never has been. This would seem highly unusual today, but it also would have been highly unusual then for the preacher to give a full sermon about demons.

In my early twenties I joined Howard Carter of London, and we traveled for years through many countries teaching and evangelizing. We spent three months in Java, Indonesia, where I had my first encounter with a demon-possessed person. She was a young girl twelve or thirteen seated on the front row in a service where I was to minister.

During the song service she slipped off the pew and began to writhe on the floor like a snake. A repulsive, green foam oozed from her mouth. She looked terrible and I felt terrible. However, the Javanese minister paid no attention and went on with the service.

When I rose to speak, something within me stirred. I was deeply indignant. Although I had had no experience with a thing like this, I said firmly, "Get back on that seat."

The Indonesian girl did not understand English, but evidently the devil within her did. Instantly she returned to her seat and remained there motionless for some forty minutes while I preached. Afterward, I prayed at the pulpit for her deliverance in the name of the Lord Jesus Christ. There was no struggle. She was instantly healed. Evidently, at my first words from the pulpit the devil knew I (through Christ) possessed authority over him.

While walking into a church in another part of Indonesia, I was approached by a woman who looked at me and said, "You have a black angel in you and I have a white angel in me."

God's power moved within me and rather than walking on toward the pulpit I immediately said to her, "No, you have a black angel in you, who is the devil. I have a white angel in me, the Lord Jesus Christ. And my angel being the stronger, I command this black angel to come out of you, and that you be free."

The woman instantly went into a kind of convulsion; after a few moments she became as normal as she had ever been. From that moment she was free. She confessed that she had been under the spell of a witch doctor for many years. Now Christ had set her free.

I was not taught this kind of ministry. I had read no books on the subject, except the Bible, but when I met the adversary, the Spirit within me was moved and my heart went out to the afflicted to assist them and bring them back to health.

Christ in the Conflict

As we ministered throughout the island of Java, I encountered the devil a number of times. The greatest thing I learned was that I was not personally in the conflict. It was Christ *in me.* Also, it was not the *person* who caused the battle, but the *devil* within him or her.

I discovered there was no reason to fear. I found that although they would scream and tear themselves, they did not seek to harm me or touch me. I was perfectly safe in exorcising demons. I found in most cases that the demons wanted to run away and avoid confronting me. They would often say, "We are not here; we are gone. Leave us alone." They do not tell the truth.

My Gibraltar

As I sought to confirm this ministry by the Word of God, the Great Commission of our Lord Jesus (Mark 16:15–18) in which He commanded his disciples to cast out devils became my Gibraltar.

It seems that almost every day I receive telephone calls from someone in America who is combating an evil spirit and is seeking help. Almost every day letters come to me from those who are tormented by the devil. After I appeared as a guest of Pat Robertson on the "700 Club," I received some 2,500 letters from listeners—most of them inquiring about deliverance.

These people needed deliverance. Philosophy cannot set them free. Pastoral counseling cannot deliver them. Psychiatry cannot deliver them. A psychiatrist from Chattanooga once brought four of his patients with him to my office. He had not been able to effect a cure, and he wanted me to lay hands on them and pray for them.

The church has tried to taboo the ministry of exorcising evil spirits. Ministers have tried to turn their backs on the situation and have committed sick people to mental institutions in order to forget them. Yet there is an ever-growing need for the ministry of setting people free—in the Spirit.

Those who lead the army of Jesus Christ must not simply be able to pray for the sick, but they must be able to reach into the spirit of man and set him free from evil, breaking the powers of Satan in his spirit and mind. Yet before they can do that, they must know how to discern the spirits and recognize their presence.

5

Where Satan Dwells

Leave no unguarded place, no weakness of the soul;
Take every virtue, every grace, and fortify the whole.
From strength to strength go on, wrestle and fight and pray;
Tread all the powers of darkness down,
And win the well-fought day.

—Charles Wesley, "Soldiers of Christ, Arise"

One cannot hope to deal with the subject of demon power without expecting one question above all others: Can a Christian have a demon? Can an evil spirit enter in and possess a believer?

The controversy on this issue rages around a theory of recognition and definition. Who is a Christian? What can happen in his life?

The Bible emphatically states in James 4:7, *"Resist the devil, and he will flee from you."* This is the position of the born-again believer. Jesus Christ, in His ultimate commission to the church, said, *"In my name shall they cast out devils"* (Mark 16:17).

The Christian should not fear the devil; he should cast him out, dethrone him, exorcise him.

However, a person who identifies himself or herself as a Christian and goes to fortune-tellers, plays the Ouija board, and depends on horoscopes for guidance is an open door for the entrance of the evil one. Almost every worshipper and high priest of witchcraft in Brazil will tell you he is a Christian. This is what I mean by definition. The apostle Paul had no fear of demons or their power, but the sons of Sceva did. (See Acts 19:13–17.)

We deal with this further in a later chapter, but first we should consider the "habitations of devils" about which there is no dispute. Satan himself, and the demons that serve him, inhabit the nations of this world and seek to dominate them. He is called "the god of this world" for good reason. His spirits, which no one can number, have their residence in the atmosphere of the planet Earth. His presence can almost be seen and felt in the places of this world where the gospel of Jesus Christ has not entered to challenge his ground.

The Bible says ancient Babylon had become *"the habitation of devils, and the hold of every foul spirit"* (Rev. 18:2). In Isaiah's descriptive account of the devil's origin (Isaiah 14), the devil is accused of having "weakened the nations" (v. 12). Lucifer, as he is called in this passage, *"made the earth to tremble, that did shake kingdoms"* (v. 16).

Satan's Initial Desire

Satan desired to be like the Creator. His chief ambition was to replace God in heaven. To do this, he initiated a rebellion against God in the heavens and continued to carry it out when he was cast down to earth, before the Creation. Man's history from the beginning until now is laced with conflicts and crises in which the devil is "weakening the kingdoms" by war, pestilence, famine, moral degradation, and every conceivable means.

When viewing our modern world it is not difficult to illustrate how the devil causes the earth to tremble. Recent history of Auschwitz, the Nazi blitz, and the mass purges under Stalin are already fading in the light of more current atrocities.

Cambodia

We are told by none other than Mr. Chang Song, the minister of information in the former Cambodian regime, that in the three years since 1975 some 2.3 million citizens of that "gentle land" have been killed. That is one third of the nation's population!

Godless Khmer Rouge armies enforced a total evacuation of Cambodia's leading cities when they came to power. The land resembles a wilderness more than the garden it once was. But while the Khmer appear to be the murderers there, the *real* murderer is Lucifer. Isaiah prophesied of Lucifer that he *"made the world as a wilderness, and destroyed the cities thereof"* (Isa. 14:17).

Uganda

Nightmare was the only word befitting the state of that African republic when Idi Amin seized power over its ten million people.

An Ugandan leaving the country said: "It is no good. It is Amin himself. He has a mental problem and you never know when you will die....The army can do nothing....Now they are as frightened of him [Amin] as the civilians; he has killed ruthlessly there....Who kills for him? Youngsters he has chosen and trained....they kill anyone, anywhere, for fun, and they murder at his direction."[1]

I do not believe Amin could have done what he did in that country—with the flow of blood there—had he not been possessed by the devil. Author Gwyn himself attributes the "indiscriminate killing" to "something that cannot be fully explained by Amin's own pathological example and influence." Gwyn links the use of magic and witchcraft with the killings. "It is true," he says, "that Amin is relying heavily on magic." He adds, "It is often said of these troops that 'their eyes have gone mad with blood, and magic is at work.'"

I am reminded of Adolf Hitler and Benito Mussolini. It is said that Mussolini declared, "I would shake hands with the devil if he would help me get the desire of my heart." Much of his generation trembled before that man's exaggerations. No one realized he had already shaken hands with Satan!

Christian missionaries have long been acquainted with the fact that certain nations are uniquely the devil's territory. Until recent years the majority of stories of demon possession, voodoo, exorcism, and witchcraft came from the countries of Asia, Latin America, Africa, and the islands of the sea.

Indonesia

Indonesia was the first non-Christian country I ministered in when, as a twenty-one-year-old evangelist, I began preaching overseas. In the three months I was there, and in all my travels since, I have never seen as much demon power and as many witch doctors anywhere as I did in Indonesia.

India

No country saddens my heart like India. For many years the nations of the West have been trying to help India get on her feet and develop the capability to feed her teeming masses. But it is still a losing battle. I judge that until India turns away from her three-thousand-year-old worship of 300 million idols and turns to the living God, her problems will never be solved. She is a nation under the dominion of the devil.

Tibet

Just across India's northern border is Tibet, an ancient and isolated land where Satan has reigned supreme for ages. With the Rev. Howard Carter, I traveled into Tibet during the 1930s. We could feel the strange power of the devil there. The dirt, filth, and stench were almost overpowering. Characteristic of the Lamaist temples of this mountain kingdom are the hundreds of grotesque idols—actually demon idols—that are sculpted into the interior walls of the temples.

During our stay there we slept in the heathen temples (there was no other place to sleep) and listened to strange stories of demon power. One missionary told us he had witnessed a Tibetan monk, in a frenzy of mystic power, twist a steel sword so that it resembled a corkscrew.

Guyana

In November, 1978, at Jonestown, Guyana, the leader of the People's Temple, Jim Jones, very definitely surrendered his spirit and intelligence to the devil and committed one of the greatest atrocities in history.

America

Demon power has dominated nations in the past, and it threatens to do so in America today. Witchcraft, the occult, and sensual evil has never been as blatant in America as it is right now. We are in a time when the devil is seeking to conquer America. If our generation fails to take authority over the devil and his demons, our children and their children could well live in a country that is tyrannized by a demon-possessed dictator, an Adolf Hitler or a Josef Stalin.

The Lord Jesus Christ, when He appeared to John on the isle of Patmos, issued a message for the churches in seven key cities of Asia. Nothing could more graphically demonstrate the importance He placed on the cities of the world. And Satan likewise chooses to operate from key cities.

Pergamos was one of those cities named by our Lord. *"I know thy works and where thou dwellest,"* He said to the church in Pergamos, *"Even where Satan's seat is: and thou holdest fast my name, and hast not denied my faith, even in those days wherein Antipas was my faithful martyr, who was slain among you, **where Satan dwelleth"*** (Rev. 2:13, emphasis added).

Ancient Babylon was a city under Satan's control, as we shall see. Some students of sorcery have traced witchcraft back to this great metropolitan center of the old world.

Heavenly Conflict

The prophet Daniel, in exile in Babylon, received a vision (chapters 9 and 10) that explained why he had not received an answer to his prayers of more than three weeks in duration

(Dan. 10:2). An angel appeared to him, informing him that one known as *"the prince of the kingdom of Persia"* (v. 13) had obstructed Daniel's petitions. The angel said that as soon as he would leave Daniel he (the angel) would again have to fight this spirit and another called *"the prince of Grecia"* (v. 20), but that *"Michael your prince"* (v. 21) would aid him in this battle. What we see here is the heavenly conflict between Satan's angels (or demons) and God's hosts. The princes of Persia and Grecia were undoubtedly high officers in the devil's world dominion.

The Devil Has Not Changed

The devil was very real to Martin Luther, and a letter the reformer wrote in 1524 contains the telling line: "I am having a terrible time with the Satan of Alstedt [a Saxon town]."[2]

Certain cities today are the devil's dwelling place. One of the most depressing cities in the world is Calcutta, a city named for a female goddess. Cali, the ugly, glary-eyed idol in temples there, receives worship and blood sacrifice.

A missionary told me once that when he delivered an Indian woman possessed of a demon, the evil spirit told him, "I am from Cali in Calcutta."

When the missionary asked the spirit how it had entered the woman, it answered, "She worshipped in our temple in Calcutta." The missionary replied, "Come out of her, in Jesus' name," and it came out, weeping loudly and saying, "Now I must journey back to Calcutta to find somebody else in whom to live."

Gone to the Devil

Evil spirits seem to be drawn to the cities. Since they apparently are not satisfied until they dwell within a human body, they congregate in places where humans are numerous. Their strength is most evident in cities that, for some reason, have little of the light of the gospel. Paris, New York City, Hollywood— these cities I believe are under the devil's ruling power.

It is said that a Frenchman can live all his life in a small French town or on a farm and remain pure and upright, but give him two days in Paris and he will lose his virtue. New York City does that to countless young people every year—people who go there looking for life at its best. A spirit of greed is in control of that great metropolis, and if our eyes were only able to see them, we would observe the hoards of evil spirits that make this city their dwelling.

We should weep over our cities, as Jesus did for Jerusalem, lest they become throne rooms for Satan. One reason evil becomes concentrated in big cities is because they are full of soothsayers, crystal gazers, fortune-tellers, spiritualist media, and cults of all kinds.

Man and Animal Life—The Devil's Habitations

Beasts may be possessed by demons also. Jesus encountered this phenomenon when, in the well-known case of the Gadarene demoniac (Matt. 8:28–32), he sent the legion of spirits into a local herd of swine. These pigs immediately became insane and were filled with a suicidal spirit abnormal to animals. They raced into the sea and were drowned.

A generation or two ago when Americans had a much closer relationship with animals, certain beasts often became possessed. I have seen horses that went berserk and had to be put to death. Their owners called them "mad horses." Dogs also would become suddenly abnormal and vicious.

Animals are very conscious of the presence of demons. When evil power lurks they become nervous and sometimes noisy. On the other hand, they respond to love, tenderness, and kind words. By receiving affection they may be protected from evil powers.

Parts of the human body can be habitations of devils. Several times our Lord cast out spirits of deafness and dumbness from people. He also cast out spirits of "infirmity" (weakness). Francis MacNutt says that in his experience, the spirit of infirmity will even move from one part of the body to another—seeking to avoid giving up its place in a person's body—when a Christian is commanding it to leave. Evidently, an evil spirit takes over a certain part of the body and does not relinquish it until someone rebukes it with divine authority.

Just as the Holy Spirit seeks to reside fully in and have control over a Christian's life, evil spirits also seek complete possession. Jesus encountered this immediately upon beginning His ministry. A person reading the first few chapters of Mark's gospel will be amazed at how often Jesus met people who needed deliverance. The writers of the Synoptic Gospels describe these encounters matter-of-factly, since they were common occurrences. (See Luke 4:33; 4:41; 8:2; 9:1; Matt. 12:22; Mark 1:23, 32, 34, 39; 3:11, 22).

The most revealing deliverance in the Bible is the healing of the demoniac of Gadara (already mentioned several times). The evil spirits in this wretched man told Jesus they were "Legion"; that is, they numbered between two and five thousand! But they all obediently left the Gadarene at Jesus' command, never to torment the man again.

Many—even preachers and learned religious professors—try to explain away demon possession today. They attribute disorders and illnesses to mental illness or physical causes. In many cases I do not dispute that, but this does not discount the primal cause for these often terrible conditions: Evil spirits are oppressing and possessing multiplied thousands of people today. They do not need medicine or psychoanalysis; they need a simple prayer offered on their behalf by one of Christ's believing children who will claim authority over spirits that have usurped God's place of honor and blessing.

Dramatic Deliverances!

A few years ago a woman traveled all the way from New Mexico to our church in South Bend, Indiana, to be delivered of evil spirits. She was in her forties, and the demons had been so strong in her that she had not been able to eat at the table with her husband for more than twenty years. She had a terrible pain in her abdomen and was a social outcast. This lady came to me in desperate straits, unable to live any longer, she felt, if she did not gain relief.

We documented this deliverance and later made a recording ("And the Demon Answered Back") of the actual sounds of the demons within her. She was not easily set free. It took more than one of us agreeing in prayer, with fasting, to take authority. But she was set free.

In 1963 our church hosted Arlindo Barbosa de Oliviera of Brazil and sponsored a tour of forty American cities where he gave testimony of his deliverance from evil spirits. People across the country can still remember Arlindo relating how more than five hundred devils possessed him at one time. He knew their names and worshipped them in different ways.

He told me that at times he would lie in a trance in the government office in Brasilia where he worked and receive information psychically about secrets behind closed doors in Washington. He said that at other times the spirits would cause him to eat and drink ground glass without doing himself any harm. One of the demons desired strong drink, and Arlindo drank certain types of wine when this devil was active in him. A Methodist missionary set him free, and he has been serving God ever since.

The Devil Is Real

I did not need Arlindo to prove to me that demons exist today and that they are always seeking to enter human bodies. The Christian has nothing to fear, for *"greater is he that is in you, than he that is in the world"* (1 John 4:4). But we do have to be alert. When you play with fire, you can get burned. And if you carelessly go into Satan's territory, you can open yourself up to his evil work.

Notes

1. David Gwyn, *Idi Amin: Death-Light of Africa* (Boston: Little, Brown & Co., 1977), p. 130.

2. Roland Bainton, *Here I Stand* (Nashville: Abingdon, 1951), p. 263.

6

Proven Ways to Recognize Demon Power

Humanity is preparing itself to yield to demon influences in a way
that has not prevailed in modern time.

—Wilbur M. Smith[1]

In the late 1950s I wrote that we are living through the greatest spiritual crisis in two thousand years, and that in this crisis angels and demons will be known to man in an unprecedented manner. "Christians will find angels supporting and succoring them," I said. "There will be more demon activity, more people oppressed and possessed, than the world has ever known."

This was before the revival of the occult had reached the proportions it has today in America. The drug traffic and pornographic publishing racket, although they were forces to reckon with, were not directly affecting millions of young lives as they are now. Films like "The Exorcist" and "The Omen" were no more than dreams in the minds of a few writers.

What has happened? Is it only for box-office profits and newsstand sales that today's generation is inundated with details about the demonic? Or is there something sinister and real and incomparably evil out there?

In crises of the past, an unusual display of angelic power was accompanied by extraordinary activity of demons. Such phenomena were well documented in the lifetime of Jesus Christ. More angels were in evidence from the time of His announced birth until His ascension than in the entire four thousand years of Old Testament history. At the same time, demon power was more in evidence during that period than at any previous time.

The Final Crisis?

A great number of Bible-believing Christians are convinced that we are now living in the final crisis of mankind. The irony and tragedy is that the less the church teaches about demon power, the more control Satan takes over society. Half the world is possessed by the devil and the other half doesn't believe the devil exists—and the devil sees to it the two never meet!

In recent years, a half-dozen excellent books about the devil and demon power, written from conservative evangelical viewpoints, have been published. I take this as an encouraging sign that the Lord is preparing His people to do battle in these last days. In order that we will not be jousting at windmills and seeking demons in every house and home, in this chapter I will point out how demon power may be recognized in society today.

Crime

I begin with crime for obvious reasons. Demonic power can be seen more easily and more often in crimes against persons, property, and society than anywhere else.

This comes as no surprise to those who know the Bible. Jesus said the devil is *"a thief"* whose threefold work is *"to steal, and to kill, and to destroy"* (John 10:10). To the unbelieving Jews of His generation Jesus said, *"You are of your father the devil, and your will is to do your father's desires. He was a murderer from the beginning, and has nothing to do with the truth....When he lies, he speaks according to his own nature, for he is a liar and the father of lies"* (John 8:44, RSV).

Writing under divine inspiration, Isaiah described the conditions existing in his day—conditions that are still true today. *"For your hands are defiled with blood and your fingers with iniquity;*

your lips have spoken lies, your tongue mutters wickedness. No one enters suit justly, no one goes to law honestly; they rely on empty pleas, they speak lies, they conceive mischief and bring forth iniquity" (Isa. 59:3–4).

Anyone who considers the immensity of crime in America today is compelled to admit that demons are a driving force. When Jesus declared that in the last days "iniquity will abound," He was speaking in terms broader than man's inhumanity to man. Satan, knowing his time is short, has unleashed his demon forces to do violence and take peace from the earth.

Almost every day the newspapers or news magazines report crimes that defy description—deeds that can only be accounted for through demonic power. A mother strangles her little child to death and later confesses to police, "A voice told me to do it." The voice of the devil told her to destroy her child.

The big cities of America have become unsafe; quite a few have been terrorized by one or more madmen. Boston has had its Strangler, Los Angeles its Manson murders and the "Hillside Strangler," and New York its "Son of Sam," the .44-caliber killer. The convicted "Son of Sam" slayer testified in court that at the command of a dog he went out to murder young women in New York City in 1977 and 1978.

During a recent crusade in Manila, I again visited Dr. Mariano Lara at Bilibid prison. After a friendly greeting he said, "Mr. Sumrall, I surely wish you had been here a day earlier." When I asked why, he took me to the morgue and showed me the mutilated bodies of two small children.

He explained that the parents of these children had come home from a spiritist meeting under a spell and imagined the children were actually devils. The parents grabbed their young son and daughter and stuck objects down their throats, up their noses, and in their eyes and ears. The children screamed in pain until they died. When police arrived the parents said they had found two devils in their house.

"But these are your own children," the police said.

"No," the parents insisted. "We found two evil spirits in our house and sought to subdue them."

The illicit and criminal use of drugs has contributed to the current dramatic rise in all kinds of crime. The wide use of hallucinogenic drugs that created the "beat generation" and later spawned the hippie cult promised grand benefits. Beyond the immediate sensation of carefree ecstasy there were new horizons for the soul, expansion of the consciousness, and contact with eternity. But it was all a lie of the devil. True, these drugs did grant immediate breakthroughs, but with immeasurable harm to the users.

Strangely, the use of drugs and heavy addiction continues despite an intensive educational program by the government, the church, the media, and such Christian groups as Teen Challenge. Politicians have compromised themselves so much that many no longer can distinguish right from wrong; they continue to yield to pressure to legalize "less harmful" drugs. (Indeed, with our nation's indefensibly lax attitude toward alcohol and tobacco, it makes poor logic to mount a campaign against the availability of marijuana, heroin, and cocaine.)

A CBS *Sixty Minutes* program showed the unpredictable and destructive effects of a drug substance known as PCP. Two young men interviewed on the show told grisly tales of murders they committed while high on PCP. Satan has tremendous power to tempt man with drugs, and in our day this has become a fearful weapon. The whole scene—the drug substances and their empty claims, together with society's inability to control them—is demonic in origin. As we approach the end of the age, crimes will become more ghastly and the human heart will become harder.

Moral Sins

While it is true that people have always been morally delinquent, we are approaching a time when the world will be under fierce attack by immoral spirits. We can expect homes in America to continue to fall apart. At the pace the devil is working now, there soon will not be many decent homes left—home life as we have known it in the past. People will live on an animal level, changing homes every night. Satan is determined to "Hollywoodize" the homes of America.

Adultery is a spirit. Men have told me, "I would give anything in the world if I could quit my immoral life, but I cannot." Immorality has a strange hold upon them. Such a person is possessed with a spirit of adultery.

I do not believe statistics that suggest one of every ten Americans is homosexual. Three decades ago the Kinsey Report found that "four percent of all men and significantly fewer women are homosexual throughout their lives...that figure is considered too high by most sociologists. The more recent Hunt study...put the incidence among men at three percent, of which perhaps one percent are openly active in a gay community."[2] Yet the so-called "gay" community is large, more visible, and apparently on the increase.

I believe that sodomy is a spirit. It is unnatural for a man to have sexual relations with another man, or a woman with a woman. It must be from an evil spirit. This horrible sin is causing consternation throughout the world. In my ministry I have at times prayed for a number of perverts, and they have told me of the craving and compulsion that keeps them bound. They recognize it is from the spirit world.

The Lord Jesus Christ said, *"As it was in the days of Lot...even thus shall it be in the day when the Son of man is revealed"* (Luke 17:28, 30). In Lot's day, sodomy was the prevailing sin, and it is rapidly becoming so in our day. God hates it no less today than He did in Lot's day when He brought awful judgment upon them. Those who indulge in it are demon possessed, I believe, and need divine deliverance. Psychiatry cannot deliver a person; only the power of Christ can set him free.

The church has been infiltrated with this spirit. In recent years we have witnessed a pitiful thing—major denominations spending large sums of people's tithes and gifts to prepare position reports on homosexuality. I approve of efforts we in the church can make to communicate an open, compassionate, loving attitude toward homosexuals as persons, but it should be very clear that the Bible condemns the spirit and practice of homosexuality. That there is now a Metropolitan Community Church in Los Angeles with twenty thousand professed "gays" as members is but one example of the fulfillment of Paul's writing in Romans 1. He showed that when man would not believe the light of divine revelation and obey the gospel, *"God gave them up in the lusts of their hearts to impurity, to the dishonoring of their bodies among themselves...to dishonorable passions. Their women exchanged natural relations for unnatural, and the men likewise gave up natural relations with women and were consumed with passion for one another, men committing shameless acts with men and receiving in their own persons the due penalty for their error"* (Rom. 1:24, 26–27 RSV).

Pornography and obscene movies are evils out of the pit of hell. Perhaps enough has been written of them to make their nature clear. But the "respectable" moral sins of greed (about which I will say more), racial bigotry, affluent apathy toward the poor, and dependence upon military force and power instead of God are also symptomatic of an evil spirit of the age.

Love of Money

Writing to the Colossian church, Paul warned against covetousness or greed, which he equated with idolatry (Col. 3:5). And in 1 Corinthians he equated idols with demons (1 Cor. 10:20). Insatiable covetousness, the love and lust for money, is without question a spirit; it is another area in which we may expect increased demon power in the days ahead.

The Bible says the love of money is the root of all evil (1 Tim. 6:10). Someone may say, "I cannot see demon power in the area of money." But many people are addicted to money; greed is as much a narcotic to them as heroin is to the dope addict. And it is of the devil. Because of money, people abuse their families, cheat and lie, and sell their reputations as well as their bodies and souls. In fact, almost every evil in the world can be traced to the love and lust for money. It breaks up homes, causes people to rob and kill, and destroys the good things of life.

Too many Americans have allowed the dollar to become their master. A man came to my office in South Bend and asked if he could talk with me about his marital problem. He had heard me preach on the radio. He told me the story of his shattered marriage.

"I have worked like a slave all my life," he said. "For a number of years I worked at two jobs—sixteen hours a day. I built a beautiful home in South Bend and a cottage at the lake. I have a late-model car. I thought I was doing all this for my wife. I thought she wanted it, too. But one day while I was at work, a salesman came to my house. My wife let him demonstrate his sweeper and before he left they had committed adultery. Taking advantage of my absence, he returned to my home time and again, and quite often the two of them would go out to the lake cottage and commit sin."

He sobbed out his story, pausing momentarily to control his emotions.

"I am so brokenhearted that I don't know what to do," he continued. "I didn't believe it could happen to me. I see now that if I had not been so greedy for money and for material things, I would still have my wife. I put money first and her second. I was never as loving as I should have been. Now I have lost my wife, for she has left me for this other man. She told me she would rather live in a one-room apartment with someone who loved her than with an old miser who worked sixteen hours a day. I tried to tell her I was doing all this just for her, but she laughed at me and said she never got any of it."

The love of money can and does become an evil spirit. It can cause a man in New York to steal a million dollars in the stock market, only to confess later, "Why did I ever do it?" He did it because he was possessed with a spirit and lost control of his life.

In Joseph Borkin's book, *The Corrupt Judge* (Clarkson N. Potter, 1962), a Washington attorney tells of three highly respected federal judges in New York and Pennsylvania who, over a period of twenty years, bought and sold "justice" in local bankruptcy and embezzlement cases.

In the high reaches of the federal judiciary, one of the judges attempted to build a corporate empire on "loans," "advance payments on contracts," and plain bribes accepted from people appearing before his court of appeals.

Another judge frequently accepted payments of money in rolled-up newspapers in the dark hallway of the federal court building, while a third judge terrorized all the lawyers in his district for twenty years until he was finally caught by the U.S. Department of Justice.

Some public officials are honest and decent, yet corruption of this sort permeates all levels of government, business, and society in America. It threatens to ruin the nation.

Apostasy

The apostle Paul wrote, *"Now the Spirit speaketh expressly, that in the latter times some shall depart from the faith, giving heed to seducing spirits, and doctrines of devils"* (1 Tim. 4:1).

The Spirit mentioned here is the Holy Spirit, the third person of the Trinity, who speaks with great emphasis and concern. He has a specific message for the church concerning the *"latter times."* We can be sure that if there ever will be *"latter times,"* they are now.

The Holy Spirit gives His message: In the latter times some will depart from the faith and allow themselves to be seduced by the subversive doctrines of devils. This departure is called apostasy—"abandonment or renunciation of one's religious faith or allegiance."

No one can depart from something they have not had. These people whom the Holy Spirit identifies know the truth, yet deliberately depart from the faith just as Adam and Eve disobeyed God in the Garden of Eden.

These people are not mere backsliders. God's Word says they give "heed"; in other words, they give their whole attention and mind to seducing spirits and doctrines of devils.

A seducing spirit is a lying spirit, a deceiving spirit. There are many in the world today. "Doctrines of devils" means exactly what it says. Satan has now, as he has always had, a doctrine or teaching he proclaims. Satan told Eve she surely would not die if she disobeyed God. Satan asked Christ to make bread for Himself and to worship him. Doctrines of devils will take whoever believes them to hell. Is this being fulfilled today? I believe it is.

I was preaching in the state of Washington and was called to pray for a woman. I walked into her home and spent a few minutes talking to her, but I could not pray. I had a strange feeling that something was wrong. The woman was not ill; it was something more devilish.

Before I could start to pray she said to me, "Father Divine will be here in a few minutes."

"He will?" I exclaimed. "Then I will stay and see him."

In a few minutes I heard a dog bark from the front porch and an awful presence entered the room. The woman said, "Father's here."

God's anointing came upon me. I laid my hands on the woman and said, "You evil spirit, you lying spirit, come out of her." And she was instantly delivered from the power of the devil. Afterward, the woman confessed this evil spirit had come to her at four every afternoon for a long while and had taken control of her life. She had been a Bible-believing Christian, but had let Satan enter her life.

For every Father Divine or Sun Myung Moon there are a hundred—perhaps that is too conservative a guess—less prominent false messiahs. Many were once in the true church, but some false doctrine has turned their heads.

In Manila there is a movement called Manalo. The founder, who had been a member of a Christian church, decided he was an angel with a supernatural mission in life. By a strange power he caused people in his services to weep. Before he would ordain anyone to preach to his congregations, the candidate had to have the power to make the entire congregation weep. He built magnificent churches in and around Manila and across the nation. I suppose a million people in the Philippines follow him. They are swayed by his magnetic personality, and they weep as he proclaims himself an angel from heaven.

Before Moon appeared in Korea, a leader named Pak got his start in one of the Christian denominations. Through the power of the devil, he has gathered thousands of people around him. The last time I was there he was selling his bathwater in small bottles, supposedly to heal people when they drank it. He has become an exceedingly wealthy man.

In America too, people in great numbers are being deceived and spiritually seduced by lying demons. I do not wish to appear as controversial, but I do wish to be a revealer of truth. I feel that churches such as the Christian Scientists, the Jehovah's Witnesses, and the Mormons—those who add to the Bible as they wish and who take from the Bible as they wish—are part of the apostasy of the last days. And I have discovered that when Satan starts anyone in error, he leads him from error to error. Once he gets a person on the wrong road, he leads him into damnable doctrines.

Demon Worship

From her birth as a nation, America has sent missionaries to foreign lands to deliver those who were bound in the prison house of sin and demonic power. Our missionaries brought life and hope through the gospel to many people, and set them free. But today, heathen religions are invading America in large numbers. Their "missionaries," if you please, are seeking to convert the "unreached" population of America.

Buddhism, Hinduism, and Islam are growing in our cities. I visited a magnificent Buddhist temple in San Francisco and observed about three hundred Americans studying Buddhism. It is no longer a phenomenon of the West Coast; the devil's religions are making a play for the minds of all our young people, from subtle Transcendental Meditation to open Satan worship. There have been many magazine stories in recent years on Satan worship in America. This theme occasionally furnishes the backdrop for a television show ("Starsky & Hutch," "Medical Center," "Barnaby Jones").

Noted Bible scholar Dr. Wilbur M. Smith wrote, "It is most significant that all specific demon activity referred to after the ascension of our Lord is to be found in relation to the end of this age."[4] From Scripture he concludes we are right in believing that demon activity will be prevalent, powerful, and violent. In the closing days of the age, demons set the stage for the Antichrist, and the chief "props" in this grand deception are religion and demon worship. Jesus told His disciples that *"false Christs and false prophets"* would arise, showing *"signs and wonders, to seduce, if it were possible, even the elect"* (Mark 13:22).

Persistent rejection of truth destroys one's sense of truth and lays a person open to *"deceivableness of unrighteousness"* (2 Thess. 2:10), and to the *"working of Satan with all power and signs and lying wonders"* (v. 9). As already pointed out, it is to be deplored, but expected, that large cities in America have become centers of false cults and demon worship. Heathen priests from India and other lands use the Saturday religion pages of daily newspapers to propagate their doctrine of reincarnation. When false teachers advertise that "the promised one of all religions has come," it is not surprising that confused and deceived men and women flock to such meetings.

An empty and confused soul becomes a sign to the devil, "House to Let," as it were, and Satan and his demons take up the vacancy. (See Luke 11:24–26.) This explains why we are seeing such widespread activity of demons in religion and worship. "As the soul of man becomes increasingly depleted spiritually and the idea of God grows dimmer and dimmer in the souls of men, man's soul becomes, as it were, an undefended fortress into which these evil powers have easy access," said Dr. Smith. "Humanity is preparing itself to yield to demon influences in a way that has not prevailed in modern times."[5]

Inexplicable Cases of Demon Possession

Some people are tormented by the devil and it seems impossible to find any reason for it.

Consider a person injured in an automobile collision. Although the injury was physical, a few months later this person becomes irritable and unbearably antisocial. What was a physical condition ends with an evil spirit. After the accident occurred, the devil moved in through a physical weakness.

Years ago one of my best friends, Go Puan Seng, the owner and publisher of a newspaper in the Philippines, called on me for help. One of his daughters became possessed with evil, and their fine Christian home was thrown into an uproar. This lovely girl lost her loveliness. She would beat the piano rather than play it. She choked the cat until it died and beat her head with her fists until she fell unconscious. Finally she refused to eat altogether. For three months her physician kept her alive with intravenous feeding. She claimed something was in her throat and stomach that would not permit food to enter.

If this case had happened today her condition would probably be diagnosed as *anorexia nervosa,* about which much has been written in recent years. But the doctor and the family did not know what to do or where to turn. Her father realized that a spirit possessed his daughter.

To test the father's faith, I told him I would fast for two days and then pray for the girl "under one condition," I said. "You prepare a dinner and after I pray for her deliverance, the girl must eat."

Mr. Go was agreeable. "My wife and I will also fast," he said.

For two days I fasted and prayed for God to deliver this Chinese girl, and then I returned to their home. Although no one from the house could see who was at the front gate, the girl screamed when I arrived. "I will not see him," she said, and ran into the basement.

Her father supposed I could not pray for her now, but I was ready. "I have fasted and prayed for two days," I said. "I must pray for her now."

I agreed with him that I would not be offended at anything she would do to me, nor was he to be offended at anything I would ask of her. I walked into the basement to find her. She was standing in a corner, and I went over to speak to her. Suddenly she brandished a knife and tried to strike me with it.

Shaking the knife from her hand, I began to pray. God's mighty power came into the room. Her mother and father were present and the three of us saw visible movements in her stomach as the evil spirit came out.

Instead of having the meal prepared in his own kitchen, Brother Go had arranged for it to be catered. We sat down to a Chinese feast. For the first time in three months this poor little girl, weighing less than sixty pounds, began to eat. As she ate she said, "Now I am going to die. All my intestines are flat and have not had anything in them for so long."

I turned to her and said, "You are not going to die; you are going to live." I laid my hands on her and asked God to create the digestive juices needed in her body.

We slowly went through course after course of this dinner. I was seated beside her and put the food on her plate. She turned to me and said, "I feel I am going to vomit. I cannot stand this food in me."

"None of that," I said. "If you become nauseated, you will have to start over again. You must eat."

Following the meal, I took her arm and walked with her in the garden, talking with her about the power of God and the promises of God and how she must now live for God. With every step she became stronger. She was healed. Great joy returned to the family.

Not all stories end like this. But some years later I was permitted to assist in performing her wedding. She married a fine Chinese student at the University of California. She was a lovely bride; no one would ever dream she once looked anything like the person I found in the basement of her home that morning.

Even in America I have heard of many situations of demon possession that have no explanation. Recently in South Bend, a mother brought her eleven-year-old daughter to me, telling me the girl had become overwhelmed by some kind of evil power. She could no longer attend school, for she disrupted classes with her fighting and screaming. She would not obey her parents, refusing to do what they told her. She would sit in the middle of the floor and throw a tantrum. Her parents were sure it was an evil spirit.

I was asked to pray for her in front of the church. As I laid my hands on her head she began screaming, throwing herself about in a violent way. I commanded the evil spirit to come out of her and she became subdued and her mother took her home.

A few weeks later someone came running up to me as I revisited the church. It was this little girl, beautiful and normal.

"Are you well?" I asked.

She replied, "I'm so happy."

Her mother told me that her daughter had been delivered of this evil spirit and her healing had brought great joy into the home. No one knew why this thing happened. All the parents knew was that suddenly everything went wrong inside their little girl.

Everywhere I go in my travels I find similar conditions. It is indeed sad to see people become victims of satanic depression and obsession. Every home should be covered by the blood of Christ, for I know the devil cannot harm the members then. A Christian has no reason to fear, because He that is in us is greater than he that is in the world. However, Christians do need to be aware of the protecting blood of Christ and of their right to the power and authority of Jesus' name. We are told to rebuke the devil, and he will flee from us.

Every Christian will rejoice on that glorious day when Satan will be bound. (See Revelation 20:1–3.) The deceiver of the nations will cease all his activities. In the meantime, there is one refuge from the lies and deception of the wicked one, and that is Jesus Christ. This is an hour to know you are in Christ, to live for Him, and to win souls for Him.

Notes

1. *World Crisis and the Prophetic Scripture* (Chicago: Moody Press, 1951).

2. Ken Ross, "Gay Rights: The Coming Struggle," *The Nation,* Nov. 19, 1977.

4. Smith, World Crisis and *the Prophetic Scripture.*

5. Ibid.

7

Going to the Devil, Step-by-Step

Yield not to temptation for yielding is sin,
Each vict'ry will help you some other to win;
Fight manfully onward, dark passions subdue,
Look ever to Jesus—He'll carry you through.

—H. R. Palmer, "Yield Not to Temptation"

The devil seldom takes a life all at once. He does it a little at a time, step-by-step. Sometimes he is able to assume complete control rapidly, but usually it is a slow process over a period of weeks, months, or even years.

He is like the proverbial camel who first puts his nose in the Arab's tent, then slowly moves all the way in. The devil is like a cancer—he devours the human personality bit by bit. The steps he uses to destroy human life fall into a definite pattern, which I call the seven steps toward full demon possession.

The steps to possession follow a logical order to a final conclusion. They begin with the smallest amount of demon power that hurts a person and continue until the person is completely overwhelmed. I explain this not to frighten people, but to reveal an antidote that can heal. We must know how the devil attacks and harasses the human personality. We also must be confident that Jesus Christ can set us free from anything the devil tries to do. Lucifer hates us because we are the sons and daughters of God. He wants to destroy us, but it is our prerogative to attack and defeat him.

I do not mean to suggest that in every case of demon assault these seven steps, or stages, will be readily evident. And on the contrary, there might be some intermediary steps not discussed here. Perhaps in some cases it may even appear that the steps occur in a different order from the progression I have outlined.

Regression

I call the first step of the devil's attack regression. It is a battle against a person's God-given abilities of release and expression. To regress in the human personality is to go backward in spiritual force and power. Men and women are built for progress, advancement, and understanding. When this goes into reverse it is the first warning that negative powers are evident.

A small boy once helped solve a great engineering problem. A bridge was to be constructed across a deep chasm and the engineers could find no way to stretch their heavy cables across the span.

"I can do it," said the lad.

Attaching a cord to the tail of a kite, he let the kite soar over the chasm, carrying the cord to men on the opposite side. Then a rope was tied to the cord and pulled across. The heavy cables were then attached to the rope and stretched into place. First a string, then a rope, then an unbreakable cable.

The devil works in a similar manner. He first binds his victims with a light cord of regression; the prisoner could snap his bonds and be free. Then the evil one adds heavier bonds, until the ropes of oppression are securely in place. It is still possible for the victim to free himself by resisting with all that is within him. But soon the devil adds heavier bonds, until the victim is helplessly bound by the cruel cables of complete demon possession. Then only a fearless servant of God can break the bonds and set the prisoner free by the power and authority of God.

As you read, you will realize that today the devil is still doing the same kind of thing he did throughout history. He will deceive you as he did Eve in the Garden of Eden. He will seek to destroy you as he did the little boy brought to Jesus. His father said the devil threw the lad into the fire and into the water, but Jesus healed him. Satan will seek to disgrace you as he did the demoniac of Gadara, who left his home and friends, tore off his clothes, and lived in the cemetery. And he will try to damn you as he did Simon Magus, the sorcerer who tried to purchase the gift of God from Simon Peter. We must know these things about demon power and understand them before we can combat the devil and win.

Repression

Demon power is not spoken of in many religious circles today. Many people seem afraid of demons. Others simply don't believe in demons, so the subject is not mentioned. But I have noticed that the less we say about demons and the less we expose them, the more control they assume over human destiny. It is only when we pull the drapes back and expose demon power that we can set people free.

It is very interesting to me that God makes every human an expressionist. The moment a baby is born, the doctor spanks it. He wants expression. If he doesn't get it, he suspects the baby might be dead!

God desires exuberant expression from us. He wants our eyes to talk, our faces to light up. He made us to express something. Anyone who represses that function is doing the work of the devil.

It is a bad sign when a person becomes silent. A soul in solitude is headed for trouble. Eyes that gaze in a fixed stare reveal bondage of the soul. To lose the good spirit of joy and happiness is to take the road to a ruined personality. One who represses all his inner feelings becomes a walking dead man. The Bible commands us not to "grieve the Holy Spirit" (Eph. 4:30). I believe the word *"grieve"* could mean "do not repress" the Spirit.

To repress a person is to destroy the natural expression God gave him at birth. To repress a person is to check by power, to restrain from without. To repress a personality takes away the joy and gladness of that life. God did not create human lives to be restrained by an abnormal environment.

This second step toward demon possession is often found in churches and religions. Some people go to church and never experience the joy of salvation. Consider a man who goes to a worship service and takes with him a little boy or girl. They walk along the sidewalk chatting and laughing, but within fifty steps of the church something suddenly happens to the man. His eyes go into a fixed gaze and his body becomes rigid.

He walks softly into the church, finds his pew, and sits down. For the next hour he sits there like a mummy, expressionless. When the meeting is over he leaves. As he gets about fifty steps away from the church, he sighs and says, "I'm glad that's over for another week."

Much of religion today expresses nothing to the spirit of man. Instead, formal religion suppresses and drives inside a person's fervent feelings toward God. In my services we often sing happy choruses because God's joy comes to us from expressing ourselves.

Many church members go to church as though it were a funeral parlor. If God did manifest Himself in any manner, it would scare them to death. According to the Bible, real worship is different. When the people dedicated Solomon's temple there was much expression—musical instruments and singing of praises to God. Many such illustrations can be seen throughout the Bible.

Sometimes repression begins at home. Every home should take a survey of its members. A child can be the repressor. When something goes wrong he flies into a tantrum and it takes everyone in the home to get things normal again. Sometimes it can be a wife and mother who causes the family to tiptoe around. When something displeases her she makes the home a miserable place for a week.

It can be a belligerent husband. The family may be happy and singing until he opens the door. Then he bellows and yells until everyone just dies inside. That man represses what could be a happy home.

Repression can happen at work. A foreman can be "as mean as the devil" to the men who work for him. He can curse and scream at the men until they are nervous wrecks. Eventually the men even hate to go to work. When they do go, they won't smile and will barely speak when the foreman is around. They become repressed.

You ask, "But what has this to do with the devil?" It is the devil who makes people act like this. Satan wants to steal all the joy and happiness from every human. We should be careful not to repress others, but rather let them express themselves under God.

Suppression

To suppress means to abnormally squeeze down, to crush, to conceal, as to suppress information.

Satan is very keen on suppression. It represents another step toward deterioration of emotions and the destruction of complete personal happiness.

Suppression comes from without. It is an unholy action because God and the entire Bible reveal dynamic expression with openness of desire and exuberance of feeling. When feelings are not expressed, they are suppressed or kept back. Let us realize that the devil causes suppression of the spiritual life.

Suppressed people are not energetic or enthusiastic about anything. A suppressed individual becomes listless and inactive—even disinterested in what goes on around him. If enough Christians were suppressed, Satan would have free rule in the world, with no one to oppose him and thwart his evil plans to control the world and its people.

Almost everyone has feelings of suppression at some time. The average person overcomes it after a few hours, or at most after a day or two. A word of comfort or encouragement from a friend, a passage from God's Word, a good night's rest, or a change of scenery is usually enough to bring new hope and renewed strength to begin living again. If suppression and melancholy hang on, however, the victim may be headed for serious trouble.

Depression

A man came into my office one day and said, "If you can't help me, I'm going to commit suicide."

He confessed that he hadn't kissed his wife in ten years. He would go for months without speaking to her. He would come home at night and read the newspaper while he ate. Then he would get up from the table, take his newspaper with him into his bedroom, lock the door, and retire. The next morning he would eat his breakfast, reading again, and then walk out of the house for work.

Looking at that man was like looking at death. I have never seen a man more depressed. There in my office I laid hands on him in the name of Jesus and prayed a prayer of deliverance for him. Instantly a cloud left his mind. Joy came into his heart. He went home and became reconciled with his wife. He became a new creature. He began to work for Jesus.

The depression under which this man was living was humanly unbearable. He had decided it was better to be dead than alive, and he was ready to commit suicide. Christ broke the bondage of that depression and set him free.

It is sad to observe the great number of people in America today who are depressed. Depression is a broken spirit. A person is pressed down until his spirit is crushed. To remain depressed for a long period of time is of the devil and is not natural to life. God does not want anyone depressed and sad. Anyone who stays depressed for an extended time is sick. The devil takes advantage of those people and moves in with conflict and confusions that will destroy their happiness, their homes, their businesses, and maybe even their lives through suicide.

Traditions can contribute to depression. While I was holding meetings in a church in another city, I met a Christian woman who was still deeply depressed over the loss of her husband six months earlier. Her pastor told me her husband had been a fine Christian businessman and that she was a very capable businesswoman herself. She had no problem financially, but following tradition she had dressed in black from head to toe. Every day for more than six months she had been in mourning. I could see she was carrying a burden of depression.

"Why are you wearing black?" I asked her.

"Oh," she said, "I'm in mourning for my dead husband."

"Was he a sinner?"

"Oh, no!" she exclaimed.

"Then why do you look so sad about his going to heaven?"

This was the first time anyone had spoken the truth to her about her melancholy. I asked her if she thought they wore black in heaven. She replied, "No, I think they wear white up there."

"Then why don't you dress cheerfully if your husband is in heaven where there is life? If he could see your sad face and those mournful clothes, it would make him sad even in heaven."

Why did I talk to this lady so plainly? She was going downhill, fast becoming a recluse. She felt that if she smiled or laughed it would be disrespectful to her husband in heaven.

In the next service she came dressed in white from head to toe. She became one of the most inspiring Christians in the community. She now works in her church and leads a victorious Christian life. The devil was simply destroying her Christian witness with depression.

Tradition often demands a long face and a sad countenance, but the Bible says, *"A merry heart doeth good like a medicine"* (Prov. 17:22).

Many times depression is triggered by loss or serious trouble. Heavy financial burdens, family problems, or disappointments can depress a person, leaving him dejected and forlorn.

Depression is dangerous because it often brings about an abnormal state of inactivity. People may sit staring into space, hearing nothing, saying nothing, and doing nothing. Inside they feel a sadness too deep to express, too painful for tears. Their problems seem too desperate and complex to be solved. They have reached a point where they see no need in even trying any longer. They have lost hope. This is a big step toward complete satanic control of a personality.

Are you depressed constantly? Then you need deliverance. And only Christ can deliver you. The cure for depression is to call upon Christ and place all your problems and heartaches and worries in His keeping. *"Casting all your care upon him; for he careth for you"* (1 Pet. 5:7). Be encouraged and say with the apostle Paul, *"I know whom I have believed, and am persuaded that he is able to keep that which I have committed unto him against that day"* (2 Tim. 1:12).

When the devil tries to weigh you down with sadness and perplexity, rebuke him in the name of Jesus. Say, "I am trusting in God, and I don't have to be worried or anxious or sad or depressed. Go away, Satan, in Jesus' name!"

Some people are religiously depressed. They think there is great holiness in a long face. There is no biblical basis for this idea. God does not depress mankind; the devil is the depressor of human life.

By experience I have discovered that a downcast face and a sad soul won't help to resolve problems. It won't pay bills! It does no good at all.

In Psalm 103, King David says, *"Bless the LORD, O my soul: and all that is within me, bless his holy name"* (v. 1). That is the way you should get up every morning! Start the day blessing the Lord.

Oppression

The fifth stage through which the devil drags a person to destroy and possess him is what I call oppression.

To oppress someone is to weigh him down with something he is not able to carry. The children of Israel were oppressed in Egypt. They were treated cruelly, beaten unmercifully, and crushed down until they could carry their burdens no longer.

God the Father sent Jesus to this earth to heal all who were oppressed of the devil (Acts 10:38). This suggests that oppression can be in the realm of disease. Millions are oppressed in America. I do not believe disease is natural any more than a beautiful tree is natural with every kind of bug and disease covering its branches. I believe it is natural to be healthy and unnatural to be unhealthy. Disease is one of the devil's tools.

Millions of people are oppressed by fear. Some worry about going out of their minds. The devil wants them to think that. But God's Word says Satan is a liar and the father of lies. He wants to torment people. He wants to hurt them. And he wants to mock and laugh at God while he does it. But God's people do not have to suffer this terrible fear. One of the great blessings of Christianity is a strong mind that is capable of rejecting the unreasonable demands of fear.

A few years ago a woman came to me and said, "Brother Sumrall, my home is breaking to pieces. I can't stay in my house. When my husband leaves home to go to work in the morning, I just start shaking and I go to pieces. I have to run out the back door and go to my neighbor's. And I don't walk back into that house until my husband gets home.

"When he comes home from work, the dishes are just as they were when he left. I'm afraid to stay in my own house alone. What am I going to do?"

"Well," I said, "did you come to talk or to get help?"

"If you can help me," she answered, "then I want you to."

"Then you must do as I tell you after I have prayed. Tomorrow morning when your husband gets ready to go to work, go to the front door and kiss him good-bye. And since he usually closes the door, you say, 'Honey, I'm closing the door today.'

"Then you step back and close it just the way a fourteen-year-old would do it. [They know how to close doors. Some of them never open again!] After the door is shut, step back into the middle of the room and say, 'Devil, I'm staying in this house all day long. You get out of here. Jesus is here. In His name I command you to leave.' And when you say it, let the devil know you mean business. Then start singing. Sing our church songs all day long. When your husband comes home, he is going to be the most surprised man in town."

I was conducting a revival meeting, and the next night the woman came back. She was free. She said she had enjoyed a glorious day.

"I did exactly as you told me," she said. "I screamed out that I was going to stay in that house, looked around, and just cleaned and sang hymns all day long. It has been a wonderful day."

Two or three days later she assured me she still had no trouble.

The devil is an oppressor. God never intended for us to be slaves of oppression. We are His sons and daughters!

Satan may use many means to try to destroy you. He may try to crush your spirit through people you thought were your friends. He may seek to trample you down through disaster and woes. He may try to overpower you with a great display of demonic power that hurts you on all sides until you feel helpless against his cruel onslaught. He might weigh you down with an awesome sense of responsibility for all the people and actions in your family or community. He might even burden you with a feeling that all your trouble and misfortune is punishment from God for some great sin.

All these things fall into the category of demonic oppression. And oppression can be overcome. Exercise your Christian dominion over the devil's power. You do this by faith, prayer, and action. Ask God for faith to command His power in your life. Pray to strengthen your inner being. And act to overcome and destroy the works of the devil.

If the devil is oppressing you with disease, with fear, with nerve problems, with anything—receive deliverance now. Christ will set you free (John 8:36)!

Obsession

Jesus was obsessed with His own destiny of saving the world. The apostle Paul was obsessed with the Gospel of Jesus Christ so much that a Roman governor told him he was a madman. These were magnificent obsessions.

But there is also a negative obsession that destroys the human personality.

At this stage of demon domination, I doubt that the individual being hurt by Satan could be delivered without the assistance of another. I feel sure that a person who has regressed or is repressed can shake it off in Jesus' name and be free. I believe that a person who is suppressed or depressed, when reminded of the danger, can rid himself of it and have a joyful spirit. And it is possible for one who is oppressed to help himself.

But when we get to the sixth stage—obsession—then outside help is necessary. The reason for this is that obsession changes the mind. Black becomes white and white seems black. A straight thing is now crooked and a lie becomes the truth. This loss of perspective causes the person to be out of step with everybody else around him. He does not realize he is obsessed with some wicked thing.

What is obsession? By definition it is an "act of an evil spirit in besetting a person or impelling him to unreasonable action." The dictionary also says it is a persistent and inescapable preoccupation with an idea or emotion. This preoccupation usually has no relationship with reality.

I met a little lady in Chicago when I was speaking to a group of Christian businessmen there a few years ago. She weighed less than a hundred pounds, was poorly dressed, and her face registered deep apprehension. After the program she came up to me, looked around at the prosperous businessmen, and said, "All these people are against me."

I decided to go along with her. I looked up and asked, "They are? Which ones are against you?"

She pointed at the man who was in charge of the meeting. He was a very wealthy man, and probably did not even know the woman. She said, "I have to hide from these people who are against me," and with that she slipped out, going out of the building. It would have been useless for me to say, "No one wants to hurt you," for in her warped mind she was sure everyone was seeking her destruction.

Obsession can come by believing a lie. If what we believe is out of line with what others believe, we should check our beliefs and seek to know the truth. Otherwise, the devil may deceive us with an evil obsession.

Obsession can come through jealousy. A wife or husband may get an idea that their spouse is not loyal to them. This thing preys on the mind. The devil makes the idea take root and grow like a strong vine. Finally, every time the mate turns his back, the jealous one says, "Now he has done something wrong." Their very lives can be destroyed because of the evilness of jealousy.

I believe hatred can be an avenue to obsession. One can believe others dislike him and begin to hate them until he cannot think straight. He cannot see what is true because hatred has blinded him.

Certain sins can become an obsession. One may become overwhelmed by his immorality and be unable to see anything pure and holy because he is blinded with this obsession.

The devil has many avenues to invade the human personality. When someone develops a complex in any form, that person should pray, read the Word of God, and consult a minister or a Christian friend whom they trust and can confide in.

An obsessed person eventually has no willpower. He has no strength to resist and he becomes a slave. His mind gets on one track and it is impossible to change his thinking.

Willpower is one of the great gifts God has given to us. We should never lend it to anybody through hypnotism, fortune-telling, drugs, alcohol, or anything else. Anything that can destroy your willpower should be avoided. God wants His children to be men and women who know right from wrong. They must let no obsession take over the mastery of their soul.

Once a person has fallen prey to demon obsession, he must draw close to Jesus Christ. He needs a man or woman of faith to pray a prayer of deliverance for him and ask God to set him free.

Possession

In this area extreme caution is necessary. The step from obsession to possession is a long one. The devil would like to push every obsessed person fully and finally into his clutches of full possession.

Up to this stage, a person is not truly demon possessed. I do not find many people in this final state, although there are hundreds in the other stages.

The demon-possessed person is under the absolute, total, complete jurisdiction of the devil. At this point he has no mind of his own. Satan is now the master of all that person's thinking and doing. He has full control of that life. The person has no spirit to reach out for God, no soul to pray for help! He is helpless in the hands of a diabolical monster.

There are many ways we can know when a person is demon possessed.

I have observed in dealing with demon-possessed persons that often the devil uses the person's voice and throat to speak. I have heard men under the influence of demon power speak to me with the voice of a woman. I also have heard a woman speak with the gruff voice of a man.

Demon possession sometimes reveals itself in forms of insanity, both temporary and complete. Doctors who work in institutions and asylums know that a patient's mind may be very clear at one time and at another time the person becomes like an animal. This is the coming and going of demon power within the person. These people who are lost in a world of gloom and darkness and misery have the saddest faces in the world. They have lost the power to rise above their problems. The devil has actually captured them and they live in his chains.

Often demon possession is easily observed in the eyes, for a person's personality frequently is projected through them. A demon-possessed person cannot look at others straight. He cannot hold up his head to you, for the devil will not let him.

The surest way to tell if one is demon possessed is spiritual discernment. If God's Spirit is within me and the devil's spirit is within another person, when we meet there is a tremendous clash of spirits. It has nothing to do with personality; it is the warfare of opposing spirits.

Satan's power is as contagious as the measles. Those under his power want others under it too. A drug addict deceives others until they too are "hooked." Sexual perverts look for the unwary, to lead them into sin. Latent victims are urged into the trap by aggressors. People with fear and depression may have an unreasonable desire that others suffer as they do. So the first stages of demon possession often result from association with others already under the devil's control.

To some people the words "demon possession" mean something dirty or immoral. But we need to change our thinking about this subject. Some of the finest people in the world have been assaulted by the devil, and in some instances conquered. They need the help of Christ and the church right now. The Lord is just as willing to heal a person who is tormented by the devil as a person with a bad cold. Deliverance comes through the same kind of power, with the same anointing, and the same kind of faith. There is no difference whatsoever.

The Holy Spirit can resolve all problems. The church is commissioned to cast out devils. We must fulfill this commission.

I believe it is time for a great freedom action to be set in motion. Men and women of courage should set out to bring freedom to those who are regressed, repressed, suppressed, depressed, oppressed, obsessed, or even possessed by the devil's power. The same Christ who set the prisoners free two thousand years ago can set them free today.

8
Can a Christian Have a Demon?

Come, Holy Spirit, heavenly dove,
With all Thy quickening powers,
Kindle a flame of sacred love,
In these cold hearts of ours.

—Isaac Watts,
"Come, Holy Spirit, Heavenly Dove"

The May 1978 issue of *The Tennessean* magazine carried a feature story about an east Nashville housewife who had evidently become possessed by a demon or was experiencing a vicious satanic attack. The woman, identified as Ann H., told the editors of *The Tennessean* her bizarre story, which had already made headlines in the Nashville papers.

According to Ann, a "lady" appeared in her bedroom one night. Ann had undergone surgery a few weeks earlier, and that particular evening she had taken antibiotics and dropped off into a sound sleep. Some time later she was awoken by the barking of dogs in the neighborhood. Then the thin bedroom curtains bloused out and a "lady" and two children appeared.

To Ann's horror, the "lady" moved to her bedside.

"I was praying, 'Lord, let me wake up!'" recalled Ann. But the figure moved closer. Ann described this spirit as having an almond-shaped face and pointed ears. Her mouth was similar to that of a rat, and her hair (under a cape) was pulled up on top of her head. The eyes were "intense, like fire."

According to Ann, the "lady" beckoned for her to go with her, assuring her that her worries and suffering were over. (Ann's husband, a building contractor, had not been able to find steady work; Ann herself had not been well.) As the "lady" moved still closer, Ann heard a voice say, "You and your damned God. You don't need God. You're with me." As this figure bent over her bed, Ann was gripped with fear, but suddenly she was enveloped by a peace she had never before experienced.

This was the first of numerous encounters this housewife claims to have had with the "lady." The children who first appeared with her never reappeared, and as far as I know, Ann does not know the identity of either the "lady" or the children.

Ann told reporters that the encounter may have been brought on by what had happened to her a few weeks earlier when she shared a room with an elderly woman in Nashville's General Hospital. The woman seemed to notice Ann, but did not say anything for the first two days. Then, Ann says, "She turned toward me, and began to move her lips. No sound came out....I told her I'd try to call the nurses, and I did. And then woman said, very distinctly, 'You're doomed to hell.' Just as she said that, her eyes locked on me and she died."

The "lady" has developed a jealousy about Ann's husband and children, reported *The Tennessean*. "She has a temper and when she's mad she sometimes touches me violently. If feels like dry ice...and she always wants to take my breath; she seems to need it," Ann says.

One winter night Ann was awakened and told, evidently by the "lady," to turn off the gas logs in the living room and then turn on the gas. She obeyed. Had not her husband awakened and smelled the fumes, all of the family might have perished.

Once, Ann stopped breathing and felt she had "physically died," and remembers "looking back on my body lying in bed and my husband and two of my children trying to revive me." Ann felt "warm and secure" wrapped in the lady's cape, but on seeing her husband and children crying she knew she had to return to them.

Following several attempts to remove the "lady" (who has physically abused her), Ann now says, "I've gotten to where I just accept her. I know she'll be with me as long as I live."

The magazine says Ann is a Southern Baptist, and that more than once pastors and "groups of people of various denominations" have prayed with her, but to no avail.

No doubt this case of an apparently Christian woman has stirred thoughtful interest among people in Nashville. The magazine judged interest so keen that it followed with another story in July. Seventeen prominent ministers and psychiatrists (including two hypnotists) were asked if they thought it "possible for a person to be possessed by a demon." None of the clinicians answered a definite yes, although some gave a qualified yes. Replies from pastors and rabbis ranged from two who said no to seven who responded with a definite yes.

One pastor answered as I would have many years ago. He said he did not believe a Christian can be possessed. "They can be oppressed and they can be under attack," he said, "but you cannot be possessed by Jesus Christ and by a demon...."

Definitions

Can a Christian be demon possessed? It becomes a matter of definitions when you really study the question carefully. What is a Christian? When you start dealing with definitions you are dealing with problems, because there are too many definitions.

A person may belong to First Church and think he cannot be demon possessed. That has nothing to do with the problem at all. If he is hurt he needs help. You reach people when you deal with them in relation to their needs rather than their tags.

The Bible teaches very strongly the security of the believer. No devil ever wanted to get inside Paul. They wanted to run from him as far as they could. And nowhere does the Bible tell anyone to be afraid of the devil. *"Resist the devil, and he will flee from you"* (James 4:7). We have a right to make him run. But when we start playing in his territory, we are in danger.

Leave the Devil's Territory Alone!

Not long ago on a Sunday night in our church, several people came forward for prayer at the close of the service. Among them was a Sunday school teacher. When it came time for me to pray for her I had no freedom to pray. Something was wrong. Finally I asked what the matter was and to my surprise a man's voice answered out of her mouth.

"She came to see the movie in the adult theater and I entered her," the spirit said. "I had every right to her."

When I asked the woman if this were true, she admitted it. She said she had felt that she needed to know what went on in the movie houses that show X-rated films in order to teach against it.

"No you didn't," I said. "You went in there and enjoyed what you saw." She nodded her head.

I believe that when she stepped into the theater she entered Satan's territory and opened herself to a demon. Knowing this, I laid my hands upon her and commanded the evil spirit to leave. It obeyed.

This opened an avenue of thinking to me. I began to understand that when a Christian goes into the devil's territory, unless intending to do battle and rescue lost souls, that Christian becomes vulnerable to whatever Satan offers, even to being invaded by an evil spirit.

While Louise and I lived in Hong Kong we never feared Communist China. From our apartment we could see the harbor where the American Seventh Fleet had its aircraft carriers, destroyers, and many submarines. When we would go about the city, at certain places we could see large numbers of crack British troops and large guns. We felt secure as long as we stayed within the borders of Hong Kong.

At one place where there is a bridge a sign was posted that said, "Communist China ahead of you. Do not advance further unless you have credentials to do so." If I had ventured to the border and entered Red China, I would have cancelled my right to protection by American and British forces. The same is true of Christian living. When you play with sin you can cancel not your salvation, but the covering of the blood to keep Satan from doing as he pleases.

I am personally convinced that anger can be a spirit, and that if a Christian allows himself or herself to vent anger without restraint, there is a very real danger of the entrance of a spirit of anger.

I am convinced that adultery is a spirit. A prominent pastor told me that for more than a year he was within the grips of a spirit of adultery. It was so strong that cold perspiration would run off his fingertips until he yielded to his forbidden desires. Only a prayer of deliverance finally set him free.

Professing church members can open themselves to a spirit of jealousy. Some women have a jealous spirit. They can have the best husband in the world and still accuse him whenever he walks in the door. The only explanation is a spirit of jealousy.

There is such a thing as a spirit of blasphemy. It is evident everywhere today, and Christians need to be on their guard. Foul language and cursing has gushed up from the gutters and back alleys until today it has entered our living rooms and become commonplace in the media. Some people cannot speak a sentence without blaspheming the name of God. These evil spirits must be cast out before people can be free.

Ananias and Sapphira were a part of the first church in Jerusalem. When they saw how Barnabas received such acclaim for donating his property, they decided to sell theirs. But they could not bring themselves to give away all of the money. They brought part of it to the apostles and pretended it was the full amount. The Holy Spirit showed Peter it was a lie. (See Acts 5:1–11.) Both Ananias and Sapphira were struck dead for their lies.

A lying spirit haunts God's children today. It is a terribly deceptive spirit, and many children of God need to be set free from its curse.

In summary, I am of the opinion that evil spirits can invade and enter the life of a believer. Paul warned that *"the servant of the Lord must not strive; but be gentle unto all men...in meekness* *instructing those that oppose themselves; if God peradventure will give them repentance to the acknowledging of the truth; and that they **may recover themselves out of the snare of the devil, who are taken captive by him at his will**"* (2 Tim. 2:24–26, emphasis added). If we obey the command to *"be filled with the Spirit"* (Eph. 5:18), then we give no place to the devil in our lives.

9
Satan's Subtle Snares

Regard not them that have familiar spirits,
neither seek after wizards, to be defiled by them:
I am the LORD your God.
—Leviticus 19:31

The devil advertises his services to today's society in dozens of ways. Never out in the open, he nevertheless is not far from the surface. In the newspapers he charms millions with the so-called guidance of the ages, written in the daily horoscopes. Bookracks at the supermarkets and newsstands hawk his wares, inviting the reader to dabble into themes on exorcism, witchcraft, and the like. Movie theaters do his bidding, enticing the vulnerable young and old alike to explore the world of the unknown, the weird, and the devilish. And television joins the trend by highlighting Satan worship in a cops-and-robbers evening show. The mail dispenses the devil's products, offering a full set of encyclopedia on the supernatural or the latest slick porno magazine.

Is It Really Harmless?

An unsuspecting tourist brings home a souvenir amulet or idol from another country and places it innocently in the living room, never suspecting that by doing so he may be playing with the devil. Much of Satan's activity dazzles the senses. It seems so harmless. But is it?

When one of our three sons was thirteen, he and his friends became enamored with the Beatles' music for a time. Word got around high school that there was a secret message on one of their records if it were played backwards, so the boys tried it. All Sunday afternoon they tried to decipher a message.

My wife and I were sitting downstairs that evening as my son rushed into the room, frightened, and cried, "Dad, the devil's in my room!"

I didn't know what to make of it. "Well, if he's there, then you're going to have to tell me how he got there," I said.

He told me what he and his friends had been doing. I could see that he was in no shape to return to the room, so I prayed with him and told him he would sleep with his mother and I would go upstairs to his room.

When I reached the room I knew a devil was there. The feeling was strange. It made my flesh seem to crawl. But I had dealt with the devil before and so I wasted no time in taking charge. Slamming the door, I said, "You wicked devil, what right do you have coming into my house! This house is cleansed by the blood of Jesus Christ. I want you to know I've already claimed the covering of Jesus' blood for my son, and now I'm ordering you to get out of this house and never return. Furthermore, I'm sleeping in this room and I will not be bothered by you. I'm not afraid of you; now get out, in the name of Jesus."

I slept in my son's room that night, and the devil never bothered us again.

A few years ago, three girls from our church in South Bend were attending Bible school in the Midwest when they received a terrible scare. For fun, they had begun fooling around with a Ouija board. In the evening they would sit around, place their fingers on the board, and ask, "Who is my boyfriend?" or "What will I do when I get out of school?"

This went on for several weeks until one night one of the girls asked, "Who are you? Who is giving us these answers to our questions?" The answer came: "I am Satan."

This so terrified one of the girls that she called home and her mother called me and asked for prayer. The girls never dreamed they were making contact with the evil supernatural world.

Shortly after his conversion, Arlindo Barbosa de Oliviera of Brazil came to America at the invitation of our church and told his personal story. He had been a witch doctor for forty years and had been baptized to the devil. As a member of the large spiritist cult in Brazil, he said he had heard the voice of the devil hundreds of times while in a trance, and had drunk flaming rum and eaten ground glass. After serving the devil all those years, he says Jesus Christ appeared to him and he was saved.

We recorded Arlindo's story and produced the "Witch Doctor" record. One of our youths, who was attending a Christian university, owned a copy of this record. One night in his dormitory room he played it for two of his friends. The two boys began to mock and laugh at what they were hearing. But while the record was playing, they went berserk. Afterward, both of them had to receive psychiatric care before resuming their studies. The boy who had played the record got on a train and came home, and his mother called me to pray for him. He was badly shaken by the incident.

It had seemed such an innocent thing to mock at the devil's voice on a recording, but the devil is not to be taken lightly.

America's climate today makes such "harmless" activities as these fairly commonplace. The influence of godliness and righteousness in our nation has waned; most people are spiritually starved, although forty-three percent attend church with some degree of regularity. This moral bankruptcy fosters the ideal environment for the occult and superstitions.

Forbidden Territory

African slaves with their voodoo brought much superstition and fear with them in the early days of America. The native Indian's life has always been heavily burdened by witchcraft, evil spirits, and magic. From England, America inherited ghost stories that abound in superstition. And today people by the thousands are turning back to these things rather than to the living God.

The Bible is very clear about the occult. It is forbidden. In Leviticus 19, Moses commanded the Israelites not to regard those who have familiar spirits or seek after wizards. "I am the Lord your God," he said. It was not the Lord's will for his people to turn to a negative, lying, demonic source. He was available for them and their future was in His hands.

Superstition Analyzed

The dictionary defines superstition as "an irrational attitude of mind toward the supernatural, nature, or God, proceeding from ignorance, unreasoning fear of the unknown or the mysterious; a belief in magic or chance, or the like." Our English word is taken from the Latin *superstitio,* which means "a standing over or above, as in wonder or awe." Superstitions are traditions, old tales, and theories still lacking proven truth.

Superstition has to do with charms, spells, good and evil spirits, foretelling of events, unusual forces, and powers operating in objects and beings. They often reveal strange and seemingly inexplicable powers and energies that, as we will see, find their beginnings in ignorance, selfishness, greed, and cultish worship.

It is a remarkable paradox that although we live in history's most scientific age, there is more superstition today than ever. Millions are probing astrology, occult faiths, Indian mysticism, and all kinds of strange and seemingly mystic powers. There is actually an army of fortune-tellers, clairvoyants, palmists, crystal-ball gazers, astrologers, and gurus marching across the stage of the modern world, begging to be heard and exhibiting their strange wares.

Man can reach supernatural elements through the realm of demon power. In giving one's life over to the devil, one has the possibility of reaching into the realm of demonic power. Superstition could open the mind's door to believe the lies of Satan. Error often begins with ignorance. One who is ignorant of God and begins seeking hidden realities without God or without the Bible may end up with the devil leading him around as if he had a hook in his nose.

The Age-Old Enemies

Divine faith and superstition are age-old enemies. Faith is the living, dynamic relationship between man and his resurrected Savior, while superstition is the willful desire of unregenerate man to rule the invisible world without a divine Savior. The sinner seeking the supernatural has one purpose in mind: to control mystic powers for self-gratification, not glorification of the Lord. In superstition there is no spiritual life, there are no morals, and there is no character.

Superstition was born because man in his deepest being longs for the supernatural. God made him this way. The spirit and soul of man disdains the material way of life.

Superstition and Fear

Ministering in a large number of countries of the world for more than forty years, I have come to know the deep fears in the hearts of the heathen. They are afraid of God and of demons. They are afraid of the dead and departed spirits. They live in mortal fear of the unknown and of the future. They are tortured by a multitude of superstitions handed down to them from generation to generation.

All superstition is motivated by fear. The traditions and legends surrounding Friday the thirteenth are good examples. The word "Friday" comes from the German goddess Freya, who was supposed to be the goddess of love, matrimony, and the home. The horse was the goddess Freya's sacred animal. It was sacrificed and eaten on her feast day at special celebrations such as weddings. Because of this the early church, especially the Roman Catholic Church, would not allow meat to be eaten on Friday. From this superstition, Friday the thirteenth became known as an unlucky day. The number itself took on many superstitions. I have sat at a table with influential people when there were thirteen at the table, and one was asked to leave and sit by himself!

Superstitious fears can ruin a person's health. A businessman I know of went to a doctor because he was nervous, frustrated, and on the verge of mental collapse. The doctor could find nothing wrong physically, but he did discover that the businessman was an ardent believer in astrology. He had come to believe that because of the opposition of the planets Mars and Saturn and the unfavorable position of the moon, his condition was incurable. Nothing the doctor could say would sway the man's opinion, and I do not know if he was ever cured.

The devil loves to destroy a life through superstition. Multitudes in this country follow the phantoms in the sky out of fear, rather than letting their loving Creator guide and direct their lives.

Hypnotism

There is a strong hint of hypnotism in the very beginning of time. In the Garden of Eden, is it not possible that the serpent hypnotized Eve, even as a snake petrifies a rabbit with its piercing gaze and magnetic rhythm? Lucifer, master of all fallen wisdom, whispered the illegal suggestion to Mother Eve. Gripping her mind through his devilish eyes, did he induce the state of unconcern that made her forget God's command? We know that he lied to her. "You will be like gods, and God doesn't want you to be like him. So He's holding information back from you!" And Eve, paying heed to the seducer's voice, did what he suggested. Sin entered the human race.

A hypnotized person is in a state of abnormal concentration induced by an operator—a description that could be used with equal accuracy to explain the condition of a demon-possessed person. Medical doctors know that hypnosis brings a change in a person's conscious awareness. The consciousness narrows, much as it does during a dream or a vision. But the hypnotized person is different from a sleeping person. He or she can walk, talk, write, or remain quiet. In most cases he will obey suggestions given him by the hypnotist.

It has been said that no subject can be induced to do anything contrary to his own moral principles. Scientists have proven, however, that hypnotized persons can and will perform antisocial and even self-destructive acts under deception by the operator.

A normally modest woman, for example, would refuse point-blank to remove her clothing under hypnosis if the suggestion were made directly. But if the operator suggested she was in the seclusion of her own bathroom, she might well disrobe before an audience of people. The subject, then, is at the mercy of the operator to a considerable degree—much more than anyone should be!

The Lord Jesus, speaking of the end of this age, warned his disciples, *"Take heed that no man deceive you"* (Matt. 24:4). Hypnosis is a form of deception. It has no divine life that can make a man better or cleaner or happier. All it can do is open the soul's door to possible demon invasion. Your mind must not be clouded by fear and phobia. It must not be confused by conflicting ideas. It must not be yielded to strange, psychic powers. At all costs, your mind must not be destroyed because it is the seat of your will. With your mind you must make all the proper decisions about how to live and prepare yourself to meet with God at the coming of our Lord Jesus Christ.

I prophesy that in the days ahead, before Jesus Christ returns, millions in America will have turned to every kind of spiritism, including hypnotism. Man will be offered religion that soothes the conscience, seemingly smoothes the rugged path of sin, and leads into sweet forgetfulness and eternal reincarnating bliss—bliss without the blood of Jesus and ecstasy without eternal life.

I urge Christians, indeed all people, not to offer their minds to anyone who wishes to hypnotize them and never to attend a meeting of oriental cults, which are demon-inspired. Rather, I urge you to keep yourselves clean and pure before God, and to walk in His ways and to serve Him.

I challenge you to have the mind of Christ: a strong mind, a dedicated mind. In Genesis 1:26–27 it is recorded that God created man to have dominion on earth. This dominion is achieved through your mind.

With Christ in your heart you do not need other guidance. He will guide you to a joyful tomorrow. The Bible declares that our Christian life is to be a walk of faith, but God has promised to be with us every step of the way. In these last days, may the Lord Jesus Christ keep you—your mind, spirit, soul, and body—by His mighty power. *"Finally, brethren, whatsoever things are true, whatsoever things are honest, whatsoever things are just, whatsoever things are pure, whatsoever things are lovely, whatsoever things are of good report; if there be any virtue, and if there be any praise, **think on these things**"* (Phil. 4:8, emphasis added).

Destroying Emblems of Demon Power

God warns His people against all supernaturalism that is not of Him. In the first century, Paul warned against idols that are symbols of evil supernaturalism. *"What say I then? that the idol is any thing, or that which is offered in sacrifice to idols is any thing? But I say, that the things which the Gentiles sacrifice, they sacrifice to devils, and not to God: and I would not that ye should have fellowship with devils"* (1 Cor. 10:19–20).

God has His symbols of power. In the Old Testament, the ark of God symbolized His presence and His holiness. When the Philistines captured the ark of God they placed it inside their temple, beside their god Dagon. The next morning Dagon lay broken on the ground at the foot of the ark. The presence of God in the symbolic ark destroyed Dagon.

The devil has symbols of power also. Perhaps the most easily recognized symbols are the idols made of clay, stone, wood, or iron. These idols have been brought to America and sold. Unsuspecting tourists have brought them back from Asia and other parts of the world, not knowing that there is evil attached to these symbols of power in the devil's realm.

A teacher in a British Bible school told me that each morning his students became drowsy and some fell asleep while he was teaching. At first, he said, he thought the students were having too much for breakfast—but no one gets too much breakfast in Bible school!

He began looking around the classroom; on a window ledge he discovered a bronze serpent from India—a coiled cobra, worshipped in India as a god. Without telling anyone that he was doing so, he removed the idol from the room. No one became drowsy the next morning or thereafter.

In China I visited a large Buddhist temple where the priests showed me their gods, many of which were ugly, frightening idols with eight or ten arms. Pointing to one about sixteen feet high I asked the priest, "How can that idol help you?"

He was very polite. "You don't understand, being a foreigner," he replied. "That idol does not have power. We all know that. The spirit of that idol is elsewhere right now, but if I were to bring incense and food and place it before that idol and start praying, something would start happening."

Then he took me to the rear of the idol and pointed to a hole. "That is where the spirit goes in and out," he said. "It wants worship. If I come and kneel here and offer an offering and burn incense or candles, immediately the spirit comes and communicates with me."

The idol was a symbol for the demon spirit. The grotesque face of that idol was something the artist designed under the power of the devil. A Christian should have no such idols in his home, office, place of business—anywhere.

While I was pastoring in Manila, we helped build a tribal church in the headhunter country of Luzon in the Philippines. While preaching there they showed me a tree where the spirits live. It is a symbol of demon power. It did not have a leaf on it and was greasy in appearance, probably because the worshippers had wiped their hands on it. The boughs were gnarled and crooked. The tribe said their spirit gods lived in the tree and that they offered incense and offerings at the foot of it.

Even the cross can be a symbol of Satan's power. When praying for Clarita Villanueva in the Bilibid prison, I noticed she wore a strange metal cross around her neck. Once she climbed under the desk of the chief of police and complained that she had lost her cross. The chief kicked her and said, "Come out from there; I don't know anything about your cross."

To prove that he did not know anything, he turned both of his front pockets wrong side out and shook them. Then he put his pockets back and Clarita said, "Look again." The policeman plunged his hand into his pocket and found her metal cross. It frightened him, and four days later he died.

The crystal ball is another device of Satan's power. With such a ball Jeanne Dixon and others who claim clairvoyance make predictions. They also use a deck of cards for fortune-telling. When one touches that deck of cards, they tell one's fortune. Many Christian households have some professional playing cards. Almost every witch doctor and fortune-teller in the world uses these to help them in their business. They have no place in the home of a Christian.

Is there any biblical basis for destroying the symbols of demon power? In the early church at Ephesus the power of God became so strong that Luke wrote, *"And many that believed came, and confessed, and showed their deeds. Many of them also which used curious arts brought their books together, and burned them before all men: and they counted the price of them, and found it fifty thousand pieces of silver. So mightily grew the word of God and prevailed"* (Acts 19:18–20).

This was a great fortune. At that time, thirty pieces of silver was the price of a slave. This means that with fifty thousand pieces of silver they could have bought 1,666 slaves!

If the early Christians were careful to clean out every symbol of the devil's power around them, you and I must do the same. We must clean out our hearts, what we wear on our bodies, and our homes. We must dig out the very roots of superstition and all that has to do with the devil's power. Believers must place their lives in the hand of God to guide them every day. We don't need to know what is going to happen tomorrow. If we did, we would not need to walk by faith. Unwarranted curiosity about the mysterious unknown may lead the believer into one of Satan's subtle snares.

10
Taking Authority over Demons

And though the fiends on every hand
Were threatening to devour us
We would not waver from our stand
They cannot overpower us.
This world's prince may rave,
However he behave, He can do no ill.
God's truth abideth still.
One little word shall fell him.

—Martin Luther
"A Mighty Fortress Is Our God"

During the time when "The Exorcist" was popular, I received a call from the David Susskind television show in New York, asking me to appear on his program. When I wanted to know why they were inviting me, they said they had read a booklet I had written and that they wished to bill me as an exorcist. I agreed to go on one condition—that I not be singled out as some phenomenon. I told them there is nothing peculiar about an exorcist and that every Christian could be one. I said I had never gone about looking for devils, to cast them out. They must have changed their minds and decided they didn't want me after all. Apparently I wasn't peculiar enough.

Every Christian's Right

I meant what I told them. I have had forty years' experience in taking authority over demon power, but I do not consider myself unique. Dominion over Satan is every Christian's right by the blood of Jesus Christ.

A Christian who exercises dominion knows how to appropriate the fullness of God's provision for discipleship. He lives a victorious life above and beyond fear and phobias, superstition and evil curses. He is radiant and forceful in Christ.

Dominion Defined

Dominion extends to the believer much like links in a chain. It begins with God the Father who is supreme, all-powerful, all-wise, and everywhere present, the Creator of all things. God possesses infinite dominion.

The chain of dominion moves to the Lord Jesus Christ in whom dwells *"all the fulness of the Godhead bodily"* (Col. 2:9). Jesus exhibited dominion in every stage of His life. His virgin birth transcended the known laws of nature. (See Luke 1:31–35.) He further demonstrated dominion over nature by turning water into wine, walking on the sea, multiplying bread and fish to feed more than five thousand hungry people, and calming the tempestuous sea. Jesus showed His dominion over sickness and disease by never failing to heal those brought to Him (Matt. 8:16). He even asserted dominion over the grave by rising from the dead (Luke 24:6).

Throughout His life, Jesus demonstrated His supreme dominion over devils. Even though they would rage against their victims, making a final effort to keep them in bondage, every one of them yielded to the Lord's command and begged for mercy as Jesus cast them out.

No man ever lived and taught dominion as Jesus did. The Bible says that in Him *"are hid all the treasures of wisdom and knowledge"* (Col. 2:3). He concluded His earthly ministry by declaring, *"All power is given unto me in heaven and in earth"* (Matt. 28:18). This is supreme dominion.

Great dominion resides in the blood of Jesus. He came to this world to shed His blood as a sacrifice for man's sin. The Bible says the life of the flesh is in the blood (Lev. 17:11); therefore,

Christ's blood had to be shed. Jesus said to His disciples, *"This is my blood...which is shed for many for the remission of sins"* (Matt. 26:28). The holy, saving blood of Jesus Christ has power and dominion.

There is no divine forgiveness outside the shed blood of Jesus Christ. *"But if we walk in the light, as he is in the light, we have fellowship one with another, and the blood of Jesus Christ his Son cleanseth us from all sin"* (1 John 1:7).

Peter wrote, *"Forasmuch as ye know that ye were not redeemed with corruptible things, as silver and gold, from your vain conversation received by tradition* [handed down] *from your fathers; but with the precious blood of Christ"* (1 Pet. 1:18–19).

Paul declared dominion in Christ's blood also. *"And, having made peace through the blood of his cross, by him to reconcile all things unto himself"* (Col. 1:20). (See also Rev. 1:5; 5:9, 12:11.)

There is remarkable dominion in the Bible. It is the only living Book known to man, possessing great power to preserve itself and to bless all humanity. The Bible is God's inspired Word. I believe with the writer of Hebrews: *"For the word of God is quick* [living and active], *and powerful, and sharper than any twoedged sword, piercing even to the dividing asunder of soul and spirit, and of the joints and marrow, and is a discerner of the thoughts and intents of the heart"* (Heb. 4:12).

Since the Bible is the Word of God, it has unique authority over all books. God has invested dominion in his written Word.

Jesus said of His prophetic Word, *"One jot or one tittle shall in no wise pass from the law, till all be fulfilled"* (Matt. 5:18). The eternalness of the Word is demonstrated when Christ said, *"Heaven and earth shall pass away, but my words shall not pass away"* (Matt. 24:35).

God spoke worlds into existence by His Word (Heb. 11:3). Peter and James declared we are spiritually born by the Word of God (1 Pet. 1:23; James 1:18). God's Word makes a believer a partaker of His nature (2 Pet. 1:4). Faith comes through hearing God's Word (Rom. 10:17), effects cleansing (Eph. 5:25–26) and gives assurance of everlasting life (1 John 5:13). When Christ answered Satan during the great temptations, He declared, "It is written....It is written....It is written...." In this way He defeated the devil. There is great dominion in the Word.

The Holy Spirit is also an important link in the chain through which dominion extends to the believer. He has the power to do great miracles. He moves and no one can hinder Him. The Holy Spirit, as the third person of the Triune God, knows no limit in time, energy, or space. He is the Comforter (John 14:16, 26); He guides the believer (Rom. 8:14); He convicts the sinner (John 16:8); He is the Spirit of truth (John 16:13).

Through the divine operation of the Spirit, a disciple can possess dominion and be the final link in the chain. The Lord Jesus Christ perpetuated dominion on earth by giving power to His disciples. *"Behold, I give unto you power to tread on serpents and scorpions, and over all the power of the enemy: and nothing shall by any means hurt you"* (Luke 10:19).

Church leaders in every age have recognized the evil presence of man's great foe, the devil, and have exerted dominion over him. In the fourth century, Augustine wrote:

> What spirit can that be which by a hidden inspiration stirs men's corruption, and goads them into adultery, and feeds on the full-fledged iniquity, unless it be the same that finds pleasure in such religious ceremonies, sets in the temples images of devils, and loves to see in play the images of vices; that whispers in secret some righteous sayings to deceive the few who are good, and scatters in public invitations to profligacy, to gain possession of the millions who are wicked?[1]

Thomas Aquinas (1225–1274) assumed the reality of demons, spoke of exorcisms, and had no doubt that their power was greater than that of man, although not as great as God's.

Many popes wrote letters dealing with the devil and witchcraft. John Calvin frequently referred his readers to Ephesians 6:11–12, which starkly sum up the human battle with evil spirits.

No Christian of earlier times, perhaps, surpassed Martin Luther in the serious manner in which he perceived the devil's attacks upon himself. Historian Roland Bainton quotes one method Luther used in taking authority over Satan:

When I go to bed, the Devil is always waiting for me. When he begins to plague me, I give him this answer: "Devil, I must sleep. That's God's command, 'Work by day, sleep by night.' So go away." If that doesn't work and he brings out a catalog of sins, I say, "Yes, old fellow, I know all about it. And I know some more you have overlooked. Here are a few extra. Put them down." If he still won't quit and presses me hard and accuses me as a sinner, I scorn him.[2]

In the same context, Bainton points out that Luther did not necessarily follow his own advice. "Don't argue with the Devil," he would say. "He has had five thousand years of experience. He has tried out all his tricks on Adam, Abraham, and David, and he knows exactly the weak spots." All the more reason to know how to take dominion!

Dominion Is for You

Who may exercise authority over demons? Is the victorious life only for a chosen few, for Paul and Luther, for Amy Carmichael and Corrie ten Boom, for pastors and missionaries? I believe the promises of the New Testament are always to any and every true disciple. Christ said, *"Behold, I give unto you power to tread on serpents and scorpions, and over all the power of the enemy: and nothing shall by any means hurt you"* (Luke 10:19). Dominion is for you if you are seeking to be a disciple of Jesus.

After a person is converted, the devil attempts in every way to continue deceiving him. He promotes the idea that Satan is not real. Failing that, he tries to keep the new Christian from knowing there is dominion over the devil. Satan knows that when the believer is aware of his privileges and power, he (Satan) will be completely defeated and his works destroyed.

An age-old strategy of the devil is to attack the believer in the area of how he represents himself or his "confession." He knows a person will never rise above the quality of his faith. Instead of making the promises of God what he lives by, a believer may only bemoan his sickness and faults and weakness. Therefore, if you do not claim the promised power of God in your life, the devil can keep you in bondage.

People do not like substitutes. For this reason an automobile dealer will display a sign over his business that reads "Authorized Dealer." The sign means a consumer can expect genuine parts for his car and factory-trained mechanics to install them. In the spiritual realm, Bible-believing Christians are God's authorized dealers of His dominion. They have what God wants this world to have. It would be most fitting, therefore, for the church to put out a sign saying, "Authorized Dealer of God's Spirit and Power."

The early church had this dominion. Before He ascended to heaven, Jesus Christ said, *"Ye shall receive power, after that the Holy Ghost is come upon you"* (Acts 1:8). The world has known of that power.

That this dominion was to continue after Pentecost is evident. Peter said, *"For the promise is unto you, and to your children, and to all that are afar off, even as many as the Lord our God shall call"* (Acts 2:39).

The New Testament emphasizes that this divine dominion was not exclusively for the apostles. (See Acts 6:8; 8:5–8.) I have always encouraged church members to pray not only for themselves, but also for others who are sick or in need—and to expect miracles from God. Quite often these lay people report dramatic answers to their prayers. Clearly, dominion is not for a select few; it is for every disciple of the Lord Jesus.

Boundaries of Dominion

Only Christ Himself can set the boundaries or categories of the dominion of His disciples. The *"keys of the kingdom of heaven"* (Matt. 16:19), which He delivered to Peter, show us what these boundaries are.

First, on the day of Pentecost, Peter used a key of the kingdom by preaching the great prophetic message that inaugurated the New Testament church. Second, at the Beautiful Gate of the Jerusalem temple Peter used another key. The lame man who had never walked was instantly healed. This miracle opened the door of the kingdom for healing during the dispensation of grace. What a thrilling key! Third, on the housetop of Simon the tanner Peter received the revelation of world revival and global participation in salvation. With his revelation key he freed the prisoners of the nations. These keys of the kingdom have forever been and still are in the church of Jesus Christ.

In Mark 16:16, Jesus said, *"He that believeth and is baptized shall be saved."* This is the key every gospel preacher can hold. But He also said, *"He that believeth not shall be damned."* This is the ministry of binding and loosing. Whatever is bound on earth will be bound in heaven, Jesus said; and whatever is loosed on earth will be loosed in heaven (Matt. 16:19). Christ recognizes the believer's authority to preach the gospel, and when sinners make their decision either for salvation or against Christ, heaven accepts the verdict.

Spiritual dominion is not exclusively a communal or collective power, it is for the individual as well. Many times a person must fight and conquer alone. The tendency today is to identify with large groups. People wish to be associated with big organizations. In much of modern warfare soldiers may never see the enemy at all; their guns and rockets and bombs are for long range. But the spiritual battle is for the individual. To win this battle you must personally have dominion from Christ. If we can see that our personal conflict must be a personal victory, we are a long way toward dominion.

Dominion over Sin

We don't have to be a slave to sin. We don't have to yield to temptation. Paul declared, *"For sin shall not have dominion over you"* (Rom. 6:14). David prayed, *"Order my steps in thy word: and let not any iniquity have dominion over me"* (Ps. 119:133). When our steps are ordered by Jesus and when His Word is a part of our very beings, we are invested with might and authority.

Dominion over Thought Life

Our minds should not be garbage containers. We cannot avoid temptation and enticement, but we do not have to give in. A well-known saying goes, "You can't keep the birds from flying over your head, but you can keep them from building a nest in your hair." Every disciple can and must assert dominion, bringing every wild and unspiritual thought into captivity. (See 2 Corinthians 10:4–5.)

Dominion over Disease

Sickness can be made obedient to the Word of power and authority. In the Great Commission Jesus said, *"These signs shall follow them that believe....They shall lay hands on the sick, and they shall recover"* (Mark 16:17–18).

Centuries earlier, Moses said sickness is a curse (Deut. 28:59–61). All curses lose their power over a child of God. *"Christ hath redeemed us from the curse of the law, being made a curse for us"* (Gal. 3:13). We are *"bought with a price"* and therefore we are to glorify God in our bodies and our spirits, *"which are God's"* (1 Cor. 6:20). It glorifies God for you to have dominion in your spirit and in your body.

The devil has power, as he did with Job, to bring disease upon you. But as a Christian you possess divine authorization to rebuke, renounce, and destroy all the authority of the devil. You must exercise your rights. If necessary, quote the source of your power. Just as a policeman says, "In the name of the law, stop," you as Christ's disciple must say, "In Jesus' name, I am healed."

God promised that none of the diseases of Eygpt would come upon the Israelites. Jesus came into the world to destroy the works of the devil. Christians who are not grounded in the Word are not aware of their dominion in this strategic area. They do not know they have authority to resist the devil and works of Lucifer. I find that the devil is an expert in fifth-column tactics. He sneaks in unaware. He comes in with his camouflage. He is a deceiver. The devil convinces man of his (Satan's) power, and by this means creates fears, phobias, confusion, and a feeling of helplessness.

This happens not because the devil cannot be overcome, but because man listens to his voice. We need to train ourselves to hear Jesus saying, *"All power is given unto me"* (Matt. 28:18).

There are times God does not see fit to heal, even when a child of God fulfills all of the conditions for exercising dominion. It is a mystery held within God's sovereign hands. Satan uses such things to tempt us to doubt God, but we know that God must have a higher plan.

Undoubtedly, God chooses to glorify Himself through the grace and peace He gives to His children—and sometimes this grace is made most impressive through a suffering saint. I have seen many of God's children walk through life in such an afflicted manner, and even in their weak condition they are not miserable victims. They have victorious faith. Theirs too is dominion.

Dominion over Devils

The Christian community must recognize that an aggressive warfare is being waged on all fronts by unseen and formidable foes. We must exercise dominion over the powers of the spiritual world in order to reach the masses of this generation for Christ.

Many men and women of this world are more aware of the spirit realm than are many Christians. This very ignorance places the believer in a losing position in the battle with *"the rulers of the darkness of this world"* (Eph. 6:12). We must know our enemy in order to defeat him. We must also be familiar with the clear New Testament pattern of exercising authority over devils. The apostles set men and women free and wrought tremendous victories for the kingdom of God. It must be the same today. Whenever a possessed person comes in contact with a Spirit-filled disciple, there must be an instantaneous battle for deliverance. If not, the evil spirit will always openly mock the disciple.

When I am confronted with people whom I suspect may have an evil spirit, I ask them if they would accept Christ as their Savior. It doesn't matter what former experiences they have had; I ask them if they would accept Him then and there. And I ask them to say the sinner's prayer.

If they have a spirit in them, the thing often starts acting up immediately. It starts squealing, screaming, writhing, or something similar. After they have told me their story, I lay hands on them and command the spirit, whatever kind it is, to loose them and let them go free. And they are delivered.

In the Bible it never took a long time to set anyone free. When we start working with a person for a long time, we are not doing it the biblical way. If we pray for a person and he is not delivered, we had better back off by ourselves and talk to God personally and then come back to them. Having a possessed person roll on the floor, screaming and yelling, is not what sets him free. Faith sets people free.

Instruments of Dominion

Without dynamic faith, born in the Christian heart at conversion and nourished through the Word of God, a believer cannot successfully battle against demon power and win. When a person is challenged by temptation or disease or the devil, his faith must constantly come into focus. He must have faith to command God's power. God explains that He desires we command Him. *"Thus saith the* LORD, *the Holy One of Israel, and his Maker, Ask me of things to come concerning my sons, and concerning the work of my hands command ye me"* (Isa. 45:11).

Abraham exemplified this ministry of commanding God. When he and the Lord were looking down upon Sodom and Gomorrah and God said He would destroy the cities, Abraham begged God for the salvation of the people there, saying if there were only fifty good people—or forty, or thirty, or twenty, or even ten—that God would not destroy them. Each time God was willing to meet Abraham's demand. (See Genesis 18:20–33.)

Man has never fully taken advantage of the true power of faith. God still waits for heroes of faith to use the divine dominion He gave Adam in the Garden of Eden. In the New Testament church, faith enabled Peter to tell the dead woman, Lydia, to rise up. By faith Paul cast out the powers of divination from the fortune-telling girl. Faith is the key that unlocks the generosity and strength of God. *"Without faith it is impossible to please Him"* (Heb. 11:6).

Prayer is one of the most powerful instruments of the disciple. Prayer is actually the council chamber where divine commands are issued. In prayer the believer receives the solution to his problems. In prayer he receives the "infilling" of divine energy. Jesus revealed this when He prayed and fasted for forty days and then met Satan alone in the greatest spiritual struggle recorded in history.

Elijah demonstrated the power of prayer when he locked and bolted the heavens for three years with a single prayer. He further demonstrated this tremendous force when he called upon God to send rain upon the land. The apostle James specifically says Elijah was a common man as we are. The difference is that *he* knew how to pray.

In the New Testament, Paul and Silas used this tremendous instrument of dominion when locked in the inner cell of the Philippian jail. At midnight they sang songs and prayed. The strength of their prayer shook the jail itself. It even resulted in the jailor's salvation.

All that prayer can accomplish has never been defined. It is still a great realm for research and exploration. But you must pray without ceasing if you wish to have dominion in prayer.

Still another instrument of dominion is action. God does not give power to the inactive. Jesus said, *"He that believeth on me, the works that I do shall he do also"* (John 14:12).

Dominion implies action. It is an act and not an idea. All through the Word of God we see that those who had dominion were men and women of action for God. God told Moses to have the people step into the water and He would do the rest. Jesus told a man with a withered hand, "Stretch it forth." He did the rest. In both instances, action was necessary before dominion was realized.

It is true that works alone are not sufficient for salvation. But some action is necessary, even vital. Paul reminded the Corinthian Christians that there is work to do for the kingdom of God. *"For we are labourers together with God"* (1 Cor. 3:9). In James' epistle even stronger language is employed. *"What doth it profit...though a man say he hath faith, and have not works?...Faith, if it hath not works, is dead, being alone"* (James 2:14, 17).

It is not enough to know God's will. You must do it. One could know he had money in the bank and still go hungry and cold. He must go to the bank, withdraw some cash from his account, and spend it for food and warm clothing before his needs are met. Having it is not enough. Knowing about it is not enough. There must be action before it is of any value.

And so it is with Christian dominion. Before it pays off with bountiful blessings, dominion must be put in force with action on the part of the believer. In reality, dominion is an instrument to better enable the disciple to work for God and to obey His commandments. And His commandments have always been: "Go...do...give...work...."

By using the three instruments of dominion—faith, prayer, and action—we can be triumphant Christians. I urge you to stand up and have dominion with Christ, to be an overcomer and a blesser of mankind all the days of your life.

We can rejoice in the fact that the day is coming when the devil shall be bound (Rev. 20:1–3) and ultimately destroyed (Rev. 20:10). What a glorious hour this will be when there will be no devil and, because of that, no fear, no torment, no sin, and no sickness. Christian dominion over evil by the blood of Jesus Christ is not only meant for this life, but will carry into the world beyond the planet Earth. At this time Satan and his demons will have received their final reward in the lake of fire and will have eternally lost the earth to God and His saints.

We greatly rejoice when we read the last page of THE BOOK. For you see, the saints win!

Notes

1. *City of God,* Book 2, Chapter 25.

2. *Here I Stand* (Nashville: Abingdon, 1951), p. 362.

Appendix
Names for Satan and Demon Spirits in the Bible

Names for Satan

1. Abaddon (Apollyon)

"And they had a king over them, which is the angel of the bottomless pit, whose name in the Hebrew tongue is Abaddon, but in the Greek tongue hath his name *Apollyon*." (Rev. 9:11)

2. Accuser of the Brethren

"For the *accuser of our brethren* is cast down, which accused them before our God day and night." (Rev. 12:10) (See also Job 1 and 2.)

3. Adversary

"Be sober, be vigilant; because your *adversary* the devil, as a roaring lion, walketh about, seeking whom he may devour." (1 Pet. 5:8)

4. Angel of Light

"And no marvel; for Satan himself is transformed into an *angel of light*." (2 Cor. 11:14)

5. Anointed Cherub

"Thou art the *anointed cherub* that covereth; and I have set thee so: thou wast upon the holy mountain of God; thou hast walked up and down in the midst of the stones of fire." (Ezek. 28:14)

6. Beelzebub

"But when the Pharisees heard it, they said, This fellow doth not cast out devils, but by *Beelzebub* the prince of the devils." (Matt. 12:24) (See also Matthew 10:25.)

7. Belial

"And what concord hath Christ with *Belial?* or what part hath he that believeth with an infidel?" (2 Cor. 6:15)

8. Corrupter of Minds

"But I fear, lest by any means, as the serpent beguiled Eve through his subtlety, so your *minds should be corrupted* from the simplicity that is in Christ." (2 Cor. 11:3)

9. Devil

"And the great dragon was cast out, that old serpent, called the *Devil*, and Satan, which deceiveth the whole world." (Rev. 12:9)

10. Dragon

"And there appeared another wonder in heaven; and behold a great red *dragon*, having seven heads and ten horns, and seven crowns upon his heads." (Rev. 12:3) (See also Revelation 20:2-7; Isaiah 14:29.)

11. Enemy

"The *enemy* that sowed them is the devil; the harvest is the end of the world." (Matt. 13:39)

12. God of this World

"In whom the *god of this world* hath blinded the minds of them which believe not, lest the light of the glorious gospel of Christ, who is the image of God, should shine unto them." (2 Cor. 4:4)

13. King

"And they had a *king* over them, which is the angel of the bottomless pit." (Rev. 9:11) (See also Ephesians 6:12.)

14. Liar

"Ye are of your father the devil, and the lusts of your father ye will do. He was a murderer from the beginning, and abode not in the truth, because there is no truth in him. When he speaketh a lie, he speaketh of his own: for he is a *liar*, and the father of it." (John 8:44)

15. Lucifer

"How art thou fallen from heaven, O *Lucifer*, son of the morning! how art thou cut down to the ground, which didst weaken the nations!" (Isa. 14:12)

16. Murderer

"He was a *murderer* from the beginning, and abode not in the truth." (John 8:44)

17. Oppressor

"How God anointed Jesus of Nazareth with the Holy Ghost and with power: who went about doing good, and healing all that were *oppressed of the devil.*" (Acts 10:38)

18. Prince of the Air

"...the *prince* of the power of the air." (Eph. 2:2)

19. Prince of Darkness

"...against the *rulers of the darkness* of this world." (Eph. 6:12)

20. Prince of this World

"Now is the judgment of this world: now shall the *prince of this world* be cast out." (John 12:31) (See also John 16:11.)

21. Roaring Lion

"Be sober...because your adversary the devil, as a *roaring lion,* walketh about, seeking whom he may devour." (1 Pet. 5:8)

22. Satan

"Now there was a day when the sons of God came to present themselves before the Lord, and *Satan* came also among them." (Job 1:6) (See also Revelation 12:9.)

23. Serpent

"But I fear, lest by any means, as the *serpent* beguiled Eve." (2 Cor. 11:3) (See also Genesis 3:1, 14; Revelation 12:9.)

24. Tempter

"And when the *tempter* came to him, he said, If thou be the Son of God." (Matt. 4:3)

25. Thief

"The *thief* cometh not, but for to steal, and to kill, and to destroy: I am come that they might have life, and that they might have it more abundantly." (John 10:10)

26. Wicked One

"When any one heareth the word of the kingdom, and understandeth it not, then cometh the *wicked one*, and catcheth away that which was sown in his heart." (Matt. 13:19)

Names for Demon Spirits

1. Spirit of infirmity (Luke 13:11)

2. Dumb and deaf spirit (Mark 9:25)

3. Unclean spirit, used 22 times (Matt. 12:43; Mark 1:23; Luke 9:42)

4. Blind spirit (Matt. 12:22)

5. Familiar spirit (Lev. 20:27; Isa. 8:19; 2 Kings 23:24)

Anglican evangelist Trevor Dearing says these "are evil spirits (not human) who are familiar with a dead person's appearance, habits, and life. They imitate the deceased in order to lead mourners astray—into occultism. Such experience is both real and supernatural. It also is false. It deceived my friend at St.

Paul's, Hainault, who thought the medium was in touch with his wife and he became interested in the occult. Thousands have been tricked by this most cruel of the devil's deceits. Mediums, in their seances, are possessed by those familiar spirits. Familiar spirits have been known to visit bereaved people without invitation."

6. An angel (2 Cor. 11:14)

7. A lying spirit (1 Kings 22:22–23; 2 Chron. 18:21–22)

8. Seducing spirits (1 Tim. 4:1)

9. Foul spirit (Mark 9:25; Rev. 18:2)

10. Jealous spirit (Num. 5:14, 30)

60 Things God
Said about Sex

Contents

Introduction

Our modern world is glutted with talk about sex. The entertainment media, commercial advertising, even our schools' textbooks are brimming over with it. Raucous voices chatter about sex nearly everywhere you go. It seems to be the favorite topic of conversation.

Much of the talk you hear is cold and factual, even clinical, because people are fascinated by the simple mechanics of sex. Some are eager to compare notes about sexual techniques. Others like to tell jokes with sexual overtones—jokes that arouse sexual desires or assume that the listener has a perverted view of sex. And quite a bit of the "sex talk" surrounding us isn't talk at all, but a series of subtle allusions to sex: a well-timed pause, a wink, or a furtive gesture.

Most of the people who like to talk about sex ridicule the secrecy of the Puritans or the Victorians; but ironically, they are just as secretive about sex themselves! They can only discuss sex in a cryptic, suggestive way because they don't really know (or can't express) what sex means to them. They haven't come to grips with the real purpose of sex.

They are still like awkward adolescents who giggle and blush when they think about the facts of life. Sad to say, many Christians are still at this stage.

And so sex has become the most discussed but least understood aspect of human life. I think it is fair to say that we at the end of the twentieth century are living in the Sexual Dark Ages. We hear more about sex than our parents or grandparents ever heard, but we understand much less. Why? Because we have forgotten the *raison d'etre* of sex, the reason it exists.

513

Imagine you were a jungle native who found a Cadillac air-lifted into the Amazon for a TV commercial. You would talk with your friends about it from daylight to dark. You would touch its shiny finish and peer into its plush interior. You would develop a strange attachment to it, a mixture of both curiosity and fear. *But you would not know why it was there.* You would know just as little about Cadillacs as you ever did—even less, because you would have acquired some strange misconceptions in the meantime!

And so it is with sex. The average person talks sex, sees sex, thinks and dreams sex, but is totally ignorant of God's purpose for sex. And so we have a whole new constellation of "helping" professions that try to untangle the knot of America's confused sexual mores. Family lawyers wade through a morass of hotly contested divorce cases, many of them directly related to sexual problems. Psychiatrists' waiting rooms are full of people agonizing over sexual problems. Social workers offer birth-control devices and free abortions to teenage girls, and their telephones ring twenty-four hours a day.

All this agony, all this confusion, all this ignorant babbling about sex just breaks my heart. I find myself saying, "Lord, help me tell these people the truth about sex. Let me show them what your Word says about it. Open their eyes to the joy and fulfillment of sex as You meant it to be."

Our country needs to hear what God says about sex. He has not changed His moral standards to suit a profligate generation. He has not changed His plan for men and women to find sexual happiness in marriage. God made us sexual creatures, and we ought to understand the pattern He intended for us to follow in our sexual relationships. God says, *"My people are destroyed for lack of knowledge"* (Hos. 4:6). Sex is a perfect example of the truth of this statement; we desperately need to seek God's purpose in this area of our lives.

God's Word includes an amazing abundance of information about sex. Nearly every book of the Bible mentions sex, either directly or indirectly. In the following pages, we will look at sixty key Scriptures concerning sex and sex-related morals. This study is by no means exhaustive, and I encourage you to dig into the Word to learn more of what God says about sex. But I hope you will be enlightened and challenged by the studies in this book, just as I found new insights by preparing them. I believe they can help you find a happier, more meaningful life.

—Lester Sumrall

1
The Sex Drive

Sex should be used, but in its proper place and time, according to
God's plan. Within that plan the sexual instinct is a good thing,
a powerful source of life and unity between two beings. Outside
of God's plan, it quickly becomes a means of division, a source of
cruelty, perversion, and death.

—Walter Trobisch[1]

The Bible is a book about sex. It is a book about God's creation of humankind and His ongoing relationship with us, touching every aspect of our lives. It is a book about birth, growth, maturity, and death; a book about love, hate, despair, and hope; a book about hunger, pain, pleasure, and ecstasy. And a book about sex.

The Bible talks honestly about the human sex drive. In fact, it is more forthright and honest in describing the sex drive than many of the so-called sex manuals published in recent years. For example, take a look at Judges 14:1–2. This passage describes how a young Israelite named Samson visited the Philistine territory of Timnath. Notice what happened when Samson went back home. As soon as he met his mother and father, he said, *"I have seen a woman in Timnath of the daughters of the Philistines: now therefore get her for me to wife"* (v. 2).

Doesn't that sound familiar? A young man sees an attractive young woman and on first impulse he says, "I want her!"

It reminds me of the story about an old hermit and his son who lived far back in the mountains, away from any other human beings. The boy had never seen another person besides his father. Finally, the old hermit decided to take the boy into town on his birthday to give him his first taste of civilization. Walking down the street, they passed a couple of pretty girls and the boy said, "What in the world are those?"

The old hermit was caught off guard. "Er, uh...That's nothing, Son," he said. "Just a couple of geese."

The boy seemed to accept that explanation, so they went on.

The pair spent a full day browsing around town, visiting the different shops. Some of the places they stopped were the livery stables, the sawmill, and the blacksmith shop. At last they decided to head for home. But before they left, the old hermit said, "Son, I'd like to get you a birthday present. Did you see any-thing here that you'd like to have?"

"Sure!" the boy said. "I want a couple of geese!"

No matter who you are, no matter what your background is, something inside you draws you to the opposite sex. God made you that way. All of His creation is interrelated. All of His crea-tures have mates designed especially for them.

Consider the plant kingdom. Any farmer will tell you that plants must have male and female organs in order to reproduce. Unless the pollen touches the stamen, unless the sperm reaches the seed, the plant cannot reproduce itself and there will be no crop the next year.

Or consider the animal kingdom. For every male there is a female, and vice versa. When you find a peacock in the wild, you can expect to find a peahen nearby. When you find a lion, a lion-ess won't be far away. The two sexes live together, protect one another, and bring new life into the world. This is the pattern God established when He created the world.

The same is true of human beings. God created us as males and females, and He intended for us to be attracted to one another. God gave each person an endowment of physical forces—psychologists call them "drives"—that enable him or her to live and grow. One is the drive for *self-preservation*, the com-pulsion to protect oneself, find food for oneself, and find shelter from bad weather. Another is the drive for *religion*, a way to sat-isfy one's awareness of the spiritual realm. Yet another strong drive, and perhaps the one that is most misunderstood, is the human desire for *sex*. This is the compulsion to seek out and mate with a member of the opposite sex, to enjoy the physical pleasure of sex, and to produce offspring.

Many Christians believe that the sex drive is evil, so they attempt to repress or ignore it. Some even believe that sexual intercourse was the original sin. That idea deserves special attention, because it has affected the sexual behavior of Christian people for centuries.

St. Augustine, one of the great theologians of the early church, felt that sex was sinful. Augustine believed that the account of Adam and Eve's sin against God (see Genesis 3) uses symbolic language and that the "forbidden fruit" actually stands for sex. He thought that Eve conceived and bore children in pain (Gen. 3:16) because sex is sinful, and any kind of sexual activity brings pain. According to Augustine, human beings should ask God's forgiveness for even thinking about sex and abstain whenever possible. In fact, Augustine said, men and women who want to be righteous in God's sight should live in celibacy (that is, without any sexual contact); his adherents believed their leaders should live in church monasteries and convents, without even conversing with the opposite sex.

Augustine was a keen theologian, and his ideas were well-respected. His understanding of sex became a standard church doctrine, and we are still feeling the effects of his teaching. In his book on Western sexual morality, C. W. Lloyd says:

> Augustine's writings have probably exerted more influence in the West on love and sexual practice than those of any other man. The clearest expression of the innate evil in sexual passion, even within marriage, is set forth. These teachings...gave theological structure to feelings of guilt and shame in a biological drive. However, the enforcement of the doctrine of sexual guilt was difficult. The struggle to impose celibacy on the clergy...was only moderately successful until well into the Middle Ages.[2]

In other words, Christians had a hard time accepting Augustine's ideas about sex. They weren't certain that God wanted them to live in celibacy. The church had to struggle to keep its leaders obedient to this rule; in fact, the sexual prohibition was one of the first doctrines that Martin Luther and the other great Reformers broke away from. (Luther himself left a monastery to marry a nun.)

Either Augustine was wrong, Luther was wrong, or both of them were terribly confused about sex. Was sex the original sin? Is the sex drive something evil? Notice what God says:

> *1. So God created man in his own image, in the image of God created he him; male and female created he them. And God blessed them, and God said unto them, Be fruitful, and multiply, and replenish the earth....And God saw every thing that he had made, and, behold, it was very good.* (Gen. 1:27–28, 31)

This passage indicates that the creation of man was very special in God's sight. God used His hands to make man (Gen. 2:7), which also manifests how important and precious we are to God. Everything else He created by giving His command: He spoke the stars into existence; He spoke the sun, the moon, and earth into existence; He spoke the plants and animals into existence. But He made man with His own hands, shaping him out of the dust of the ground. He breathed the breath of life into man's nostrils. He created a beautiful garden where man could live (Gen. 2:8). Obviously, God was pleased with the person He had made. He set out to make man in His own image, and He was satisfied with the results; He felt that man was "very good."

What else does the Bible tell us about this person whom God created *"in his own image"*? We learn that He created *two* people—people of opposite sexes. And right after God created the first man and woman, He told them, *"Be fruitful, and multiply, and replenish the earth."* God *commanded* the man and woman to have sexual relations with one another to bring children into the world. It would have been sinful for them *not* to have intercourse. They would have been disobeying a direct order from God if they had not conceived children through sex.

No other creature in the universe can bring another human being into existence. Angels cannot do it, animals cannot do it, no creature of any kind can do it—except man and woman. God gave us this special distinction. We are the only creatures who can bring into this world another creature with an immortal soul. We are God's partners in spiritual creation. Isn't that awesome? And it should impress us once again with God's divine purpose in giving human beings a sexual nature, a sex drive.

Never forget: The sex drive is God-given. You did not create your own sex drive. It was not made by TV, the movies, or dirty magazines. God made it! And God made it *"very good"*!

Controlling the Sex Drive

Even though the sex drive is good, it must be controlled. This is true of any biological or psychological drive that God has given us. Imagine what would happen if you did not control the drive to eat. You would be eating constantly, indiscriminately. I've heard it jokingly said that some people "eat anything that doesn't eat them first"; well, if you didn't control your drive for food, that would literally be true. You would pile your plate high repeatedly, and you might even try to eat the plate itself. You would be obsessed with eating. Even though hunger is a healthy drive—a drive we must satisfy in order to survive—it can destroy us if we let it run out of control. The same is true of the sex drive.

Carnally-minded humanity would like to give free rein to the sex drive, as can be seen in much of society today. Nearly every town has a strip of massage parlors, peep shows, and brothels—where people go to indulge themselves sexually without inhibition or control. They would let their sex drive run wild day after day, twenty-four hours a day, if they could. One British writer wistfully concluded:

> It would be much easier if, like our monkey relatives, we...were more truly biologically promiscuous. Then we could extend and intensify our sexual activities with the same

facility that we magnify our body-cleaning behaviour. Just as we harmlessly spend hours in the bathroom, visit masseurs, beauty parlours, hair dressers, Turkish baths, swimming pools, sauna baths, or Oriental bathhouses, so we could indulge in lengthy erotic escapades with anyone, at any time, without the slightest repercussions.[3]

God's Word condemns this kind of thinking. An uncontrolled physical drive will destroy the body. At first such indulgence may seem enjoyable; in the end, it will destroy you.

We will come back to this matter of promiscuity—letting the sex drive run uncontrolled—in a later chapter. For now let us consider why the sex drive should be controlled and how it can be controlled.

We have already seen that God says sex is a very beautiful and wholesome thing. He intended from the very beginning for us to have a sex drive. But He also tells us that the sex drive must be used for the purposes He intended:

> *2. If a man find a damsel that is a virgin, which is not betrothed, and lay hold on her, and lie with her, and they be found; then the man that lay with her shall give unto the damsel's father fifty shekels of silver, and she shall be his wife; because he hath humbled her.*
> *(Deut. 22:28–29)*

Here God deals with sexual intercourse between two unmarried people who mutually agree to have intercourse. Today we hear some people say that "consenting adults" should be free to engage in any kind of sexual activity they want, even though they are not married; but God says no. Why? Because this kind of sexual relation "humbles" the woman. (The Revised Standard Version translates the word as "violated"; it would be just as accurate to say that the woman is "humiliated.") Her integrity is destroyed; her self-worth is cheapened by having sexual relations with a man who is not her husband and who refuses to become her husband. Such a man treats her as just another morsel for his sexual appetite. He does not love her; he loves the pleasure he gets from her. God says this is not what He expects a man and woman to do with their sex drives.

Dwight Hervey Small, a pastor and counselor who has taught for many years at Wheaton College, sheds more light on the problem:

> Sexual intercourse is an act which affects the whole personality, a personal encounter between a man and a woman in the depths of their being, which does something permanent to each, for good or for ill. Hence it cannot be treated merely as a sensual indulgence, the effects of which pass with the act.[4]

God intended sex to be this kind of personal encounter, a kind of interaction which is only proper in marriage.

"But," someone may think, "Who's to say what is 'proper'? Why is intercourse in marriage the only 'proper' use of sex?" God made sex for the purpose of marriage; any other usage perverts this purpose. You can use a claw hammer to scrape ice off your sidewalk, but that's not the proper use of a claw hammer. The hammer wasn't made for scraping ice, and using it that way will ruin it for its intended purpose. The same is true of sex: There is one proper use of sex and many improper uses. God says we should control our sex drive for its proper use.

Realizing the proper use of sex is the first step toward controlling the sex drive. When you know how God wants you to use the sexuality He gave you, the goal is set. The standard is established. You then know that anything that undermines or hinders the proper use of your sexual powers should not be done; by the same token, anything that helps you fulfill or enrich the proper use of your sexual powers should be done. Like any other human drive, the sex drive can be trained and enhanced by new experiences and skill. You can learn techniques that will make your sexual relationship more enjoyable and rewarding, and in so doing you honor the Creator who gave you this wonderful ability we call "sex."

The Sex Drive and the Total Person

As Reverend Small noted, sexual relations involve the total personality. We need to understand the full-orbed nature of the sex drive and how it interacts with other components of the personality. We need to appreciate the spiritual effects of the sex drive, as well as the physical effects. Otherwise we will be unable to control and utilize the sex drive to its utmost potential.

We might say that the sex drive functions in three worlds, or in three different planes of the human personality. In my book *Ecstasy,* I explain how each person is three-dimensional: Each person has a body, a soul, and a spirit.[5] These three components make up the whole person.

Sex and the Body

We know, of course, that sex involves the *body,* the physical component of our being. A sexual relationship is the most intimate physical bond that can exist between two human beings, as a man and woman use their bodies to express their love and appreciation for one another. All five physical senses are involved:

—*Seeing* the physical charms of your loved one.

—*Hearing* your mate's words of endearment and desire.

—*Smelling* the scent or fragrance that uniquely belongs to your mate.

—*Tasting* the sweetness of each kiss.

—*Feeling* the caresses of your loved one's hands.

A sexual encounter is probably the most remarkable experience any person can enjoy on this earth, because it involves every aspect of the physical self. Howard and Charlotte Clinebell, a husband-and-wife team of Christian marriage counselors, have well expressed the physical joy that many couples have found:

Sexual intimacy is more than the bringing together of sexual organs, more than the reciprocal sensual arousal of both partners, more even than mutual fulfillment in orgasm. It is the experience of sharing and self-abandon in the merging of two persons, expressed by the biblical phrase "to become one flesh."[6]

They are referring to one of the most candid statements God's Word ever made about sex. It comes just after the Bible tells us how God created woman as a "fit helper" for the man:

3. Therefore shall a man leave his father and his mother, and shall cleave unto his wife: and they shall be one flesh.
(Gen. 2:24)

In other words, the physical tie of a man and woman through sex is even stronger than the physical tie of a child to his parent. The bond of sexual intimacy takes a higher priority than the affection you have for your father or mother. So far as God is concerned, a man and woman who enter into sexual union have become "one flesh"—they are one physical person. And if you must choose between honoring your parents or honoring your mate, God makes it crystal-clear that your mate comes first.

Many marriages fall apart because one or both mates fail to realize this! They are unwilling to put Mom or Dad in the proper place, below husband or wife. But God's Word says that a person who marries should leave his or her parents and set up house-keeping somewhere else. A house isn't big enough for two men, and it's not big enough for two women. If you want to have sexual relations with someone, you ought to get married; and if you are to get married, you ought to leave your parents and find a place of your own. That's the only way you can have physical intimacy.

Sex and the Soul

The sex drive also involves the *soul.* Your soul is composed of your mind, emotions, and will; all three of these are affected by the sex drive.

The *mind* weighs everything that goes into decisions. It considers the facts; it measures the pros and cons; it evaluates your feelings. Some conscious decisions are made about your sexual desires; but sex influences many of your everyday decisions, whether you realize it or not. Your mind acts like a referee in the midst of your will, your emotions, your opinions, and many other competing influences—including your sex drive.

The *emotions* are very clearly affected by the sex drive. Sexual motives can cause a person to swing from one emotion to another. Perhaps you've seen your mate turn from happiness to disappointment, or even to anger, because of a sexual problem between the two of you. It can happen very easily, and you may not discern the reason for the sudden change. At a time like this, you need to have a heart-to-heart talk with your mate to learn what's behind his or her feelings.

The *will* is also strongly influenced by the sex drive. The will is your self-guidance system; it asserts what you want to do, regardless of what the mind may objectively tell you to do or what the emotions may try to sway you to do. The sex drive can persuade your will to desire sexual satisfaction.

These three components—the mind, the emotions, and the will—comprise the soul, the element of your nature that gives you your own unique identity. Your soul may be dedicated to God or it may be unregenerate and sinful. Either way, the sex drive influences your soul, and your soul directs how you will use your sex drive.

Sex and the Spirit

You are also a spirit. God created your body and soul; but the God-breathed, eternal essence within you is your spirit. The spirit is the divine element that reminds your soul of God's will for your life. Your soul will be held accountable for the decisions it makes, for the Bible says, *"The soul that sinneth, it shall die"* (Ezek. 18:4). The spirit, though, does not die; it returns to God. (See Ecclesiastes 12:7.)

Is the spirit involved in sex? Yes! The ecstasy of your spirit, your consciousness of faith in God, and all the other aspects of your spirit are involved in the sex act. Your spirit can employ the sex drive to honor God—if your soul permits it.

A Serious Matter

The sex drive, as we have seen, touches every component of the person. For that reason the sex drive must be handled with care and respect. If abused or allowed to have its own way, the sex drive can destroy you completely. It can not only debilitate your body, it can corrupt your soul and alienate your spirit. Our handling of the sex drive is a very serious matter.

I am afraid that our generation has played with the sex drive as if it were a toy. Men and women have pretended that the sex drive is just basic instinct that should be freely gratified, like the animals gratify theirs. This is a fallacy. The human soul is immortal, and anything that affects the soul should be taken seriously.

God has given us in His Word some very direct, explicit commands regarding sex. If we keep His commands, we will enjoy happy lives on this earth; we will have beautiful children and grandchildren; we will see generation after generation of our descendants cross the stage of human drama. If we ignore what God says about the sex drive, we place ourselves under His judgment. He tells us what the penalties will be, and we must expect to pay them if we disobey. God's spiritual laws are just as immutable as His physical laws. You might jump off a cliff and say, "Look! I'm defying the law of gravity!" You will still fall. The same thing happens when you defy God's spiritual laws. It is not your opinion about sex that matters. It is not the opinion of a cheap novel or magazine that matters. Only God's law matters. You can either conform to His law and enjoy sex as He intended it to be enjoyed, or you can defy His law and bring suffering on yourself.

The sex drive is not dirty. The sex drive is not sinful. The sex drive is a precious gift from God, to be used for His glory and our enjoyment. We need to respect it, control it, and obey God's laws concerning it.

Notes

1. Walter Trobisch, *I Loved a Girl* (New York: Harper and Row, 1965), p. 3.

2. C. W. Lloyd, *Human Reproduction and Sexual Behavior* (Philadelphia: Lea and Febiger, 1964).

3. Desmond Morris, *The Human Zoo* (New York: McGraw-Hill, 1969), p. 121.

4. Dwight Hervey Small, *Design for Christian Marriage* (Old Tappan, N.J.: Spire, 1971), pp. 92–93.

5. Lester Sumrall, *Ecstasy* (Nashville: Thomas Nelson, 1980), pp. 21–31.

6. Howard J. Clinebell and Charlotte H. Clinebell, *The Intimate Marriage* (New York: Harper and Row, 1970), p. 29.

2

Why Is God So Protective about Sex?

A Christian is one who can wait...wait for the complete union. By not
waiting you will gain nothing and you will lose much.
I will put what you would lose into three words:
freedom, joy, and beauty.

—Walter Trobisch[1]

Only God has the right to make a final statement on anything. God is the only final authority, the only One who
can enforce His will in the end. He has the final word
because He had the first word. He created this world and everything in it. He created you and me. He is the Maker of our lives,
so He is the only One who can say how we should live them. For
this reason, what the Bible says about sex has an air of finality, a
tone of absolute authority.

If you know that God is the final authority about sex, you
won't get upset with His instructions. You will know He is telling you the truth about sex. You will realize that if you follow
His rules, you will enjoy sex to the fullest as it was meant to be
enjoyed.

Of course, human logic often leads us to different conclu-
sions about sex. For example, logic would suggest that since a
single person has a sexual nature just like a married person,
a single person should engage in sexual relations. God's Word
says *no*. Logic would indicate that if some persons enjoy physical, sexual contact with members of the same sex, they should be
allowed to have that. God's Word says *no*. Logic would say that

if a person can enjoy sexual intercourse with a marriage partner, that person could enjoy it just as much—maybe more—with someone else. Again God's Word says *no.*

We find that God often overrules our own reasoning in matters of sex. When He does, He's usually less permissive than we would be. His rules are much tighter than we would make them. He is much more protective than we are inclined to be.

Why is God so protective about sex? Why does He govern sex with such strictness and care?

Societies' Restrictions

Even primitive societies that have never heard the gospel of Jesus Christ impose some limitations on sexual conduct. In fact, all known societies have regulated sex in some way, either with written laws or unwritten customs and taboos. This shows that we human beings know, deep down inside, that sex is a very important and serious matter.

I once attended a jungle wedding in Paraguay. The boy wore only a string around his waist and the girl had a waistband and a simple band across her breasts. Yet despite the crude simplicity of that occasion, they stood before a campfire with reverent solemnity and pledged to take one another as husband and wife. Their family and friends were witnesses. After they exchanged their vows, the boy and girl danced around the campfire while their friends laughed and cheered. Then the couple walked down a jungle path to the simple hut he had prepared for their honeymoon night. It was a very simple wedding without many of the formalities we know in America.

However informal in some ways, some customs were absolute. The villagers did not permit the boy to touch any girl except the one he planned to marry. This strict regulation protected the virginity of the girls and kept order.

In Muslim countries, every unmarried woman must wear a veil to conceal her beauty from any men she might meet in her village. The enjoyment of a woman's charms is a privilege reserved for her husband alone.

In ancient China, the parents of a boy chose his bride while he was still a child, but the youngsters were not allowed to see one another until their wedding day. Why? To preserve their sexual purity.

Anthropologists have found similar laws and customs in every known society, both ancient and modern. Many of these communities had never heard of God, and certainly had never read the Bible; yet they knew by instinct that they should safeguard the dignity of sex. They knew it should be protected and used for the right purpose—within marriage.

God's Protective Rules

So you see, God is not being overly protective about sex. He wants us to be happy. He has established His regulations about sex to reserve sex for its best use, within the intimacy of marriage. Even the primitive tribesmen know that sex can be vulgarized and cheapened, and in their own way they try to protect their young people from the painful consequences of vulgar sex. So why shouldn't God, who created sex and knows more about it than anyone, be even more protective about it?

God's specific regulations about sex show what great care He takes to preserve sex for its proper use. In the following chapters, we will make a more thorough study of God's regulations for sex in marriage. For now let's consider God's law against adultery. This protective law reveals why He is so concerned about our sex lives.

4. Thou shalt not commit adultery.   *(Exod. 20:14)*

That's all. Now that's simple, direct, and to the point. It's also very protective. God knew that sexual fidelity was so important that He devoted one of His Ten Commandments to it. He put sexual infidelity alongside murder and robbery as a crime so serious that He simply said, *"Thou shalt not."* He did not give any reason for His command, because the reason was self-evident. As a country farmer might say, "Anybody with a lick of sense ought to know that." Anyone with the slightest idea of what sex is all about, of how deep and intimate the sexual relationship is, should know that adultery is a crime. But because we're trying to understand why God is so protective, let's review the reasons for this law.

First, adultery is a crime because it destroys a sexual relationship. We've already suggested that such a relationship is the most beautiful and meaningful bond that two human beings can have; it is a relationship of full commitment to one another. The man and woman give themselves wholeheartedly to one another, holding nothing back. Nothing is "saved" for someone else. Their complete and total sharing explores all areas of intimacy. When one partner leaves to have sex with someone else, the relationship is destroyed. The "one flesh" is torn apart.

Dr. Charles L. Allen has counseled scores of married couples during his years as a pastor. Notice what he says about adultery:

> In marriage there are two things which must exist. First, a solid affection, a love for each other entirely different from the love for anyone else. Second, complete trust in each other. Adultery destroys both.[2]

He's right! Adultery destroys the trust and confidence that is the foundation of any marriage relationship, any sexual relationship. It is an act of betrayal, a way of pulling back your commitment to the person who has your all. It rips up your *covenant* with the human being who has shared more than anyone ever shared with you.

Second, adultery is a crime because it denies a person's God-given duty to raise children. In this day of popular birth-control devices and abortion, many people don't link sex with bearing children. Bringing children into the world is still God's primary purpose for sex!

> On this basis, the love relationship between man and woman cannot be regarded as "fleshly"; it is in the highest sense the fulfillment of God's purpose in creating men and

women. In entering this relationship, Christians are committing themselves to their part in fulfilling the plan of God for
mankind....It is a sign of commitment before God and an affir-
mation that this couple views its relationship as a part of God's
will for his people.[3]

God gave man and woman a duty with the gift of sex; He
commanded them to "be fruitful." If one mate decides to find
sexual enjoyment elsewhere, he is ignoring the duty that came
with his gift.

Third, adultery is a crime because it perverts the spiritual
truth that sex symbolizes. God's Word compares the sexual bond
between a man and a woman to the spiritual bond between
Christ and His church. Read the following statement along with
God's command in Exodus 20:14 if you want to understand why
adultery is so sinful in God's sight:

> 5. *For the husband is the head of the wife, even as Christ*
> *is the head of the church: and he is the saviour of the*
> *body. Therefore as the church is subject unto Christ, so*
> *let the wives be to their own husbands in every thing.*
> *Husbands, love your wives, even as Christ also loved the*
> *church, and gave himself for it....For this cause shall a*
> *man leave his father and mother, and shall be joined unto*
> *his wife, and they two shall be one flesh. This is a great*
> *mystery: but I speak concerning Christ and the church.*
> *Nevertheless let every one of you in particular so love his*
> *wife even as himself; and the wife see that she reverence*
> *her husband.* (Eph. 5:23–25, 31–33)

Adultery shouts to the world that Christ is going to turn His
back on the church, or that the church is going to "fall in love"
with someone besides Christ. That's heresy! A barefaced lie! Yet
that's exactly what adultery is saying. It is a theological statement.

The poet Walter A. Kortrey expressed the cynicism of a
non-Christian world when he said:

Why Is God So Protective about Sex?

If loving God
Is nothing like
The love I have for her—
Then you can have it.[4]

But God says His love for us is *exactly* like the love of a man and woman. A man and woman sharing the joys of nuptial sex portray the love of Christ and His church. They demonstrate how Christ and the church give themselves completely to one another. Sexual love is a holy symbol.

True, only Christians realize this; but any couple that breaks up to find other sexual partners is blaspheming the truth of God's love. To put it bluntly, they act as if Jesus were a gigolo or the church a prostitute. The very idea is repulsive.

Do you begin to see why God is so protective about sex? He is interested in the physical happiness of men and women, but He's also interested in guarding spiritual truth. He knows that sex enters both planes—the physical and the spiritual.

We find this again in the prophecies of Ezekiel. Here God puts a spiritual truth into sexual language; He calls the disobedient city of Jerusalem a "harlot." As He describes what He will do to Jerusalem, we see His protectiveness toward His people's spiritual life as well as their sexual life. His treatment of the spiritual harlot, Jerusalem, gives us an inkling of how a physical harlot will be treated:

> 6. And say, Thus saith the Lord GOD unto Jerusalem...When I passed by thee, and looked upon thee, behold, thy time was the time of love; and I spread my skirt over thee, and covered thy nakedness: yea, I sware unto thee, and entered into a covenant with thee, saith the Lord GOD, and thou becamest mine....But thou didst trust in thine own beauty, and playedst the harlot because of thy renown, and pouredst out thy fornications on every one that passed by; his it was....And I will judge thee, as women that break wedlock and shed blood are judged; and I will give thee blood in fury and jealousy.   (Ezek. 16:3, 8, 15, 38)

God says that a woman who breaks wedlock is judged like a woman who sheds blood. An adulteress is just as bad as a murderess; both of them must pay with their lives. This is what He means when He said, *"I will give thee blood."* We will see in a later chapter that the penalty for adultery in Old Testament times indeed was death. We will also see that the adulterer still dies in other, less obvious ways. One should notice, though, how God describes adultery in such clear, graphic terms.

Read the entire sixteenth chapter of Ezekiel and you will get the full picture. There God punishes infidelity, whether it's spiritual or sexual. He just won't allow it, because He knows the consequences. Infidelity will destroy the person who does it, pervert the other persons involved, and make a mockery of God Himself. So God said, *"I will judge you* [spiritual harlots] *as women who break wedlock and shed blood are judged"* (Ezek. 16:38 RSV).

A Christian's Concern

Our spiritual welfare and our physical welfare are equally important to God. He loves us and cares about us, so He's keenly concerned about both aspects of our lives.

We Christians need to realize this, because we often are so concerned about another person's spiritual life that we ignore the physical life. When we counsel with someone, let's not tune out any clues of sexual trouble. God cares about His people's sex lives, and so should we.

Pastor Tim LaHaye tells of a friend who was holding evangelistic services in a certain city and staying with a fine Christian couple who were leaders in the local church. After breakfast one morning, the evangelist casually asked his hostess, "How are things going?" She broke down in tears. Her husband was a very aggressive man, she said, and in their sexual contacts he moved too fast. She did not really enjoy their relationship, but she submitted to him out of love. She asked the evangelist to pray that God would help them. Pastor LaHaye tells what happened:

Why Is God So Protective about Sex?

That night as he was getting ready for bed, the minister stepped into the bathroom to brush his teeth. Since the bathroom was between the two bedrooms, without trying to eavesdrop he could clearly hear his friend perform what he called "making love to my wife." It was all over in three minutes! It was nothing more than physical satisfaction of the masculine mating urge.

The next morning the evangelist asked his friend to stay home from work, and they talked in the backyard for two hours. To his amazement, this college graduate who dearly loved his wife didn't even know anything was wrong. Neither of these young people had read a book on the subject of sex and they had never been given marriage counseling. When the preacher finished the long-overdue counseling session, the young man was heartbroken. He confessed his selfishness to God and asked for divine wisdom in being the kind of husband that God wanted him to be.[5]

Yes, God is very protective about sex. It is a wonderful gift that we should also cherish and protect.

The Sanctity of Human Life

Sex is important because human life itself is important to God. Human life is holy in God's sight.

"Alright," you may say, "but doesn't the Bible tell us that the human heart is *'deceitful above all things, and desperately wicked'* (Jer. 17:9)?" Indeed it does, and carnal man is a corrupt and despicable creature. But God does not want us to be like that. He created us in His own image, as a reflection of His own divine nature. And even though man has fallen from grace and lives under God's condemnation, each person still has the capacity for pure and holy living. Each person's life is priceless in the eyes of God. Speaking through the apostle Paul, God said:

7. Do you not know that you are the temple of God and that the Spirit of God dwells in you? If anyone defiles the

> *temple of God, God will destroy him. For the temple of God is holy, which temple you are. (1 Cor. 3:16–17 NKJV)*

This applies to sex as well as to any other aspect of our physical lives. We are not free to do as we please with our bodies; they are dedicated to God. Each one of us has a spirit, a divine element within us. We should handle our bodies in a way that will honor the spirit within, bringing glory to the God who made us.

You probably have seen pictures of the temple ruins of Greece. The Parthenon and other great buildings of the classical age are now crumbling. Their twisted columns lie scattered about the city of Athens like a child's broken toys. Once they were tall and beautiful, their polished marble arches shimmering in the afternoon sun. Centuries of war and riots and vandalism have left them a rubble. The "temples" of peoples bodies can be just like that. God intends for them to be strong and beautiful for His sake; but if we neglect or abuse them, they will bring honor to no one.

When God created Adam and Eve, He made their bodies pure, holy, and clean. He gave them their own unique sexual powers and brought them together into the intimate relationship of marriage. Their bodies were holy, their sex drive was holy, and their marriage was holy.

God warned them not to violate His commands, which reflected His own moral nature; yet they disobeyed Him and were banished from the Garden of Eden. Their souls became rebellious and corrupt. They passed that corruption on to their descendants, but that did not make their *bodies* corrupt! It did not make the sex drive corrupt. Granted, the descendants of Adam and Eve made corrupt use of their bodies—the generations leading up to the Flood were full of unspeakable immorality. Yet the human body itself did not change. It could still be used for holy or unholy purposes, whichever a person chose.

Several years ago, a major network staged a radio drama called "The Cartwheel." It was about the career of a silver dollar (back then they were so big that people called them "cartwheels"). The drama showed how this coin passed through the hands of first one person, then another, until it had been used by almost every type of character you could imagine. A bridegroom used it to pay for his honeymoon suite. (You can tell this was back in the 1930s!) A faithful parishioner dropped it in the offering plate at church. A gambler used it to bet on a crap game. A drunkard used it to buy a pint of whiskey. On and on it went. Obviously, the cartwheel could be used for almost any purpose, depending on its owner's inclination.

The same is true of the body. God created it to be a holy, wholesome thing. He created it to bring honor to Him. He has given us many guidelines to help us preserve and strengthen every function of the body—including the sexual function. Yet we alone decide what to do with it.

God knows everything about sex, and He intended for us to be very careful about how it's used. His rules for sex are very protective. Shouldn't we heed these rules?

Notes

1. Walter Trobisch, *I Loved a Girl* (New York: Harper and Row, 1965), p. 87.

2. Charles L. Allen, *God's Psychiatry* (Old Tappan, N.J.: Family Library, 1974), p. 69.

3. Howard Clark Kee, *Making Ethical Decisions* (Philadelphia: Westminster Press, 1957), pp. 36–37.

4. Walter A. Kortrey, "Agape and Eros," *The Christian Century,* July 18, 1973, p. 749. Reprinted by permission.

5. Tim LaHaye, *How to Be Happy Though Married* (Wheaton, Ill.: Tyndale House, 1968), p. 72.

3
Sex in Marriage
(Where Else?)

[Marriage] was a divine plan and a God-given provision for His
creature—man. He who would corrupt this union is guilty
of affront to God, and he who despises the relationship
despises God who gave it.

—Paul Wilson[1]

D id you ever stop to think that the first two people in the
world were married? Today we hear a great deal about
the single lifestyle; many people think it's more fun to be
single than to be married. But this was not God's original plan.
After God created Adam, He said:

*8. It is not good that the man should be alone; I will make
him an help meet for him.*   *(Gen. 2:18)*

The term *"help meet"* literally means "an appropriate partner." The Revised Standard Version says *"a helper fit for him."* In
other words, God was a matchmaker. He made a woman who
would be just what the man needed, and then He brought them
together. They became lifelong mates and raised the very first
family in the world, without the help of any marriage counselors
or self-help books or even "Dear Abby." God matched them very
well. In what ways was Eve "meet" or "fit" for Adam?

It seems clear that she was a good helper in the manual labor that Adam had to perform; after they left Eden, she became the very first farmer's wife, and that's not an easy job. I can imagine her making their clothes, foraging for firewood, threshing and storing the field crops that Adam brought in. No one had ever done this type of work before, but Eve seemed well suited to the task.

Also, she was a fit companion and adviser. She did not always give Adam good advice, but she did try to help him make decisions. She weighed theological questions in her mind, such as whether they should obey God's commands "to the letter," or follow the serpent's interpretation. She tried to steer Adam in the most sensible, reasonable direction. We would have to say that she was well matched to Adam in intellect.

She was also a fit partner in her sexual role. Her female charms were a perfect match to Adam's male features. She opened up a whole new realm of physical pleasure that Adam could not have known if he had spent the rest of his life alone. She was well matched to Adam in the sexual sense.

In every way, the first marriage brought together two people who needed each other. It mated two individuals whose lives would have been limited and lacking had they not been married. Adam and Eve had a successful marriage, even though they were failures in other respects. One important reason for this success was the fact that they were well matched sexually.

With the couples I counsel for marriage, the question of compatibility always comes up. The young man and woman want to know, "Are we right for each other?" So we talk about the things that ought to matter in a marriage, to see whether they "match up."

First of all, we talk about their spiritual life—Are both of them Christians? If not, do they realize the problems caused by being *"unequally yoked together"* (2 Cor. 6:14)?

We talk about their life's work—Do they know each other's plans for the future? (You'd be surprised how many engaged couples don't know!)

We also talk about sex—Are they attracted to one another sexually? Do they see in one another the physical qualities they think they will enjoy? Have they talked about the purpose of sex and the proper role of sex?

Many times they haven't. Christian couples are especially prone to think that if they're well matched in every other way, their sex life will just naturally fall in line. They don't talk about it. They don't think about it. And after they're married they get a rude awakening.

This doesn't mean that partners-to-be must be in perfect agreement about everything. In fact, I don't think that is ever the case. My wife and I have enjoyed a wonderful marriage for the past thirty-five years, but I still can't say that we're in total agreement about everything. We *complement* one another. The strengths of one offset the weaknesses of the other. I believe that should be true in every married couple's life.

A prospective husband and wife can save themselves a lot of unnecessary grief if they will have an honest, straightforward talk about what they expect from their relationship. The range of subjects most certainly must include the sexual aspect. Pastor Tim LaHaye says:

> Physical adjustment in marriage can be properly compared to the instrumental adjustment necessary for an orchestra to produce a beautiful, harmonious symphony. Contrary to popular opinion, "doing what comes naturally" does not automatically guarantee physical harmony in the marriage relationship.[2]

In other words, you may not *seem* like a perfect match sexually. But can you make the adjustments necessary? Are you willing to be patient with your spouse while you learn to satisfy each other's needs? A computer dating service will never be able to tell you this kind of thing: You must learn from each other how flexible you are—learn by praying about it and talking honestly about it *before* you marry.

Sex Expresses Love

Perhaps no word in the English language is so misunderstood as the word "love." A secretary turns to her friend in the elevator and says, "Oh, Myrtle! I just love your new outfit!" A prizefighter scowls at his opponent and says, "I'd love to punch you in the mouth!" Starry-eyed young girls sigh and say, "I'm in love!"

What does "love" mean anyway? Particularly, what kind of "love" is married love? John Powell, a well-known Roman Catholic writer, says this:

> The young man who professes to love a young woman may often be deceived in thinking that the gratification of his own egotistical urges really constitutes love. The young woman who finds the voids of her own loneliness filled by the companionship and attention of a young man may well mistake this emotional satisfaction for love....The critical question always remains that of self-forgetfulness. Does the young man or woman...really forget himself and his own convenience and emotional satisfaction, to seek only the happiness and fulfillment of the beloved?[3]

That's a pretty tough standard, isn't it? Everyone likes to think of his own needs and wants; everyone takes for granted that "happiness" is a matter of satisfying those needs and wants. But true love forces you to go beyond yourself. It makes you think about the needs and wants of someone else. More important, it may cause you to sacrifice your own comfort and pleasure to give enjoyment to the one you love.

God's Word gives us a beautiful description of love, and it's one of the most important things God has ever said about sex:

> *9. Love suffers long and is kind; love does not envy; love does not parade itself, is not puffed up; does not behave rudely, does not seek its own, is not provoked, thinks no evil; does not rejoice in iniquity, but rejoices in the*

> *truth; bears all things, believes all things, hopes all things,*
> *endures all things.*   *(1 Cor. 13:4–7 NKJV)*

Here is the perfect description of the role of sex within marriage. Your sexual relationship should express this kind of pure and selfless love for your mate. Otherwise you've missed the mark.

"But wait a minute, Dr. Sumrall!" someone may say. "I thought you told us that sex was for bearing children." Yes, that is the primary reason God gave us our sexual nature. But He also expects us to use sex to express our love for our mate. His Word says:

> *10. Let the husband render to his wife the affection due*
> *her, and likewise also the wife to her husband. The wife*
> *does not have authority over her own body, but the*
> *husband does. And likewise the husband does not have*
> *authority over his own body, but the wife does.*
>   *(1 Cor. 7:3–4 NKJV)*

A married couple should have sexual relations, not just to conceive children, but to show one another their complete love and devotion.

Marriage is the most unique relationship on earth. It is above all other human relationships. Only in marriage do two people share their minds, their souls, and even their bodies. Only in marriage do two people pledge their lifelong loyalty, "forsaking all others," as the wedding vow says. Only in marriage do two people join with God to bring other human beings into this world—others who are created in the image of God.

Married love is holy because God created the marriage bond. He authorized the first wedding, and He is the only One who can rightfully authorize a wedding today. This is why Christian marriages should not be performed in some court clerk's office, on a judge's back porch, or in the couple's favorite social spot. The marriage is not designed to honor the state or honor the couple; it is designed to honor God. It should express the unselfish love that only God can give. So the wedding should be performed where God is publicly worshipped, asking God to sanctify it. God should be invited to "tie the knot" that no one can untie.

Sex Is a Dialogue

Marriage is a lifelong conversation. It's an exchange of ideas, a sharing of joy and sorrow. When a man and woman pledge to "cleave only" to one another, that wedding vow means they will share their innermost thoughts and feelings with one another. They will communicate. Or to put it in a spiritual context, they will *commune* with one another.

> *11. Nevertheless neither is the man without the woman, neither the woman without the man, in the Lord. For as the woman is of the man, even so is the man also by the woman; but all things of God.*   *(1 Cor. 11:11–12)*

Here the Word of God reminds us that man and woman are physically tied to one another, all the way back to Creation. The woman was created from a rib that God took from man's side; the man has been born of woman, ever since Eve. Man and woman are intimately related; they are incomplete without one another. It is foolish to think that marriage is simply a partnership of two self-willed, independent people.

Husband and wife must share their total lives, and the sexual relationship is an important way of sharing. It demonstrates in a literal, physical way that they are one. It is a kind of physical dialogue. The Reverend Small says:

> Dialogue takes place when two people communicate the full meaning of their lives to one another, when they participate in each other's lives in the most meaningful ways in which they are capable.[4]

That's a good description of the sexual relationship. It is a way of participating fully in another person's life without fear or selfishness. It is true dialogue.

Like any other kind of dialogue, the sexual relationship must observe certain courtesies. If you were having a conversation with another person, would you insist on "being in charge"? Would you refuse to hear what the other person says? Would you turn and walk away when you're through, regardless of whether the other person is still speaking? Of course not. That would not really be a "conversation." The same is true of the sexual relationship. Each partner must be sensitive to the other's needs, ready to respond, patient in letting the other express himself (or herself). Howard and Charlotte Clinebell describe a typical situation in which sexual dialogue breaks down. We might call it a sexual "communication gap":

> It is important for the husband to understand that his wife literally can't respond as she and he would like, when her feelings are hurt, the bedroom is cluttered, or the children are stirring in the next room. It is well worth the effort to create the needed atmosphere to allow her romantic side to flower. Many women experience sexual arousal more slowly than their husbands and respond to considerable tenderness, caressing, fondling, and reassurances of love in the full enjoyment of intercourse.[5]

So many couples become frustrated by their sexual differences and seek relations with others, instead of learning how to truly commune with one another. This kind of adjustment is a natural part of becoming a mature person. It is a part of learning to love. God says:

12. Drink waters out of thine own cistern, and running waters out of thine own well....Let thy fountain be blessed: and rejoice with the wife of thy youth. Let her be as the loving hind and pleasant roe; let her breasts satisfy thee at all times; and be thou ravished always with her love.
(Prov. 5:15, 18–19)

I firmly believe that the men and women of America would have much more enjoyable sex lives if they would take time to learn how to really communicate in marriage, rather than "shopping around" for better sex mates. A man who patiently learns the sexual language of his wife will always be ravished with her love. The woman who tunes her ear to her husband's sexual messages will be fully satisfied. But it takes time. It takes patience.

Several years ago, Charlie Shedd wrote a series of letters to his young son-in-law to be, and they have become a classic in the Christian literature about sex. One of Dr. Shedd's most startling statements was that a husband and wife may need a "twenty-year warm-up" to learn real sexual enjoyment together. He said:

> Freedom to express your desires is a great goal, but, for the first twenty years,...it's more goal than reality.[6]

Many couples will be able to establish the lines of sexual communication much sooner than that, but it's still good advice. Husband and wife need to be patient in their sexual dialogue, even if it takes years to learn how to communicate.

Sex Brings Pleasure

The carnal world would have us believe that pleasure is the *only* purpose of sex. Some prudish Christians think that pleasure has *nothing* to do with sex. Both are wrong. The sexual relationship is a very pleasurable one, and it should bring a great deal of enjoyment to a marriage. But we need to get the pleasurable aspect of sex in proper perspective, according to God's Word.

The entire Song of Solomon describes the pleasures of sexual love. Some critics say the Song of Solomon is an erotic book that has no place in the Bible; but they obviously don't know what "erotic" means. It comes from the Greek word *eros,* which means "love for the sake of physical pleasure." The Song of Solomon certainly describes physical pleasure, but no one can say that it depicts pleasure as the "be all and end all" of sex. This book shows that sex expresses the great love a husband and wife have for one another. In fact, many Bible scholars believe it is a symbolic picture of God's love for His people, the love of Christ for His church. No matter how one interprets it—literally (concerning marriage) or symbolically (concerning God)—we would have to say that the Song of Solomon puts sex and pleasure in proper perspective.

Let us look at just a couple of passages from this remarkable book:

> *13. Tell me, O thou whom my soul loveth, where thou feedest, where thou makest thy flock to rest at noon: for why should I be as one that turneth aside by the flocks of thy companions?* (Song 1:7)

This is the bride's earnest plea to her groom. It underscores the message we have already heard from God, that a married couple should not seek pleasure with other companions. Here God puts His words in the mouth of the bride herself. She says, in effect, "Show me how I can find pleasure with you, darling. For why should I try to find it with your friends?"

I told you the Bible was very straightforward about sex, didn't I?

Read on in the Song of Solomon, and you will find the bride pleading with her husband again and again, begging him to find his sexual pleasure with her. Remember that this book was inspired by God, just like any other book of the Bible. We should watch for what He is teaching us about sex here. The bride says:

> *14. Let my beloved come into his garden, and eat his pleasant fruits....I am my beloved's, and my beloved is mine: he feedeth among the lilies....I am my beloved's, and his desire is toward me.* (Song 4:16; 6:3; 7:10)

See how the theme of pleasure runs throughout this book? Yet it is always pleasure as an expression of *love*, not just pleasure for its own sake.

In the first statement (Song 4:16), the bride invites her husband to *"eat his pleasant fruits."* This is a vivid and beautiful way of inviting him to enjoy the physical pleasures of her marriage bed. She then says that *"he feedeth among the lilies"* (Song 6:3). The lily is a symbol of purity or, in this case, virginity. The bride is happy to say that her husband is the only one who has tasted her sexual pleasures. She has saved them all for him, for she knew she would belong to him—and he to her! She says, *"His desire is toward me"* (Song 7:10). Any woman would like to say this about her husband. Despite all the other women whose physical charms might tempt him, *"his desire is toward me."* He finds his pleasure in the right place, with his wife.

Unfortunately, many Christians think that sex is a dull, mechanical sort of thing. They look on it as a duty, an obligation they have to their mate—like washing the dishes or mowing the yard. But sex is a pleasure! Sex is enjoyable! God intended sex for the mutual pleasure of husband and wife, and they should feel no qualms about exploring the many "treats" it holds for them. Tim LaHaye advises wives:

> Rid your mind of any preconceived prejudices or "old wives' tales" that tend to make you fear the act of marriage—or look on it as evil. Just because your mother or some other woman was not well-adjusted in the physical area of marriage is no reason you have to perpetuate her mistakes and resultant misery. Approach the act of marriage with pleasurable antici-pation. God meant it to be good![7]

No kind of sexual pleasure is "off limits" to husband and wife, so long as it honors God. Some people think that only one particular technique of lovemaking is "holy," and all others are sinful; but you won't find that teaching in Scripture:

> *15. Marriage is honorable among all, and the bed undefiled; but fornicators and adulterers God will judge.*
> (Heb. 13:4 NKJV)

In other words, marriage is an honorable way for anyone to enjoy sex. Some other way—whether sex before marriage (forni-cation) or sex with someone else during marriage (adultery)—is condemned by God. Moreover, the marriage bed is "undefiled." There is nothing sinful about sex in the marriage bed; there are no taboos to observe with your partner. You need only observe the courtesies of dialogue and the dignity that any divine gift deserves.

Sex Honors God

Before we leave the subject of sex in marriage, we should consider how the sex life of a Christian man and woman can bring honor to God. This is another important function of sex. God says that everything we do should honor Him:

16. Therefore, whether you eat or drink, or whatever you do, do all to the glory of God.   *(1 Cor. 10:31 NKJV)*

Everything that we do—eating, sleeping, talking with our friends, conducting business, even sexual intercourse—everything should be done in a way that will glorify the Lord. He made us and He expresses Himself through us. As Paul said, *"It is no longer I who live, but Christ who lives in me; and the life I now live in the flesh I live by faith in the Son of God, who loved me and gave himself for me"* (Gal. 2:20 RSV). Thus every physical act of the Christian should express love for the Lord. This is the final test for the Christian's sex life: Does it honor the Lord?

If a man and woman share the joy of sex in marriage as the Lord intended, and if they regard one another with the love and respect that any Christian should have for another, their sex life will be a tribute to the Lord. But if they flirt with sex outside of marriage, they have broken His command. If they desire sexual relations simply for the thrill or physical "charge" they get out of it, with no thought of mutual love, they have cheapened it. Most sex manuals would tell us that the *method* of sex is all-important, but God's Word tells us that the *motive* is just as important. If a man and woman engage in sex with selfish or perverted motives, they waste one of God's most precious gifts. They insult Him. And they will have to pay the consequences. Dwight Small says:

> The distinctive thing about the Christian concept of sex is in thus fully acknowledging it as a biological function in man, but at the same time insisting that it is a function of the total personality which at its highest is spiritual. Its physical aspects cannot be disassociated from its spiritual aspects.[8]

This is the key. Sex cannot be understood apart from all the other aspects of a Christian's consecrated life.

In marriage, sex is a normal part of daily life, just as eating or any other physical function. So we should not be reluctant to talk about it. We should thank God for sex and strive to use it as joyously and reverently as any other gift from Him.

Notes

1. Paul Wilson, *The Institution of Marriage* (Oak Park, Ill.: Bible Truth, 1969), p. 8.

2. Tim LaHaye, *How to Be Happy Though Married* (Wheaton, Ill.: Tyndale House, 1968), p. 53.

3. John Powell, *Why Am I Afraid to Love?* rev. ed. (Chicago: Argus Communications, 1972), pp. 19–20.

4. Dwight Hervey Small, *After You've Said I Do* (Old Tappan, N.J.: Revell, 1968), p. 51.

5. Howard J. Clinebell and Charlotte H. Clinebell, *The Intimate Marriage* (New York: Harper and Row, 1970), p. 145.

6. Charlie W. Shedd, *Letters to Philip* (Old Tappan, N.J.: Spire, 1968), p. 110.

7. Tim LaHaye, *How to Be Happy,* p. 68.

8. Dwight Hervey Small, *Design for Christian Marriage* (Old Tappan, N.J.: Spire Books, 1959), p. 92.

4
X-Rated Marriages

The home is basically a sacred institution. The perfect marriage
is a uniting of three persons—a man and a woman and God.
That is what makes marriage holy. Faith in Christ is the most
important of all principles in the building of a happy
marriage and a successful home.

—Billy Graham[1]

Not all marriages are made in heaven. When two unbelievers marry, or when a Christian and unbeliever marry,
they set themselves up for a lot of heartache. They soon
find themselves at odds. God can bless a marriage of His own
people, but unbelievers take their marriage out of God's hands.
Then it's by no means heavenly. In fact, it can be a hell on earth.

I call this kind of marriage an "X-rated marriage," because it
has God's clear stamp of disapproval.

Movie theaters advertise X-rated films with all sorts of lurid
"come-ons" that are supposed to arouse your interest. They tell
you from the very start that the films are unfit for family viewing. They put an "X" on the ad to warn you that the film has
carnal sex, perverted sex, or extreme violence. Yet people attend
these films anyway, filling their minds with corruption. In the
same way, God warns us against marrying unbelievers; He puts
His "X" rating on such a union. He warns us that such marriages
always bring trouble. Yet many people plunge ahead and reap
the consequences.

Notice what Abraham said to his chief servant Eliezar about marriage: *"Swear by the LORD, the God of heaven, and the God of the earth, that thou shalt not take a wife unto my son of the daughters of the Canaanites, among whom I dwell"* (Gen. 24:3). Abraham did not want his son to marry a woman who came from a pagan and immoral family. He knew that the Canaanites had loose morals. They were steeped in heathen myths and idolatry; they were ungodly to the very core. So he made Eliezar promise before God that he would not let Isaac marry a woman of Canaanite origin.

I think parents are often too careless about the kind of friends they let their children socialize with. This may sound old-fashioned, but I'll say it anyway: We need to be more careful that our sons and daughters have good Christian friends. Because Christian parents have had a "do-your-own-thing" attitude toward their children in recent years, we have seen hundreds of young people lured into ungodly marriages. Careless Christian parents have *"sown the wind, and they shall reap the whirlwind"* (Hos. 8:7).

The Sorrow of Ungodly Marriage

Ungodliness always brings sorrow. We see that illustrated throughout the world. Until India turns to God, for example, no one will be able to end its poverty and starvation. Until Americans repent and accept the Lord, they will struggle with inflation, crime, and spiritual bankruptcy. The same is true in any individual's life. Ungodliness brings sorrow.

Marriage simply redoubles the sorrow of ungodliness. It solves no problems for an ungodly person; in fact, it gives him a whole new set of problems! This is why the Old Testament patriarchs took pains to tell their children not to marry a heathen. (See Genesis 28:1.) They knew an ungodly marriage would bring their children nothing but trouble and pain.

God reminded His people of this as they prepared to enter the Promised Land. He warned them of the pagan peoples they would find in Canaan, and He said:

551

17. Neither shalt thou make marriages with them; thy daughter thou shalt not give unto his son, nor his daughter shalt thou take unto thy son. For they will turn away thy son from following me, that they may serve other gods: so will the anger of the LORD be kindled against you, and destroy thee suddenly. (Deut. 7:3–4)

Again we see God's protectiveness about sex. He would not allow His chosen people to marry just anyone, because ungodly marriages make ungodly people. Such marriages are designated "X-rated" because they will corrupt both marriage partners. God gave Israel the same warning through Joshua:

18. If ye do in any wise go back, and cleave unto the remnant of these nations, even these that remain among you, and shall make marriages with them, and go in unto them, and they to you: know for a certainty that the LORD your God will no more drive out any of these nations from before you; but they shall be snares and traps unto you. (Josh. 23:12–13)

You see, this is not only a family problem—it is a national problem. Ungodly marriages undermine the entire nation. They unravel the moral fabric of the society. They warp the values that a decent home should uphold. Why? Because they are not anchored to the rock of God's truth.

If you've never been involved in such a marriage, you may think this restriction is too harsh. You may have an optimistic attitude toward your ungodly mate, saying, "I'll be able to change him (or her) for the better." But sad to say, it usually works the other way around. The ungodly mate will discourage and corrupt the godly one. In fact, the ungodly mate will get his (or her) partner into problems that otherwise would never occur.

Make no mistake: When you marry outside God's family, you step outside His protection. You expose yourself to problems you never would have had otherwise. God says:

19. Do not be unequally yoked together with unbelievers. For what fellowship has righteousness with lawlessness? And what communion has light with darkness?

(2 Cor. 6:14 NKJV)

Marriage is not the sort of thing you should launch on a whim or impulse. When you marry, you must think not only of yourself but of your children and grandchildren; all of them will be exposed to your marriage. All of them will be affected by the mate you choose. God says that when a believer and an unbeliever marry, it's like a donkey and a camel trying to pull a plow together, they just don't match. One is too tall and the other too short; one takes long strides and the other takes short strides. They don't share the burden equally. They are "unequally yoked."

Ungodly Marriage in the Bible

In Genesis 6:1–6, we read that the *"sons of God"* married the *"daughters of men"* in outright defiance of God. Bible scholars have long speculated about who the *"sons of God"* were; some say they were a particular tribe of Adam's descendants, others that they were some sort of superhuman, spiritual beings. No matter how you interpret that phrase, it's clear that they were "unequally yoked" with their wives. Godly men married carnal women. The result? God sent the great Flood to destroy that wicked generation, saving only Noah and his family.

Can you imagine that? Ungodly marriages—X-rated marriages—caused the greatest catastrophe the world has ever known.

Samson, one of the judges of Israel, decided to marry a heathen woman from among the Philistines. You'll recall how he came back from Timnath and told his parents, *"Get her for me"* (Judg. 14:2).

Samson's parents were God-fearing people; they knew that marriage was not to be taken lightly. So his father asked, *"Is there never a woman among the daughters of thy brethren, or among all my*

553

people, that thou goest to take a wife of the uncircumcised Philistines?" (Judg. 14:3).

But Samson said, *"Get her for me; for she pleaseth me well"* (v. 3). This kind of attitude is widespread today. Young men and women care nothing about the spiritual background of their friends. When they get engaged to marry, they seldom think about what kind of family they're getting into. They only say, "She turns me on," or, "I really like the way he kisses." That seems to be their only standard for choosing a mate. But Samson's X-rated marriage caused him to lose his eyes, to lose his dignity, and even to lose his life with his wife's heathen friends.

What a tragic thing it is to get involved in an ungodly marriage! When you marry the wrong person in open defiance of God, you have no idea what the future holds for you.

It's no use to say, "That's all right. I know what I'm doing." Even King Solomon, one of the wisest men who ever lived, made a foolish mistake when he married heathen women. His X-rated marriages finally destroyed his kingdom. *"King Solomon loved many strange women, together with the daughter of Pharaoh, women of the Moabites, Ammonites, Edomites, Zidonians, and Hittites; of the nations concerning which the* LORD *said unto the children of Israel, Ye shall not go in to them, neither shall they come in unto you: for surely they will turn away your heart after their gods: Solomon clave unto these in love"* (1 Kings 11:1–2). His heathen wives persuaded him to set up altars to their gods, and they gradually got him to worship their gods. In the end, Scripture says, *"his heart was not perfect with the* LORD *his God, as was the heart of David his father"* (I Kings 11:4). What a sad commentary! Solomon was wise in statecraft and politics, but he acted foolishly in the realm of sex. He was "unequally yoked."

Practical Answers

This is not to say that a Christian who winds up in an ungodly marriage just has to "tough it out." God admonishes a Christian in such a situation to set a good example for his or her mate. Notice His word to wives especially:

*20. Wives, likewise, be submissive to your own husbands,
that even if some do not obey the word, they, without a
word, may be won by the conduct of their wives.*

(1 Pet. 3:1 NKJV)

Dorothy C. Haskin spent several years trying to win her
husband to the Lord. Both of them were unbelievers when
they married, and she was converted just one year later. At
first she tried to make him attend church services with her.
"The result was that he decided I was a 'religious fanatic,' and
he was not interested in my faith," she says.[2] But she kept
on trying. She subscribed to some good Christian magazines,
which he picked up and casually leafed through. She occasionally tuned in Christian radio programs for their leisure-time
listening. She invited him to church for some special occasions. But even though she saw a breakthrough now and then,
it wasn't easy.

> I liked to attend all the services but I realized that he
> would not. I gave up some so he would attend the others.
> Because he had to get up early Monday morning and liked
> to take his mother for a long drive after dinner on Sunday, I
> decided that Sunday school was easiest for him. So we went
> to Sunday school. Later, he decided he preferred the eleven
> o'clock Sunday service.
>
> My husband received Christ as Savior in his forties and
> was baptized. Nothing takes more tact and patience than win-
> ning a non-Christian husband to the Lord.[3]

I'm sure that many other people caught in X-rated marriages
would say the same thing. It's a long, tough battle to win an
unbelieving mate to the Lord. But if you're patient, you may see
results. *"Let us not grow weary while doing good, for in due season we
shall reap if we do not lose heart"* (Gal. 6:9 NKJV).

If you are married to an unbeliever, I want you to know that
God still loves you and cares for you. He can forgive your mistake. An X-rated marriage can bring you deep sorrow, sadness,
and even damnation of the soul. You can get so far from God

that it seems there's no way back. But God is always ready to welcome you back when you realize your mistake.

If you are contemplating marriage, be sure that you are getting married in three ways—in body, soul, and spirit. If you are married in all three ways, you are destined to have a happy marriage and a harmonious home.

Notes

1. Joan Winmill Brown, ed., *Day-by-Day with Billy Graham* (Minneapolis: World Wide Publications, 1976), May 27.

2. Dorothy C. Haskin, *God in My Home* (Anderson, Ind.: Portal Books, 1973), p. 12.

3. Ibid., p. 16.

5
Sex and Divorce

A crisis is a fork in the road—the couple turns either toward growth
or toward greater alienation.

—Howard J. Clinebell, Jr.[1]

Hardly any family in America has not been affected by
divorce. It is a problem that grips our society like an
octopus, strangling the very life out of our families. Even
Christian marriages are dissolving in divorce. In fact, statistics
show that one out of every three new marriages will end in
divorce. The problem has become a national menace.

Sex is very closely related to the divorce problem. Some
divorces result from sexual problems *per se;* in others, sexual
problems play a major role. I believe that a husband and wife
who completely share one another in the sexual relationship are
not likely to ask for a divorce. Their differences will be minimized, and any conflicts that do crop up can be discussed
openly and maturely. A healthy sexual relationship helps to
preserve a healthy marriage. By the same token, an unhealthy
sexual relationship does nothing to stop the disintegration of a
marriage—and may speed it up.

Divorce is an admission of failure. It means that a husband
and wife have failed to make the adjustments of marriage. (And
believe me, any marriage calls for adjustments!) Divorce means
that a man and woman have chosen to go their separate ways
instead of facing their problems head-on and trying to solve
them.

Immaturity

More often than not, divorce is a couple's surrender flag in the battle for maturity. It's true! Many married couples are immature from the start. They have no idea of the responsibilities marriage will entail; and when the responsibilities are dumped in their laps, they don't know what to do. Lester David tells of such a marriage:

> It was a beautiful wedding. True, the bride was only sixteen and the groom just nineteen, but they looked grown-up as they stood there, she so radiant, he so tall and protecting. No one could foretell that less than a year later this fine young man would say to this lovely girl, "I wish you were dead, because then I'd be free." Or that, later the same day, she would slash her wrists.[2]

How could such a couple stand a chance? They were scarcely adults in the physical sense, and certainly not in the spiritual, emotional, or intellectual sense. So they could not be sexually mature. They could not handle the stresses of living together day after day. They "got on each other's nerves," so their marriage became a curse instead of a blessing. Divorce was their way of withdrawing from the battlefield and nursing their wounds after her attempted suicide.

Casual Attitude

To some extent, divorce is caused by our society's casual attitude toward marriage. Many people think that marriage is simply a "convenient arrangement" that they can begin or terminate as they wish, much like signing a lease on an apartment. When you tire of the scenery, you simply pack your bags and leave. This kind of attitude shows a basic disregard for the spiritual side of marriage. Just after World War II, when the divorce rate in America was growing at an alarming rate, the sociologist Henry A. Bowman made this comment:

Marriages contracted with a civil ceremony are more likely to end in divorce than those contracted with a religious ceremony. This does not mean that an irreligious couple could increase the probability of their marital success by having a minister marry them. The type of ceremony is significant only to the degree to which it reflects the attitudes of the parties to the union.[3]

Dr. Bowman closed his remarks with this pointed note:

Those [marriages] more deeply affected by the decline of religious authority are less likely to succeed, or, at any rate, are more likely to divorce.[4]

Remember this is a sociologist speaking, not a minister. He says that couples who have little regard for their spiritual life are more likely to fail in marriage. They are more likely to break up. They lack a vital ingredient of the cement that should hold a marriage together, because they are married in only two ways—in body and soul, but not in spirit.

Remember that divorce is a breakdown of the moral and spiritual fibers that bind a couple to one another. If they cut the spiritual strands that God used to wed them as husband and wife, they will find little else in common. They will become disenchanted and dissatisfied with one another.

Misguided Ideals

Many couples wind up in divorce court because they had a misguided notion of marriage to begin with. A romanticized picture of what marriage would be like made them unable to cope with the harsh reality that they found the morning after their wedding day. Dr. Clyde M. Narramore tells of a young lady who brought a folder full of poetry to the editorial office of a large publishing house, hoping to have her work accepted for a leading magazine. When she finally was ushered into the editor's office, she gaily informed him that she had some love poems for his publication.

"Well, what is love? Tell me," the editor said.

The girl's eyes got misty and she heaved a happy sigh. "Love is filling one's soul with the beauties of the night," she murmured, "by the shimmering moonbeams on the lily pond when the fragrant lilies are in bloom, and..."

"Stop, stop, stop!" the editor exclaimed. "You are all wrong. I'll tell you what love is: It's getting up cheerfully out of a warm bed in the middle of the night to clean up after a sick child. That's real love."[5]

Thousands of young couples march down the wedding aisle with the sort of visions this girl described, only to find a couple of years later that the editor's picture of love was more realistic. It's an unpleasant surprise. And some marriages don't survive the shock.

Selfishness

Selfishness is another common cause of divorce. One or both partners begin to say, "I don't get the attention I'm supposed to get from this marriage," or "Why doesn't he (or she) give me the love I'm supposed to get?" Bickering starts. Husband and wife make subtle digs at each other. They use "hostile humor" to get revenge because they think they have been shortchanged. Just like two nations beginning a war, the minor skirmishes get worse; the mates attack each other more and more caustically. Soon the hatred boils over into divorce.

This is a symptom of the decadent society in America today. Our nation is becoming more unstable, which in turn causes individuals to become more unstable. Marriage partners begin growling and fussing at one another for any little excuse, and they are more prone to run to the divorce court for a final solution. But the courts do not solve the problem—they simply bring it to a conclusion. Lawyers specializing in divorce cases are becoming quite wealthy, and they don't do it by counseling their clients away from divorce! Judges render decisions that have no basis in the Bible or even in common human decency; they just follow precedent. They keep on repeating the mistakes of other judges before them. A judge in Ft. Lauderdale once told me, "You must realize, Mr. Sumrall, that there are times when the court is God."

"Sir, the court can never replace God," I replied.

You had better believe it! God is sovereign above all human beings, above all courts, above all cultures. Governments may rise and fall, but God remains the same. Our first loyalty is not to the law books of our land but to the Law Book of our God. When we obey His law, we will have no problem meeting the loose requirements of man's law.

God's Word on Divorce

Many marriage counselors—even some ministers—would say that divorce is the best solution for a serious marriage problem. But is that the advice God would give? What does He have to say about divorce? Jesus told the Pharisees:

21. Moses, because of the hardness of your hearts, permitted you to divorce your wives, but from the beginning it was not so. And I say to you, whoever divorces his wife, except for sexual immorality, and marries another, commits adultery; and whoever marries her who is divorced commits adultery. (Matt. 19:8–9 NKJV)[6]

A person could interpret this passage to suit his own preconceived ideas about divorce, but I think it speaks for itself Jesus is saying exactly what He means: *Divorce is wrong.*

Notice that He said, *"From the beginning it was not so."* God ordained marriage from the very beginning, but not divorce. Only later, when man and woman corrupted marriage with adultery and all sorts of perversion did God find it necessary to permit divorce. It was better to make a formal separation between a husband and wife than to let them display their corrupt relationship to the whole community. Read closely the specific law that God gave for divorce:

22. When a man hath taken a wife, and married her, and it come to pass that she find no favour in his eyes, because he hath found some uncleanness in her: then let him write her a bill of divorcement, and give it in her hand, and send her out of his house. And when she is departed out of his house, she may go and be another man's wife. (Deut. 24:1–2)[7]

God said that if a man found *"some uncleanness"* in his wife—if she were an adulteress—he did not have to live with her. He could give her a *"bill of divorcement"* and make a formal end to their marriage. That was the only reason for which God allowed divorce.

Yet the people of Israel took advantage of this statute. They began to grant divorces over very trivial things. The rulers took liberty with the phrase, *"she find no favor in his eyes,"* and interpreted it to mean any sort of dislike or displeasure the husband had with his wife. In fact, many Jewish women lived in terror of their husbands, always fearing that they would be divorced in a fit of anger, being left to fend for themselves. So God spoke through the prophet Malachi to clarify this law:

23. The LORD hath been witness between thee and the wife of thy youth, against whom thou hast dealt treacherously: yet is she thy companion, and the wife of thy covenant. And did not he make one?...And wherefore one? That he might seek a godly seed. Therefore take heed to your spirit, and let none deal treacherously against the wife of his youth. For the LORD, the God of Israel, saith that he hateth putting away: for one covereth violence with his garment, saith the LORD of hosts: therefore take heed to your spirit, that ye deal not treacherously. (Mal. 2:14–16)

God hates divorce! He is not pleased when a husband and wife sever themselves from one another. Frankly, I would do everything I could to avoid doing something that God hates; I would try to find some other way to rectify the situation. Divorce is the great "cover-up" of marital sins—yet God sees right through the cover! He knows what really happened, and He hates it.

God gave the Israelites strict rules to prevent any slaphappy use of divorce. For example, a bride's family was supposed to keep the bedding from a couple's wedding night. Then if the man falsely accused her of fornication, they could show the bloodstained evidence of her virginity:

> *24. If any man take a wife, and go in unto her, and hate her, and give occasions of speech against her, and bring up an evil name upon her, and say, I took this woman, and when I came to her, I found her not a maid: then shall the father of the damsel, and her mother, take and bring forth the tokens of the damsel's virginity unto the elders of the city in the gate: and the damsel's father shall say unto the elders, I gave my daughter unto this man to wife, and he hateth her; and, lo, he hath given occasions of speech against her,...and yet these are the tokens of my daughter's virginity. And they shall spread the cloth before the elders of the city. And the elders of that city shall take that man and chastise him; and they shall amerce him in an hundred shekels of silver, and give them unto the father of the damsel, because he hath brought up an evil name upon a virgin of Israel: and she shall be his wife; he may not put her away all his days.* (Deut. 22:13–19)

Some people get married and at first things seem to go well; but eventually they start blaming and accusing one another. They try to say their spouse has ruined the marriage by having sex with someone else. But God will expose the truth, either now or later.

I did say He was protective about sex, didn't I?

God also laid down strict rules to govern remarriage after divorce. You will recall, for example, that the passage from

Deuteronomy 24 allowed a divorced woman to remarry. But take a careful look at what God then says:

> *25. And if the latter husband hate her, and write her a bill of divorcement, and giveth it in her hand, and sendeth her out of his house...her former husband, which sent her away, may not take her again to be his wife, after that she is defiled; for that is abomination before the LORD.*
>
> *(Deut. 24:3–4)*

You see, God does not approve of any Hollywood-style marriages. Capriciously marrying one person after another is an "abomination" in His sight. So far as He is concerned, a divorced woman who has remarried is now "defiled" unto her former husband, and her first husband would corrupt himself by marrying her again.

Even when God permitted divorce, He regulated it to make sure that no one used divorce as an excuse for promiscuity.

Better Solutions

If you are having problems with your marriage, consider your alternatives besides divorce. By all means, seek the advice of a capable Christian counselor. Your pastor may be able to do this; if not, he should refer you to someone who can. But the first step in dealing with your problem is being able to talk about it, and a good counselor can help you do that.

If you have children, your counselor might even recommend family counseling; in other words, he may want to bring the whole family together in his office to talk about your problem. You may not want to do that in order to protect your children from the hurts of your marriage. But whether you like it or not, the children are a part of the hurting, and it's best to let them be a part of the healing. The noted family counselor Virginia Satir says:

> Once the therapist convinces the husband that he is essential to the therapy process, and that no one else can speak for

him or take his place in therapy *or* in family life, he readily enters in. The wife (in her role as mother) may initiate family therapy, but once therapy is underway, the husband becomes as involved as she does. Family therapy seems to make sense to the whole family. Husband and wife say: "Now, at last, we are together and can get to the bottom of this."[8]

Both of you need to face your problem and admit that it is a problem. Your family needs to face it. In fact, you may find that your family grows stronger as you sit down together and talk through your marital trouble.

Have a forgiving spirit toward one another. Don't be afraid to reconsider what you've done and say, "You know, I was wrong. I am sorry." This kind of spirit would eliminate the vast majority of all divorces. But an obstinate, unforgiving spirit continues to drag old problems up out of the cellar and hurl them at everyone else. The result is broken hearts and broken homes. Jesus is our example of forgiveness; if we imitate His spirit of love and understanding toward our mates, we will bring harmony back to the most disharmonious situations.

Speaking of forgiveness—notice that adultery can be forgiven, just like any other sin. Some Christians think that God requires divorce for adultery, even if the sinful mate repents of what he or she has done. But look back at what He said. He doesn't require divorce for adultery; He allows it. He then says that He hates divorce, period.

It is far better to forgive than to punish a person forever. If you hold a grudge against your mate, you inject poison into your own veins. You make yourself a bitter person. You cause yourself as much suffering as your mate—often more. But if you extend the hand of love to your mate, you will find your love returned. You will grow stronger and more mature as a Christian. Dr. G. Curtis Jones tells of such a case:

> I once served a church where the chief custodian had been on the staff for fifty years. During this time he had serious domestic troubles. His wife left him. Years passed. Eventually she asked to return. This splendid Christian took her back,

saying, "She is my wife and the mother of my son." Such forgiveness is reminiscent of Hosea, who received again his wife after her unfaithfulness. Little wonder that the congregation served by this man erected a plaque to his memory.[9]

If your mate commits adultery, I urge you to read the book of Hosea and learn what forgiveness really means. Think about the love Hosea had for his wife, who kept sliding back into promiscuity. The Law allowed him to divorce her, and he certainly would have felt justified in doing so. But his love won out. He forgave her and brought her back home. Together they reestablished their family.

I want your home to be beautiful. I want Jesus to bless your marriage. If you are having a marital problem, go to the Bible together and see what God says about it. Then pray together and let the Spirit of the Lord fill you anew. Let His forgiveness flow into your hearts. Then talk with each other about your problem. Take the first step to heal the wounds in your relationship by saying, "I'm sorry, Honey. I've been wrong."

"But, Dr. Sumrall," you say, "I haven't been wrong!"

Friend, it takes two people to disagree. It takes two to have discord. It takes two to break up a marriage. So no matter whether you were "right" or "wrong" about the issue that started your trouble, you were wrong to let it develop into trouble. Admit that. Ask for your mate's forgiveness. Then God can begin bringing you back together.

Notes

1. Howard J. Clinebell, Jr., *Growth Counseling for Marriage Enrichment* (Philadelphia: Fortress Press, 1975), p. 65.

2. Lester David, "Matrimony Is Not for Children," *How to Live with Life* (Pleasantville, N.Y.: Reader's Digest Association, 1965), p. 44.

3. Henry A. Bowman, *Marriage for Moderns* (New York: McGraw-Hill, 1954), p. 502.

4. Ibid., p. 502.

5. Clyde M. Narramore, *This Way to Happiness* (Grand Rapids, Mich.: Zondervan, 1969), p. 22.

6. Apparently the last portion of this text refers to a woman who was divorced for reasons other than adultery. That is to say, if a man marries a woman divorced for an illegitimate reason, he is committing adultery.

7. The last phrase of this passage does not condone adultery, because God does not condone it. The intent, I assume, is to allow a divorced adulteress who has *repented* to remarry.

8. Virginia Satir, *Conjoint Family Therapy,* rev. ed. (Palo Alto, Calif.: Science and Behavior Books, Inc., 1967), p. 5.

9. G. Curtis Jones, *A Man and His Religion* (St. Louis: Bethany, 1967), p. 65.

6
Twenty Laws against Incest

To an age which condones increasingly the exploitation of human
beings in the game of sex, [God's Word] speaks of the divine order
among men, requiring recognition of the sanctity of marriage. People
are not simply bodies to be played with.

—Jack Ford[1]

The *Phil Donahue Show* recently featured a young woman whose stepfather had sexual relations with her many times while she was a teenager. This bond of incest nearly destroyed her, emotionally and spiritually. Her stepfather repented of what he had done, and through the help of experienced counselors the young woman was able to regain her sense of dignity and self-respect.

"What I did was a terrible thing," the stepfather said. "But I hope that our telling about it will help some other family avoid this problem."

Incest is one of the "secret sins" that people seldom discuss. It is a vile sin. It destroys the family as a unit and individuals within that family. But worst of all, it offends God, who created sex for marriage.

God ordained that a man and woman who have the same parents or who are closely related by blood should not cohabit. They should not share sexual intimacy. They should not produce offspring. A person might think that God would avoid such a delicate topic, but the Bible is loaded with God's pronouncements on incest. In fact, the Bible repeats His law against incest at least twenty times, and in two different books of the Old Testament. Read God's commandment against incest and the rationale behind it:

> 26. *None of you shall approach to any that is near of kin to him, to uncover their nakedness: I am the* LORD.
>
> (Lev. 18:6)

Scripture uses the phrase *"to uncover their nakedness"* as a tactful way of referring to sexual intercourse. God specifically says that a person should not have intercourse with someone who is *"near of kin."* Why? Because *"I am the* LORD*"*—in other words, it's so, simply because He has the authority to say so. Now notice the specific cases of incest that God forbids:

> 27. *The nakedness of thy father, or the nakedness of thy mother, shalt thou not uncover: she is thy mother; thou shalt not uncover her nakedness. The nakedness of thy father's wife shalt thou not uncover: it is thy father's nakedness.*　　　　　　　　　　　(Lev. 18:7–8)

To put it plainly, God says that a girl should not have sexual relations with her father and a boy should not have sexual relations with his mother.

"But, Brother Sumrall," someone is likely to say, "That just doesn't happen anymore!"

As a pastor, I can tell you that it happens all the time. I constantly have people coming into my office who are caught up in incest. For example, I've counseled with a young man who ran away from home because his mother insisted on having intercourse with him. The first time he ever had sexual relations with a woman was when she seduced him into her bed, and she insisted that she "teach" him the way to have sexual pleasure. Anytime she wished, she forced him into bed with her by threatening to tell his father. Don't say that God is just talking into the wind when He talks about incest; He is talking to the homes of America. He forbids anyone to defile the marriage of mother and father.

28. The nakedness of thy sister, the daughter of thy father, or daughter of thy mother, whether she be born at home, or born abroad, even their nakedness thou shalt not uncover. (Lev. 18:9)

29. The nakedness of thy son's daughter, or of thy daughter's daughter, even their nakedness thou shalt not uncover: for theirs is thine own nakedness. (Lev. 18:10)

30. The nakedness of thy father's wife's daughter, begotten of thy father, she is thy sister, thou shalt not uncover her nakedness. (Lev. 18:11)

31. Thou shalt not uncover the nakedness of thy father's sister: she is thy father's near kinswoman. Thou shalt not uncover the nakedness of thy mother's sister; for she is thy mother's near kinswoman. Thou shalt not uncover the nakedness of thy father's brother, thou shalt not approach to his wife: she is thine aunt. (Lev. 18:12–14)

32. Thou shalt not uncover the nakedness of thy daughter in law: she is thy son's wife; thou shalt not uncover her nakedness. (Lev. 18:15)

33. Thou shalt not uncover the nakedness of thy brother's wife: it is thy brother's nakedness. (Lev. 18:16)

34. Thou shalt not uncover the nakedness of a woman and her daughter, neither shalt thou take her son's daughter, or her daughter's daughter, to uncover her nakedness; for they are her near kinswomen: it is wickedness. Neither shalt thou take a wife to her sister, to vex her, to uncover her nakedness, beside the other in her life time.
(Lev. 18:17–18)

This last law concerns incest in second marriages—incest with stepchildren or other relatives of a second wife. This is perhaps the most common form of incest in America today. With the great number of divorces and remarriages now occurring, men and women are being thrown into intimate contact with new families, and they seem to feel less guilt about having illicit sex with members of these families.

Recently a woman came to my office for counseling about such a problem. She was married and had two fine children, but she was haunted by the guilt of an incestuous relationship she had had with her stepfather.

When her natural father died, her mother remarried. One day the stepfather sent her mother out to do some shopping, and used the occasion to lure the girl into bed. She was only thirteen at the time. For the next five years, the stepfather kept on arranging these afternoon rendezvous. He said that if she told her mother, he would put the girl out of their house and she would "starve to death." She escaped from that situation only when she got married. But even now the memory of that affair makes her seethe with anger.

You know, sin is a terrible thing! Its effects linger on for years. It leaves scars that take a long time to heal.

35. And the man that lieth with his father's wife hath uncovered his father's nakedness: both of them shall surely be put to death; their blood shall be upon them.
(Lev. 20:11)

36. And if a man lie with his daughter in law, both of them shall surely be put to death: they have wrought confusion; their blood shall be upon them.   *(Lev. 20:12)*

37. And if a man take a wife and her mother, it is wickedness: they shall be burnt with fire, both he and they; that there be no wickedness among you.
(Lev. 20:14)

38. And if a man shall take his sister, his father's daughter, or his mother's daughter, and see her nakedness, and she see his nakedness; it is a wicked thing; and they shall be cut off in the sight of their people: he hath uncovered his sister's nakedness; he shall bear his iniquity. (Lev. 20:17)

These laws spell out the penalties for incest. While the laws of chapter 18 simply say that God forbids incest, chapter 20 shows us the consequences of breaking His Word. Obviously, incest was a serious matter. It was punishable in Old Testament times by death—even the torturous death of being burned alive.

But some of God's laws suggest a spiritual penalty for this kind of perversion. We caught a glimpse of that in verse 17, when God said that a man who commits incest with his sister will *"bear his iniquity."* Read on and it becomes clearer that incest brings a spiritual as well as a physical punishment:

39. And thou shalt not uncover the nakedness of thy mother's sister, nor of thy father's sister: for he uncovereth his near kin: they shall bear their iniquity. And if a man shall lie with his uncle's wife, he hath uncovered his uncle's nakedness: they shall bear their sin; they shall die childless.   (Lev. 20:19–20)

40. And if a man shall take his brother's wife, it is an unclean thing: he hath uncovered his brother's nakedness; they shall be childless.   (Lev. 20:21)

Not only would the community punish people guilty of incest, but God would punish them by leaving them childless. Incest was such an abomination in His sight that He refused to grant even the normal biological results of intercourse. He would not countenance bringing children into the world under those circumstances.

Unfortunately, that is not true today. Children sometimes are born to incestuous couples. I don't know why God allows this now; perhaps it is because we live in a new era of grace, when everyone has the opportunity to know His law. Perhaps He expects us to be more responsible than the children of Israel were, so He lets us live with the results of our sin. Whatever the reason, I think you would agree that incest brings great spiritual harm as well as emotional harm to the people who are involved.

The book of Deuteronomy is a review and summation of the law that God gave His people at Mount Sinai. This is how the book got its present name, "Deuteronomy" (Greek, "second law"). As we read God's laws against incest in Deuteronomy, we find that the laws of Leviticus have been expanded and clarified at some points:

41. A man shall not take his father's wife, nor discover his father's skirt. (Deut. 22:30)

42. Cursed be he that setteth light by his father or his mother. And all the people shall say, Amen.
(Deut. 27:16)

43. Cursed be he that lieth with his father's wife; because he uncovereth his father's skirt. And all the people shall say, Amen. (Deut. 27:20)

44. Cursed be he that lieth with his sister, the daughter of his father, or the daughter of his mother. And all the people shall say, Amen. (Deut. 27:22)

45. Cursed be he that lieth with his mother in law. And all the people shall say, Amen. (Deut. 27:23)

The first of these laws simply declares that incest is wrong—emphasizing once again that it is wrong just because God says so. But the next four laws put incest in a community perspective. Each one says that the people of Israel were to condemn incest as being *"cursed"*; they were supposed to add their *"amen"* to the priest's pronouncement of the curse. They were responsible for enforcing God's law. The same is true today; God expects us to enforce His laws of sexual morality and condemn any uncleanness that creeps into our society. This is one reason why I felt such a burden to write this book!

Bible Case Histories

The Bible gives us some case histories of incest, real-life examples of what happened when people ignored God's law. We won't dwell on these long. But I think we should examine how God's laws on incest can protect us from some very foolish and destructive mistakes.

Genesis 35 records a case of incest among the twelve sons of Jacob. Notice what happened:

> *And it came to pass, when Israel [Jacob] dwelt in that land, that Reuben went and lay with Bilhah his father's concubine: and Israel heard it.* (Gen. 35:22)

We read nothing more about this incident until several years later, as Jacob lay on his deathbed. He gathered his twelve sons around him and began to give them his final blessing, Reuben being the first:

> *Reuben, thou art my firstborn, my might, and the beginning of my strength, the excellency of dignity, and the excellency of power: unstable as water, thou shalt not excel; because thou wentest up to thy father's bed; then defiledst thou it: he went up to my couch.* (Gen. 49:3–4)

Can you imagine the shame Reuben must have felt? He was the firstborn son, the legal heir of Jacob's finest possessions; yet Jacob could not bless him because of his incest. Reuben's father revealed his sin in front of his brothers. He said, *"He went up to my couch."* Things probably got so quiet you could hear a pin drop! The brothers were astonished to hear about the crime, and Reuben himself was shamed into silence.

But this wasn't the end of it. Generations later, a Jewish chronicler put this sad note in the record:

Now the sons of Reuben the firstborn of Israel, (for he was the first-born; but, forasmuch as he defiled his father's bed, his birthright was given unto the sons of Joseph the son of Israel: and the genealogy is not to be reckoned after the birthright.) (1 Chron. 5:1)

Reuben lost his birthright. He lost his rightful inheritance because he had an affair with his father's concubine. So the chronicler begged our indulgence to list Reuben's descendants. "After all," he says, "I have to do it because the genealogy is reckoned according to the firstborn, not according to the birthright." Reuben put a blight on his family—a blight on history itself—by indulging himself in an impulsive fling with his father's mate.

Another case of incest is recorded in 2 Samuel 16. This occurred in the family of David, the greatest king of Israel:

Then said Absalom to Ahithophel, Give counsel among you what we shall do. And Ahithophel said unto Absalom, Go in unto thy father's concubines, which he hath left to keep the house; and all Israel shall hear that thou art abhorred of thy father: then shall the hands of all that are with thee be strong. So they spread Absalom a tent upon the top of the house; and Absalom went in unto his father's concubines in the sight of all Israel. (2 Sam. 16:20–22)

Absalom wanted to start a rebellion against his father, so he asked the king's counselor (who was plotting with him) how to get the people stirred up. "That's simple," the counselor said, "just pitch a tent on top of your father's house, where everyone can see you, and have sex with all of his mistresses!"

So Absalom took the advice. He committed incest with his father's women. And the nation erupted into a vicious civil war that ended only with Absalom's death. Actually, this was a ful-fillment of prophecy. When King David had conspired to get the wife of Uriah the Hittite, the prophet Nathan confronted him with these words:

Thus saith the LORD, *Behold, I will raise up evil against thee out of thine own house, and I will take thy wives before thine eyes, and give them unto thy neighbour, and he shall lie with thy wives in the sight of this sun.* (2 Sam. 12:11)

When sin comes back to you, it comes back with a vengeance. No one learned this lesson more painfully than David.

At least one case of incest is recorded in the New Testament. In fact, Paul devoted an entire chapter of his first letter to the Corinthians to this problem. He wrote,

It is actually reported that there is sexual immorality among you, and such sexual immorality as is not even named among the Gentiles; that a man has his father's wife!...Deliver such a one to Satan for the destruction of the flesh, that his spirit may be saved in the day of the Lord Jesus. (1 Cor. 5:1, 5 NKJV)

The man committing incest was a Christian. We know this because Paul mentions him again in 2 Corinthians 2 and calls him a "brother." Yet the man was living in sin with his father's wife, and the church did nothing to correct it. So Paul rebuked them. He said, *"Do you not know that a little leaven leavens the whole lump?"* (1 Cor. 5:6 NKJV). In other words, if they let one man live in incest, they would soon have other Christians living in adultery or homosexuality or Christian girls walking the streets as prostitutes. They had to get rid of the sin. So Paul told them to expel the man from their fellowship. It was better to make him live outside the church without all the physical benefits that the first-century church provided, and hope that he would realize his sin and repent.

In fact, that's what happened. The church put him out. And apparently the man repented, for in Paul's next letter he said,

This punishment which was inflicted by the majority is sufficient for such a man, so that, on the contrary, you ought rather to forgive and comfort him, lest perhaps such a one be swallowed up with too much sorrow. (2 Cor. 2:6–7 NKJV)

God's forgiveness is that complete: He can forgive any sexual sin, even incest, if a person repents of it. God says that we are not to pervert the purpose of sex by having intercourse with our parents, our children, or other next of kin. Sex is not just another family entertainment. It is a holy and wholesome thing that ought to be respected and used reverently.

Notes

1. Jack Ford, "The Book of Deuteronomy," *Beacon Bible Commentary,* vol. 1, ed. A. F. Harper (Kansas City: Beacon Hill, 1969), p. 578.

7
Sexual Perversion Bears a Curse

Some people are building chicken coops when they ought to be erecting mansions. Remember you will have to live in what you build. You can build a chicken coop and be cooped up all your life, or you can build a mansion and enjoy the freedom of its comforts.

—Carl C. Williams[1]

No person has ever been born a homosexual. Yet thousands of people in our country believe they are different by design. They believe there is some natural alteration in their body chemistry that draws them to persons of the same sex, and they say they ought to have a free and open homosexual relationship. But God's Word says they are wrong. A homosexual becomes so through lust, which leads to experimentation, or through the pressure of homosexual or bisexual friends or relatives. It is not what God intended.

Before the slogans of "gay rights" became so popular, homosexual acts were called "sodomy." That term comes from the city of Sodom, which the Bible describes as one of the most wicked cities on the face of the earth. Genesis 19 tells how God sent two angels to visit Lot in that city. As they sat around their evening meal, the men of Sodom pounded on the door and demanded that Lot send his visitors out so they could have sexual relations with them. Lot begged the men to take his daughters instead. But the mob was intent upon having the men. While they argued about it, the angels struck the crowd blind. Then they warned

Lot to gather his family and flee from the city, saying that God had sent them to destroy it because of its great sinfulness.

This account proves that sexual perversion did not begin in the twentieth century; it has been with us ever since the Fall of Adam and Eve. But it is just as foul and damnable today as it was in the days of Sodom.

God's Word for "Gays"

God has given us a very explicit ruling on homosexuality. Read what His Word says:

> *46. Thou shalt not lie with mankind, as with womankind: it is abomination....Defile not ye yourselves in any of these things: for in all these the nations are defiled which I cast out before you: and the land is defiled: therefore I do visit the iniquity thereof upon it, and the land itself vomiteth out her inhabitants.* (Lev. 18:22, 24–25)

God wiped out entire nations because they practiced homosexuality. Did you know that was in the Bible? It's a terrible thing to think about.

Amidst all the clamor for "gay rights," we ought to pay careful attention to what God says about homosexuality. God takes this problem seriously, and He deals with it firmly. He classes homosexuality among the most vile sins of humankind.

> *47. For even their women exchanged the natural use [of sex] for what is against nature. Likewise also the men, leaving the natural use of the woman, burned in their lust for one another, men with men committing what is shameful, and receiving in themselves the penalty of their error which was due....those who practice such things are deserving of death.* (Rom. 1:26–27,32 NKJV)

Would God say this about homosexuals if some people were *born* this way? I think not. He is trying to protect us from unnatural passions. Homosexuality is just as perverse as prostitution; both warp the purpose God intended for sex. Read what He says:

> *48. There shall be no whore of the daughters of Israel, nor a sodomite of the sons of Israel.*   *(Deut. 23:17)*

God uses strong language to denounce the perversion of sex. As we have seen so many times before, God is very protective of sex. He leaves no room for behavior that is motivated by twisted lust.

I have had enough face-to-face encounters with homosexuals to know what a sad and desperate life they lead. While I was walking through the streets of Jerusalem, for example, I was approached by several young boys offering to have sexual relations with me. These were very young boys—about ten years old. I can't tell you how much this grieved my heart. But I put my arm around the shoulders of each little boy and said, "Son, I don't know what kind of men you've met before, but I am a godly man, and I want you to know that what you're doing is wrong. It is wrong to offer to do such a thing—it is wicked. You go right home and tell your parents what you've been doing, and ask God to forgive you for this."

This kind of thing has gone on for centuries, and is now common in America. Homosexuality is drawing thousands of men and women into its spell.

> *49. Do you not know that the unrighteous will not inherit the kingdom of God? Do not be deceived. Neither fornicators, nor idolaters, nor adulterers, nor homosexuals, nor sodomites, nor thieves, nor covetous, nor drunkards, nor revilers, nor extortioners will inherit the kingdom of God.*   *(1 Cor. 6:9–10 NKJV)*

This is the worst thing about homosexuality—the spiritual result. Granted, it degrades the individual and distorts his moral values. Sex becomes a flippant kind of physical recreation that can be enjoyed anytime, anywhere, with anybody. These results are bad enough. But the clincher is what homosexuality does to the soul of a person, leading him or her into gross sin.

The Bible says that homosexuality ranks beside drunkenness, extortion, and idolatry as a despicable form of ungodliness. It declares that a homosexual cannot inherit the kingdom of God, anymore than a common thief could. If you think God is being too harsh at this point, remember the basic purposes of sex:

—*To bring children into the world.* Homosexuals and lesbians cannot fulfill God's first commandment regarding sex (Gen. 1:28). They cannot *"replenish the earth"* through their perverse cavorting. In fact, if everyone thought homosexuality was the ideal model for sex life, humanity would die out in one generation.

—*To give pleasure to married partners.* Some homosexuals try to circumvent this by staging "gay marriages"—actually getting married to their sexual partners. But God still says it is sinful for two people of the same sex to "make love" to one another (Lev. 18:22), and the sanction of an attorney or justice of the peace doesn't make it less wrong.

—*To symbolize Christ's relationship with His church* (Eph. 5:23–25). In this respect, homosexuality is an outright blasphemy against God. It suggests, in effect, that Christ has no love for His church or that the church has no need for Christ. Either statement is a lie. A homosexual is perverting the truth of God as well as perverting sex, the gift of God. This sin must be named for what it really is.

Yet even the sin of homosexuality can be forgiven. Leaders of the "gay rights" movement insist that homosexuality is something that a person must live with forever; but God doesn't say that. He says, *"Come now, and let us reason together...though your sins be as scarlet, they shall be as white as snow; though they be red like crimson, they shall be as wool"* (Isa. 1:18). God is ready to forgive any sin, no matter how vile and offensive it is, as soon as we confess our sin to Him. He loves us that much. One of my favorite verses of the Bible says, *"If we confess our sins, he is faithful and just to forgive us our sins, and to cleanse us from all unrighteousness"* (1 John 1:9). It's true! When we confess our sins to the Lord, He will forgive us and wash all the sin out of our lives—even the sin of homosexuality.

Don't be fooled into thinking that homosexuality is something in your genes, something that can't be changed. It is a sin. And thank God, sin can be wiped out when we confess it to Him.

Prostitution

I have focused a lot of attention on the perversion of homosexuality simply because God's Word is being challenged so boldly on that point these days. But we ought not to overlook other forms of sexual perversion that are just as sinful and devastating. One of these is prostitution.

Prostitution is the selling of one's sexual favors. It is the merchandising of sex—having intercourse with someone for money or some other privilege. There are both female and male prostitutes, and they operate in all levels of society. A federal judge was recently indicted on charges of taking sexual favors from female defendants. A wealthy prostitute in Washington, D.C., named several high-ranking politicians as her customers in a scandal just a few years ago. Many movie stars and corporation executives keep their prostitutes in well-heeled comfort, letting them live in expensive apartments and be chauffeured about town in plush limousines. Prostitution is not just a Skid Row enterprise anymore. One sociologist has made this cold assessment of the problem:

> Prostitution has perdured [sic] in all civilizations; indeed, few institutions have proven as hardy. The inevitable conditions of social life unfailingly produce the supply to meet the ever-present demand.[2]

He goes on to recommend that, since prostitution is so widespread, we should abolish our laws against it! While I don't agree with his solution, he has certainly appraised the problem accurately. Since Adam and Eve left the Garden of Eden, there have always been some people desperate enough to sell their bodies on the open market. Today prostitution has a more professional look, but its motive is still the same. Men and women still enter prostitution because of financial problems, family pressures, or some other breakdown of normal life. Seldom does a person become a prostitute on a whim. It is a deliberate, often unwilling, step that a person takes. But once a prostitute has started to sell sex, it becomes an accepted way of life; the cycle is hard to break. What does God say about this problem?

> 50. *Do not prostitute thy daughter, to cause her to be a whore; lest the land fall to whoredom, and the land become full of wickedness.*   *(Lev. 19:29)*

God calls prostitution "wickedness." He does not allow us to send our daughters into prostitution because it is a "wicked" thing to do. Also, the book of Proverbs gives very strict warnings to any man who feels tempted to patronize a prostitute:

> 51. *Let not thine heart decline to her ways, go not astray in her paths. For she hath cast down many wounded: yea, many strong men have been slain by her. Her house is the way to hell, going down to the chambers of death.*
> *(Prov. 7:25–27)*

That's putting it bluntly, isn't it? God says that the prostitute will take you to hell; she will destroy the soul as well as the body. The greatest hazard in visiting a prostitute is not the disease you might contract (although that certainly is a hazard); the greatest danger is that you will lose your soul by corrupting yourself with such a person.

Again, God is ready to forgive a prostitute who repents. He loves the prostitute, and He is ready to cleanse him or her of all the guilt and suffering this sin has created.

Remember the sinful woman who came and knelt at Jesus' feet, washing them with her tears? The people around Jesus criticized Him for associating with her. But He said, *"Her sins, which are many, are forgiven, for she loved much; but he who is forgiven little, loves little"* (Luke 7:47 RSV). Many times a person who has been deep in sin, like the prostitute, becomes one of the most radiant Christians because Christ has forgiven so much. God's promise is sure. He will forgive anyone who is truly sorry for the past. (See Colossians 2:13–14.)

Bestiality

Now we look at something that will really shock you. Forgive me for even mentioning it, because it is repulsive; but deal with it we must, because God deals with it in His Word.

I am talking about bestiality—having sexual relations with animals. This perversion of sex was much more common in the ancient world than it is today, but some people still practice it. Pornographic movies and magazines use scenes of bestiality for "shock value," and some people decide to experiment with it. God speaks very frankly about this practice:

52. Neither shalt thou lie with any beast to defile thyself therewith: neither shall any woman stand before a beast to lie down thereto: it is confusion. (Lev. 18:23)

And if a woman approach unto any beast, and lie down thereto, thou shalt kill the woman, and the beast: they shall surely be put to death; their blood shall be upon them. (Lev. 20:16)

Bestiality is an unspeakable perversion of the divine gift of sex. I can hardly find words to express how sickening this practice is to any decent-minded person, much less to Almighty

God. Yet some people do it. Once again we have an example of how sex is cheapened by the carnal mind, how it is considered a plaything for the idle. Bestiality proves how far the ungodly mind will descend into degradation.

The Freedom and the Curse

When God gave us sex, He gave us the freedom to choose how we would use it. His guidelines are here before us, but He will not force us to follow them. We must decide on our own.

> God cannot deny man the right to do wrong. Such inhibitions would reduce man to the level of animals or insects. The same freedom of choice which permits a man to be noble and compassionate also allows him to be greedy and hateful.[3]

This freedom is the most exhilarating aspect of being a man or woman. A sense of dignity is created that no other creature can know. But when we use that gift to deny the Giver, we have acted very foolishly indeed. We bring upon ourselves the curse of the consequences.

Perhaps you have been caught up in some type of perversion. Perhaps you have fallen prey to the spirit of lust, which leads to frustration, condemnation, depression, and finally death. If so, I have good news for you—Christ can set you free from it. I have prayed for hundreds of people to be delivered from homosexuality, and God has answered in marvelous ways.

Regardless of how faithful you have been to the church, if you are perverting sex you will never enter the kingdom of heaven. That's what God says. Sexual perversion is an insult to God.

But God forgives a sinner who repents. I have seen homosexuals give their lives to the Lord and right away they begin to change; their faces look different and their entire beings take on a different countenance. Men become more masculine and women become more feminine. This is what God's forgiveness can do.

If you have this kind of problem in your family, I urge you to use the Bible as your standard. Find God's final word on sex and sexual perversion, and cast out the perversion in Jesus' holy name.

Notes

1. Carl C. Williams, *Chicken Coops or Sky Scrapers?* (Anderson, Ind.: Warner, 1973), p. 12.

2. Sanford H. Kadish, "The Crisis of Overcriminalization," *Crime, Criminology, and Contemporary Society*, ed. Richard D. Knudten (Homewood, Ill.: The Dorsey Press, 1970), p. 8.

3. Mort Crim, *Like It Is!* (Anderson, Ind.: Portal Books, 1972), p. 32.

8
The Deceptions of Sex

Joy is often confused with simple pleasure. The joy of which
the Bible speaks fills one from the inside out.

—Cyvette Guerra[1]

S atan can fool you into thinking that sex is the answer to
all your problems, but this is a delusion. In fact, it can be
another one of your problems! God wants men and women
to live together and love together in the context of marriage.
Since the beginning of time, though, Satan has tried to deceive
us into using sex for illicit reasons. He has tried to turn one of
Gods greatest gifts to his own advantage. Unfortunately, he has
often succeeded.

People who come to me for counseling say, "I wanted a little
extra joy, a little extra excitement from sex. Instead it turned out
to be a nightmare." They are talking about their illicit use of
sex, their desire to try something different from what God had
intended.

Satan has deceived men and women about sex in many ways.
Let us examine some of his favorite deceptions.

Sex Is Not a God

In some parts of the world, sex is worshipped. Two thousand
years ago, for example, the people of Ephesus worshipped a sex
goddess called Diana who was supposed to have twelve breasts.
(See Acts 19.) I have visited the ruins of Diana's temple. Beside

the temple was a den of prostitutes; men who came to the temple had sexual relations with the prostitutes as part of their "worship."

In India, I have seen temples to the sex goddess Cali. (The city of Calcutta is named after her.) Worshippers will slit the throat of a goat and let its blood run under the idol of Cali, so that she will allow a woman to conceive a child. They believe that Cali controls the use of sex.

In their own way, many Americans also worship sex. They wear clothing that accentuates their sex organs and arouses the lust of the opposite sex. They read salacious magazines and attend X-rated movies to indulge their restless appetite for stimulation. Women undergo surgery to enlarge their breasts, while men take hormone shots to boost their virility. It's all done in the name of the great god Sex.

Sex is not a god. Sex is a servant of mankind. God designed sex to undergird the unity and happiness of the home, to provide a new generation of men and women. When we are dead and gone, our children and grandchildren will follow us in the long procession of God's people; the gift of sex, insures that the procession will continue.

Sex is a beautiful and holy gift, but it is not to be worshipped.

Perversion Brings No Satisfaction

Satan tricks many people into thinking that sexual perversion will make them happy. Normal sexual relations do not satisfy them, so they try all sorts of perverted lifestyles in an effort to find what's "right for me."

Entire books have been devoted to the topic of how to have a homosexual affair, how to lure a married man into bed with you, how to practice good hygiene as a prostitute, and so on. These filthy books fill their readers' minds with perverse ideas they would not have gotten otherwise; it is a tragic error even to read them. A healthy, godly person doesn't gain anything from reading literature about abnormal, perverted sex. There is little value in sex manuals that teach all sorts of strange, exotic positions for intercourse. I firmly believe that marriage partners can teach one another much more than they can ever learn from a book. Professor Andrew M. Greeley of the University of Arizona recently said:

> Sophisticated lovers know that in the bedroom or anywhere else gentleness has incredible erotic power. A kiss at the nape of the neck, a contact of two hands, fingers brushing lightly and quickly...all of these subtle actions have much more powerful erotic impact than do the acrobatics and gymnastics of the sex manuals performed without tenderness. If what happens in the marriage bed is not pervaded by gentleness, sexual relations are likely to be both unsatisfying and infrequent.[2]

Sexual perversion and sexual experimentation cannot take the place of honest, open sexual relations between husband and wife. Sex was created for marriage, and that is where it gives the greatest fulfillment.

We also need to keep these things in proper spiritual perspective. God tells us that:

53. Angels who did not keep their proper domain, but left their own abode, He has reserved in everlasting chains under darkness for the judgment of the great day; as Sodom and Gomorrah,...having given themselves over to sexual immorality and gone after strange flesh, are set forth as an example, suffering the vengeance of eternal fire. (Jude 6–7 NKJV)

People who pervert sex to "go after strange flesh" are destined to die. God places them in the same pit with the rebellious angels who defied His will in heaven. That's what sexual perversion is—a defiance of God's will. The people of Sodom and Gomorrah were deceived into thinking that prostitution, homosexuality, bestiality, and other perversions were more fun than sexual relations in marriage. But they were destroyed for it! They will be sent to hell for what they did.

You may say, "I don't believe in hell." But that makes no difference. You may not believe the sun will rise tomorrow, but that won't stop it from happening. What you believe has nothing to do with God's enforcing His will. The strands of history are running forward to their inevitable conclusion, and the end will bring judgment upon those who have profaned God's gift of sex.

Multiple Mating

Satan has deceived many people into thinking that they will enjoy sex more if they have sexual relations with several people. This might be called "multiple mating." We see it expressed in the prostitution, promiscuity, and adultery that stains every level of our society.

In biblical times, the most common form of multiple mating was polygamy—the practice of marrying more than one wife. It was permitted in the Old Testament world; in fact, custom dictated that a wealthy man should have many wives. The first recorded polygamist in the Bible was Lamech (see Genesis 4:23–25); he had two wives. Some men, such as King Solomon, had hundreds of wives. As a missionary in Hong Kong and Manila, I met quite a few polygamous couples. Not one of them was happy. I believe their problems were typical of those anyone in the United States encounters in multiple mating, even though it's practiced differently here.

No woman wants to receive half a man's love and no man wants to receive half of hers. True love—especially when it is expressed sexually—is a total giving of oneself to someone else. It isn't something that gets more enjoyable as you "spread it around."

Yet God's Word says that we can expect more multiple mating as we approach the final judgment. Read what He says through the prophet Isaiah:

54. And in that day seven women shall take hold of one man, saying, We will eat our own bread, and wear our own apparel: only let us be called by thy name, to take away our reproach.   *(Isa. 4:1)*

As we approach the end of time, people will become more desperate for sexual fulfillment. During the great Tribulation, which will precede the Lord's return, wars and famine will ravage the male population. There will be fewer men to act as fathers. So several women will go to a man and say, "Give us children. You don't have to support us, you don't even have to love us—just help us conceive children. We can't bear the shame of being barren." They will try multiple mating, and they will find sex to be less fulfilling than ever. That's what God predicts.

A Price to Pay

Have you ever seen people play "the old shell game"? It seems very simple. Someone places a pea under one of three walnut shells, then shuffles the shells back and forth across the tabletop. The object is to guess which shell has the pea under it. But no one can. The operator's hand is "quicker than the eye," and he can trick you into thinking the pea is where it isn't.

That's exactly what Satan tries to do with sex. He tries to trick us into thinking that real joy and satisfaction are found in lust, carnality, and perversion. But it just isn't true. These are deviations from the sex life God intended us to have; they will bring us nothing but deformed bodies, feeble minds, unsatisfied desires, and slavery to sin.

Don't get caught in Satan's "shell game." Listen to what God tells you about sex, and you will find the satisfaction you long for.

Notes

1. Cyvette Guerra, *The Joy Robbers* (Nashville: Impact, 1979), p. 10.

2. Andrew M. Greeley, "To Increase the Enjoyment of Sex in Marriage," *Reader's Digest,* September 1978, p. 113.

9
How Jesus Dealt with Sex Offenders

If I close down, there'll be another porno movie house open
tomorrow. Look, you can't tell other people what's for them....
These creeps come in here and masturbate or worse while the
picture's on. But so what? It's a free country....

—A theater manager[1]

esus Christ cares about what is happening to the sex morals
of our world. During His earthly ministry in Palestine, He
often confronted people who indulged in adultery, prostitution, and other kinds of sexual perversion. He criticized the
Pharisees for being too lenient about divorce. He explained what
creates a happy, harmonious life in every respect—including
sex.

As we study Jesus' dealings with sex offenders, we find that
He used loving firmness to call people back to the proper use of
sex. This gives us valuable insights into Jesus' overall teachings
about sex. We see how deeply Jesus cares about our sex lives.

We find a good example of Jesus' concern for sex offenders
in John 8, which tells how the scribes and Pharisees brought to
Him a woman they had caught in the act of adultery. Scripture
tells us that they had taken her *"in the very act"* of having adulterous intercourse with another man (v. 4). There was no question about her guilt since they had seen her sin firsthand. After
bringing the adulteress to Jesus, the men reminded Him that
God's law required them to stone such a person. "What do you
say?" they asked.

Notice that they weren't interested in the woman; they were interested in proving a point of law. As far as they were concerned, she was just another case, an exhibit for "Show and Tell" at their Pharisaic law school. They couldn't care less whether she lived or died; testing Jesus on a point of law interpretation was their entire purpose.

Jesus could see through all of that. He said, *"He who is without sin among you, let him throw a stone at her first"* (v. 7 NKJV). He didn't question the law; He didn't deny the Scripture. He knew that His heavenly Father had given the law against adultery for a good reason, to prevent a total breakdown of marriage. But He also knew that arguing the case with His enemies would not achieve what the law intended; it would not restore the woman's marriage or protect anyone else's. So Jesus focused on the real problem—the Pharisees' cold, impersonal attitude about sex. The eminent Bible scholar Raymond E. Brown develops this further:

> Jesus...recognized that, although they are zealous for the word of the Law, they are not interested in the purpose of the Law, for the, spiritual state of the woman is not even in question, or whether or not she is penitent.[2]

God is always just, but loving; He always condemns sin, but forgives the sinner who repents. The Pharisees were too narrow-minded to see that. They could only shake their heads and walk away. And Jesus told the woman, *"Go, and sin no more"* (John 8:11).

Only Jesus Christ could forgive sex offenders like that. Only He could see beyond the sin and shame that covered their lives to uncover the child of God within—the person who was hungry for love. Jesus knew what was happening inside a person's life. We see this again in His Sermon on the Mount:

55. You have heard that it was said to those of old, "You shall not commit adultery." But I say to you that whoever looks at a woman to lust for her has already committed adultery with her in his heart. (Matt. 5:27–28 NKJV)

That's a strong statement, but it shows us once again that Jesus looks at the inward life; He teaches inward strength and godliness. No matter how pure and godly you may seem, if you think lustful thoughts you are guilty of lust.

Lust is common in our world today. Men sit on benches outside the supermarkets and watch the women stroll by, thinking to themselves, "Man, wouldn't I like to have her! Wouldn't I like to take her to bed!" These men do not realize that they are sinning against God just by thinking that. They are toying with the idea of infidelity. They are entertaining Satan's delusions.

Jesus said that adultery is not just a physical act; it is a defilement of the heart. If you wish to do it—even if you think about doing it—you have already betrayed your true sex partner. You are just as guilty of adultery as if you had paid for an overnight motel room and taken the woman with you. Jesus Christ judges you for what you really are.

Satan will try to plant evil ideas in your mind; no matter how righteous you are, Satan will tempt you to lust after the opposite sex. Whenever that happens, start to pray. You can say, "Lord, take it away. I don't want to be that kind of person. I'm not a carnal person on the outside, and I don't want to be carnal on the inside. So take that thought out of my mind." You know what will happen? The Lord will make you clean again.

Joseph confronted this kind of problem. His master, Potiphar, placed him in charge of his house and all his possessions while he was away on business. Potiphar's wife began to lust after Joseph, and one day she said, *"Lie with me"* (Gen. 39:7). It would have been so easy for Joseph to give in. He could have rationalized his sin and said, "Oh, well, I'd better do what my master's wife says!" But Joseph knew this was nothing more than lust, and he put it right out of his mind. *"How then can I do this great wickedness,"* he said, *"and sin against God?"* (v. 9).

Joseph realized that lust was not simply a sin against Potiphar or Potiphar's wife—it was a sin against God! It insulted the Lord of his life. It offended the One who made Joseph's sex drive. Regardless of how pleasurable it might have seemed for the moment, Joseph knew this affair was a "great wickedness," and he put it out of his mind. Potiphar's wife kept trying to seduce him, but he kept turning his back on the temptation. Finally, she grabbed his clothes to pull him into her bed. Joseph tore out of his clothes and ran away!

Now that's what I call fleeing temptation!

How to Avoid the Offense

Satan will get you into embarrassing situations like that, and you will have to decide what to do. He will test your morals. He will try to destroy you. But Christ teaches us to resist Satan every step of the way.

We can resist Satan's temptations in several ways. First, we can avoid situations that might get us into trouble. I have been in the ministry for quite a few years, and I have learned never to be alone with a woman who might ask me to go to bed with her. That way I give the devil no chance to do his dirty work. I deal with people openly, honestly, and straightforwardly. My ministry is clean because I don't let Satan get his foot in the door.

Second, we can avoid temptation by keeping our thoughts where they ought to be. The prophet Isaiah said, *"Thou wilt keep him in perfect peace, whose mind is stayed on thee"* (Isa. 26:3). It's difficult for Satan to break through that kind of relationship; he has a hard time turning our thoughts to lust if we are meditating on God and His will. Jesus followed this course when Satan tried to tempt him in the wilderness. (See Matthew 4.) Every time Satan started to whisper in His ear, Jesus turned His thoughts to Scripture. The moment Satan started to say, "Think how much fun it would be to do such and such," Jesus bounced it back to him with the Word of God. Try that the next time you are tempted.

Third, we can resist temptation by putting our lives in the eternal perspective. By that I mean we should constantly think about the eternal consequences of what we are doing. We should always ask ourselves, "Is this going to make me any happier in heaven?" Believe me, that throws cold water on any wild impulses. When Satan lulls you into fuzzy thinking about sex, that one question can snap you back to reality.

Jesus did this on at least one occasion. He put marriage and sex in eternal perspective, saying, *"In the resurrection they neither marry, nor are given in marriage, but are as the angels of God in heaven"* (Matt. 22:30).

There will be no sexual relations in heaven; there will be no procreating of children there. Why? Because everyone will be like angels. Our immortality will make reproduction unnecessary. Everyone's enjoyment of the presence of the Son of God will take away the need for physical pleasures. The purpose of sex will be ended, just as the purpose of marriage will be ended. In that light, any thoughts about multiple mating seem very foolish indeed.

As the old gospel song says, "This world is not my home; I'm just a-passin' through." Sex and marriage seem terribly urgent now, but they have very little value in the eternal scheme of things. I'm not making light of sex and marriage. To the contrary, God says that our behavior in this area will affect whether we go to heaven or hell. But Christ says that gratifying our sexual desires is not all-important. While we think the world revolves around sex and marriage, Christ sees the end of the world. He says, *"Heaven and earth will pass away,"*—yes, even sex will pass away—*"but My words will by no means pass away"* (Matt. 24:35 NKJV). A. W. Tozer gave this graphic description of the attitude many Christians have toward the present, physical life:

> Men think of the world, not as a battleground but as a playground. We are not here to fight, we are here to frolic. We are not in a foreign land, we are at home. We are not getting ready to live, we are already living, and the best we can do is rid ourselves of our inhibitions and our frustrations and live this life to the full. This, we believe, is a fair summary of the religious philosophy of modern man.[3]

But this is a delusion! We are not at home in this present world. We are not entitled to look after our own comfort while the rest of the world goes to hell. We are on assignment here; we have a mission to fulfill for the Lord. There are many things more important than working through our sexual frustrations and fantasies. Our sexual hang-ups will mean nothing in eternity, because there will be no sex in eternity. When we hold this fact firmly in mind, sexual temptation loses its allure.

Forgiveness for Offenders

While we are thinking about Jesus' teachings on sex, we should take special note of the way He forgave sex offenders. He shows us once again that God is ready to welcome back anyone who repents of sin—even a sexual sin.

When Jesus traveled through the region of Samaria, He stopped at a well to get a drink. A woman came to dip her jar in the well, and Jesus struck up a conversation with her. This was highly unusual because Jews had a deep resentment of the Samaritans, who were a mixed breed, half-Jew and half-Gentile. But Jesus was so interested in this woman's soul that He didn't let racial differences stand in the way. He talked to her. And after discussing theology for a few minutes, Jesus said, *"Go, call your husband, and come here"* (John 4:16 NKJV).

The woman must have smiled as she said, *"I have no husband"* (v. 17 NKJV).

"You have well said, 'I have no husband,'" Jesus replied, *"for you have had five husbands, and the one whom you now have is not your husband; in that you spoke truly"* (v. 17–18 NKJV).

Notice that Jesus did not condemn her for her sin. He did not shame her for what she had done. But He did confront her with the truth; He told her pointblank that her sex life needed to be straightened out. He let her know that He was well aware of her promiscuous life, and He wanted her to "come clean" before God.

Earlier I mentioned the incident in which a woman anointed Jesus' feet with tears (Luke 7:36–50). The Bible simply says that she was *"a woman in the city who was a sinner"* (v. 37 NKJV). The Bible commentator Charles L. Childers says, "Such an expression as this, in New Testament terminology, means a prostitute."[4] Dr. Childers' interpretation seems confirmed by the way the Pharisees reacted to this woman. They said, *"This man, if He were a prophet, would know who and what manner of woman this is who is touching Him, for she is a sinner"* (v. 39 NKJV).

The Pharisees were careful students of the Law. They did not want to defile themselves by touching anyone who had violated God's commandments. So they would have nothing to do with the woman.

But observe Jesus' attitude. He watched her kneel at His feet and weep unashamedly in front of all the men; then she let down her long hair and used it to wipe His feet, washing them with her tears. Jesus had compassion on her. He could see through her sin of prostitution and discern the needs of her heart. So He said, *"Your sins are forgiven....Your faith has saved you. Go in peace"* (vv. 48, 50 NKJV). The master expositor Matthew Henry writes:

> Let who will object, Christ will bid the penitent that applies to him depart in peace, partaking of salvation through faith in his name. But may we not with shame confess, that while we hope our offenses are freely pardoned, we love but little?...Instead of grudging greater sinners the mercy they find with Christ, upon their repentance, we should be stirred up by their example to examine ourselves, whether we are indeed forgiven, and do love Christ.[5]

This is God's grace at work. By no means do we see Jesus treat sexual offenses in a casual, halfhearted way. He takes sin seriously, but He also takes repentance seriously. Whenever a sex offender comes to Him and says, "Lord, I'm sorry for what I've done," Jesus is ready to forgive. He is ready to forget the offense of the prostitute, the adulterer, the homosexual, or the person guilty of any other sexual offense. Sexual sins are very grave matters in God's sight; but He is just as willing to forgive the sex offender as He is to forgive the "smallest" sin of a godly person.

Christ can make "something beautiful" of your life. No matter what your sins have been—even if you have been sexually immoral in the vilest way—Jesus stands ready to forgive you and cleanse you of your sin. He can wipe the evil deeds and evil thoughts out of your life forever, if you give Him a chance.

Notes

1. Paul Moore and Joe Musser, *Shepherd of Times Square* (Nashville: Thomas Nelson, 1979), p. 152.

2. Raymond E. Brown, *The Anchor Bible,* vol. 29 (Garden City, N.Y.: Doubleday, 1966), p. 388.

3. Warren W. Wiersbe, ed., *The Best of A. W. Tozer* (Grand Rapids, Mich.: Baker, 1978), pp. 85–86.

4. Charles L. Childers, "The Gospel according to Luke," *Beacon Bible Commentary,* vol. 6, ed. A. F. Harper (Kansas City: Beacon Hill, 1964), p. 485.

5. Matthew Henry and Thomas Scott, *Commentary on the Holy Bible,* vol. 3 (Nashville: Thomas Nelson, 1979), pp. 247–48.

10
Sex and Spiritual Reality

Under the figures of the tenderest affection...the Divine love is represented [in the Book of Hosea] as ever enduring in spite of all indifference and opposition; and, on the other hand, the waywardness, unblushing faithlessness of the loved one is painted in colors so repulsive as almost to shock the moral sense.

—James Robertson[1]

The Bible uses sex to portray the deepest spiritual truths. God has some very practical things to say about sex; this is because God is intensely interested in our well being and happiness, and He knows that sex is a vital part of our happiness. But we would be shortchanging ourselves if we did not notice the spiritual side of God's Word on sex. He uses sexual symbols to convey some of the most stunning pictures of the gospel.

The relationship between a person's sex life and his or her spiritual life also needs to be pursued further. This is one of the most misunderstood aspects of human sexuality. The popular sex manuals would have us believe that sexual fulfillment is simply a matter of biology or emotions; but it is also a matter of the spirit. If you are not in harmony with the God who made you a sexual creature, you cannot expect to be in harmony with your sex partner. Besides that, sex can affect your spiritual growth.

Sex as a Spiritual Symbol

The Bible often uses marriage, adultery, prostitution, and other sex-related acts to illustrate spiritual truth. Perhaps the best-known example of this is found in the book of Hosea. Here the prophet Hosea is told to marry a prostitute in order to illustrate God's love for His rebellious people. The result is one of the most bizarre yet beautiful stories of the entire Bible.

> *And the Lord said to Hosea, Go, take unto thee a wife of whoredoms and children of whoredoms: for the land hath committed great whoredom, departing from the Lord.* (Hos. 1:2)

Imagine what Hosea's neighbors thought of this course of action. A handsome young prophet marries a prostitute and says, "The Lord told me to do it." I suspect his friends said, "Ha! That's what he says! I wonder what the real story is."

But God had indeed told Hosea to marry this "woman of the night." He commanded the preacher to become a living example of how God was going to treat the wayward nation of Israel. Preachers can have some very tough assignments, but I can't imagine a more difficult calling than Hosea had. God made Hosea and his wife Gomer an object lesson for the entire nation. Hosea was able to tell his people, "Look! You have made yourselves prostitutes with all sorts of pagan gods, just as Gomer made herself a prostitute with other men. But God loves you and will forgive you, just like I forgave Gomer and married her."

Gomer proved unfaithful again. After she bore children to Hosea, she left home and became the concubine of another man. Hosea corrected her and purchased her from the other man, bringing her back into his home once again. He never stopped loving her, despite her unfaithfulness. As one commentator notes, his love for her was "a beautiful equilibrium of loving tenderness and severe judgment."[2]

I cannot think of a more dramatic way to describe how God loves us and redeems us from our unfaithfulness to Him. When a husband forgives an adulterous wife and brings her back into his home, that's true forgiveness and love.

We find another stunning sex-related spiritual symbol in Revelation 17, where John sees a vision of a great harlot riding on a scarlet-colored beast. John said:

The woman was arrayed in purple and scarlet, and adorned with gold and precious stones and pearls, having in her hand a golden cup full of abominations and the filthiness of her fornication. And on her forehead a name was written: MYSTERY, BABYLON THE GREAT, THE MOTHER OF HARLOTS AND OF ABOMINATIONS OF THE EARTH. I saw the woman, drunk with the blood of the saints and with the blood of the martyrs of Jesus. (Rev. 17:4–6 NKJV)

This is a vision of what will happen at the end time, just before Christ returns to earth. John said that at the end time a profane and sinful power will arise upon the earth, like a great harlot, who will wreak havoc upon the church of Jesus Christ. This sinful power will kill saints by the thousands; it will all but wipe out Christianity as we know it today. The figure of the harlot is a striking contrast to the bride of Christ—the faithful church that will consummate her love with Christ at the end of time. (See Revelation 21:9–21.) Indeed, I believe the harlot symbolizes an unfaithful church, a church that prostitutes itself by following other lords besides Christ. The harlot stands for a "world church" inspired by Satan himself, which will ally itself with the Antichrist and blaspheme the holy name of Jesus. This "world church" will deny the Virgin Birth. It will deny the miracles of Jesus; in fact, it will deny the Bible itself. Giving itself to all kinds of unclean practices, it will ride upon the system of the Antichrist, the Beast. God calls this unfaithful church a harlot because she will sell her soul to the devil.

My friend, terrible times are coming to this earth. As we will see in the next chapter, we are about to enter a time of great suffering and tribulation that leads up to the return of Jesus. Many people won't survive. Many Christians will fall away from the Lord. Unbelievers will cast their lot with the unfaithful church, the "great whore," instead of following Jesus. And they will be destroyed in the end. We ought to pay careful attention to these sex-related symbols, because God can use them to teach crucial lessons to us.

Another sex-related symbol of the end time is found in Matthew 25, where Jesus describes what will happen just before He returns. He says that the kingdom of heaven will be like ten virgins waiting for their prospective husband. Five of the virgins are wise; they buy a generous supply of oil to last through the night, so they will be sure to have their lamps burning when the young man comes. But the other five virgins are foolish, because they let their lamps burn with a meager supply of oil, hoping that the young man will come soon.

The night wears on, and the young man is delayed. At midnight they hear an attendant shouting, *"Behold, the bridegroom cometh; go ye out to meet him"* (v. 6).

Suddenly the five foolish virgins realize that their lamps are out of oil. They beg the five wise virgins to give them some. But they answer, *"Not so; lest there be not enough for us and you"* (v. 9). Then the five foolish virgins rush down to the lamp shop and buy a fresh supply of oil, while their five friends go into the banquet hall with the eligible young bachelor. When the five foolish virgins return, the banquet hall is locked; they pound on the door and shout to be let in. But the young man says, *"Verily I say unto you, I know you not"* (v. 12). (Perhaps he thinks they are prostitutes, for what other kind of woman would be roaming the streets at night?)

The moral of the story, Jesus said, is that we must always be ready to receive Him. No one knows when Christ will return to earth to claim His people.

Notice once again how vividly God has illustrated this spiritual truth by using the symbol of sex. A virgin is an unmarried woman who keeps herself free from illicit sex. She has not indulged in premarital sex or promiscuous flirting; she has kept herself pure for the man she knows will someday ask her to marry him. In the same way, Jesus says, we should keep ourselves spiritually pure until He returns to claim us for His own.

Sex and Your Spiritual Life

We could examine several other examples of how God used sex to drive home a spiritual message. The Bible is full of such passages, and the ones I have cited just give you a taste of them. For now, though, let us think about the link between sex and your own spiritual life. How does your sexual behavior affect your relationship with God?

Even in Old Testament times, God showed His people that their sex life and their spiritual life affected one another. This connection is why God laid down so many regulations concerning marriage, why he was so protective in matters of adultery and promiscuity. He gave men and women the gift of sex for wholesome and holy reasons, and He did not want to see it profaned. Moreover, He knew that a wayward sex life would lead a person to dishonor God in other areas; it would be the first step toward wholesale spiritual decay. So God regulated the conduct of a person's sex life with great care.

The book of Leviticus contains some very interesting laws that reveal the tie-in between the sexual and the spiritual. For example, Leviticus 15 prohibits a man from worshipping at the temple if he has recently had sexual intercourse or if he has touched a woman during her menstrual period:

56. And if any man's seed of copulation go out from him, then he shall wash all his flesh in water, and be unclean until the even. And every garment, and every skin, whereon is the seed of copulation, shall be washed with water, and be unclean until the even. The woman also with whom man shall lie with seed of copulation, they shall both bathe themselves in water, and be unclean until the even. And if a woman have an issue, and her issue in her flesh be blood, she shall be put apart seven days: and whosoever toucheth her shall be unclean until the even. (Lev. 15:16–19)

Scholars argue about what this passage means; surely it cannot mean that these natural processes are evil. I think it shows that God expected a person to spend some time in meditation and prayer, preparing for worship before actually coming into the house of God, and God knew that a person who was overly concerned with physical things could not worship Him wholeheartedly.

Perhaps Matthew Henry's comment is also helpful at this point. He says, "These laws remind us that God sees all things, even those which are concealed from human eyes, and escape the censures of men."[3] As we have been saying all along, God makes no separation between a person's physical and spiritual life: Both are part of the same life. Anything that you do sexually will affect every other aspect of your life, including your worship. God wants to keep you mindful of that.

In Paul's letters, he often warns the early Christians to keep their sex lives pure because of the effect this will have on their spiritual lives. Here is such a warning from Paul's first letter to the Corinthians:

> 57. Flee sexual immorality. Every sin that a man does is outside the body, but he who commits sexual immorality sins against his own body. Or do you not know that your body is the temple of the Holy Spirit who is in you, whom you have from God, and you are not your own? For you were bought at a price; therefore glorify God in your body and in your spirit, which are God's.
>
> (1 Cor. 6:18–20 NKJV)

Many of us have memorized verse 19, which says, *"Do you not know that your body is the temple of the Holy Spirit...and you are not your own?"* I have heard this verse quoted to condemn cigarette smoking, drug abuse, and drinking. All of those are valid applications—but the original application was to sex! God tells us that our bodies are holy temples where He can live and reign; but we defile these temples if we indulge in promiscuity. Loose living exposes our bodies to venereal disease and infection leading to heart disease, blindness, or insanity. To put it bluntly, *promiscuity can destroy the temple of God.* It can ruin any chance we have to serve God with our physical bodies. So promiscuity raises both a physical danger and a spiritual danger, demonstrating once again that sexuality and spirituality cannot be neatly broken apart.

Anyone who lives a life of sexual perversion cannot be a victorious Christian. That should be obvious. A prostitute does not glorify Christ by the way he or she lives; a homosexual does not honor the Lord with the temple of his or her body. You do not have to be a theologian to realize that. Any practice that abuses or corrupts the bodies God has given us is a shame and mockery to the gospel. It cuts off the testimony that a person could otherwise give to the Lord. Christians must purge them out of their lives; they must get rid of any sexual deviancy or sin in order to live lives that are holy unto the Lord.

Moral Lawlessness

Sexual immorality has spiritual consequences for nations as well. Ungodly people make an ungodly nation, and God will not fail to punish a nation that turns away from Him. D. Elton Trueblood pointed this out in his book entitled *Foundations for Reconstruction,* written just after World War II.

> Sexual corruption is one of the chief symptoms of a sick and decaying society. The right ordering of the relations between the sexes is so important to a culture that any culture which fails to deal realistically with the problem is likely to go to pieces.[4]

Isn't that what we see in America today? Families are breaking up, businesses are falling apart, and the government itself is sliding into graft and corruption because of immoral sex and the selfish attitudes that accompany it. We live in a hedonistic age that defies the moral laws of almighty God. But no one can revoke God's laws. The sexual deviant, the prostitute, and the adulterer don't negate Gods law—they simply illustrate it. Their stories will not be finished until the day of reckoning when Christ returns.

Several years ago, when I was a missionary to South America, I lived on a compound with eight or ten other missionary families. One of the women was an incurable socialite; in common parlance, she was a "rounder." I think this woman went to every party within driving distance of our mission station. She was rarely around her cottage because she spent most of her waking hours gallivanting around town in her husband's jeep "looking for action." To be honest, she was not a very spiritual person, and I suspected that she had some habits that were very unbecoming to a Christian.

One day this lady became ill and sent word for me to come and pray for her. I replied that I was busy and could not come. Again she sent a message for me to come, and again I declined. Finally, her husband came and said, "Aren't you going to come and pray?"

"Yes, I will," I said. "But I'm in no hurry."

"Why not?" he asked.

"I've been holding revival meetings for several days, and I have yet to see her in church," I said.

"But she's been busy!"

"Brother," I said, "your wife has been doing ungodly things with ungodly people and living an ungodly way of life in town instead of going to church. Do you think that just because she snaps her fingers I ought to jump?"

My friend didn't expect that. He walked away with a dazed look on his face.

At last I went to the woman's bedside. She said, "Oh, thank goodness you're here! Pray for me, Brother Sumrall. Pray for me!"

"No," I said, "I would rather talk to you. Why haven't you been in church?"

"Oh, I've been so busy I just haven't had time to come," she said. "Maybe I've been a little bit too busy."

"Well, it looks to me like you intend to stay too busy," I replied. "God has put you where you won't be so busy."

"Aren't you going to pray for me?"

"Yes, I'll pray with you after I finish talking with you," I said. "Are you ready to repent of your sins?"

She didn't answer.

"Are you ready to ask for God's forgiveness? Are you?"

Tears welled up in her eyes, and I could tell she was finally facing up to her sinfulness. "Yes," she said, "I want to repent. I'm sorry for what I've done."

So I led her in a sinner's prayer, asking God to forgive her sins. Then I laid my hand on her forehead and prayed earnestly that God would make her whole again. The Spirit of the Lord moved mightily, and I could feel His power flowing into her body. She was healed within the hour!

You cannot escape God's moral law, no matter how "slick" you are. The day will come when you must admit all of the sins—even the secret, sexual sins—standing between you and God.

Your Spiritual Life and Sex

Yes, the sexual life can affect the spiritual life; but the reverse is also true. Sex is predominantly a spiritual thing, and the breakthrough for sex problems often begins with prayer.

We find a touching example of this in the Old Testament, which tells how a woman named Hannah went to the temple and prayed that God would let her conceive a son. Her husband had another wife who bore him children, but Hannah was barren; the Bible tells us that the other wife *"provoked her sore, for to make her fret, because the L*ord* had shut up her womb"* (1 Sam. 1:6). The Israelites believed that God controlled a person's sex life; they trusted Him to bless their marriages with children, and they saw barrenness as a curse. So Hannah wept and prayed that God would give her a child. Here is what happened:

> *And they* [Hannah and her husband] *rose up in the morning early, and worshipped before the L*ord*, and returned, and came to their house to Ramah: and Elkanah knew Hannah his wife; and the L*ord

remembered her. Wherefore it came to pass, when the time was come about after Hannah had conceived, that she bare a son, and called his name Samuel, saying, Because I have asked him of the LORD.

(1 Sam. 1:19–20)

Millions of women have received children in this same way. They know that sex is God-given, that children themselves are God-given, so they are not ashamed to bring their request to the Lord. I have personally prayed for many women who could not conceive, and God has allowed them to bear children. I know that a person's relationship with the Lord can affect his or her sexual life.

If you face a sexual problem that seems to have no solution, take heart—God can work a miracle for you! He can free you from inhibitions and fears about sex. He can take away the lustful desire to engage in illicit sexual relationships. He can give you the ability to have children, to enjoy sex with your mate, to become a better sexual partner yourself. He can do all these things because your sex life is all wrapped up with your spiritual life.

But be careful not to let sex become the chief purpose of your life. It's important to remember that sex is a gift, not a goal; it is a way station, not the Way. The chief goal and purpose of your life should be to honor and glorify the Lord.

Sometimes it is even necessary to abstain from sex to realize that goal. We find this in one of God's instructions to married couples:

58. Do not deprive one another except with consent for a time, that you may give yourselves to fasting and prayer; and come together again so that Satan does not tempt you because of your lack of self-control. (1 Cor. 7:5 NKJV)

In other words, there may be times when a couple decides to abstain from sexual relations to devote themselves to a season of prayer about a special concern. This does not mean that sex is evil, just as fasting does not mean that eating is evil. This kind of abstinence simply means that a person is willing to put aside the normal functions of the body for a short time, in order to concentrate more completely on prayer and meditation. This is a good discipline, but like fasting, it should only be done for a limited time. Just as a prolonged fast can destroy the body, prolonged continence can destroy a marriage.

While we are on this subject, you might be interested in the reasoning behind the Roman Catholic rule of celibacy. As you know, the Catholic Church does not permit its priests, nuns, or monks to marry. Many of them live in monasteries or convents, virtually cut off from contact with the opposite sex. You might think this is because the Catholic Church thinks sex is evil; but just the opposite is true. In fact, a little research shows that this custom grows out of a deep respect for the sexual relationship in marriage. Catholics follow the rule of celibacy because they know that sex should demand the full commitment of a marriage partner. Pope Pius XII explained it in these terms:

> For the duty of the married life...clearly demands: "They shall be two in one flesh." For spouses are to be bound to each other by mutual bonds both in joy and in sorrow. It is easy to see, therefore, why persons who desire to consecrate themselves to God's service embrace the state of virginity as a liberation, in order to be more entirely at God's disposition and devoted to the good of their neighbor.[5]

I am not a Catholic and I certainly don't agree with Catholic dogma, but I find this statement extremely fascinating. It affirms the fact that sex demands a one hundred percent commitment of a person's life. Catholic Church leaders abstain from sexual relations all the time to be sure that they are not distracted from God's work, because they know that sex and the spirit are interrelated.

Sex is indeed a one hundred percent commitment. It involves every bit of a person's character. If you want to have a healthy sexual relationship, you can't just think of sex in terms of biology. Think in terms of psychology, because of the involvement of the emotions. Think in terms of philosophy, because of the involvement of the mind. And think in terms of the Bible, because of the involvement of the soul. Sex causes two persons to commune with one another on the deepest levels of their being—and commune with God at the same time.

Notes

1. James Robertson, "Hosea," *International Standard Bible Encyclopedia,* vol. 3, ed. James Orr et. al. (Grand Rapids, Mich.: Eerdmans, 1939), p. 1426.

2. Francis Davison, ed., *The New Bible Commentary* (Grand Rapids, Mich.: Eerdmans, 1954), p. 682.

3. Matthew Henry and Thomas Scott, *Commentary on the Holy Bible,* vol. 1 (Nashville: Thomas Nelson, 1979), p. 260.

4. D. Elton Trueblood, *Foundations for Reconstruction,* rev. ed. (Waco. Tex.: Word, 1972), p. 71.

5. Anne Fremantle, *The Papal Encyclicals in Their Historical Context* (New York: Mentor-Omega, 1963), p. 301.

11
Sex and the Last Days

At a time in history when standards of conduct are at an all time
low, and when the barriers of holiness are being broken down by
licentiousness, impurity, and sexual irregularities, Christians ought
to rise to the challenge of living for God in such a way that the world
will know they are true followers of Jesus Christ.

—Harold Lindsell[1]

I have felt deeply impressed to prepare these studies on sex
at the present time. Never before have Christian morals
been under such heavy attack. Lewdness and immorality are
paraded before our eyes every day—in bookstores, on television,
even on public streets. Sociologists tell us that our country has
experienced a sexual revolution and so we can expect radical
changes in the way we use sex. But God sheds a different light
on the subject. According to His Word, the profligate sexual lifestyles of our day are a signal that His Son, Jesus Christ, is about
to return and judge the world. You can read it in your Bible:

*59. And as it was in the days of Noah, so it will be
also in the days of the Son of Man: they ate, they drank,
they married wives, they were given in marriage, until
the day that Noah entered the ark, and the flood came
and destroyed them all. Likewise as it was also in the
days of Lot: They ate, they drank, they bought, they sold,
they planted, they built; but on the day that Lot went out
of Sodom it rained fire and brimstone from heaven and*

destroyed them all. Even so will it be in the day when the
Son of Man is revealed.   *(Luke 17:26–30 NKJV)*

Think about this for a moment. Think of the situation in our land today and compare it to the world of Noah's day. Compare it to the atmosphere of Sodom and Gomorrah just before God rained His judgment down. Do you see any similarities?

My friend, we are living in those last days. We are about to see the Lord Jesus Christ return to gather His people. I want you to be ready for His coming. I want your life to be pure and holy in God's sight, so that He will look at you and say, *"Well done, thou good and faithful servant"* (Matt. 25:21).

The sinners of Noah's day did not give up their sin, even though Noah warned that God would destroy their world. The homosexuals and prostitutes of Sodom paid no attention to their godly neighbors like Lot until it was too late to change their ways. And so it is today. The people who pervert sex just laugh at their Christian friends; they ridicule what God is trying to tell them. They boast about their "newfound freedom" and encourage other people to join them, tempting even Christians to adopt their wayward lifestyles.

Remember Lot's wife. She was being delivered from the terrible judgment God poured out on Sodom and Gomorrah, but at the last minute she looked back. Curious to see what would become of her sinful neighbors, she wondered whether they really would be punished as harshly as God said. She looked back longingly. She became a pillar of salt.

Let me say it again—we are living in the last days. So don't contaminate yourself with the sins of this world. Do not study them with idle curiosity. Do not cozy up to illicit sex and say, "Maybe it's not so bad." Sin is always bad. Sin will destroy you. God says, *"The wages of sin is death"* (Rom. 6:23), and that's the price you can expect to pay for immoral sex.

60. But know this, that in the last days perilous times
will come: For men will be lovers of themselves, lovers

of money, boasters, proud,...lovers of pleasure rather than lovers of God, having a form of godliness but denying its power. And from such people turn away!

(2 Tim. 3:1–2, 4–5 NKJV)

"Lovers of themselves....lovers of pleasure rather than lovers of God." How well that describes many people of our day! Self-centered and self-loving, they think that sex is just an exercise in self-gratification. But despite all these efforts to build up the self, they are more lonely and dissatisfied with life than anyone has ever been. They have found exotic sex to be just as disappointing as all the other popular "ego trips." In the process their lives have become a pathetic waste.

Ironically, many pleasure-seekers go through life *"having a form of godliness but denying its power."* They go to church on Sunday and sing "Amazing Grace," but their way of life denies that God has done anything amazing to them. The search for fulfillment is in sex, in drugs, in high-minded learning, or in any number of other things, but it is futile. God predicted this course of events. He foretold in His Word that the pleasure-seeking unbelievers would become more and more dissatisfied as we approach the end of time. That prophecy is coming true right now.

Millions of Americans are living in immorality. Sociologists tell us that half of the brides who walk down the wedding aisle today are not virgins; they have had premarital sex. About ninety percent of young men have engaged in premarital sex. To put it in biblical terms, these men and women have committed fornication. Then they wonder why marriage disappoints them. In the words of Jesus, they *"do not know the Scriptures nor the power of God"* (Mark 12:24 NKJV). They have not listened to what God says about sex.

We can expect things to get worse. Our society will slide into gross immorality and people will take for granted their right to live in perversion. Do not be surprised if Satan's agents get "gay rights" written into the Constitution. Do not be surprised if they start selling do-it-yourself abortion kits. Do not be surprised if they make intercourse a required "final exam" for high-school sex education courses. Such things seem wild and fanciful now, but who would have thought twenty years ago that hospitals would have to give teenage girls abortions on demand? Our nation's sexual morals are on a long downhill slide, and they will slide faster as we get nearer to the time of the Lord's return.

> The end of the age will manifest these qualities in worse ways than has been done so far. This is why the Christian does not for a moment believe that men are getting better or that a golden age is around the corner. For the people of God these developments should not be looked upon as a misfortune, although they will suffer grievously. Rather, they should regard them as a sign of hope portending the soon return of the Lord. They are to look up, for their redemption draws near—indeed, it may be nearer than men think![2]

Dr. Lindsell is right. The rotting moral fiber of our time reminds us Christians that our deliverance is almost here. Our Savior is about to return. We are about to consummate the most glorious spiritual event that sex represents—the union of Christ with His bride, the church. It will be the happiest "wedding" this universe has ever known. It will bring us together with Christ in true intimacy and commitment, and we will know firsthand the love that human marriage has foreshadowed for all these centuries. Then sex will pass away. Immorality will pass away. Marriage will pass away as we go to live and reign with Christ.

Are you ready to meet the Lord, or are you one of the sinful signs of His coming? Are you ready to inherit the kingdom with Him, or will the lamp of your soul burn out before He comes? One way or the other, you will be involved in His return. No one will be left out.

If you are not living a life that's worthy of His bride, let Jesus come into your heart right now. Prepare yourself to enjoy the pleasure of His presence forever and ever. Be ready for the day when all the physical concerns of this life—including sex—will be no more. The joy of sex will end, but it will be replaced by the Lord's *"joy unspeakable and full of glory"* (1 Pet. 1:8). That joy can be yours.

Notes

1. Harold Lindsell, *The World, the Flesh, and the Devil* (Washington, D.C.: Canon, 1974), pp. 110–11.

2. Ibid., pp. 216–17.

My Challenge to You

If Jesus should come today, would you be ready? If you are not sure, I invite you to receive Jesus as your Savior now. You will be filled with hope and peace that only Jesus can offer.

Pray this prayer out loud.

"Dear Lord Jesus, I am a sinner. I do believe that you died and rose from the dead to save me from my sins. I want to be with you in heaven forever. God, forgive me of all my sins that I have committed against you. I here and now open my heart to you and ask you to come into my heart and life and be my personal Savior. Amen."

When you pray the Sinner's Prayer and mean it, He will come in instantly. You are now a child of God and you have been transferred from the devil's dominion to the kingdom of God.

Read 1 John 1:9 and Colossians 1:13.

—Lester Sumrall

About the Author

Lester Sumrall (1913–1996), world-renowned pastor and evangelist, entered full-time service for God after experiencing what he recalls as the most dramatic and significant thing that ever happened to him.

At the age of seventeen as he lay on a deathbed, suffering from tuberculosis, he received a vision: Suspended in midair to the right of his bed was a casket; on his left was a large open Bible. He heard these words: "Lester, which of these will you choose tonight?" He made his decision: He would preach the Gospel as long as he lived. When he awoke the next morning, he was completely healed.

Dr. Sumrall ministered in more than 100 countries of the world, including Soviet Siberia, Russia, Tibet, and China.

He established Feed the Hungry in 1987. In addition, he wrote over 130 books. His evangelistic association (LeSEA), headquartered in South Bend, Indiana, is still actively spreading God's Word. Dr. Sumrall's goal was to win 1,000,000 souls for the kingdom of God, and the ministry continues this vision. LeSEA ministry includes such outreaches as the World Harvest Bible College, radio and television stations, a teaching tape ministry, and numerous publications.

ANOTHER POWERFUL BOOK
from Whitaker House

Handbook for Healing
Revised Edition
Charles and Frances Hunter

Presented here are the keys to healing that Charles and Frances
Hunter have found in the Bible and through the discoveries of
medical science. You, too, can find that God can use you to
bring healing to family, friends, and people you meet. No longer
will you have to stand by, helpless, when people are hurting.

ISBN: 0-88368-705-4 • Trade • 224 pages